# The Age
# of the Muscle Car

# THE AGE OF THE
# MUSCLE CAR

## CLAY FEES

*Forewords by* John Kraman
*and* Diego Rosenberg

McFarland & Company, Inc., Publishers
*Jefferson, North Carolina*

*This book has undergone peer review.*

Library of Congress Cataloguing-in-Publication Data

Names: Fees, Clay, 1972– author.
Title: The age of the muscle car / Clay Fees ; forewords by John Kraman and
Diego Rosenberg.
Description: Jefferson, North Carolina : McFarland & Company, Inc., Publishers, 2022 |
Includes index.
Identifiers: LCCN 2021052755 | ISBN 9781476678146 (paperback : acid free paper) ∞
ISBN 9781476642451 (ebook)
Subjects: LCSH: Muscle cars—United States—History—20th century.
BISAC: TRANSPORTATION / Automotive / History
Classification: LCC TL23 .F387 2022 | DDC 629.222—dc23/eng/20211208
LC record available at https://lccn.loc.gov/2021052755

British Library cataloguing data are available

ISBN (print) 978-1-4766-7814-6
ISBN (ebook) 978-1-4766-4245-1

Front cover: 1970 Plymouth Road Runner
(courtesy of Fast Lane Classic Cars, St. Charles, Missouri)

Printed in the United States of America

*McFarland & Company, Inc., Publishers
Box 611, Jefferson, North Carolina 28640
www.mcfarlandpub.com*

For my parents,
who encouraged my love of these old cars
and taught me so much about them;
my Uncle Roger,
who helped me so much with my first one;
my daughter
whose childhood (and passing interest)
in cars encouraged this book;
and finally my wife,
who indulges this hobby and perseveres through it,
and who encouraged me to persevere
through the completion of this project.

For my mentor and friend Mrs. Webb
(whom I will never be able to address as Vicky),
my 3rd grade teacher and again in 8th grade,
and my mentor teacher at the outset of my teaching career.
She waited on this book to see the fruits of her efforts,
but she just couldn't wait any longer.
Thank you, Mrs. Webb.

# Table of Contents

# Acknowledgments

I am not a professional writer, and this work represents a hobby. As such, I could not have done this without the help of many, many people.

I first have to thank Andrea Foster, who was a tremendous resource and guide in this project. She taught several classes at Canadian Valley Technology Center in El Reno, Oklahoma, instructing novices such as myself on how to write and publish a book, but the greatest benefit of her classes was her enthusiasm and ceaseless encouragement. Andrea goes above and beyond for her students, and our projects are very much her projects. Without these classes, my fellow students and the Creative Quills group, this would never have come to fruition.

I want to thank my editor, Kelly Rogers Rupp, in whose Freshman Composition I class I was enrolled at Redlands Community College in the fall of 1991, and who gave me as one of her first assignments a three-page informational paper. I ended up writing 10 pages about cars, and that was in a real sense the first version of this book. Aside from this history with Kelly, she also gave this thing a final editing polish, and was responsible for editing the pictures in this work as well. Kelly has been a friend for nearly 30 years and was an invaluable partner in this project.

I also want to thank the professional organizations and businesses that were invaluable in helping me collect pictures of the vast array of cars about which I wrote. My goal was to make this work comprehensive, and to include a picture of every vehicle I mentioned and with few exceptions, I succeeded. I could not have done so without the help of the following organizations, and I want to extend my most sincere gratitude to the following:

Barrett-Jackson Auction Company, Scottsdale, Arizona
Fastlane Classic Cars, Inc., St. Charles, Missouri
Fort Pitt Classic Cars, Sharpsburg, Pennsylvania
Gateway Classic Cars, St. Louis, Missouri
Hanksters Hot Rods, Indiana, Pennsylvania
MJC Classic Cars, Lakeland, Florida
Sam's Alignment and Brake, Tulsa, Oklahoma
Motor Car Company, San Diego, California
Pontiac Oakland Museum, Pontiac, Illinois
Red Hills Rods and Classics, St. George, Utah
Streetside Classics, Charlotte, North Carolina
Tanner's Classic and Performance Motors, Carlisle, Pennsylvania

Tom Mack Classics, Prosperity, South Carolina
Vanguard Motor Sales, Plymouth, Michigan

I would like to acknowledge and thank Tim Dye and the Pontiac-Oakland Museum in Pontiac, Illinois, for his unwavering willingness to help in this book. Tim and I first came to know each other as members of the Indian Nations Pontiac Oakland Chapter of the Pontiac Oakland Club International (POCI) back in the early 2000s. Likewise, I would like to thank that chapter and my friends in the Indian Nations chapter of POCI, and Larry Crider, POCI president, in particular.

I would like to thank *Hemmings Motor News* for its massive archive of articles, contemporary sources, and other invaluable information and its past articles—accessible for free—that has served as an invaluable font of information upon which I relied very heavily in the completion of this project.

Finally, I also want to thank the scores of muscle car enthusiasts across this great county who helped me by submitting pictures of their vehicles. These were private individuals happy to share pictures of their "baby." Regretfully, I could not use all of the pictures that were submitted to me but I thank and appreciate everyone and the car clubs that submitted pictures to help me with this project.

Alexander Automotive of Downtown
  Franklin, Tennessee
Loren Alexander
Rimas Alinskas
Mark Ascher
Phil Aubrey
Allen Bates
Doug Bender
Keith Blasius
David Browe
Ron Brundies
Tammy and Shane Bryant
Marty Burke
Shirley Burner
David Butler
Daniel Centurioni
Brian Clark
Brown's Classic Autos
Central Oklahoma Mopar Assn.
Tom Coppa
Kathy Cox
Larry Crider
Ken and Elsa Dages
John Dallain
Rick Duden
Tim Dye
Ronald Eichler

Edwardene Fees
Lynn Fees
Roger Fees
Steve Fox
Franks Car Barn
Tammy Bryant
Jim Fura
Stephen Gewecke
Charles Gibson
Craig Gould
Jim Grisham
Gaylene Grossen
Rob Guzanek
Gary Hiltunen
Todd Hollar
Ron Holzschuh
Dennis Jones
John Kearney
Stan Kelly
Cam Kings
Chuck Knudsen
Gregory Langston
Jeff Larger
Leaded Gas Classics, Alabaster, Alabama
Leake Auction Company, Tulsa,
  Oklahoma
Mark Lenhardt

Diane Lents
Ralph Lopez
James Lusk
Steven Maas
Kervyn Mach
Tim Madigan
Chris Mazzili
Dale McIntosh
Miller Brothers Auto Sales
Brad Myers
Edward Nagel
Scott Nickett
Steve Nickett
Sara Oaks
Gary Parente
Vicki Parker
Chuck Patten
Pontiac Oakland Club Intl.
Joe Puleo
Kenneth Pylant
Vicki Rahmer
B.J. Raymond
Joe Razumich
Diego Rosenberg
Rocky Rotella

Route 36 Motor Cars, Dublin, Ohio
Frank St. Elmo
Joe Salvo
Sam's Alignment and Brakes, Tulsa,
   Oklahoma
David Saunders
Richard Savage
Andrew Selig
David and Ginamarie Shaw
Marty Sinzig
Chris Smetana
Bill Soman
Mike Spangler
Suzanne Steczak
Anthony Steiner
Frank Szymkowski
Charles Tran
Rick Treworgy
V8Buick.com
Tommy Wallace
Adam Wichard
Darla Willhite
Jerry Wilson
Gregory Winters
Glenda Yoder

# Foreword

by John Kraman

I love cars and I always have. My mom enjoyed telling stories about how, when I was two years old in the late 1950s, my first words, other than Mommy and Daddy, were the names of cars. My first memories as a toddler also revolve around cars. I clearly remember the TootsieToy and Midgetoy diecast cars I played with on the linoleum kitchen floor of our new midcentury ranch-style home in Rockford, Illinois. This was the beginning of a classic baby boomer obsession that continues to this day.

In the '60s I started building model kits in ¼₄ scale and racing slot cars in both HO and ⅓₂ scale, while starting to read the various car magazines. But after a move to Los Angeles in 1963, when I was the tender age 7, my dad found work as a salesman at Harry Maher Pontiac, located at 4245 Lankershim Boulevard in North Hollywood. This was right at the early stage of the explosion of style, performance and image from Pontiac that earned the coveted third place in sales behind Ford, and Chevrolet at #1.

As a result of the demise of the Pontiac brand in 2010, this location is now home to Universal BMW/Mini but parts of the original dealership still remain. I spent countless hours at the dealership in the various departments, but the showroom was heaven to me. The cars, promotional wall displays, and the colorful and informative brochures were simply irresistible to me. Even my Dad would enlist me to help explain the features and benefits of the Pontiac line-up to customers, and when it came time to close the deal, I was not afraid to ask for the sale.

Right down the street from the dealership, on Riverside Drive was Barris Kustom City founded by "The King of the Kustomizers," George Barris. Yes, it's still there, now headed by his daughter Joji. My wife Christine and I are good friends with her and her husband Barry to this day. I would walk past there frequently as it was on the way to the dealership from our home. I saw the faded red Lincoln Futura show car from the '50s sitting outside that eventually became the 1966 Batmobile, much to my delight. The famed Munster Coach and Dragula were also created there and were on display and visible thru the large plate glass windows in the front.

The cars I recall seeing for the first time include the landmark '63 Chevrolet Corvette Split Window Coupe, '64 Pontiac GTO, '65 Ford Mustang 2+2 Fastback and the '66 Oldsmobile Toronado with its show car looks and futuristic interior. When my 5th grade teacher, Mr. Roe, showed up with a brand-new Reef Turquoise '66 GTO hardtop I immediately declared to all that I would own a GTO myself someday. That goal became a reality in 1976, when, at age 19, I bought a '64 GTO with equipment exactly as immortalized by the hit song "GTO" performed by Ronnie and the Daytonas. I still own it today.

I also decided that cars just might be a career path for me and while in high school worked at a well known speed shop installing various typical Day Two performance goodies, such as exhaust headers, traction bars, and dual point distributors. This experience eventually led to aircraft maintenance, then aircraft sales and finally to my current responsibilities with Mecum Auctions in 2006. Mecum has grown to be the world's largest collector car auction handling over 20,000 entries and providing 200 hours of television annually.

As the Director of Company Relations and Lead TV Commentator/Analyst for Mecum, I have a unique opportunity to utilize my sliver of aptitude before a large, eager yet critical audience. I strive to be relevant and accurate. The majority of entries are from the mid–'50s thru the '70s and include a high volume of both Corvettes and Muscle Cars. Right smack dab in my knowledge wheelhouse!

So why I am telling you all this? Well, my personal automotive library has over 300 books on car history and facts as well as some autobiographies as well. The amount of information, especially from this first Muscle Car era, is immense and easily available. So when Clay mentioned to me the he was writing a book about not only Muscle Cars, but also the colorful pop culture of the 1960s, I was hooked. This is a different direction that I am used to, from the many talented auto writers who focus solely on technical data and production figures. I was there in the front row of the culture revolution of the '60s. It would be difficult to fool me if Clay wrote an inaccurate book.

So did Clay, from a later generation, accurately document an authentic view of these historic times? Absolutely. Nailed it—an entertaining, informative book that will certainly be enjoyed by Baby Boomers like me. But more importantly this book will appeal to and enrich those who were not there so they may better understand precisely the hows and whys of this significant time period. This is the book I wish I could have written. But alas my patience and word-crafting talent is well below the level of Clay Fees, so I am grateful he was able to do it. Finally, I appreciate this opportunity to provide this foreword. Let me leave you with one final thought: Life is too short to drive boring cars!

*John Kraman is director of company relations for Mecum Auctions and lead commentator/analyst for* Mecum Auto Auctions: Muscle Cars and More *on NBC Sports Network. He is also a multimedia auto journalist, a car collector and guitarist/vocalist for Redline 7000, a classic rock band.*

# Foreword

BY DIEGO ROSENBERG

Visit your local bookstore (if it still exists) and you'll find volumes on any number of vehicles from the postwar era. They could be marque-specific, an overview of a particular model, or all the minutiae of one model from a particular year. This is how it's been for decades.

But a book that explains the adjectives and adverbs of the hobby (if your grammar is weak, that would be *a descriptor for a noun or pronoun* and the *who/what/when/where/why*, respectively) has gotten lost in the shuffle in publishers' zeal to produce yet another Mustang book. *How* did high-performance cars develop? *What* is the difference between a Hardtop Coupe and a Sports Coupe? *Why* is the Plymouth Road Runner different from a GTX?

These cars were a product of their culture. Muscle cars may not have had the latest in technology (Hemi heads may have superior flow, but 4-wheel disc brakes were a more contemporary example of technology in 1968) but they demonstrated an American competency beyond the style and living-room luxury that were its *modus operandi*. The culture behind the muscle car eventually changed, as other concerns cannibalized the enthusiasts' world (though pollution itself was a world-wide issue, truth be told) but computers eventually brought performance back. Today, we have showroom-stock Honda 4-doors pulling faster ETs (elapsed times for ⅛ and ¼-mile runs) than *both* a Road Runner *and* a GTX. If that insults your sensibilities, rest assured a modern Dodge Challenger SRT Demon can do the same in under 10 seconds. In the 1960s, it took radical Super/Stock racers to achieve that kind of performance.

As the North American car hobby shifts—while Boomers continue to rule the roost, vehicles from various continents commanding a larger presence thanks to a generation of enthusiasts—fans of high-performance cars from the 1950s to 1970s are starting to feel the pinch, as new performance cars are so easy to live with and are much faster than what was offered on the showroom floor 50 years earlier. Just as December 7, 1941, is fading from infamy, classic muscle cars and the like run the risk of fading from glory over time. The time is ripe for someone to step up to the plate and explain the era of when an enthusiast could choose a performance car among at least 10 brands, specify one of five different colors for the interior, pick something with style not determined by a wind tunnel, and with model year changes that made it easy to distinguish between one year and the other.

Clay Fees has written that book. That book is currently in your hand. Enjoy the ride.

*Diego Rosenberg may have been born during the low-compression era, but he's an enthusiast of performance cars (and a lot of others) from before his time. He's also the author of* Selling the American Muscle Car: Marketing Detroit Iron in the 60s and 70s *and* Cobra Jet: The History of Ford's Greatest High-Performance Muscle Cars.

# Author's Note

Any history of the muscle car era will necessarily include figures, data, statistics and quantifications regarding the performance of these cars. The statistics cited in this book come from the individual automakers in their advertising or contemporary road tests. These statistics have been ably compiled by such sources as modern enthusiast magazines and by *Hemmings Motor News*. All of these sources have been heavily relied upon in this work and have been thoroughly checked for accuracy and reliability.

# Introduction

The great pageant of American history holds few moments more dramatic than the decade known as "the Sixties." Only the 1860s a century previous can challenge the 1960s in terms of transformative effect on the American social and cultural landscape. It was a maelstrom of momentous change and societal upheaval—much of it long in coming. The '60s were an era of unparalleled scientific achievement, expanding the boundaries of humanity's accumulated knowledge. It was a decade that demolished long held institutions, many of which kept the nation from achieving the promises set out by its founders. Even the government and its systems, the one constant institution reaching back unbroken to the founding of the nation itself, were shaken.

These changes permeated all facets of American life and were inescapable even to the most average of Americans. The great march toward civil rights, the "Space Race," and the Vietnam War—the nation's fever blister—were ubiquitous in the American consciousness. The Counterculture and the great migration of young people to its meccas like the Haight-Ashbury district of San Francisco stirred hopes of an imminent utopia. The music of the era was unique as well. Bands such as the Beatles, Rolling Stones and the Who were the vanguard of the "British Invasion." Later in the decade came the darker acid rock of groups such as the Jefferson Airplane, Cream and Strawberry Alarm Clock. At its core, the 1960s was a line of social and political demarcation, the result of the clash of cultures on either side of the chronological divide, the product of the intersection of a myriad of social currents unlikely to be seen again.

One indispensable thread in the tapestry of the 1960s was the cars. More than in any other decade since the advent of the automobile, the popular cars of the '60s were as much a part of the American experience as Neil Armstrong or Selma, Alabama. Of the myriad sizes, shapes and classes of automobiles in 1960s, the American muscle car stands out and has transcended the decades since.

The muscle car is a uniquely American breed of automobile and very much a product of the 1960s. It kindles the smoldering memories of those people who lived (and drove) through the '60s and inspires the imaginations of later generations of classic car enthusiasts, conjuring images of small-town cruise routes across the country. The mind's eye resurrects images of street battles between thundering big-block sedans or scampering pony cars powered by high-winding small blocks. Fully fifty years after its birth, the muscle car holds a place of prominence in American culture.

There are few things more American than the muscle car. The automotive equivalent of John Wayne, gun ownership and the Normandy landings, the cars of the 1960s and early 1970s were machismo made tangible. Even the way these vehicles achieved performance was typically American—big engines were designed to produce big horsepower. When more power was needed, the solution was bigger engines, and pouring more fuel into them. While European performance cars of the day embodied refinement and style, the American answer was typically American: vulgar, unadulterated power.

Even today, there is still marketing power in those long dead cars from a bygone era. These cars are regularly used in advertising. They are seen in blockbuster movie franchises. Modern day musicians use them in their videos. They are the subjects of televised auctions and even another modern American staple, the reality television show. Modern car makers are resurrecting long dead nameplates, retrieving them from the dust heap of American automotive history and attaching them to modern day offerings thoroughly qualified to wear the name "muscle car." After all, without the 1970 Dodge Challenger R/T, there would be no modern Challenger R/T.

The American muscle car is alive and well in the mind of the general public as well. Muscle cars are not reserved only for the ultra-wealthy, Hollywood studios or advertising agencies. Twenty years after Pontiac built its first GTO, arguably the most recognizable of the muscle cars, German automaker Volkswagen tapped into its mystique and reworked the classic '60s car song "Little GTO," *auf Deutsch*, into "*kleiner GTI*," or "little GTI." Muscle cars of the '60s and '70s are regularly being used to promote products or to cast an image of cool onto characters in movies and will likely continue to do so until the last of the baby boomers pass away.

But Hollywood and advertising agencies are not the lifeblood of today's muscle car hobby. Indeed, the grassroots of the muscle car community are normal, car-loving Americans. These people are called "old car people."

Old car people are a special and unusual breed. They live and breathe cars. Cars get into the blood, as if sniffing rich exhaust fumes causes some kind of incurable disease. They watch the televised auctions. They subscribe to car magazines. Old car people go to the car shows and talk about the same cars and tell the same stories about their cars or, like lost loves of the distant past, of cars they once owned. They network with each other, and they further the hobby. There are literally thousands of these automotive dinosaurs in the hands of regular people all over this country. These cars and their loving owners support a parts and restoration industry measured in the millions of dollars, and its impact on the overall economy in terms of countless body shops, mechanics and other ancillary industries is immeasurable.

Old car people all share a love of cars of the past, and true old car people understand not just the cars, but the historical context that gave them birth. Old car people come in many types, from the history-loving originality nuts that believe classic cars should be preserved exactly as they came from the factory, to the hot rodders who see the muscle car as a blank medium to express automotive and mechanical creativity. While old car people appreciate any genre of old car, such as pre–War or '50s models, they usually gravitate to a specific era. These people keep these cars and the old car hobby alive, so many years past their heyday.

But old car people don't live in a vacuum. Human nature dictates that we are creatures of community, and the old car people usually have people in their lives that are not old car people—spouses, friends, and children. These people may not understand that Old Car Fever is a virulent, incurable disease, apparently contracted by breathing copious amounts of exhaust fumes. They may not be fellow sufferers, and they may not understand the allure of these pieces of archeological iron.

And they are the audience for whom this book is intended.

This book is an attempt to explain what muscle cars were, why they came about, and what they meant to the generation that lived the era when they were new. This work is intended to provide a casual survey of the myriad makes and models to the next generation of potential muscle car fans, to the uninformed, or to the curious. To be sure, this book is aimed at today's youth, in an effort to foster interest and carry forward the next generation of old car people.

It is also intended as an explanation, a *mea culpa* to the persevering significant others in the orbit of those of us bitten by the muscle car bug—to the people endlessly dragged to car shows, or forced to watch auctions on television, or to have "car talk" droning constantly.

This book is also a history, but I hope an atypical one. There was a lot going on in the world at the time these cars were new, and muscle cars did not spontaneously appear. I attempt to place these cars in their historical context, and to describe the factors that led to their rise, the ferocity of the competition between manufacturers, and the eventual demise of the American muscle car.

I also attempt to discern the future of the old car hobby, and in some way to protect it.

There are literally thousands of muscle car books that have come before this one. Any fan knows the basics. What sets this one apart is the effort to place these cars, as a phenomenon, in their historical context. Muscle cars are much more than a collection of parts bolted together, or horsepower and torque ratings. To reduce them to such simple measurables is to dishonor them and to deny them full credit for what they were. Muscle cars were inextricably intertwined in the larger American culture of their era. They were products of their times, as much as psychedelia, Credence Clearwater Revival and draft dodging. Muscle cars influenced the culture around them, and they were in turn influenced by that culture.

To cite but one example, there is a reason that many of the cars of the era carried space related nameplates such as "Nova," or "Satellite," or "Galaxie." During the 1960s, the nation was engaged in the Space Race, a technological competition between the U.S. and the Soviet Union. The Space Race became a test of the two adversarial economic systems of capitalism and communism, freedom versus totalitarianism. It was, literally, a race to the moon. The Space Race became a part of the national consciousness, and influenced popular culture, including the cars. People were interested in the Space Race and enamored with "the final frontier," perpetuated not only by the real-life events of the Space Race, but also by fictional space-based story lines such as *Star Trek* and *The Twilight Zone*. They watched with bated breath every incremental step in that decade-long race to the moon. Car builders, seeking every opportunity to sell more cars, wished to capitalize on the high level of national interest in the

Space Race. So naturally, to name but one, Oldsmobile co-opted the term "rocket" in its marketing.

What this work is not is a technical book, full of mind-numbing technical data. That is because I am a technical novice myself, with only a casual relationship with the knowledge of how anything more mechanical than a wheelbarrow might work. You will not find many references to top dead center or ignition curves. There will be few references to foot-pounds of torque. There will be no talk of dwell times or cam-shaft specifications. Except for some necessary terminology critical for a basic under-standing, there will be none of this. That said, things like "horsepower" are vital to the understanding of performance cars of any era. Lest anyone be offended by that, let me assure you that that is the level of technicality at which I operate in the world of old cars. If reading about the muscle car hobby puts the reader to sleep, or worse, readers will be turned off. This book is for the novice or passing car enthusiast. This book is a book for beginners to the muscle car hobby.

As I type these words, I am forty-four years old. I was not personally present for the muscle car era. I was born in 1972. Most automotive historians close the muscle car era somewhere in the early to mid–1970s, so I wasn't even born until the waning days of the era, and they were long over by the time I had any memory.

I am not a mechanic, nor am I an engineer. I have never rebuilt an engine, and I only have a pedestrian knowledge of how one actually works. I cannot do paint and body. I cannot even re-cover seats. I usually have to rely on friends or family to do what needs to be done on my two muscle cars. As an attorney, I can sometimes trade legal work for work on my cars. What I am, however, is a history nerd with a love of muscle cars that spans three decades.

My relationship with old cars goes back to El Reno, Oklahoma, and my grand-mother's house. That house was the cradle of my love for old cars. Some of my earli-est automotive memories involve rides around town as a little guy in her 1967 Pontiac Grand Prix—not exactly a muscle car, but it did have a big, rumbling engine and dual exhaust—to visit the various parks all over town or to go down and watch the trains at the now long-gone Rock Island railroad depot north of town after she got finished with her customers who visited her in-home beauty shop. I used to ride around in that land yacht standing—yes, standing—in the middle of the front bench seat. For safety restraint, I relied on her seemingly spring-loaded right arm to the chest, seat-belts be damned.

My grandmother was a car person. She was crazy about cars—performance cars. As an octogenarian, she got run off the local Pontiac lot for regularly wandering the lot looking at the new models. This angered the sales manager because she never bought anything. My grandmother was sort of a less threatening version of the Lit-tle Old Lady from Pasadena, immortalized by Jan and Dean in 1964, except in her rickety old garage was not a barbarous super stock Dodge but a relatively docile little 1957 Thunderbird. My dad bought that old T-Bird in 1965 and drove it to his proms and all through high school and college. My grandmother acquired it when my mom got pregnant with me, and my dad had to sell it to finance their first house, and she agreed to buy it from him. He has since inherited it back, and it still sits in his shop, with a lot of other old cars.

**1957 Thunderbird owned by Lynn Fees of Kellyville, OK (photo by the author).**

I always liked that old T-bird when I was a kid. Like the Grand Prix, the Thunderbird wasn't a muscle car, but it was old and from another time and appealed to my developing appreciation of relics of the past. What I remember the most as a kid is the smell of its interior. Old cars have a unique, pleasant smell, and none of them smell the same. They smell like time itself. When I am visiting my parents, I wander out sometimes and open the door to that old T-bird just to smell the interior and remember being a little kid.

The Grand Prix and the T-Bird simply made cameo appearances in my life. They were but a prologue to what would come. While I would drive that Thunderbird years later to my junior prom, the T-bird and the old Pontiac primarily served to build in me a basic appreciation of old cars in general. The summer of 1986, however, again at 910 S. Shepard, saw my full appreciation for old cars, and specifically muscle cars, fully bloom.

In that summer, for some reason, my dad and uncle came into my grandmother's having bought the September issue of *Popular Hot Rodding* magazine. I have no idea why they got it or even which one of them actually bought it. My dad always liked the cars from his youth, though I didn't really know it at the time. Turns out, he knew his cars. My Uncle Roger was definitely a car guy, which I always sort of knew, as I remember when I was very young, he had some kind of hot rod, flames gracing the side. What I didn't know was that he was what was known in the 1960s as a "grease monkey," and spent a large part of his youth piddling on cars, specifically Chevrolets. This fact would prove important. I always assumed Roger, or Roddy or Rod, as he is known in the family, bought that magazine. Neither of them remembers today. Tucked inside that issue was a simple article that traced the history of Pontiac's GTO.

Somehow, I got hold of that magazine and for some reason—probably mind-numbing boredom at Granny's—I read that article. From the moment I finished that article, I was hooked on muscle cars, and GTOs in particular. Until that time, I hadn't given much thought to cars, and to this day I don't know what about that article that gave me the old car sickness, an incurable ailment that I will carry the rest of my days. It is not an exaggeration to say that magazine was one of the pivotal moments of my life. The fact that I am sitting here writing a book about muscle cars, all these years later, confirms that.

In the years since, I have read and re-read that article—I still have it—and still can't figure it out. That article was simple, but well written. Very likely the reason was that I was thirteen years old in '86. A driver's license and the freedom it represented were on the horizon, and even I, not attuned with the car world, knew the performance cars of the mid '80s weren't exactly exciting. Plus, I was a history nerd. I have always had an appreciation for the past and its relics. That article about cool cars from a lost era stirred something in me.

Regardless, I was infected with muscle car fever. I spent the remainder of that summer buying car magazines with articles about particular models of muscle cars. I asked my dad a million questions about old cars. I was like a sponge, soaking up all I could learn about Super Bees, Gran Sports, and Chevelles. I immersed myself in Fairlanes and 4-4-2s. Though things like carburetor flow rates and engine timing put me to sleep, I learned what "SS" and "R/T" meant, and I understood instinctively that, historically and culturally, the American muscle car was something very, very special.

Later that summer, we had a family reunion in Enid, Oklahoma, and we drove by a car lot, upon which sat a 1969 Dodge Charger. That Dodge was painted in full blown, gloriously offensive *Dukes of Hazzard* General Lee regalia. Dad, who, it turns out, always liked 1968 Chargers, stopped and we test drove it back to the park where the reunion was. We left Dad's 1985 Buick Regal at the lot. I remember asking Dad why they'd let us drive that obviously priceless Charger off the lot and his answer—as true in 1986 as it is incredible today—was that the Buick was worth far more than the old Dodge.

That fall, my parents took my dad's parents on a vacation to Red River, New Mexico, and we stayed with my mom's folks across town in El Reno. I made my younger brother Patrick go riding our bikes all over town looking for muscle cars (Patrick was not and is not a "car guy"). Muscle cars were relatively plentiful then. In the '80s, they were just old cars. I remember finding a '68 Buick GS, two flat-top Mustang Mach 1's and a '73 Dodge Charger, all in the same neighborhood. When he got back, I made my dad go look at them all.

He wasn't impressed. I remember he told me how all of those cars I found were "not his favorite" or that he considered "that model ugly." I didn't really care though, and I was soaking up all he had to say about them to learn as much as I could. Interestingly, I discovered that my opinion somehow mirrored Dad's. Looking back, I didn't like them only because Dad didn't like them. Nothing much has changed much from those early impressions; while I love all the old muscle cars, the '68 GS and third generation Chargers are not near the top of my list of favorites.

Really though, it all came back to the Pontiac GTO and that article. The GTO rested solidly at the top of my list. Dad didn't like GTOs that weren't 1965–1967 models. Again, I agreed (still do). Of those three, I liked the '66 best, because of its louvered taillights and black grille. I finally formed an opinion divergent from Dad's, as he liked both the '65 and '67 better.

So, come-hell-or-high-water, the hunt for a '66 GTO was on—sort of. "Sort of," because of one substantial hurdle. For, you see, I was an unemployed teenager, with limited ambition to become un-unemployed. Despite the fact that GTOs in the mid–1980s were still extremely affordable, there weren't enough aluminum cans along all the roadsides in all of Oklahoma to fund one.

Be that as it was, I was fourteen, and I was panicking. To me, fourteen was dangerously close to sixteen, and I hadn't found my GTO. Luckily, my enthusiasm sparked a latent interest in Dad for the cars of his youth, an enthusiasm I hoped to manipulate. We went looking at cars.

We found a 1968 GTO convertible in the Route 66 town of Chandler, Oklahoma. They wanted $2500, which is insane to think of today, but Dad didn't like '68s, so I didn't like '68s either. Nevertheless, I had a '68 in right there in front of me. It had the three little white letters in the grille that called out GTO. It might as well have said "Holy Grail." Could Dad not see that beautiful pot metal GTO crest on the fender? That '68 GTO suddenly became my favorite car in the whole world, and I wanted it, but Dad sure as hell wasn't going to pay the outlandish sum of $2500 for an ugly '68 GTO.

We looked at a '66 GTO convertible—my ultimate GTO—in a salvage yard in Drumright, Oklahoma. Time and the elements conspired to make that GTO too much of a basket case, but it became my favorite car in the world. I wanted it. Dad didn't buy that favorite car in the whole world either. I did manage to pry the GTO crest off of its fender. I took it home and used plastic model paint to refurbish it the best I could, because it came from a GTO. That pitted old GTO crest might as well have been a piece of the True Cross. I still have it somewhere.

We looked at a 1968 Dodge Charger in Tulsa, painted Plum Crazy, a popular Chrysler color back in the '60 and early 70s. The Charger became my favorite car in the whole world. I just knew Dad couldn't resist the siren's song of a '68 Charger, one of his favorites. He passed on that favorite car in the whole world too.

We found a 1968 Plymouth Satellite near home in Sapulpa. That old Plymouth was red, and I can still point to the exact spot in the parking lot where it sat where a used car dealership used to be. That Satellite was my favorite car in the whole world.

Nope. Didn't get the Plymouth, either.

Despite my shifting opinion on my favorite car in the world, I really wanted that '66 GTO, but I wasn't finding one. I scoured the *Tulsa World* and *Daily Oklahoman* Sunday classifieds. I bought *Bargain Post* classified ads and pored over them, every week, looking for the perfect GTO, and by perfect, I mean one that was either free or cheap enough that Dad would buy for me. I didn't find one.

But I did run across an affordable 1968 Plymouth Road Runner. I had read an article in *Hot Rod* magazine on the year-to-year history of the Road Runner, and we had earlier found a used car dealer in Oklahoma City that had a 1970 Road Runner and also a 1970 Super Bee (Dad would buy neither—they wanted $2500, for God's sake). So I knew Road Runners. I liked Road Runners. A Road Runner wasn't a GTO, but it would suffice. If I had run across a Chevy Nova, or a Buick Gran Sport, or an Oldsmobile 4-4-2, they would have sufficed too, but I didn't. I ran across a 1968 Road Runner.

I didn't really know much about Dad's opinion of 1968 Road Runners. The closest we came to discussing Road Runners was when he obliterated my hopes of driving that '68 Satellite. Aesthetically speaking, '68 Satellites and Road Runners are of the same Plymouth line, so they look a lot alike. For some reason, Dad had enough of a level of interest to at least go look at the car.

The Road Runner was way the hell out in a western Oklahoma town called Waynoka. If God hadn't totally forgotten about this town, He certainly hadn't thought of it in a while. The Road Runner would start and propel itself—a good start—was dressed in crappy paint and was equipped with a 4-speed transmission and a non-original 440 cubic inch engine. It had the personal touch of class of someone hand painting "440" on each fender. In retrospect, that Road Runner was a mechanical turd, but it was cheap, and at fourteen, I could feel my biological clock ticking. I NEEDED that car. For some reason I still can't fathom, Dad was willing to buy that car, and I had my old car. Not a '66 GTO, but an old car.

That Road Runner was the car I drove in high school. My Uncle Roger painted it in his garage in the winter of 1987, and there I learned that being a Chevy disciple like he was mandated that you hate Chryslers. I thought he simply hated that particular Chrysler, which over time showed us there was plenty about which to hate, but I have since learned that, no, Roger hated *all* Chryslers.

Roger made me sand it, though I know now that he did much more sanding on that thing than I did. When you are hand sanding a 1968 Road Runner, you realize just how big the cars of that era are. It was a hell of a long way around that car. The red dust we sanded off infiltrated his entire house through his ventilation system. This caused, I feel certain, some significant marital strife when everything in my Aunt Christy's house was tainted pink. Roger's distaste for that car was such that for Christmas of 1988, he thoughtfully gave me a "Mopar Repair Kit" made of items lovingly acquired and assembled personally. The "repair kit" consisted of a steel ammunition box, painted the same red as my car, and a hand grenade.

By the time I was sixteen, the Road Runner was wearing the new paint—Roger truly had done an amazing job. It sported wide hood stripes that weren't available until the 1969 model year. I didn't care about such things then. With that 440 growling through twin pipes, that old Plymouth was a true hot rod. Though the car was of a previous era, I immediately began "updating" it with cheap accouterments of the 1980s. I installed a whole host of cool gear ordered right from the J.C. Whitney catalog, such as hood pins and a top of the windshield shade that said "Plymouth." It had the sound system mandatory for the late 1980s: 6 × 9 speakers in the package tray, and Alpine stereo with equalizer and amp. With its '60s muscle era performance and adorned with '80s crap, my Road Runner was truly intergenerational. That car went a significant distance to making me cool, a Herculean feat.

...When the damn thing ran, anyway. It was an old car, and old cars are persnickety by nature. At some point in its past, that Road Runner had a hard life of putting distance on the odometer a quarter mile at a time. I had a propensity to burn up clutches racing the car against various pretenders to my small town drag racing throne. In my hometown of 5,000, that amounted to exactly three pretenders. I could beat two of them. Sandy Holmes was the third. She had a gear-head dad who was confined to a wheelchair, and he taught her to build cars. She, herself, built a 1970 Camaro that I raced exactly twice. She beat my ass the first time, and my testosterone-fueled pride wouldn't stand for that. After she beat me worse the second time, I decided discretion was the better part of valor and went back to regularly beating up on the other two.

The author and his 1968 Plymouth Road Runner on the way to the Kellyville (OK) High School Senior Prom in May of 1991.

Having the second quickest of four cars wasn't good enough for me. With my friend Tommy Turner and his '70 Pontiac LeMans, I used to sneak off to the Tulsa Speedway to the Midnight Drags. There we would beat up on preppy kids from South Tulsa in their mommy's Mercedes or the "performance" cars of the early 1980s, like six-cylinder Camaros and Pontiac Fieros. There was, however, a '59 Ford Ranchero with the bumpers that had to be chained on the car with which we quickly learned not to mess. My folks didn't learn of my drag racing career until the waning years of the Obama Administration. Dad was paying for my insurance back then.

I enjoyed that old Road Runner, driving around listening to Cream and Jimi Hendrix and imagining it was 1968. I got detention for "corrupting other students" by listening to Eric Clapton's "Cocaine" too loudly in the parking lot. I drove that car to my senior prom. We cruised Friday and Saturday nights in Sapulpa. We had a lot of fun when it ran, but it ran so infrequently that my mom once bought potted mums to put all over it, stating that if it were going to be a lawn ornament, she wanted it to be a pretty one. The Road Runner was a great high school car and was as much my childhood friend as Tommy Turner.

I sold that car in the fall of 1991 when I started college, but unlike amputating a gangrenous limb, old car fever cannot be cured by removing the infecting object. After I sold that old Road Runner, I missed it. When I approached graduation from college, I began looking for a new old car to present to myself as a graduation present.

I found a new old car in the fall of 1995 in Lawton, in southwest Oklahoma, and with it I had finally caught my chimera. I had found my long sought-after 1966 GTO. The car was a unique example—it came with a laundry list of optional equipment, such as air conditioning, roof rail lighting, AM/FM radio, power steering and power brakes. This was because the original owner was nearly fifty years old when he bought it. It was being offered for sale by his widow.

Having not yet graduated, I had yet to embark on the career of whatever one

**With his grandmother and his '66 GTO in the fall of 1995, the author undertakes what was assuredly a counterproductive repair effort while grandmother Ruby Fees enjoys a glass of iced tea (photo by Roger Fees).**

does with a political science degree (which, turns out, is nothing), I was going to be a college graduate, with all the honors, rights and privileges that came with it, one of which was a great political science-y job making lots of money. I didn't need Dad's help to buy this car.

But, as I was yet to land that lucrative political science job, whatever that was, I didn't quite have the funds on hand. So, I turned to my car crazy old grandmother for a loan, secured with the riches aboard my ship that was soon to come in. She bridged the gap between the $2000 I had and the $2500 purchase price I negotiated as a graduation present to myself.

Over the next few years, I restored that GTO and took it to various local car shows. I was soon joined by my dad, who found and bought a nice 1967 GTO. My Chevrolet loving uncle got into the game as well, inexplicably buying a '65 GTO convertible. I didn't understand that, as I assumed he knew GTOs are made by Pontiac. His daughter Desiree and her husband also bought a 1967 GTO. For a few short years, my family was a traveling GTO exhibit.

While my uncle and cousin have since sold their cars, I still have my '66 GTO. That old GTO is showing its age and in need of some serious freshening up. Dad still has his '67 GTO, but he has added a 1966 Corvette convertible. He still has his high school Thunderbird. My youngest brother owns a 1978 Pontiac Trans Am. We are an old car family.

When a young person is lucky enough to own or be able to drive one of these cars, or any unique automobile, the car literally becomes a part of one's identity.

The Fees GTO collection, circa 1999. Left to right: The author's 1966 hardtop; his cousin Desiree Walling's 1967 hardtop; Lynn Fees' 1967 coupe; and Roger Fees' 1965 convertible (photo by author).

When my dad, who graduated from high school in 1966, sees people with whom he went to high school, they never fail to ask if he still has that old Ford. Though the T-Bird wasn't exactly a "muscle car," it was unique even in the mid–1960s. More than fifty years later the car is what people remember when they see Dad. When I see people with whom I went to high school, they don't remember how cool I was (not a lot to remember), or that I played varsity baseball, or if I had 3rd hour Geometry with them. They remember that I drove a '68 Road Runner. Some of them still call me "Road Runner," which was my nickname back then. When I think of Sandy Holmes, I think of her Camaro and its rapidly disappearing taillights the time I raced her. Certainly in the '50s and '60s, and up to at least the '80s, cars became a part of the greater individual, of a person's identity. Cars were cool, and if you had a cool car, you were cool by extension, even if you were a nerd in every other way. I am a living example of that.

In 2005, I bought another Road Runner, this time a 1969 model. As will be seen in the following pages, the 1968 and 1969 Road Runners are very similar, and I bought it because of the 1968 model I had but didn't really want back in 1987. I was approaching forty years old and I had come full circle and wanted a car like the one I drove in high school. I call it the "Midlife Chrysler." I understood then why these cars mean so much to the people who were young when these cars were new.

Sitting behind the wheel of my new purchase, staring across the cheap Plymouth instrument panel and out across the hood, I understood. Sitting there in that car, I was transported to 1990 and I felt young again. In that car, I was the Road Runner again. I thought of racing Tommy Turner's 1970 LeMans at the Midnight Drags. I remembered cruising the drag in Sapulpa, from the Tru Discount grocery parking lot to the big parking lot near Braum's ice cream and dairy store. I thought of my friend Ross, who wanted a cool car like I had and sometimes helped me wash it before we went out cruising. Sitting there made me miss those days. It made me miss the cruise circuit in Sapulpa, now long dead, and of frantically racing back home to beat my curfew, having seen the time on the big clock on the American National Bank building. My "new" Road Runner gave me a connection that spanned the decades back to my youth. Though I wouldn't go back if I could, it made me miss being young.

In the decades since the September 1986 issue of *Popular Hot Rodding*, I have planned, attended or judged more car shows than I can count. I have attended car shows all over this country. I have read more books and articles on muscle cars than I can recall. I have helped friends shop for and purchase cars of their own. I am a guy that loves these old cars, cantankerous and unreliable as they are today. And that is the story of how I became an old car person.

# 1

# A Look at the World
# of the American Muscle Car

Today the term "muscle car" is used collectively to refer to many cars in different classes from the 1960s and 1970s, from full-sized performance cars like Chevy's Impala and Ford's Galaxie to short wheelbase "pony" cars, like Mustangs, Challengers and Barracudas. Today, even two seat Corvettes are considered by some to be muscle cars. Strictly speaking however, the purists' definition of "muscle car" is a mid-sized, or intermediate, car with a large cubic inch engine, at least a four-barrel carburetor, and dual exhaust. While there is no set requirement in terms of numbers of cars built, muscle cars were mass produced and generally available to the public at large.

That is not to say that there weren't other performance cars out there. Chevrolet had what is still the premier American performance car, the Corvette. The popularity of the Corvette is such that it had no American competition after Ford quit trying with the end of the 1955–57 "baby bird" Thunderbirds. After 1957, having destroyed the Corvette in terms of sales, Ford dusted off its hands and took its T-bird in search of new worlds to conquer, leaving Chevrolet to pick up the shattered fiberglass pieces. From then on, the Corvette wouldn't have an American competitor until 1992 when Dodge unveiled its Viper, and even then, it wasn't serious competition.

Thankfully for today's muscle car market, there aren't many "purists." The "purist's" definition excludes other cars that people traditionally consider muscle cars, such as full-sized offerings from all the car makers, as well as the class of car birthed in 1964 called "pony cars." At about the same time Pontiac was planning the GTO, over at Ford, another of the gods of American automotive history, Lee Iacocca, unveiled the most popular car in history, the Mustang. It hit the streets late in the 1964 model year, and it took the world by storm as well; more so, in fact, because the Mustang was far more popular than the GTO in terms of sales numbers. Mopar guys cringe at the Mustang being called the progenitor of the pony car. They know that the Plymouth Barracuda, the Mustang's whipping boy for the next ten years, was released before the Mustang, but the little Valiant based Plymouth looked like a mechanical genetic experiment gone wrong, in which a large go-cart somehow impregnated a greenhouse. The early Barracudas didn't sell well, at least in relation to the Mustang, and the 1964 Mustang has banished at least the early incarnations of the Barracuda to the dark recesses of memory to all but the most ardent fans of the Pentastar.

Pony cars were smaller and lighter than midsized cars, and in the early days

1954 Chevrolet Corvette, owned by Bill Soman of St. Augustine, FL. The inaugural 1953 Corvette was identical (photo by Bill Soman).

The Corvette's main competition in the American sports car market was the wildly popular two seat 1955–1957 Ford Thunderbird. Pictured is a 1955 model (courtesy Vanguard Motor Sales, Plymouth, MI).

of what is considered the muscle car era, they were equipped exclusively with small-block engines, producing much less power than their bigger brethren. Later, Ford's competitors tried to cut into the Mustang-dominated pony car market with cars like Chevy's Camaro, Pontiac's Firebird, the AMC Javelin and later, Dodge's Challenger. By the 1967 model year, Ford began stuffing big-block engines into the Mustang, kicking off a trend that would effectively put the pony cars, at least the big-block ones, under the muscle car umbrella. From that point, the pony cars began slowly to grow, both in size and power, to such an extent that but for the Mustang badging, the Mustang of the last years of the muscle car era are hardly recognizable from those of 1965. While they don't meet the purist's definition, the pony car competition between the car makers should be considered its own theater in the muscle car wars.

* * *

It is important to understand something about the auto industry in that time. Back then, there were three major American car manufacturers—and one little one. The big ones were Ford, General Motors (called "GM" or "The General"), and Chrysler (also referred to colloquially as "Mopar"). The small one was American Motors. (A fifth manufacturer, Studebaker, ended production in 1966.) Each of these major manufacturers was subdivided into divisions that aimed at particular segments of the car buying market, from entry level vehicles up to full-blown luxury barges that generally could only be afforded by old people with plenty of money.

The General had Cadillac, Buick, Oldsmobile, Pontiac, and Chevrolet. GM also had a division that made only trucks—GMC—obviously irrelevant in the muscle car wars. Ford had three divisions—Ford, Mercury, and Lincoln. Only the Ford and Mercury divisions of the Ford Motor Company produced true performance cars in the muscle car era. Chrysler had four lines—Plymouth, Dodge, Chrysler and Imperial. Only Dodge and Plymouth competed in the muscle car arena. American Motors didn't have any divisions; the entire company was smaller than some divisions of the Big Three. AMC was better known for building sensible cars and, after 1970, the indestructible Jeep than for '60s performance cars. American Motors was purchased by Chrysler in 1987, and all that is left of AMC's storied history is Chrysler's Jeep line.

These divisions among the manufacturers were semi-autonomous and had a degree of independence from their cousins. For example, Pontiac and Chevrolet were corporate cousins, both being General Motors divisions, but they were generally autonomous from each other. Pontiac built its own engines and designed its own cars and competed against Chevrolet, and Oldsmobile, and Buick, though they were all of the same corporation. All the GM mother ship cared about was that its divisions were selling cars. This was a great time for car buyers, as each manufacturer was always trying to one up the other in performance and style.

Each make of car, and sometimes their owners, had nicknames on the street. A Chevrolet was a "Chevy," and guys who liked Chevys were sometimes called "Bowtie Boys," because Chevrolet's symbol resembles a bow tie. Pontiacs were called "ponchos" or "tin Indians," because the division was named for a 1700s Ottawa Indian chief. Fords were called "Blue Ovals," because Ford's symbol was, and still is, a blue oval. Unfortunately for AMC, people still called them "Ramblers" from a previous incarnation of American Motors that was known for magnificently unexciting cars. Oldsmobiles were called Olds, Dodge and Plymouth drivers were "Mopar guys," and so on.

Sometimes, car makes were referred to by where the corporate headquarters were located. For example, references to Ford were made in terms of "Dearborn," meaning Dearborn, Michigan, where the corporate headquarters of Ford was located. Same thing for Kenosha, Wisconsin, and AMC, though Kenosha is only where AMC cars were built; AMC was headquartered in Michigan. Pontiac is the easiest, because Pontiac's headquarters were helpfully located in Pontiac, Michigan.

People were fiercely loyal to their chosen brand, many for life. Often fans of one make failed to see the appeal of others. The rivalry between Ford and Chevy was (and is) perhaps the most intense, but there was no love lost between fans of any of the major car makers. Ford drivers informed Chevy and Mopar fans that they'd rather push a Ford than drive a Chevy or a Mopar. Mopar guys might retort that if one owned a Ford that is likely exactly what they'd be doing, and the Chevy guy might declare that Ford was an acronym for "Found on the Roadside Dead."

Each of these car makers aimed at a different customer demographic. Chevrolet, Plymouth and Ford aimed for the younger, first-time car buyer on the bottom end of the pricing scale. This didn't mean they didn't build nicer, more luxurious cars, but that wasn't their bread and butter. Other divisions within the mother corporation would take care of other buying market segments. Aiming for a little older and more refined demographic were Dodge and Pontiac. Up one more rung were Mercury and Oldsmobile and then Buick, who built more luxurious and opulent cars than Dodge and Pontiac but filled the niche below Lincoln, Cadillac, Chrysler or Imperial, which built exclusively full-sized luxury cars aimed at the older, wealthier crowd who would have no interest at all in quarter mile times. When it came to muscle cars, Chrysler, Imperial, Lincoln and Cadillac didn't even try.

This isn't to say that one couldn't get a Chevrolet or even a low-rung Plymouth decked out nearly as opulently as a Buick. By checking the right boxes on the option sheet, you certainly could. Bucket seats, power windows, power steering, power brakes, air conditioning, power antennas and so forth were generally available on all cars, but opulent cars didn't pay the bills at Plymouth; basic transportation did. Conversely, an Oldsmobile could be ordered as stripped down as the cheapest Chevrolet, but one would have to work at it and take on a lot of "no cost" options like a bench seat rather than standard buckets, or an automatic gear selector lever on the steering column rather than on the floor, which was standard. And Oldsmobile didn't lower the price any for these "no cost" options. "No cost" meant just that: it didn't cost anything to opt for less luxury, but the car was priced as if those options weren't chosen. Additionally, higher-end marques came with styling features that couldn't be opted out of, but raised the price of the car nonetheless, such as faux wood grain paneling in the interior or full vinyl seating.

Today, cars that are in the neighborhood of fifty years old all look the same to a novice car enthusiast. To one used to looking at modern vehicles, there isn't much obvious difference between a bare-bones 1970 Pontiac GT-37 and a plush '70

Oldsmobile 4-4-2. All things being equal, a pristine, bone-stock 1968 Dodge Super Bee—near the bottom of the ladder among muscle cars with respect to price—is typically worth more today than a 1968 Buick GS 400 in identical shape, though when they were both new, the Buick commanded a higher sticker price.

What made the high-end muscle cars that much different than the bare-bones stripped down models? What features, specifically, differ between the two that made the high-end cars expensive and the cheap cars cheap? One factor was body style. Muscle cars came in three basic body styles: pillared coupe, hardtop and convertible. The pillared coupe, or simply coupe, was usually the cheapest of the three. With vertical pillars forming the door frame from the base of the body to the roof, it was also the lightest and most rigid, making it popular with racers. The hardtop, considered by many to be the more stylish non-convertible body, lacked this pillar, and the door and quarter glass could therefore be rolled down to create an unbroken space—a design that did require reinforcement elsewhere, since the car's roof was now supported only by the four pillars framing the windshield and rear window. Convertibles were by far the heaviest of the three body styles, as they required heavy boxed frames to compensate for the lack of structural integrity the roof would have provided.

Other factors are the features, and the builders, of the cars themselves. Consider the two cars in the photographs that follow. The first is a 1969 Buick GS, at the top of the muscle car market's ladder in terms of luxury and comfort. The second is a 1969 Plymouth Road Runner, at the opposite end of the spectrum and among the cheapest and most basic of all the muscle cars in stock, optionless form. It is worth noting that muscle cars' base prices were competitively set within a narrow range, with the incongruous result that adding a few options to the budget-oriented Road Runner would put it above a base-level GS. In practice, though, Buick buyers were the ones more likely to opt for such extras as an automatic transmission, power steering and brakes, and air conditioning.

**The Buick Gran Sport represented the pinnacle of style and comfort of the muscle car era. Shown is a 1969 model GS 400 (courtesy Gateway Classic Cars, St. Louis, MO).**

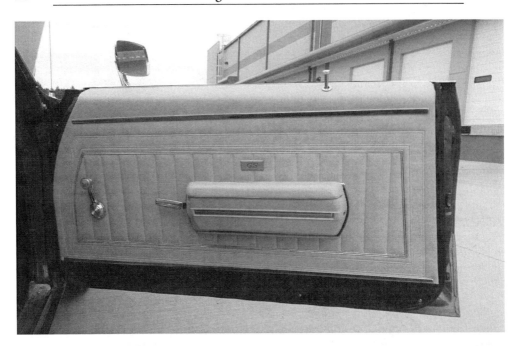

*Top and above:* The 1969 Buick GS interior. Door paneling covers the entire door with vinyl, and has large armrests, GS badging and stainless accents. The bench seat, rare for a Buick, was covered in full vinyl. Bucket seating and a console were much more common in an upscale Buick (courtesy Gateway Classic Cars, St. Louis, MO).

*Top and above:* The driver's area sports a bright three-spoke tilt sport steering wheel, air conditioning vents, and automatic transmission. The instrument panel includes plenty of brightwork around the radio, lower dash and air conditioning vents. The power steering pump and power brake booster can be seen on the left side of the engine compartment and the air conditioning unit on the opposite side of the engine (courtesy Gateway Classic Cars, St. Louis, MO).

The Buick is adorned with a full vinyl top with stainless trim, a chrome grille surround and sculpted lines arcing from the rear fender down through the doors and into the lower forward quarter panel. It also sports stainless steel molding around the wheel wells, and even the hood scoop is adorned with brightwork. On the inside, the Buick came standard with bench seating in full vinyl trim, though many Buick buyers opted for the more plush, optional bucket seats. The GS sports deluxe, full vinyl door paneling adorned with GS badging, as well as carpeting and extensive padded dash pad and Buick symbology on the instrument panel. Unseen is thicker (and heavier) sound deadening material inside the dash and inner spaces of the body. Optional for '69 were power steering, power brakes, air conditioning, power windows and seats, and AM/FM stereo with eight-track tape deck.

In contrast to the '69 Buick Gran Sport, the '69 Plymouth Road Runner was Spartan by design and represented perhaps the cheapest cars of the muscle car era. Simply but ruggedly built, the first-generation Road Runners were built to be affordable performance, with a stated goal of providing quarter mile times of less than 15 seconds for less than $3,000. This example is the pricier hardtop as opposed to the base coupe body style, and sports Magnum 500 road wheels, an expensive option over dog dish hubcap covered steel wheels standard on the Road Runner (courtesy Gateway Classic Cars, St. Louis, MO).

*Opposite, top and bottom:* The interior of the 1969 Road Runner is austere. A bench seat and manual transmission were standard. In contrast to the Buick's instrument and door panel, the Plymouth appears primitive. Only roughly ¾ of the door panel is vinyl covered, the remainder being cheaper painted steel. Rather than rally style gauging, the Plymouth's simple bar-style instrument panel featured idiot lights for oil pressure, and a cheap block-off plate to the far right when the optional tachometer was omitted. The steering wheel did feature a Road Runner badge in the center, but the interior was otherwise devoid of badging or brightwork, save for a Road Runner sticker on the passenger side of the dash panel. By 1969, the Road Runner did come with carpeting standard, with the standard rubber floor mat of '68 being deemed too cheap even for Plymouth. The Road Runner floor mats shown on this model are aftermarket (courtesy Gateway Classic Cars, St. Louis, MO).

In contrast, the Plymouth has practically none of this. Intentionally built as affordable muscle, Plymouth was aiming at the youngest and most frugal performance car buyer. In base form, the Road Runner was essentially a high-powered taxicab. Initially, Road Runner could only be had in the cheapest of body styles, the pillared coupe. The coupe reached new levels of cheapness in that the rear quarter

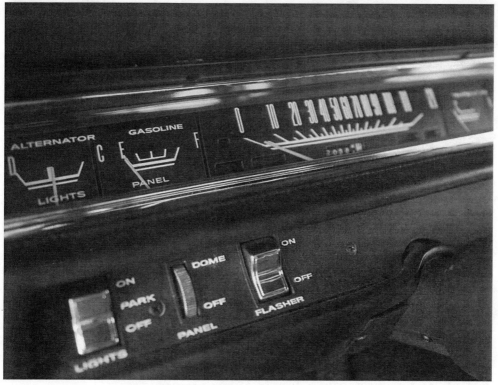

*Top and above:* Plymouth austerity continued under the hood and on the body. Gone are the rocker panel moldings and plentiful badging found on the Buick, though Plymouth added a colorful Road Runner sticker. The base 383 engine is devoid of power sapping—and expensive—accessories such as power steering, air conditioning or power brakes. Plymouth even thought to omit the chrome air cleaner and valve covers found on most muscle car models (courtesy Gateway Classic Cars, St. Louis, MO).

glass couldn't even be rolled down, and instead popped out, saving the expense—and weight—of roll-down mechanisms. By mid–1968, Plymouth offered a more expensive hardtop and '69 brought a convertible, but the pillared coupe remained the standard.

Standard seating was a cloth and vinyl bench seat, and carpeting was optional, replacing the standard rubber floor mat. Door panels were vinyl and cloth as well. Air conditioning, power steering and brakes, and upgraded seating were available as added cost options. The exterior offered no body sculpting save for a gentle crease along the fender and quarter panel, and certainly nothing like what was found on the Buick. Stainless and chrome trim was minimal. Due to a lack of sound deadening, riding in a '69 Road Runner was like riding in a railroad freight car. Cheap decals of Warner Brothers' bird were used on Road Runners; in 1968 they weren't even in color. By 1969, the bird appeared in full Technicolor regalia, but Plymouth continued to make short use of more expensive metal badgework.

Though the Road Runner and other low end, budget muscle cars could be outfitted similarly to the higher end cars like the Buick GS, the beautifully molded and stylish GS and the primitive Road Runner stand in stark contrast as two ends of the spectrum of available muscle during the era.

Many of the car companies that built muscle cars and muscular ponies do not exist anymore. Beginning in the 1970s competition from Japanese, European and later Korean manufacturers started to cut into the American companies' sales, so they had to streamline to cut the fat and get rid of the overlap. The first to go was tiny little American Motors in the 1980s. It was bought by Chrysler, and the only thing that AMC built that Chrysler kept was Jeep. In the early 2000s, Plymouth and Oldsmobile went away. In 2010, the U.S. federal government ordered GM to kill Pontiac as part of GM's Chapter 11 bankruptcy. Ford shut down the Mercury brand around the same time, early in the 2011 model year. To a car person, the death of such immortal marques as these, which spawned such legendary models as the refined muscle of an Olds 4-4-2 or the David-against-Goliath courage of AMC's Javelin is lamentable. In fact, one of these dead brands—Pontiac—gave birth to the entire muscle car era itself and has since suffered the indignity of resting beside automotive failures such as the Edsel in the boneyard of American automotive history.

* * *

The concept of a "line" or "family" of cars is important to understand as well, because most of the muscle cars were a model in a manufacturer's line. Car makers back in those days made a lot of different models of cars, in all different sizes. For example, Chevrolet in 1964 produced diminutive Chevy IIs, intermediate Chevelles, car/truck hybrid El Caminos, little two seat Corvettes, hulking full-sized Biscaynes, and revolutionary Corvairs, not to mention its truck line. Each of these models represented a "line," "series" or "family" of cars.

Within each line were various trim levels or performance variants that pretty confusingly may have carried a different name plate and therefore appeared to be an entirely different car, though in reality it was still a part of a specific car line. For example, Chevrolet had its Chevy II line, within which were several models, differentiated by their trim level—meaning level of luxuriousness in the interior—or by engine and driveline. There was even a Chevy II based station wagon. The top-of-the-line Chevy II was the Nova. An "SS" or "Super Sport" package could be had on the Nova. Until late in the muscle car era, Chevy's SS package indicated high performance, but an SS Nova still belonged to the Chevy II line; it was just a highly optioned, high-performance Chevy II.

Staying in the Chevrolet family for another example, consider the Chevrolet full-sized line. The Chevy family included the basic, low-optioned Biscayne and went all the way up to the sporty Impala Super Sport. While the patrician SS Impala and the plebeian Biscayne were of the same line, sharing a chassis and essentially the same body design, the two were entirely different cars in terms of performance, style and comfort. The Chevelle had its family, and all the manufacturers, more or less, did the same thing. The GTO was the top dog in Pontiac's Tempest family, and so on. All the cars in the family looked very much alike from the outside, with small differences between the cars of the line. The most important differences were in the interior and the drive lines. From the outside, there wasn't much difference to the untrained eye between a 1967 Buick Skylark and a 1967 Gran Sport 400. The driveline made the difference.

Related to car lines are the interesting similarities between cars of different makes, or brands, of the same corporation. These similarities illustrate a family resemblance across divisions within the same size class of cars. In much the same way that cousins might share physical features, many times divisions would share body panels—usually roofs or doors—to save the parent company costs in fabrication and design. For example, the 1966–1967 lines of the Pontiac Tempest/LeMans, Olds Cutlass/F-85, Buick Skylark and Chevrolet Chevelle/Malibu all shared rooflines. The same is true of the 1968–1970 Chrysler B-body lines.

The family resemblance has since spawned a huge industry in fraud, in which basic, non-performer cars of a given line are "cloned" into something more desirable. There are many, many GTOs that began life as lowly Tempests, only to be fitted with the drive line from a wrecked 389-powered Bonneville, and rebadged as indistinguishable from the Tempest's more lethal sibling. "Cloning" a car is not nefarious in and of itself, but it is when a Tempest is sold as a GTO, since the GTO itself began as an up-engined option on the lowlier Tempest LeMans before becoming its own legendary model in Pontiac's line. Since "clone" has become somewhat of a dirty word in the car world, the term has morphed into less-fraudulent sounding terms such as "tribute car." Many an unwary buyer has purchased a "clone" or a "tribute car," and the most scrupulous car sellers or restorers will acknowledge up front the actual identity of the car they are selling. There is nothing inherently wrong with clones; they are a cheaper way for entry level enthusiasts to have the fun and attention of driving a genuine muscle car, but such cars must be marketed for what they actually are, or, more importantly, what they aren't.

Car lines that share characteristics are referred to in terms of "generations," with similarly styled vehicles of a given manufacturer grouped together. Each car maker had multiple generations of muscle cars during the muscle car era. First generation A-body GM muscle cars included the '64 and '65 model years. The second generation

*Top and above:* The "family resemblance" in the 1969 Chrysler B-body lines. At top is a 1969 Plymouth Road Runner, a B-body of the Belvedere line that included the base Belvedere, Satellite, Road Runner and GTX. Bottom is a 1969 Super Bee, of Dodge's Coronet line. The two car lines shared the basic body lines and in particular the roofline (courtesy Vanguard Motor Sales, Plymouth, MI).

*Above and opposite:* "Family traits" of GM's 1966–67 A-body muscle car lines. Clockwise from top left: 1967 Oldsmobile 4-4-2 of the Cutlass/F-85 line, 1967 Malibu of the Chevelle line, 1967 Buick GS California of the Skylark line, and the 1967 Pontiac GTO of the Tempest line. All models shared identical rooflines, drip rail trim and doors, among other body panels (SS and GTO photos courtesy Gateway Classic Cars, St. Louis, MO; 4-4-2 and GS photos courtesy of Streetside Classics, Charlotte, NC).

was '66 and '67, and the final generation of A-body muscle cars lasted through 1972, though some muscle car nameplates, like the GTO and 4-4-2, went on for several more years after the end of the muscle car era. For the Ford intermediate family, the '64 and '65 models constitute a generation, as do the '66–'67, '68–'69, and the '70– '71. Chrysler B-body generations were '64–'65, '66–'67, '68–'70, and the diminishing

*Top and above:* The shared DNA of the 1969 Ford midsized line is readily apparent in the Ford Torino GT (top) and Mercury's Cyclone. The Blue Oval didn't do much to hide that the Mercury was a virtual clone of the Ford, with the cars sharing not only the roofline, but identical doors, glass, deck lid and quarter panels. Even the molding aft of the quarter glass was identical (courtesy Vanguard Motor Sales, Plymouth, MI).

performance mid-sized nameplates of '71–'72, though, again, some muscle car names went on long after the end of the muscle car era.

Pony cars were grouped into generations as well. The '65–'67 Mustangs are considered a generation, as are the '68–'70s, though they are still pretty similar to the first gen Mustangs. Cougar generations were '67–'70 and '71–'72. The first-generation GM ponies were the '67–'69 models, and the second generation included the '70 and beyond, up through 1981. Plymouth's Barracuda line had three muscle car generations—'64–'66, '67–'69, and the beautiful '70–'74. The late coming Dodge Challenger had only one generation ('70–'74), as did the AMC Javelin ('68–'70) and AMX ('68–'70) before the two lines were merged in 1971.

* * *

Finally, a few words must be said about the various muscle cars in relation to one another. Many observers of the muscle car era and its cars fall victim to the habit of simply reducing the various cars to a collection of numbers representing various characteristics, such as engine displacement, curb weight, horsepower or torque, tallying them up, and declaring whichever car has the best numbers to be superior. This approach fails to take into account the myriad of factors which go into the actual performance capabilities of a given car, and it cheapens them all.

Many would consider the 1970 LS6 454 SS Chevelle to be among a very few cars that can be declared the greatest muscle car of them all. On paper, that assertion would be correct. The LS6 recorded the greatest horsepower of any muscle car engine, and it was stuffed into a relatively light body, but to end the analysis there is lazy and fails to take in the variables. There may be a world of difference between two 1970 LS6 SS Chevelles in terms of performance: one may be a stripped down, bench seat, four speed equipped with a low-geared positive traction rear end and no horsepower sapping power options, while the other may be a high geared, open rear end car with automatic, heavy bucket seating, and a whole lot of power-this and power-that drawing horsepower from the engine. On paper, and probably in real life, the former will whip the latter.

Chrysler provides another example. The 426 Hemi was one of the most fearsome engines of the era, and Hemi-powered Mopars are considered to reside in the same rarified air as the LS6 Chevelle, but the Hemi was a disagreeable, barely civilized engine, and very difficult to keep in tune. The six-barreled 440 surrendered 35 horsepower to the Hemi, but many Mopar folks preferred it to the Hemi, because it was easier to keep running, even with the challenge of keeping an array of three two-barreled carbs in tune. The 425 horsepower rating on the 426 Hemi assumed it was in perfect tune, and it rarely was. A smooth running, well-tuned 440 Six Pack was a better performer than a Hemi that wasn't running right.

All things being equal, betting on the cars with the better stat sheet was usually the safe route. All things, however, were rarely equal. It was nowhere near unusual for base model muscle cars to outrun what on paper, and in reality, were more powerful cars. It all depended on the variables. Tires, tune, weight, power options, transmission, rear end, and many others weighed into the equation. And the one variable that could never be equalized, because no one can drive two cars at once, is the skill of the driver. The driver is perhaps the most important variable of all, though big displacement and big horsepower and torque can cover a multitude of driver sins.

All of that is to say that regardless of how they are equipped, from the lowliest Plymouth or Chevy to the most opulent Buick, all of these cars are members of an elite class and were the greatest of performers of their day. The differences between them are measured in degrees, particularly fifty years removed from their heyday. Today, it does not matter much. A muscle car is a muscle car. It would take an individual of particular bravery, or some might say stupidity, to beat on a vintage muscle car with its original driveline like they were beaten on in their time. Whether in base form or decked out with all the options available, or any combination in between, they were—and are—all awesome.

With the preliminaries out of the way, it is now time to begin the survey of the history of the rise and fall of the American muscle car and the times which gave birth to those tremendous vehicles.

# 2

# Genesis

## *The Genealogy of the American Muscle Car*

In order to understand the American muscle car and its rise and its fall, one must have an understanding of the times that gave it birth because, without the 1960s, there would be no American muscle car. One must understand the times and the context and the state of the nation overall through the years when the streets were ruled by large cube, high horsepower vehicles. To understand this contextual history is important, because with as much fond nostalgia as we have for the 1960s, many tend to forget that in the 1960s the United States came as close to coming apart at the seams as at any time in a century.

When we look back at the 1960s through the hazy lens of more than fifty years, we tend to see that era through the eyeglass in reverse—that is to say, we focus on the quaint, the interesting, or the iconic. We don't look back and think of the daily struggles of black Americans forced to drink from specified water fountains or to use segregated bathrooms. We don't think about what went through the minds of any specific individual denied a seat at the lunch counter in Woolworth's. We remember the big events—the beatings on the Edmund Pettus Bridge, the Selma to Birmingham March, and the speeches of Martin Luther King, Jr. We don't remember the fear that parents had of their children contracting some horrendous disease by engaging in the free love of the time, which we see now as quaint. We remember the moon landing, but forget what an accomplishment that was, and that people died in the Apollo program. The space shuttle and the projected manned trip to Mars have eclipsed it as much as the first vehicle eclipsed the development of the Conestoga wagon. We remember the highlights—the British Invasion, the clothes, girls stuffing flowers in soldiers' rifle barrels, civil rights, and the cars—we don't remember the mundane happenings that fill the drab space in between. We know that two Kennedy siblings were assassinated, as well as an icon of the Civil Rights Movement, but don't remember the details. We watch *Easy Rider* or footage from Woodstock and think that is the '60s. For many, the first half the decade is the Civil Rights Movement, and the last half is the war, and then on to overly simplifying the '70s, reducing that decade to Watergate, stagflation and gas lines.

What we don't think, because our social memories are clouded with nostalgia and the passage of time, is that the country was on the brink of self-destruction. This was due to the largest social shift in generations, as the young, having been coddled and spoiled so they would not have to endure the hardships their parents had, rebelled against "the system." This wildly divergent intergenerational worldview was further exacerbated by the war in Vietnam and by the Civil Rights Movement. No event better represents the gulf of difference between the younger generation and the older than the war. By and large, the older generation that had supported the war effort against Fascism twenty years earlier also supported the war in Vietnam. Some of that generation fought a similar conflict against communism in another Asian country, Korea. The youth, however, opposed the war in Vietnam, and by a wide margin. This was understandable because they were the ones to fight it, and many were drafted to do so against their will.

1968 exposed the substantial fissures in the nation's society. President Lyndon Johnson, having prodded the nation headlong into war and, for great swaths of the nation, "forced" civil rights upon them, declined to run again and see the mess through to the end. The most visible figure of the Civil Rights Movement, the Rev. Martin Luther King, Jr., was shot dead by career reprobate James Earl Ray in Memphis in April of that year, sparking widespread race riots and adding further turmoil to a country quickly wearying of it.

In the scramble to claim Johnson's smoldering throne, Robert Kennedy, younger brother of the president slain in 1963, surged to an early lead in the Democratic primary. In May, fresh off his victory in the California primary, Kennedy was himself shot dead by Palestinian Sirhan Sirhan, a very early version of assassinations motivated by the Arab-Israeli conflict that would be repeated to the present day. The Democratic National Convention that summer was marred with protests, riots and violence and eventually resulted in a split in the Democratic electorate. The uninspiring but mainstream Hubert Humphrey was nominated, while Alabaman and staunch supporter of segregation George Wallace broke from the Democratic Party and ran as an independent, drawing off Democratic support in the Deep South. The result, in the short term, was the thorough trouncing of both by Republican Richard Nixon. Illustrative of the angry mood of the country and its dissatisfaction with eight years of Democratic governance was the election of a man the nation had rejected way back when things looked much better in 1960. Nixon's election made no one on the left even remotely happy and further divided the country, and though they didn't know it, Americans still had Watergate to which to look forward. In the long term, Nixon's election set in motion the long, slow drift of the South from the Democratic Party, where it had been strong since the founding of the party. A straight line can be drawn from Donald Trump and the divisions the country faces today back to the election of 1968.

The 1960s were far more than music festivals, LSD, war protests, civil rights and psychedelic Volkswagen micro-buses. The decade was a combination of these things and many, many more that produced the totality of circumstances that we call the '60s. An unavoidable shortcoming of the study of history is that we only remember the highlights or the lowlights. Acknowledging that, try as we might and as much as we might want, we cannot reproduce an era or a moment in time once it has passed, and to do so becomes more difficult as more and more moments in time separate us from the one we wish to recreate. However, to do our best is incumbent upon those who study or are interested in the history of a given era.

The performance mid-sized and pony cars of the 1960s, more popular now than they ever have been, played a role in the great tapestry that makes up the history of the 1960s. This in brief is their story.

\* \* \*

More than any other nation, America has always had a love affair with its cars. From its earliest days, the American automobile represented freedom. Cars were a convenient and more efficient departure from previous animal powered modes of transportation. Cars afforded ordinary Americans a way to experience first-hand the amazing variety of people and places that the country had to offer. Cars spurred the American imagination and provided the means for Americans to discover whether those imaginations were close to the mark. Cars have always been an integral part of the American experience.

But cars were much more than a means of recreation. Very early on, the automobile became a tool of nation building, and in a very real sense, of national power. During the early 20th century, the automobile became an integral part of American commerce. Cars were a means of transporting goods across the net of roads that traverse the vastness of the nation, and were therefore vital to the exponential growth of the national economy in the first half of that century. Cars were a means of economic mobility that Americans used to improve their station, whether desperate Okies fleeing the Dust Bowl, desperately trying to improve their economic station by moving west, or people moving to far-flung areas of the country to change jobs with relative ease. The American automobile was a weapon of war and moved the victorious troops and the gear they needed to fight the nation's battles. Indeed, the American automobile even provided transport to other armies: the Soviet troops that brought down the Third Reich moved primarily in American made trucks. In the post-war years, the American automobile hit its stride. In those prosperous years, finally free from the apprehension of the previous twenty years that saw economic calamity followed by war, Americans took to the roads. These are the halcyon days of Route 66 and U.S. 41, no longer avenues of desperation, but of recreation. This new freedom and the cars that provided it birthed an entire industry that catered to their drivers—mechanic shops, roadside cafes, "service stations," and motor hotels—"motels"—with eye piercing neon signage along the concrete and asphalt arteries of commerce upon which the car roamed. By the 1950s, the automobile had become a ubiquitous part of American culture.

The history of the American automobile and the old car hobby itself is subdivided into various groups of similar cars or cars from a specific era or decade. For example, there are "pre-war" vehicles, which is a catch-all term that encompasses any car made before production of vehicles for civilian consumption shut down during World War II. Cars of the 1950s are lumped together, as are those of the '70s and the '80s. The subdivisions go on, but one of the most significant subdivision is the American muscle car of the 1960s and early 1970s.

The muscle car is a uniquely American creature. To begin with, there were no "import" muscle cars. Muscle cars are 100 percent American. The muscle car is the mechanical representation of a national confidence that emerged from the trials of the 1930s and 1940s. The American muscle car came into being during a time in American history between two eras of national trial. These young people who bought the American muscle car or who were fans of it did not suffer the '30s and '40s. They had yet to be scarred by the tragedy and defeat of the Vietnam War, the body blow of public confidence that was Watergate, or the general national malaise of the 1970s. The muscle car represents the last gasp of an era in which the United States exuded masculinity and an arrogant confidence about its place in the world. In an era of John Wayne, the Apollo missions and the confident belief that the United States was the only nation capable of saving the world from Communism, the muscle car played its part to assert the swaggering confidence of the most super of superpowers.

The 1950s and the 1960s have proven to be the high watermarks for the American automobile in terms of its place in popular culture and enduring influence. One doesn't have to look far to see the enduring popularity of these cars. There are literally thousands of websites dedicated to the cars from this era. The muscle car restoration industry is measured in the millions of dollars. A casual glance at the magazine section of a local bookstore will reveal title after title of magazines dedicated to the cars in general or to specific makes. Nearly every small-town festival across the country includes a well attended car show. On any given weekend, people can tune in and watch muscle cars being sold at auction, in real time. Most people with even a basic grasp of automobile knowledge have heard of the legendary cars of the era, such as GTO or Mustang.

The cars are arguably more popular now than they were in their own time. These cars came from an era in which all the cars did not look the same and where there was a definable difference between them in terms of styling and performance. Generally speaking, the grayheads that own and enjoy muscle cars today could only wish they could have afforded them when they were new. They have since had fifty years to build careers and to accumulate the disposable income to own now what they wanted to own back when they were mainly worried about their draft lottery number. There were dedicated Chevrolet guys, or Chrysler guys, or Ford guys, and they had their reasons for their staunch support of their brands and were very vocal about their loyalties.

More importantly, these cars represent a time that is long gone, a nostalgia that is yearned for today in this era of economic instability, global terror and general uncertainty. They represent a past that will not return, a time of national naiveté in terms of what would come over the next five decades. Back then, the bad guys were bad, and the good guys were good, and you knew exactly who they were. The country did not yet have endless partisanship in Washington, too-big-to-fail banks, and a national debt measured in tens of trillions. That was a world before global economies and internet interconnectivity and one that rarely expanded beyond the sphere of influence of one's hometown.

That is what these cars represent. A simpler time. It was a time of foot operated dimmer switches and roll down windows. For people of that generation, sitting behind the wheel of a long-retired boulevard brawler is to sit in a time machine. Driving one puts one back in a different place in time, where the concerns and fears of a modern world, often difficult to understand, cannot penetrate the protective veil of sound produced by a large cube V-8 engine snarling through dual exhaust.

* * *

To understand the muscle car era and the fertile soil from which it sprang, one must understand the decades before 1964, when what is now generally recognized as the first true muscle car arrived on the scene to leave its indelible mark on the history of the American automobile. This is necessary because history is nothing but an endless cycle of cause and effect relationships. The muscle car era did not just spontaneously happen. No auto executive suddenly woke up one day and decided to build a muscle car. The American muscle car was the product of its time; like all such "times," they were the product of a historical evolution and an intersection of a myriad of historical and cultural factors.

When asking a historian to describe the history of anything, one always runs the risk of getting far more description than that for which one bargained. To a historian's mind, to start a history at any point after Creation, or the Big Bang, if that is preferable, is simply to pick an arbitrary starting point in the history of the thing and to tell an incomplete story. A historian describing the history of the development of satellite communications that didn't go back and start the story with the Roman system of roads would be shortchanging the story. This is the danger of attempting "brief" history.

In the interests of time, space and attention span, the arbitrary starting point for the brief history of the muscle car era will only go back to the 1930s and '40s. To understate things, the 1930s in the United States were not happy times. The 1930s saw the worst economic conditions in U.S. history, an era known as the Great Depression. Despite what was bandied about by the media and politicians in the last years of the first decade of the 2000s, 2008 was not the worst economic time the U.S. had suffered. The '30s were. At points during the Great Depression, unemployment approached 25 percent, and people lost homes and farms by the millions. As hard as it is to believe today, Americans were literally starving to death.

The good news was the Depression of the 1930s didn't last forever. It did come to an end. The bad news is the end of the Depression is marked by the beginning of the most devastating bloodletting humankind has ever seen, a little six-year barrel of fun called World War II. Though the exact number is unknown, tens of millions of people lost their lives in this war, which finally ended with twin atomic mushroom clouds and the deaths of more than a hundred thousand Japanese in 1945.

These two events, the Depression and The War, piggy-backed each other and directly on a single generation of Americans, and they profoundly changed people and their worldview. The generation that survived these twin catastrophes tended to be very conservative. They were not risk takers, because experience taught them that all good things could go to hell in an instant. The economy of the 1940s rebounded from the Depression, driven by the U.S. and allied governments buying billions and billions of dollars in materiel to fight the Nazis, Italians and Japanese. If one were not one of the millions of Americans mobilized by the War, the economic boom of the 1940s provided jobs for just about anyone who wanted one, including groups that

**An "Okie" family with a broken down "jalopy" heading west in search of a better life during the Great Depression (Library of Congress).**

historically had been shut out of the work force, such as blacks and women. That was good, but history had taught that generation that economic stability was fleeting indeed. Better to play safe and conservative and plan for the worst. People of this generation understood economic calamity, starvation and war.

The years after the war were the beginning of the Baby Boom years. Soldiers, when they are away soldiering, get homesick. They miss the comforts of home. Living the austere life of a soldier in constant danger of violent death has that effect. One of the comforts sorely missed was female companionship, and when these soldiers came home, they were very glad to see their wives, girlfriends, or someone else's' wife or girlfriend. The ritual is as old as war itself: soldiers coming home from wars to reunite with the woman (or women) they left behind and to suddenly find themselves in the market for diapers and bottles. In the years following the war, there were babies. Lots and lots of babies. This generation, currently hard at work bankrupting Social Security, are collectively known as the Baby Boomers.

The parents of the Boomers, these very conservative people that had lived through war, famine, and depression, were now raising millions of kids, but in an era entirely unlike that which these parents had ever known. From 1929 to 1949—twenty years—there were exactly four years without one hardship or another—the last four years of that period. They tried to instill in the Boomers their hard-earned values of hard work and responsibility. They tried to teach them that you should get a job as early as you can and be damn glad you had one. To work hard, and for God's sake, don't do anything out of the ordinary to get fired. You may not get another job. Even worse, in that era there was the ever-present threat of nuclear annihilation in the emerging Cold War between former World War II allies the U.S. and the Soviet Union. There may not be a world at all tomorrow. Conform and be happy with your lot in life. After all, the baby boom years were also economic boom years. There were plenty of jobs and prosperity.

The cars of a given era can tell a lot about what is going on in society, culture or the economy, if one knows for what to look. For example, the tiny, underpowered economy cars of the mid–1970s told of the Arab Oil Embargo and the relative scarcity of gasoline. The 1950s were no exception.

The new-found and previously unexperienced prosperity, after decades of depression and war, was reflected in the cars of the 1950s. The 1950s were good times. Unemployment was low. There was plenty of money to be made and spent. The cars of the late '50s reflected this. They were land rockets—behemoth cars with curb weights measured in tons, obscene amounts of chrome and absurd tail fins supposedly inspired by the fighter aircraft of World War II. In terms of resource use, they were ridiculously wasteful of everything. They were the product of prosperity and were a tangible representation of the celebration after the years of turmoil. Those cars said, "We made it. Let's celebrate."

A terrific example of this came courtesy of the mad scientists at General Motors at the tail-end of the decade. The 1959 Cadillac El Dorado was a monument to '50s styling taken to its logical extreme, all of twenty feet long and weighing nearly 5000 pounds. Its tail fins approach two feet in height, each sporting two bullet shaped taillights perched halfway up. Each seat had its own power adjustment and cigarette lighter. The chrome alone, generously hung anywhere on the car it could fit, weighed in the neighborhood of a modern import. It may have made it to eight miles per gallon of gas, going downhill and with a good tail wind, but who cared? Money was plentiful, and gas was cheap. There was, in fact, an endless supply of gasoline pumped out of the ground in what twenty years earlier had been the Dust Bowl wasteland of Texas and Oklahoma. Cars of the 1950s dripped in chromium plated opulence. The 1959 Cadillac was the automotive expression of the newfound American prosperity.

By 1960, as if ashamed of itself, the American car industry dialed things back a bit in terms of styling. Fins were still around, but they were more subtle, or at least as subtle as a tail fin could be. In the late 1950s and early 1960s, the Baby Boomers, that huge demographic wave of humanity, grew up and began to approach driving age.

**1959 Cadillac El Dorado Biarritz, owned by Joe Puleo of Watchung, New Jersey (photo by owner).**

Like any generation, the Boomers grew up in a different environment and with a different set of experiences than their parents. Boomers had never seen the level of hardship their parents had, and, luckily, avoided the painful lessons their parents had learned. Boomers had only known peace and prosperity. Parental guidance, admonitions and advice based on past experiences fell on the deaf ears of the Boomers, as they do on any generation. They didn't see the point. Didn't everyone always have a house with a garage, a good job, and a giant chrome car? Insulated against hardship, never having known the need for the conservatism of their parents, the Boomers began to rebel against it. That way of thinking was outdated and obsolete. Boomers had never made a desperate flight to California with everything they possessed stuffed into a jalopy or seen people starve. Likely, they were unfamiliar with the term "jalopy."

Culturally and politically, the late 1950s and early '60s were transitional times and set the stage for more uncertain times later in the decade. In 1960, grandfatherly President Dwight Eisenhower, who had not only vanquished the Nazis but also presided over the gloriously stable and prosperous 1950s, was gone. In his place America elected a young, dynamic, handsome president named John Kennedy, who had a beautiful wife. Kennedy was a sharp change from the older, dour, sage men who had typically occupied the White House. While not a Boomer, Kennedy better reflected the Boomers than the man he defeated in 1960, Republican Richard Nixon. Nixon was another curmudgeonly, dour Republican of the old guard, and had served as the equally curmudgeonly Eisenhower's vice president. Elvis introduced Rock and Roll, and white people were beginning to appreciate what black people had always appreciated in blues and music from the Motor City. Kennedy challenged Americans to do things unheard of, such as walk on the moon and initiating the "space race" with the Soviet Union, giving focus to America's slumbering prowess in science, mathematics and engineering.

Times were rapidly changing by the early 1960s. They were good times. The nation began to get militarily involved in some unknown place called French Indochina, or Vietnam, or something, but that was all the way around the world and out of people's minds. Americans had good jobs and money. Good jobs and money meant plenty of leisure time to do enjoyable things. The money the parents were making trickled down to the Boomer kids, and because there were plenty of job opportunities, the kids got jobs of their own. Many of those Boomer kids spent their time and money on cars.

Cars were a vital part of the culture of the early to mid–1960s. Musical groups had hit songs on the radio about drag racing on killer curves or Ford Thunderbirds. Racing was popular, either drag racing or stock car racing, in what would be recognized as NASCAR racing today. The car manufacturers cashed in on the Space Race and its inherent coolness and named their creations accordingly. People were known by their cars, and the cars themselves, if particularly notorious, were maybe even better known than their drivers.

The importance of drag racing on the evolution of the muscle car cannot be overstated. Drag racing was a popular pastime in the late 1950s and early 1960s;

1963 R–Code Galaxie, owned by Todd Hollar of Thackerville, OK (photo by owner).

sometimes officially sanctioned, and sometimes, perhaps most times, not. In those days, thousands of small dragstrips dotted the countryside, and people, professional and amateur alike, raced their cars. Drag racing also took place on the streets, when the cops were not around. Drag racing became popular, aside from the rush of adrenaline, because drag racing was easily done on any street. No high banked superspeedway was needed, just a quarter mile strip of pavement and someone to tell the racers when to start. In bigger towns, this wasn't even needed because stop lights were used.

In the late '50s and early '60s, the kids who raced for fun usually raced some car they built or worked on and heavily modified. Back in those days, people could work on their cars. Changing a carburetor, or exhaust, or even entire engines, was easy. Guys tuned their cars throughout the week, and then they took the cars out to the local drag strip, or simply to the nearest cruise circuit, and they raced, and then they started the whole process over again the next week. That's what kids did, then. Today, they play on social media. Back then, they raced.

Speed was generated relatively simply then. There were no computer-controlled fuel injection systems—there were only carburetors. There were no racing tires, which were the result of millions of dollars of research and development; there were F70–14 bias ply tires. By today's standards, driving to the Dollar General for a case of Cokes on bias ply tires is a harrowing experience; the width of the lanes is barely wide enough to contain the random wanderings of those old tires. There were no turbocharged, intercooled engines. Modern technology taken for granted today was still decades in the future.

The Ford Galaxie's 427 engine displacement callout (courtesy Todd Hollar of Thackerville, OK).

Back then, speed was achieved by generating horsepower. Without the benefit of modern technology, horsepower was produced with engines of huge displacement, and bigger generally meant better. An engine's size or displacement—the volume of fuel-air mixture drawn into the cylinders during one full revolution—was measured in "cubic inches." Big engines meant more capacity for fuel and air, which was detonated inside them, and that meant more horsepower. More horsepower meant more speed. That's somewhat of an oversimplification, but it's true. Today's technology allows cars to produce three times the horsepower from half the engine size. Back then, horsepower was generated very bluntly—bigger engines using more fuel.

For people into cars and racing, engine displacement was an important factor. In fact, it may have been *the* important factor. Displacement became as important an identifier as the make and model of the car in which the engine was sitting. For example, there was no such thing as a '63 Chevy Biscayne or a '64 Ford Galaxie. When cars were referred to or talked about, there was an engine displacement figure attached to the make and model. The Biscayne wasn't a Biscayne; it was a 409 Biscayne. The Ford was a 427 Galaxie. In many cases year, make and displacement were enough. All anyone needed to know was that it was a 409 '63 Chevy. No one talked about the bad '62 Pontiac Catalina from the next town over that was beating everyone on the street. They talked about the bad '62 Super Duty Pontiac from the next town that was beating everyone on the street. One immediately knew not only the car that was beating everyone, but also why. In the early '60s, "Super Duty" and "Pontiac" were all that needed to be said. No one really cared the identity of the guy piloting the Pontiac.

The racing trend wasn't lost on the car builders. In the late 1950s and especially into the early 1960s, car companies began to make limited edition, full-sized vehicles with high-performance engines, and specially modified, lightweight frames or aluminum body panels. These cars were hard to get, however. The car makers didn't make many of them, and they were expensive. They weren't widely available to the public; many times these cars were sold to only particular dealers or racing teams.

The general buying public was increasingly into racing and performance cars, the younger buyers in particular. Drag racing and stock car racing were many times broadcast on television, and when they were, they were widely watched, spurring

1962 Super Duty Catalina (courtesy the Pontiac-Oakland Museum, Pontiac, IL).

**1963 SS 409 Impala owned by John Dillman of Crosby, Texas (photo by Kenneth Pylant).**

the interest in performance cars. Today, hundreds of television options are taken for granted; in those days, there were only three major channels. Car makers used racing in their advertisements, applying the marketing adage of "Win on Sunday, sell on Monday." Relative to their parents at the same age, young people had money, but the new, high-performance cars available in the early 1960s were still out of their reach, if they were available at all.

Some people built their own race cars. These people used what was coming from the factories as a starting point. In the late '50s and early '60s, however, big-block power was only available in the land yachts—the full-sized cars. People pulled those big engines from those big cars—to do so was easy then—and stuffed them into smaller vehicles. This required a lot of work and at least two cars. The cost wasn't cheap, even if the job was relatively easy.

A person could do a lot with those engines to improve their performance; the level of technology at that time made the various mechanical components that make up a car relatively simple. There just was not a lot to them, and compared to today's cars, they might as well have been something Fred Flintstone would drive. Regardless of the miracles those shade tree mechanics were able to work on those drive trains, those were still huge cars. Some pushed north of 4,000 pounds. Those old engines, tuned and modified to the outermost limits of the available technology, would dutifully fling huge cars like Buick Wildcats and Chrysler's various land barges down the track at a surprisingly good clip, but to do so was a lot of work.

**Early Chrysler full-sized performance: Dodge's 413 powered 1963 Polara (courtesy Gateway Classic Cars, St. Louis, MO).**

The American car builders took notice. Two of them in particular, Ford and the Pontiac division at General Motors, suspected the presence of an emerging youth market for performance cars. Cars were increasingly becoming a part of the youth culture. The band Jan and Dean kept singing about cars. Market research indicated that more women were buying cars and that younger people were increasingly buying a second car. The Beach Boys sang a song called "Shut Down" about nothing but a drag race between a fuel injected Corvette and a 413 powered Super Stock Dodge. Kids talked about racing in the high school halls. People, particularly young ones, flocked to the local drag strip on the weekends, or "cruised" their town's "main drag" and challenged each other to stop light to stop light drag races. Young people were increasingly identified by their cars.

Car companies are companies, and by definition they want to sell things. The emerging youth market was largely untapped, because the car companies didn't want to take the plunge. Selling what would be essentially factory race cars was just too risky and out of the ordinary—against tradition. The auto executives that were making such decisions were from the generation before—the conservative folks that had lived through the Depression and World War II. While the car companies would build some low production, high-performance full-sized cars like the Chrysler "letter" cars, Super Duty Pontiacs, Ford Thunderbolts, or wedge-powered Plymouth Belvederes, they weren't willing yet to commit to the mass production of factory racers.

All of that was set to change as the curtain was raised on the 1964 model year. The market was ripe for a mass produced, affordable performance car, the result of a perfect intersection of several popular cultural factors. The storm that broke in 1964 would mark a revolution in the American auto industry, the first volleys of the muscle car wars.

Pontiac's warning to the street (photo by author).

# 3

# Opening Salvo

### *Pontiac's Rebellion and Wild Horses*

Looking backwards through the lens of history, the decade of the 1960s is undoubtedly one of the most transformative in American history. Virtually every single year of that decade saw cataclysmic events that shaped—or scarred—the American psyche. (Historian's note: 1961 was the first year of the 1960s and 1970 the last; despite the hysteria of December 31, 1999, decades, or millennia, end in multiples of 10, and not with a 9.)

The muscle car wars arguably started in 1964. Some historians of the era date the start earlier, but virtually no one dates it later than 1964. Culturally speaking, 1964 was a bridge year. One end of the bridge was firmly grounded in the waning days of a 1950s culture that was reluctant to die, and the other end stretched unseen in the swirling maelstrom that was the future of the '60s. 1964 was far more similar to the late 1950s than it was to 1968, having yet to endure the bleeding cultural abscesses that scarred American consciousness and that lay a few short years ahead.

Retrospectively viewed, 1964 was a calm before the breaking of a furiously gathering storm. The country was emerging from the trauma of the November 1963 killing of its young and energetic president, John Kennedy. Kennedy's slaying ushered in the hugely influential administration of Lyndon Baines Johnson, one of the most controversial presidential administrations in the nation's history.

It did not take long for the Johnson Administration to get itself in gear. In Southeast Asia, after years of smoldering on the back burner and out of people's minds, Johnson placed the decades old communist insurgency in Vietnam squarely on America's front pages. The Johnson Administration continued Kennedy's policy of sending military equipment and U.S. "advisors" to prop up a corrupt but rabidly anti–Communist regime in South Vietnam. In August, after an alleged attack on the U.S. Navy destroyer *Maddux* by the North Vietnamese Navy, Congress gave Johnson a blank check for direct action in Vietnam, known to history as the Gulf of Tonkin Resolution. Like it or not, and in 1964 polls said most people did, the U.S. was being drawn more and more heavily into Vietnam's nasty little civil war.

At home, Congress, spurred by the President's cajoling of reluctant Southern Democrats, passed the Civil Rights Act. The result of the years-long Civil Rights Movement highlighted by violence and obstinate foot dragging across the states of the Old Confederacy, the Civil Rights Act represented a great leap forward for the civil rights of African Americans toward a social equality supposedly established a century earlier. A relatively unknown fighter known in 1964 as Cassius Clay—who took on the name of Muhammad Ali after a conversion to Islam—defeated Sonny Liston to become heavyweight champion of the world. The United States suffered the first English invasion since 1814, this time in the form of mop headed boys from Liverpool called the Beatles; rather than burning the White House again, this British invasion's casualties were merely swooning teenage girls and the introduction of a Baskin Robbins ice cream flavor called Beatle Nut. Things were hopping in New York, as the City That Never Sleeps hosted the World's Fair and plans were announced for the world's tallest skyscrapers, known as the World Trade Center, to be built in lower Manhattan. The Warren Commission determined that Lee Harvey Oswald and only Lee Harvey Oswald killed President Kennedy, and the Surgeon General couldn't make up his mind whether smoking actually caused lung cancer.

Particularly because of the burgeoning involvement in Vietnam, 1964 marked the beginning a cultural transformation in the United States. It didn't have the momentous events of 1963, 1968 or 2001, but was an interesting year.

\* \* \*

Mark Twain once accurately observed that history does not repeat itself, but it rhymes. History is replete with rhyming irony; an endless cycle of events, of cause-and-effect relationships, sometimes separated by hundreds or even thousands of years, that appear to bear a remarkable similarity to one another through an alignment of factual circumstances.

The first sound in a particular historical rhyme took place in 1763 in the old growth forests of the old Trans-Appalachian West in what is now southeast Michigan. In that time and place, an Ottawa warrior named Obwandiyag, Anglicized to *Pontiac*, shattered a post–French and Indian War peace by leading a revolution against the English settling in that vast territory. English encroachment in the Trans-Appalachian West had been forbidden by the Crown with the Proclamation of 1763, with the area to be set aside as a perpetual Indian reservation. But the Crown's reach did not extend further than its grasp, and the fertile river valleys and rolling hills of the Indians' sanctuary proved to be irresistible to white settlers and speculators sifting west through the Appalachian Mountains. Pontiac unified several tribes in opposition and led an attack on an English fort near present-day Detroit. History marks this attack as the beginning of an event known to posterity as "Pontiac's Rebellion."

History's rhyme came exactly 200 years later, when a GM division named for the courageous Ottawa planned its own rebellion, again just outside Detroit. This new rebellion by Pontiac was mechanical, an automotive rebellion against its corporate overlords at General Motors and against the status quo of American car making. Where the original Pontiac was ultimately unsuccessful in driving out the British, its modern analog successfully changed the American cultural landscape. The result of the 20th century Pontiac uprising was the legendary GTO. The GTO was the first mass produced, affordable factory super automobile. The GTO was the first muscle car.

In 1963, at roughly the same time President Kennedy was putting the final touches on a Dallas itinerary for later that fall, a relatively obscure engineer at Pontiac was developing a car that would appeal to the emerging youth performance market that Pontiac had correctly identified and that had thus far been left untouched. That engineer was a man named John DeLorean, and long before he built the signature car from the 1980s *Back to the Future* movie franchise, he was dutifully plugging away designing Tin Indians.

DeLorean believed that the youth market would buy performance cars from the factory, in the vein of the Super Duty Pontiacs, SS Impalas and big Chrysler letter cars that had ruled the streets since the mid–1950s. Young performance drivers had only a couple of options in those days, drive Daddy's big car, assuming one was available, or build one, which took a certain skill set not everyone had. Alternatively, they could buy a performance full size car of their own—an expensive proposition that precluded all but the most fortunate.

In order to tap into this invisible market, DeLorean and his team came up with a simple, yet forward thinking concept. Pontiac would take its reliable old 389 cubic inch engine that since 1959 had labored to push its big, full-sized cars and stuff it into something smaller and lighter. The chosen receptacle was the LeMans, the top of the mid-sized Tempest line, now part of GM's new 115-inch wheelbase A-body platform. Mating the increased horsepower from the 389 with the lighter, 3,400-pound intermediate Tempest was revolutionary in its simplicity. It was a matter of simple power to weight.

The result—for the first time—was a car that was capable of not simply competing with, but outperforming, the bigger, full-sized cars of an earlier era right off the dealer's lot. No mechanical skill was needed to achieve instant street credibility, and the car was relatively cheap, coming as it did with Spartan accouterments such as a standard 3-speed manual transmission and lightweight pillared coupe body style. With the right options checked on the order sheet, the little Pontiac could be upgraded with speed items like multiple carburation—the legendary Pontiac Tri-power—4-speed manual transmission with top-of-the-line Hurst shifter and a limited slip rear end. The result was the quickest of regular production cars. The mid-sized Poncho may have had a tough time with some of the limited production cars of the same year, such as Ford's Thunderbolt Fairlane, 426 Mopars or the final 409 Impala from Chevrolet, but these cars weren't produced en masse, and they weren't affordable like the little Pontiac. Those behemoths were few and far between.

The designation "GTO" was brazenly stolen from a contemporary Italian supercar built by Ferrari, the *Gran Turismo Omologato*. Because Americans are generally averse to big words from other languages, Pontiac just went with "GTO," launching arguably one of the most revered name plates in American automotive history. Never satisfied to just call something what it was, car circles came to know it as the "goat," a sort of out-of-order acronym for "GTO." That goats have a reputation for eating anything they come across probably helped settle the nickname.

DeLorean's concept was not without its problems with the higher ups at General Motors. By the mid–1950s, the Pontiac brand had become stale, and simply wasn't selling. To generate excitement, Pontiac developed its "Wide-Track" campaign in 1959, and to support its performance image, Pontiac got heavily involved in

1964 Pontiac GTO coupe (courtesy Pontiac-Oakland Museum, Pontiac, IL).

racing. By 1963, in part due to Pontiac's resurgence, General Motors occupied such a large percentage of the market that the federal government was threatening it with anti-trust action, which is difficult to imagine given that the federal government actually saved GM from bankruptcy in the late 2000s (one result of the restructuring was the death of Pontiac as a GM division). The powers that were at GM, not wanting to draw unwanted federal attention through an inherently dangerous, corporate sponsored racing program, banned corporate involvement in auto racing, a pastime in which Pontiac had enjoyed considerable success. GM also banned any engine larger than 330 cubic inches in intermediate cars. In 1964, days of limited technology and when the most effective and efficient way to produce horsepower was with ever bigger engine displacement, this was a pretty significant hindrance. Math tells us that 389 cubic inches is more than 330, so the latter of these two millstones should have effectively put the kibosh on the GTO concept.

Never one to let rules stand in his way, John DeLorean—whose alleged dalliances in the cocaine trade caused him to narrowly avoid marking time turning big rocks into little rocks in federal prison in the 1980s—would not be denied. The 330 restriction was set in stone, but DeLorean had a workaround: to simply make the GTO an option package on the Tempest. This would effectively frustrate the GM restrictions; technically, an option package is not a car at all, any more than air conditioning or a trailer towing package was a car. There was no car called a GTO; the GTO was just a Tempest. A really hot little Tempest.

In addition to the 325-horse base 389, Pontiac gave the car fake hood scoops and fender badges calling out the engine displacement in Euro-cool metric liters. The American car buying world may have been unfamiliar with the metric system, but they knew enough to know that 6.5 liters was probably a lot. The GTO came with upgraded suspension and brakes. The horses could be boosted to 348 with the multi-carbureted Tri-power option, which topped the intake manifold with three two-barrel carburetors. The standard 3-speed manual transmission could be upgraded to a 4-speed manual or two-speed Powerglide automatic. A host of luxury options was available from Pontiac's extensive list, such as power assisted steering and brakes, bucket seating and air conditioning, and the GTO could be had in coupe, hardtop and convertible body styles. In its base coupe form, the GTO weighed in 300 pounds, or roughly ten percent, lighter than a base full-sized Chevrolet SS Impala, and with a larger engine producing more horsepower.

The GM brass was not pleased, but grudgingly gave the car the go-ahead with a production restriction of only 5,000 cars. They rethought things once the cars started dispersing out to Pontiac dealers, where they didn't stay long, and onto the streets. With substantial support from an aggressive marketing campaign headed by advertising whiz Jim Wangers, demand for the revolutionary car went through the roof. Sales skyrocketed, and the 5,000 car cap was gleefully lifted. People flocked to the revolutionary GTO. The higher-ups at General Motors may not have been pleased with DeLorean's chicanery in circumventing their rules, but the sight of more than 32,000 sets of GTO taillights rolling out of the factory doors made them feel quite a bit better about it.

The GTO gave the non-gearhead public the opportunity for an instant increase in cool factor. With the GTO, one didn't have to have any real mechanical ability. One didn't have to build a race car or have the knowledge to do so. No longer were cool and impressive rides the province of the grease monkeys and the guys who hung out in the speed shops. In fact, the GTO gave coolness to people who had no interest in street racing credibility—it was enough to simply drive a car that brought its own cred. Pontiac gave those without the requisite shade tree mechanic skill set, to tweak and tune whatever car they may have had, access to purchase a ready-made, formidable performer, for a reasonable amount of money.

Pontiac had caught lightning in a bottle with the '64 GTO. The car immediately became a cultural icon and remains so today. A band called Ronny and the Daytonas made their only contribution to the landscape of American popular culture with a hit song about the "little GTO," and the much more well-known group Jan and Dean had a much less known song called "Mighty GTO." The Wangers propaganda machine was constantly reminding people who didn't have a GTO that they really wanted one. Pontiac was selling GTOs as fast as they could build them, and the other car manufacturers were left wondering what the hell had just happened. With the 1964

Pontiac's famous "3 deuce" Tri-power (photo by Darla Willhite).

Pontiac GTO—an automotive weapon of mass construction—the muscle car wars had begun.

* * *

The resounding success of the GTO caught the automotive world by surprise. DeLorean's little intermediate muscle car put Pontiac back on the performance map after its timid retreat from sanctioned racing. The GTO and its success didn't go unnoticed, particularly by the brass at Pontiac's sister divisions. Pontiac's super car for the masses may have caught everyone flat-footed in 1964, but her competitors would not stay on the sidelines long. Immediately after the release of the GTO, the other car makers, particularly within General Motors, began to plan how best to fight back.

Surprisingly, the division with the quickest reaction to the GTO was Oldsmobile. Perhaps it shouldn't have been as much of a surprise as it was, because Oldsmobile had some history of building performance cars. Olds people will argue that it was the 1949 Olds 88 that was the original muscle car, not the GTO. GM performance history was dominated by the long shadow of Chevrolet, and even more than Pontiac, Olds performance had long been hidden in the gloom. By the early '60s, Oldsmobile had a reputation, perhaps unfairly, of being a stodgy car maker that built cars that catered to older, more affluent people who really would rather have had a Buick or, especially, a Cadillac.

Oldsmobile, while crying foul at Pontiac's blatant disregard of GM's corporate

1964 Oldsmobile F-85 442 convertible (courtesy Steven Anastos, Red Hills Rods and Classics, St. George, UT).

mandates, hurriedly sifted through its parts bins to try to cobble together something to compete with the marauding GTOs. Its answer was to stuff the hottest engine it had on hand—a new for '64, 310 horse, 330 inch small block—into its A-bodied, plain Jane F-85 or more plush Cutlass mid-sized cars. They were dutifully playing by the rules in using the 330; there was no chicanery going on at Olds. The official option code for the car was B09, a police car option code, but the world has come to know the car as the 4-4-2.

The cadence-y name of "4-4-2" was derived because the car, in the early days, came with four-barrel carb, 4-speed transmission and dual exhaust (as the years went on, the options changed but the name stuck). The 4-4-2 imitated the GTO with its appeal to the youth market. The 4-4-2 could be had in coupe, hardtop and convertible body styles. Its four-barrel 330 cubic inch engine was usually only available on cars being sold to police departments, a fact Olds vigorously exploited in its own marketing campaign for the car. Circumstance made one of the fours in 4-4-2 mandatory; the automatic transmissions Olds had on hand would not handle the high revving 330. With a flood of GTOs leaving Pontiac, Oldsmobile didn't have the time to redevelop it, so the 4-speed would have to do. Aside from the lack of an automatic, other option choices were all Oldsmobile—tilt steering wheel, AM/FM radio, electric trunk opener, and air conditioning, to name a few.

With a small block engine asked to pull a car 300 pounds heavier than a base GTO, despite its respectable horsepower, the 4-4-2 was competition for the GTO only in the mind of Olds brass. The 4-4-2 didn't sport hood scoops, though it did have tricolor "4-4-2" badging that was attractive. It just didn't look the part of a muscle car like the GTO did. On the plus side of the ledger, the 4-4-2 did handle significantly better than the Pontiac, due to the lighter engine and a stiffer, sway bar equipped suspension vultured from police edition Oldsmobiles, but people comparing the 4-4-2 and the GTO weren't deciding based on those qualities. Pontiac was offering big 389 power and far sportier looks. Compared to Wangers' enthusiasm, Olds' promotional campaign was uninspired and uninspiring. These facts combined with the 4-4-2's late release in the 1964 model year resulted in 2999 models being sold.

The early tricolor badging of Oldsmobile's 4-4-2 (courtesy of Gateway Classic Cars, St. Louis, MO).

Chevrolet had always been General Motor's flagship with regard to performance, despite valiant efforts by Pontiac and Oldsmobile to de-throne the Bowtie over the years. Coming into the early '60s, Chevrolet enjoyed a stellar reputation for stylish cars powered by legendary engines. The Corvette had been released in 1953, and after Ford's Thunderbird mercifully abandoned the American two seat roadster market, the Corvette solidified its reputation as the premier American sports car. The 1955–57 full-sized line that included the iconic Bel Air has become the symbol of the 1950s and is as popular today as it ever was. The full-sized line from 1958 to 1964, including cheap Biscaynes and the stylish Impala, became legendary in their own right. The big Chevys of the early 1960s, such as the 409 immortalized by the Beach Boys, carried the banner of performance until the smaller GTO signaled the near extinction of the full-sized performance car. The great Chevrolet engines—the 283, 327, and 409—were easy to work on, and parts were abundant, making them the most popular "builders" among car guys. Chevrolet also had the advantage of being the entry level division at General Motors—their cars were affordable. Affordable performance was the *raison d'être* of Chevrolet. Pontiac, Olds and Buick had always built great cars, but when it came to performance, they were little siblings doing their best to manage in the long shadow cast by Chevrolet, standing like a colossus over General Motors performance.

The success of the GTO was not lost on Chevrolet, nor was, more importantly, the new youth market Pontiac had discovered. Needless to say, with a history of performance as decorated as Chevrolet's, the division was not pleased to be one-upped by an insurgent Pontiac encroaching on what it believed was its domain.

Like Olds, Chevrolet scrambled to put the offering together and get it into showrooms before Pontiac had eaten up the entire market. Chevrolet looked to its new-for-'64 115-inch wheelbase Chevelle as the foundation on which it would create its GTO fighter. Falling back on the tried-and-true SS badge that had been burned into the consciousness of performance car buyers since the early '60s, Chevy created the SS Malibu, an option on the Chevelle.

**1964 Malibu SS, owned by Martin Siznig of Berg, Switzerland (photo by Kai Roos).**

Chevrolet already had a range of proven power plants available on hand and offered several versions of its 327 cubic inch engine in Corvettes. Chevrolet also made available any engine offered in the Chevelle line, starting with an uninspiring six-cylinder. There were two 283s offered—a 195-horse two-barrel or a 220-horse four-barrel. Up next were a pair of 327s, producing 250 or 300 horses. The top engine offering was the L76 327. Plucked right from the Corvette, it was one of the great engines of the era, producing 365 horsepower. This engine was only briefly offered before Chevrolet withdrew the option. Very few, if any, Chevelles were ever built with the L76 327.

Like the Olds and Pontiac offerings, these cars came with heavy-duty suspensions and brakes, and came standard with a 3-speed manual transmission, though that could be upgraded to a 4-speed manual or a two-speed Powerglide automatic. Limited slip rear ends were also available. The SS Malibu could be had only in hardtop and convertible body styles, and the SS option got the buyer bucket seats, SS wheel covers, premium interior, four gauge instrument panel, as well as a console for cars equipped with the optional 4-speed or Powerglide automatic.

Chevrolet's first foray into the muscle car wars sold well, though it didn't have the panache of the GTO. Pontiac built a car specifically aimed at the younger crowd, and the GTO looked the part—hood scoops, cool badging, chrome exhaust tips, and the like. The '64 Malibu SS had none of this. It looked like a sober little sedan, dignified yet uninspiring, even with SS badging made famous on the great cars of earlier years. Additionally, the little Malibu was still a small block, even if it was Chevy's legendary 327. Despite all of this, Chevrolet found new homes for 67,085 SS Malibus with one V-8 or another.

* * *

Across town at Chrysler, the GTO was likewise seen with some alarm. The smallest and weakest of the Big Three, Chrysler usually finished a distant third in terms of sales. Chrysler was somewhat of an enigma—it had a long history of great performance engines, and a long history of styling that was somewhat unconventional. Some of Chrysler's good ideas over the years included a relatively popular push-button automatic transmission, swiveling bucket seats, lug nuts that turned the wrong way, and foot operated radio. Someone at Dodge even thought reverse tail fins were a good idea; rather than tapering in height as they stretched back to the deck lid, Chrysler's did the opposite, making cars so equipped look like big bowfin fish.

Chrysler introduced what it called its B-body in 1962, the platform that would underpin all of the great Chrysler intermediate muscle cars over the next decade, riding on a 116 inch wheelbase. For 1963, Plymouth's Sport Fury and the Dodge Polara were introduced to compete with the SS Impalas from Chevy, the Pontiac Catalinas, the Ford Galaxie, and the like. In base form, the smaller Mopars, considered full-sized by Chrysler, were lighter than these competitors, and when equipped with the potent 413 cubic inch engine, they could compete on even footing with the legendary 409 Chevys and Super Duty Pontiacs, but they just weren't as good looking. The Fords and the General Motors cars had performance and wide stylistic appeal; the Chryslers had it only half right. Most car builders understood that performance wasn't necessarily enough to win the sales wars. Style was at least as important. It wasn't entirely clear that Chrysler understood this.

Like everyone else, Chrysler was caught flat footed by the GTO and was ill prepared to respond. Their most obvious answer was to plow ahead with Plymouth's Sport Fury. Dodge's Polara 500 had suddenly grown back out to 119 inches and out of the class of the 115-inch GTO, and Dodge didn't have a true intermediate car to stack against the Pontiac, so Plymouth carried the Pentastar flag into the muscle car battle.

The Sport Fury's base engine in each was a 330 horse 383 cubic inch block—similar to the 325 horse 389 offered in the base GTO. A mid-year engine option was a 426 cubic inch, 365 horse engine that was superior to the Tri-power GTO in terms of horsepower. Either engine could be mated to an automatic or manual transmission. The car's grille was redesigned for 1964 and was referred to by literature of the era as "Chevy-like," and the slanted C-pillars were "Thunderbird style" (it says something about Chrysler's design self-esteem that the major styling features of the car were identified by referring to features of other manufacturer's cars).

The Sport Fury sold respectably in 1964 with over 27,550 copies sold in hardtop and convertible form, but the Sport Fury was no GTO. The Plymouth, despite being an inch longer in wheelbase and two in actual length, weighed 200 pounds less than the Pontiac. Its base engines were essentially the same—the Mopar producing slightly more horsepower—and the optional 426 produced eighteen more rated

**1964 Dodge Polara (courtesy Vanguard Motor Sales, Plymouth, MI).**

horses than the Tri-powered Pontiac. Perhaps the biggest hindrance working against the Plymouth was that it was a Plymouth. Fairly or not, Plymouth had the reputation of building large numbers of taxicabs and police vehicles—boring, basic transportation. People that drove Plymouths wore hard hats to work and ate their meals out of a metal lunch pail, not at the local drive-in on Saturday night. For a car to be a hot seller it takes more than just the car, regardless of how good it might be, and must be paired with a mystique. Unfortunately for Plymouth, the Sport Fury lacked the GTO's flair—no cool crests, no hood scoops or chrome exhaust splitters. Perhaps more importantly, the Plymouth had no Jim Wangers creating that mystique and telling the world how great it was. The angular Plymouth did not appeal to the younger buyer. The GTO made history, and Plymouth put all its performance and image eggs in its new performance A-body, the Barracuda. That was a misjudgment that would take Plymouth years to overcome.

Despite its inability to competently compete with the GTO in terms of a muscle car for the masses, Mopar continued its fearsome track-only cars, competing across various classes. Perhaps the most famous of these, called "Super Stocks," were based on the Dodge 330 and Plymouth Belvedere. Jan and Dean sang about a little old woman in California that somehow got a hold of one and terrorized the streets of Pasadena. The Super Stock Mopars were fearsome on the track, especially so when Chrysler began putting its terrifying NASCAR inspired 426 S and 440 cubic inch "wedge" engines in these cars. Mopar didn't make many of them, but they were practically unbeatable. In fact, in 1965 the 426 was banned by NASCAR. The Super Stocks weren't produced in the numbers the GTO was and therefore were not true

**1964 Plymouth Sport Fury convertible (courtesy Vanguard Motor Sales, Plymouth, MI).**

competitors for the Pontiac, but the lightweight 426 and 440 powered mid-sizes were the advanced shock troops of the full-scale attack Chrysler would unleash later in the muscle cars wars.

* * *

General Motor's longstanding arch-rival, the Blue Oval of Ford, did not miss the significance of the GTO, and tried, however feebly, to match it in the mid-sized performance car arena. Ford's intermediate efforts were distracted, however, by a nasty little surprise it was planning to unleash on the American car market, and therefore it did not field an intermediate car capable of competing with the virile Pontiac or even the 330 powered Oldsmobiles or 327 powered Malibus. Much like Chevrolet, Ford was still stuck in an early '60s mindset, and its larger performance car was still the powerful but heavy Galaxie, built to run with the full-sized Chevys, Pontiacs and Ramcharger Mopars that Ford still believed made up the performance car universe.

What Ford had to offer was a performance version of its popular Fairlane line. The Fairlane came in several different incarnations, from basic grocery-getter to station wagon. The performance Fairlanes were the Fairlane 500 and Fairlane Sport Coupes. These models were available only as hardtops, and with their thick C-pillars, round taillights and horizontal dual headlamps set in a stainless steel grille, the Fairlane looked an awful lot like its bigger brother, the Galaxie. All of this made the Ford an attractive car in 1964, but it simply was not built to competently compete with the GTO.

This is primarily because its top engine offering was a "K-code" 289 cubic-incher

**1964 Ford Fairlane, owned by Elsa L. Dages of Souderton, PA (photo by owner).**

producing 271 horsepower—one of the legendary Ford engines of the 1960s—and exhaling through dual exhaust. Three or 4-speed manual transmissions were available, as was the 3-speed Cruise-O-Matic automatic, but that little 289 could not reasonably be expected to propel a 115.5-inch wheelbase car weighing nearly 3,000 pounds down the track with anywhere near the velocity of the GTO.

The Fairlane that could be expected to do so, however, was known as the "Thunderbolt," a Fairlane two door post built specifically for the track with fiberglass hoods and fenders and without things such as carpeting, radios or sun visors, among other things. The Thunderbolt's engine bay was stuffed with Ford's new 427 cubic inch engine, fed through two four-barrel carbs and cold air induction. With fewer than 130 of them built and intended specifically for the track, they were not really a true competitor of the GTO, but they were fearsome cars to behold.

The more garden variety Fairlanes were attractive cars and could be had with bucket seating and a host of other luxury options, but they were not in the same universe as the GTO. Ford built more than 64,000 Fairlane hardtops in 1964, a respectable number, but this includes all engine options all the way down the line. K-code cars were significantly less common. The 1964 Fairlane did, however, establish itself as a name, and in the coming years would evolve to be a true competitor capable of running with the various GM offerings of later models.

\* \* \*

The GTO and the various mid-sized efforts to catch it were only half of the story of 1964. Ford's nasty surprise was the other half, and it came about late in the model year. The long-term effects would impact the American automobile industry even more than the GTO and the resultant muscle car wars. Late in 1964 model year came the second of the seismic happenings in the American automotive world. The event was the release of the Ford Mustang, a car destined to be the most popular American car ever built and a nameplate that survives to the present day in substantially its original concept.

By the early 1960s, automotive wizard Lee Iacocca at Ford, like DeLorean across town at Pontiac, was sensing a growing youth market as the Boomers began to come of age. There was clamoring for a return of the two-seat Thunderbird, there were more women buying cars, more people were buying second cars, and market forecasts indicated that the coming ten years would see more money spent on cars than any other ten-year period in history. To Iacocca and his band at Ford, this all led to the same conclusion at which DeLorean had arrived, if not the same concept for an answer: if they could design and build the right car, there were a hell of a lot of them to be sold. Their answer was the Mustang, an all-American car if there ever was one.

The idea of the Mustang was very simple: take an existing platform—in this case, the uninspiring but popular Falcon—and build an affordable, sporty car that could be equipped with a huge variety of options that allowed the buyers to tailor the car to whatever they wanted it to be, from cheap but attractive grocery duty to genuine performance car to a miniature Thunderbird in terms of opulence. Thus, the car would appeal across a wide spectrum of the market, including women, a demographic decidedly forgotten by the GTO that veritably sweated testosterone. The Mustang would do all of this affordably; the Mustang's base price was well under $2,500. After some initial hesitation about introducing a new car line so soon after Ford's late '50s Edsel debacle ("Edsel" would become synonymous for "failure"), the Mustang became an unrivaled success, claiming Car of the Year honors from *Motor Trend* magazine. The Mustang has never looked back.

So popular was the car that it spawned a new class of car named for itself—the Pony Car, which is somewhat ironic because the Mustang was not named for a horse but was an attempt to harness the mystique of the P-51 Mustang fighter plane from World War II. The pony cars were a class of performance cars that were smaller and nimbler than the intermediate muscle cars, but sportier and better performing than the base level compacts such as the Falcon, Mercury's Comet or Chevy's Nova. Its smaller size allowed it to position itself as a poor man's Corvette, but without the drawbacks of only two seats. It couldn't equal the Corvette's performance, but then, it didn't cost nearly as much as the Corvette. In terms of sexiness per dollar, the Mustang was a better buy.

It is a considerable exercise in imaginative gymnastics to class the 108-inch wheelbase 1964½ Mustang a muscle car on par with the thundering GTO. The Mustang didn't have the attributes available to make it so, such as the availability of a big-block engine. But, it did offer performance at a reasonable price for a younger market, and as such, it was a rival of the GTO in sales. The Mustang platform would serve as a blank palette of sorts for Ford's engineers, and as the '60s wore on, and as the performance wars escalated, the little pony would be enlisted in the struggle and would eventually grow, literally and figuratively, into a muscle car in its own right.

* * *

Any Mopar fan with even a passing knowledge of the history of Chrysler offerings of the muscle car era knows that the pony car class should more appropriately be called something ichthyologic because it wasn't the Mustang that fired the opening salvo of the pony car front of the muscle car wars, but Plymouth's little Barracuda. Iacocca and DeLorean weren't the only ones to recognize the emerging youth market for budget friendly performance cars. Chrysler's designers were tracking pretty much parallel with Ford's evaluation of the market, and two weeks before the launch of the Ford Mustang, Plymouth set the Barracuda loose.

In concept, the Barracuda was very similar to the Mustang, or perhaps the Mustang was very similar to the Barracuda. Plymouth took an existing compact chassis— the Valiant—and draped it with new sheet metal, which for the Barracuda meant a fastback design that integrated the most enormous back glass ever installed in an American car. The Barracuda shared doors, quarter panels, hood, bumpers and most glass with the Valiant. It was truly the result of an economy of effort at perpetually cash strapped Chrysler. The Barracuda offered the Valiant's range of engine choices as well, from a pair of six-cylinders to the top of the line, a new 180 horse 273 cubic inch V-8, which was at least in the same conversation as the Ford's top engine, the 210 horse 289. It could be had with a full range of luxury options, including the unique push-button automatic transmission. It was in most ways the same idea behind the Mustang—a very affordable small, sporty car that could be a blank canvas for option choices, allowing the enthusiastic Mopar pony car buyers to build essentially what they wanted.

Turns out, there weren't too many of those. Plymouth sold only 23,443 Barracudas. This number is actually respectable for a first-year rollout of a new model, but not when compared to the number of Mustangs Ford sent out the door. The Barracuda was perceived by many to be a singularly ugly vehicle, and Plymouth didn't go to great lengths to hide its uninspiring Valiant lineage, even forgetting to delete Valiant badging. The Barracuda's reception was lukewarm. Things only got worse two weeks later when the Mustang was revealed, and the rest really is history.

Had the Barracuda been born in any other time than two weeks before the release of the Mustang, it might have enjoyed a better fate. It was a competent, if aesthetically unbeauteous car. As it is, however, the little Plymouth is better remembered for its huge back glass than for anything else, despite its otherwise commendable attributes. In fairness, Chrysler didn't help the early Barracuda as much as it could have, only offering it in fastback body style.

The 1964 model year was doubly unkind to Plymouth. The Barracuda as a competent Mustang competitor is as lost to history as is the 1964 Sport Fury as a GTO fighter. In their own rights, they were good cars, powered by indestructible Chrysler drivelines. The 1964 Plymouths were the right cars, or sort of the right cars, at precisely the wrong time, particularly for the Barracuda. The Barracuda never caught

**Plymouth's unlucky Mustang fighter, the 1964 Barracuda (courtesy Streetside Classics, Charlotte NC).**

Ford's Mustang, and while the Barracuda was relegated to history's trash heap—Plymouth was too, for that matter—the Mustang is still running strong today.

\* \* \*

Though 1964 may be best remembered for the introduction of the GTO, the final year of Chevrolet's legendary 409, and the late introduction of the Mustang, there were other things going on in the car world. The GTO and Mustang weren't the only performance cars in existence, though once those two models hit the ground, they dominated popular attention.

Chevy was still arming its full-sized Impalas, as well as the lesser models of the Chevy full-sized line, the Bel-Air and the Biscayne, with the 409. The base 409 produced 400 horses, but that could be upped to 425 with dual four-barrel carbs. Chevy full-sized cars could also be had with performance 327 blocks as well. Pontiac was building what it dubbed its "2+2" trim package on its full-sized Catalina, available with a 389 or 421, either of which could be had in four-barrel or Tri-power variants. The Ford Galaxie came with a line of performance engines, the most potent of which was the 427, producing an awesome 425 horsepower. As formidable as these and other giant performance cars were, by 1964 they were relics of an earlier era. While the revolution that the GTO started wouldn't exactly kill off the full-sized performance cars—Chevrolet produced potent 427 and 454 powered Impalas through most of the muscle car era—their production and sales numbers continued to slide as the 1960s ground on. With the history of these great cars in the early 1960s, their eclipse at the hands of the intermediate performance cars and the little pony cars truly marked the end of an era.

The compact car represented the opposite end of the spectrum from the full-sized Impalas and Galaxies, which were pushing the 4,000-pound mark. Like the waning full-sized performance cars, the sporty compacts have been lost in the furor over the mid-sized cars, particularly since the release of the Mustang.

Ford and its more upscale corporate sister Mercury were building performance compacts that warrant far more attention than they typically get in surveys of the muscle car wars. The Ford Falcon and the Mercury Comet were the brainchild of another icon of the 1960s, Robert McNamara. After his role in the Falcon/Comet project, McNamara would go on to find infamy as Secretary of Defense for both John Kennedy and Lyndon Johnson. He would partner with Johnson as the main architects for the disaster of the Vietnam War.

The Falcon and Comet were a deliberate effort by Ford to move away from a seemingly endless line of full-sized cars it offered in the late '50s and early '60s and to cut into the market share of competitor Rambler, later known as American Motors. Ramblers were seen as sensible, practical, affordable and pragmatic, and Ford wanted to get into that game. The Ford compacts debuted in 1960, and while they were generally regarded as sportier than the Ramblers, they certainly didn't set the world on fire. By 1964, sportiness was on full display in the redesigned Falcons and Comets.

Both were offered with a full range of grocery-getting power plants, but the Falcon Sprint and the Mercury Comet Cyclone were the top of the line performers. The Ford was initially offered with a 260 cubic inch V-8 power plant, and with stiffer suspension. The 289 of Mustang fame was offered in the Mercury, and later in the model year in the Falcon as well, producing 210 horsepower and outfitted with chromed engine accessories in an effort to appeal to a younger buyer.

Aiming at the same segment of the market—the sensible and practical segment—Chevrolet introduced its Chevy II line in 1962 in addition to its Corvair. The Corvair was truly a remarkable car, in the purest sense of the word, because there were a lot of remarks made about it. Not many were good. Chevrolet had the quasi-revolutionary, rear engine Corvair to compete with the Ramblers and the Falcons, but the car proved unpopular and its rear suspension design produced dangerous handling traits. Consumer advocate and future presidential candidate Ralph Nader would point out the fallacy of putting human beings inside a moving Corvair in his book *Unsafe at Any Speed* in 1965, after changes had been made to correct the issue. The Falcon hammered the ailing Corvair in sales, and going back to the drawing board, Chevrolet tried again with a compact it dubbed the Chevy II.

The little Chevy II was a plain Jane compact seemingly designed specifically to appeal to librarians and school marms, and to haul clothes to the dry cleaners. The Chevy II line was available with either four or six cylinders as well as different trim levels. The top-of-the-line Chevy II was dubbed the Nova. By 1963 Chevy offered the Nova in Super Sport trim, emulating the wildly successful SS Impalas, with a 194 cubic inch, 120-horse straight six as the most potent—to use the word

**The stylish GTO crest graced Pontiac's supercar from 1964 through 1968 and stood in stark contrast to the brutality under the hood (courtesy Vintage Muscle Photography).**

loosely—engine option. But by 1964, the little Nova SS got its first V-8 offering, with the most powerful being a 220 HP 283 cubic inch engine. It wasn't much, and it lived in the shadows of the emerging GM muscle car offerings, but it was a start. By the end of the muscle car, the SS Nova would be remembered as a legendary muscle car, even if it didn't squarely fit into either the traditional muscle car or pony car class.

* * *

Chief Pontiac met an untimely and inglorious end in 1769 at the hands of a rival warrior of the Peoria tribe. His death marked the end of one of the early movements to unify the native tribes against the hordes of white settlers swarming across the Appalachian Mountains. His namesake's 1964 rebellion was much more successful. The GTO touched off a car makers' war that would rage unabated for the next several years, reaching ever more audacious heights in terms of horsepower and styling. The performance car buying public benefited, and the great name badges of that war are legendary today. The GTO was the first salvo in what we now know as the muscle car wars.

# 4

# Rolling Thunder

*Pontiac Dominates and Detroit Responds*

The wave of cultural change in the American landscape continued into 1965. One of the main transformers was the growing Civil Rights Movement, as blacks, with the force of the Civil Rights Act, attempted to enact in reality what Johnson had signed the year before. President Johnson, fresh off his landslide victory over Barry Goldwater in the 1964 presidential election, continued his reshaping of the racial landscape. As he pushed his expansion of civil rights and government programs, 1965 saw the passage of the Voting Rights Act, which protected the voting rights of minority voters, predominantly in the states of the Old Confederacy. This top-down effort was supported by the grassroots, as Martin Luther King, Jr., led rallies in Selma, Alabama, culminating in a march into the history books in the form an actual march from Selma to the state capitol in Montgomery. In a sign of the times, the University of Alabama graduated its first African American, and a woman to boot, in Vivian Malone, much to the chagrin of Alabama's "segregation now, segregation tomorrow, segregation forever" governor, George Wallace. Not all events in the civil rights realm were positive, however, as intense riots broke out in Watts, a black neighborhood in Los Angeles, as well as in Chicago, and Black Nationalist Malcolm X was killed by members of the Nation of Islam, after an internal squabble with the organization for which he had been a spokesman.

The Space Race also dominated the news. Soviet cosmonaut Aleksei Leonov became the first person to conduct a spacewalk. Despite this success, it was in 1965 that the U.S., up to now playing catch-up with the Soviet Union, took the lead after a series of spectacular Soviet disasters. Soviet lander Luna 5, attempting a soft landing on the lunar surface, crashed. The Soviets with Luna 6 managed to miss the moon entirely by 99,000 miles; someone presumably went to a gulag for that. Then, completing the trifecta, Luna 7 suffered the same fate as Luna 5. In the meantime, the U.S. was sending spacecraft past Mars, the pictures of which disappointed legions of *Twilight Zone* fans when they failed to show the existence of green men. NASA was also conducting the first successful space rendezvous, when Gemini 6 and Gemini 7 were maneuvered within a foot of each other, setting the stage for the successful moon landings later in the decade.

Johnson also signed off on an expansion of combat operations in Southeast Asia, with the first combat troops making their way to Vietnam and the first B-52 strike. That strike was quickly followed by a sustained bombing campaign against North

Vietnam dubbed "Rolling Thunder," the heaviest bombing campaign since the Second World War. The surprise of Soviet radar-guided surface-to-air missiles, known as SAMs, rendered Rolling Thunder a strategic defeat, and there were fewer things more terrifying to airmen than the cockpit warning buzzer indicating a SAM battery's radar had locked on. Rolling Thunder was successful, however, in igniting the first of the war protests at Washington, D.C., and (surprise, surprise) the Cal-Berkeley campus. It also spurred Chinese aid to North Vietnam. The famous battle for the Ia Drang Valley, in which American forces staved off certain defeat by the first effective use of helicopters in combat, was a product of 1965's war effort.

Vietnam wasn't the only place where President Johnson was active. As if the adventures of Lyndon Johnson in Southeast Asia weren't enough, he also OK'd the invasion of the Dominican Republic, forever changing the face of Major League baseball. Aside from the Voting Rights Act, Johnson pushed for and signed acts creating Medicare and Medicaid, government sponsored programs to increase access to medical care for the aged and poor, respectively. These acts were a part of Johnson's "war on poverty" effort, a part of his Great Society program. This collection of programs served as the genesis for two things ubiquitous in modern politics: the eventual expansion of government involvement in healthcare known as "Obamacare," and politicians of all stripes using the term "the war on X," with the X usually being some group supposedly disadvantaged by nefarious members of the other party.

Also marking 1965 were the death of Winston Churchill and the debut of the rock group the Who. Astoundingly, it took a 1965 Supreme Court case, *Griswold v. Connecticut*, to establish the right of married couples to use contraceptives. Much to the joy of kids everywhere, Campbell's released Spaghetti-Os, and Kellogg's introduced Pop Tarts. The first Subway sandwich shop was opened in New York. Milwaukee was granted the rights to a baseball club to replace the Braves, who left for the sunnier clime of Atlanta, and the Brewers emerged as an expansion team in 1969. The Miami Dolphins and Atlanta Falcons were established as football franchises; the Dolphins found success relatively quickly, and the Falcons continue a half decade's worth of futility to this day.

And then there was the 1965 class of muscle cars…

\* \* \*

Coming into 1965, Pontiac was still riding the wave of its massively successful GTO, which was dominating both the streets and the sales sheets. However, Pontiac was not content with simply bringing back the 1964 model for another run. Instead, Pontiac refined the little GTO, and the result is what is widely considered to be the most aesthetically successful muscle car of the early days of the muscle car years, if not the entire era.

The 1965 GTO was simply a work of art. The same, generally boxy design was carried over from 1964 and it was again offered in hardtop, lightweight pillared coupe and heavy convertible body styles. The horizontal headlamps of 1964 were stood upright in more traditional Pontiac style, and the grilles were redesigned to give the front end a cleaner look. The hood was reworked as well, with the chrome plated, obviously non-functional scoops of 1964 being replaced by a power bulge in the

**Pontiac's 1965 GTO hardtop, owned by Richard Savage of Alden, NY (photo by owner).**

center of the hood, with twin not-so-obviously non-functional inlets. The taillights were reworked as well to wrap around the side of the quarter panel somewhat, and the car could be had with uber-cool exhaust splitters dumping exhaust just aft of the rear wheels.

Under the hood, the base engine was again the 389, but for 1965 DeLorean was given no guff from GM brass; after the success of the GTO, GM wisely figured it was in its best interest to lift the 330 cubic inch limit for its A-bodies. The 1965 version of the 389 was upped in horsepower from 325 to 335 in the base four-barrel engine, perhaps because Pontiac was lying about horsepower production in 1964 in an effort to keep the questions to a minimum after putting the 389 in the car in the first place. The three deuce "Tri-Power" carburation set up produced 360 horses, up from 348. The 1965 production year saw the introduction of one of the great names of Pontiac history—Ram Air. Available only as an accessory to the Tri-Power 389, The Ram Air system was a cold air induction system that used a foam seal around the triple carbs that seated to the hood and surrounded the twin scoops, which were made functional by cutting slats in the molding to allow cold air into the engine via negative vacuum pressure created by the carburetors.

GTO suspensions were of the heavy-duty variety, and the 389, whichever one was chosen, came mated to a 3-speed manual transmission. This could be upgraded to a 4-speed manual or a two-speed Powerglide automatic, shifted on the column or though the available console. Manual brakes and steering were standard, though power assist was available as well. A bench front seat was also standard, though most GTOs were upgraded to full vinyl bucket seating. Instrumentation occupied round, rally style gauging, and a tachometer could replace the standard clock. Pontiac offered a long list of other available options, including air conditioning, tinted glass, power antenna and rear speaker.

The little GTO, on the strength of its restyle, Ronnie and the Daytonas and Jim Wangers, led muscle car production in 1965. The 75,352 units sold more than doubled 1964 output, and helped to launch Pontiac into 3rd place in American car sales behind only Ford and Chevrolet. Today, many people consider the 1965 GTO to be the pinnacle of GTO styling, and the model, particularly in Tri-power, convertible or Ram Air varieties, commands healthy prices.

With the lifting of the 330 cubic inch displacement limit on mid-sized cars, Oldsmobile lashed back at the GTO with a 400 cubic inch powered version of its 4-4-2. The 4-4-2 option package was available on the F-85 and Cutlass line, and the Oldsmobile proved to be a powerful counterpunch to Pontiac, as the new 4 barrel 400, in base form, produced 345 horsepower, or 10 more than the base GTO. The heavy-duty suspension, initially designed for police duty and equipped with heavy-duty shocks and front and rear sway bars, gave the 4-4-2 what was arguably the best handling of the genre. The big 400 breathed through an enlarged exhaust, lessening back pressure and increasing performance over the 4-4-2's '64 incarnation.

4-4-2 originally stood for 4 barrels, 4-speed and dual exhaust, but with the replacement of the 4-speed as the standard tranny with a 3-speed manual, that definition was in need of updating. The "4" now meant 400 cubic inches. In decidedly non-performance style, the 3-speed was mounted on the column—"three on a tree"—but at least the gears were selected by a Hurst shifter. The more refined tastes of the average Olds buyer meant that the base 3-speed or far more common optional Hurst shifted 4-speed was usually mounted on the floor, inside a console. The automatic option was a two-speed "Jetaway," shifted either on the column or, more commonly, via console mounted floor shifter. A limited slip rear differential was also available, as was power assist on the standard drum brakes all the way around; disc brakes were unavailable.

Outside, the 4-4-2 was more understated than its Pontiac cousin, offering no hood scoops and instead brandishing bright trim running up the middle of the length of the hood. There were subtle faux vents just aft of the doors, with the tricolor 4-4-2 emblem. Bright molding ran the length of the car, bumper to bumper, along its lower third. Horizontal quad headlamps nestled into an unassuming grille adorned with an even more unassuming 4-4-2 badge in its lower right-hand corner. Interior accouterments varied depending on body style: cheaper F-85 based cars got a bench seat, while Cutlass based 4-4-2s got buckets. Olds being Olds, both types of seating were full vinyl. Power seats, power windows, and power steering were optional, as were air conditioning and tinted glass, among a long list of other optional items.

The upgraded 4-4-2 was every bit a match for the GTO, but sales were sluggish by comparison. Still handily topping the late arriving '64 model, created in a responsive panic to the GTO, '65 sales were 25,003 4-4-2s in all body styles. While the Oldsmobile had caught up to the GTO on the street, few knew it. The GTO had

Oldsmobile's 1965 4-4-2 hardtop (courtesy Gateway Classic Cars, St. Louis, MO).

panache, and it had reputation. The 4-4-2 would stand in the long shadow of the GTO for much of the remainder of the muscle car era, and this was a cruel fate for a superb car. For Oldsmobile, it simply was what it was. Ronnie and the Daytonas didn't sing a song about the 4-4-2. Jan and Dean didn't even sing a song about the 4-4-2.

GM's tardy entrant into the expanding muscle car battlefield was Buick. Buick was perhaps an unlikely entry into the muscle car wars, positioned as it was snuggly between GM divisions that built performance cars as a matter of course, and Cadillac, which most certainly did not. Even so, the Buick buyer had a median age of somewhere between 40 and dead.

Buick did have a mid-sized, A-body platform, like her sister divisions, called the Skylark. Figuring "why not?" Buick sifted through its parts bins and dubbed a high-performance version of the Skylark with the youth-friendly moniker of Gran Sport, and set it loose as a mid-year option in 1965. In fact, Buick got a lot of mileage out of the Gran Sport badge, as it also offered a Gran Sport option on its Riviera, a 117-inch platform 2 inches longer than the Skylark; for 1966 the Riviera would grow to a 119-inch chassis shared with Oldsmobile's new Toronado and Cadillac's El Dorado. In 1966 Buick even hung the badge on its gargantuan 126-inch wheelbase Wildcat. Muscle car history, however, only remembers the Skylark based Gran Sport.

The Skylark's Gran Sport option, known simply as Gran Sport, was a sedate looking vehicle, particularly relative to its be-scooped Pontiac cousin. Buick engineers stuffed the 4-barrel Wildcat 455 engine—confusingly referring to the block's torque output rather than the more common horsepower—into the little Skylark. The Wildcat 455 was more commonly used to haul around the much larger Buicks such as, as one might guess, the Wildcat, and produced 325 horsepower. The "nailhead" engine actually displaced 401 cubic inches, a little bit of naughtiness from stodgy, conservative Buick in the face of GM's newest 400 cubic inch limitation, and it was the only option on the Gran Sport. Transmission options were standard GM fare at the time—3-speed manual as the standard tranny, but upgradable to 4-speed manual or two-speed "Super Turbine 300" automatic. The Gran Sport's suspension and front sway bar were considerably heavier than on the base Skylark. The Gran Sport, regardless of body style, was built on the heavy, boxed frame usually reserved for convertibles. Positive traction rear ends were available as well, and brakes were manual drums all the way around, though power assist was available.

The little Gran Sport, available in hardtop, coupe or convertible form, was one of the few muscle cars to sport a hood ornament, another tribute to the upscale way Buick typically liked to do things. It shared the same straight, somewhat boxy lines with its A-body cousins, and its fenders were adorned with Buick's trademark triple moldings, called "ventiports" in Buick vernacular. The grille was clean, with quad headlamps set horizontally, and with a small Gran Sport badge on the left side, balanced by the same badge on the left side of the deck lid. Inside, it was all Buick grandeur: standard full vinyl bucket seating was standard, which was optional on lesser GM A-bodies. Buick made sure its riders were comfortable with bucket seating, directional turn signal indicator, and DeLuxe steering wheel—all of which were optional on lesser GM muscle cars. Of course, a full-length console, power seats, windows, and steering were optional, as was air conditioning. All of this interior bliss and the boxed frame made the Buick a bit of a butterball, weighing in at 3,720 pounds, or nearly 200 pounds heavier than the GTO; the Buick didn't perform on the same level as the GTO, or even the 4-4-2, but the experience going slower was considerably more comfortable.

Marketing the car simultaneously as a "super bird"—a name that would re-emerge later in the era—and a "gentleman's hot rod," Buick sold 15,780 Skylark Gran Sport cars of all body styles. Certainly not GTO numbers, but more than respectable for the mid-year release of a maiden model built by a car maker hardly known for exciting vehicles. Stripped down dragsters weren't for everyone, and the strong Gran Sport sales illustrated that nearly penniless kids weren't the only ones buying muscle cars.

The introduction of the Buick Gran Sport was interesting, but unfortunately for the Tri-Shield, it was but a sideshow overshadowed by the news coming out of the Chevrolet camp, and substantial escalation in the emerging muscle car wars that was introduced by the Bow Tie in 1965. Having been caught asleep when Pontiac released its 389 powered GTOs, the 327 powered SS Malibu of 1964 were completely outclassed by the Pontiac. But Chevrolet was GM's performance division and it had an image to maintain. Pontiac had historically been a nuisance to Chevrolet's performance dominance, but playing second fiddle to Pontiac was not a part of its image. In 1965, Chevrolet struck back.

The SS Malibu was again Chevy's champion in challenging the GTO; the utilitarian Chevelle/Malibu line included 4 door models, the car/truck hybrid El Camino as well as station wagons. The SS option could be had in hardtop, coupe and convertible forms, and netted not only higher performance engine choices, but also special SS badging, trim and wheel covers, unique instrumentation, floor shift and bucket

**1965 Chevrolet Malibu SS convertible, owned by David Browe of Cincinnati, OH (photo by owner).**

seating. It also opened Chevrolet's lengthy book of performance options, such as positive traction rear ends in a variety of gearing.

While the styling of the 1965 Malibus was relatively unchanged from the 1964 offerings, with only minor changes to the front and rear ends, the SS engine lineup most certainly got a revamp. The serious performance engines for the SS began with the 250 horse 327, as well as a 300-horse version. The top of the line 327 was taken directly out of the Corvette's stash of engines and it produced an astonishing 350 horsepower. Though equipped with a small block, the 350 HP 327 SS Malibus could run down anything on the street—even the marauding, 389 powered GTO—especially in the stripped down, lightweight versions typically ordered with the high-performance 327.

As exciting as the awesome 350 horse 327 was, Chevrolet sent a strong signal to the automotive universe that the future of its mid-sized performance vehicle was not with small block 327. With the late year release of its Z-16 engine option, Chevy declared itself to be a force to be reckoned with in the rapidly escalating muscle car wars.

Intended to be released in the 1966 model year, the 396 cubic inch Z-16 engine produced 375 horsepower and 11:1 compression ratio—unheard of production in an intermediate vehicle in 1965. The 396 was destined to be one of the most famous engines in American automotive history, and the Z-16 stuffed into the lightweight

Chevy immediately made the few Malibus outfitted with it a devastatingly effective GTO killer. Thankfully for Pontiac, and everyone else for that matter, Chevrolet only built around 200 '65 396 SS Malibus. The Z-16 was met with critical acclaim by the motor press, being described as running like a "scalded cat" and a "rocket ship on wheels." Interestingly, as strong a performer as the Z-16 396 was in 1965 and beyond, it was only in that model year that a 396 could be had in the Corvette.

Drum brakes without power assist were standard, though power was optional. Also standard was a heavy-duty suspension with front anti-sway bars. Transmission choices were the standard 3-speed manual or a 4-speed manual. Two automatics were optional as well, depending on the engine—a two-speed Powerglide or 3-speed Turbo-Hydromatic.

The 396 Malibu SS was the pinnacle of early muscle car performance and shamed anything but the most potent Ram Air GTOs. Pontiac's unquestioned dominance of the mid-sized performance market was threatened, as Chevrolet put its sister divisions on notice that it wasn't going to easily relinquish its position as GM's performance flagship.

Chevrolet produced a ton of Chevelles and Malibus of all types—more than 378,000 of the wide ranging line. Of these, 81,112 were SS equipped vehicles; though these numbers were buoyed by the availability of the SS package on any Malibu regardless of engine—even base 6 cylinders—these numbers had to cause some panic

Quarter panel identification of early Super Sport Malibu (courtesy Gateway Classic Cars, St. Louis, MO).

in the Pontiac boardroom. The SS Malibu had established itself as a bona fide threat to the GTO, both on the track and on the balance sheet.

* * *

For the 1965 model year, Chrysler, as in most model years, was behind the pack. As in 1964, Chrysler did not build any mid-sized cars specifically as performance models, and in fact didn't even offer an option package like the GM divisions did. That is not to say Chrysler didn't build any cars to compete on the emerging muscle car battlefield. Buyers just had to work a little harder for it; savvy Mopar loyalists could option intermediate Dodge and Plymouth cars to compete with the offerings GM was putting on the road. These were the Dodge Coronet and Plymouth Belvedere.

Until 1965, the Chrysler mid-sized offerings finally found lucidity after a period of schizophrenia. Through the 1964 model year, what Chrysler called "full-sized" cars were what other divisions were calling mid-sized—116 or 117-inch wheelbase cars like Plymouth's Fury or Belvedere and Dodge's Polara. All the while, Ford and GM's full-sized offerings were gargantuan cars like Chevy's Impala or Buick's Wildcat. For 1965, Chrysler drew a line of demarcation between its mid-sized models— the new Coronet line in the case of Dodge, while Plymouth's Belvedere line remained mid-sized. The Fury grew to a true full-sized model, along with the Dodge Polara, now housed in a larger, C-body frame. Excepting the Charger, which would come along in 1966, it would be some variation of the Coronet and Belvedere lines that would spawn Mother Mopar's mid-sized muscle car models for most of the muscle car era.

Both the Coronet and the Belvedere lines came in a variety of trim and luxury levels. Plymouth offered its Belvedere in base form as the Belvedere I, but buyers could step up to the more luxurious Belvedere II. Plymouth wanted a unique name for its top-of-the-line Belvedere, and it went with a moniker stripped straight from the Space Race; "Sputnik" would likely prove to be a poor seller at the height of the Cold War, so Plymouth went with the much more general, yet still very spacy, name of Satellite. Belvedere IIs and Satellites could be purchased as hardtops or convertibles, and the Belvedere I could even be had as a thoroughly unmuscular grocery fetching station wagon. The Belvedere line could be had with the full range of Mopar engine offerings, up to and including the 426 Wedge.

The 116-inch wheelbase Satellite would become the closest thing Plymouth had to a GTO hunter in 1965, as it was the most similarly equipped, with the lesser Belvedere models being more mundane. The Satellite was an attractive car, as mid-'60s Chryslers go. It featured the same basic, straight lines that were popular in the early 1960s, and a stainless steel grille that stretched the width of the car's front end, bookended by single headlamps. The trailing edge of the quarter panels featured chrome louvers, and the tail panel featured a full-length stainless steel panel that balanced the grille. The triangular shaped C-pillars housed a rounded rear glass that Chrysler seemed to love. Like the Buick Gran Sport, the Satellite featured a prominent hood ornament with engine callout. It was no Flying Lady such as graced the hoods of Rolls-Royces, or even the lighted amber Indian head of the Pontiacs of the 1950s. At least Buick had a history of luxury cars and therefore hood ornaments. Plymouth seemed to do it just because. Make no mistake, however; while the 1965 GTO was a sculpted work of automotive art, Plymouth was not interested in creating works of art. The '65 Satellite was not exactly a modern art masterpiece, and it was no 1965 GTO.

The base engine for the Satellite was the same 273 found in the hottest Barracudas, but no Satellite was going to compete with the GM offerings unless the buyer opted for the 383 Commando engine, topped with a 4-barrel carb and producing 330 horsepower. The Chrysler 383, first introduced in 1959, was one of the most venerable of Chrysler power plants and would, in some form, be the standard big block used in all Chrysler muscle cars for the entire muscle car era. A 3-speed manual transmission was standard in the Satellite, with a 4-speed manual or 3-speed automatic available as options. Unlike the GTO, manually shifted Satellites came equipped with a shifter not made by the Hurst Company, and in the 1960s, this meant something. What it meant was that it was shifted by an inferior shifter, sort of like trying to shift with a rope. The Satellite came standard with bucket seats, a console and bright trim inside, keeping with its intent of being the most upscale mid-sized Plymouth offering. With the 383 and the interior accouterments, it was a worthy competitor to the GTO.

The Coronet, Dodge's new midsized line, was the analogue to the Belvedere. The Coronet was offered in four trim levels: the base Coronet and Coronet Deluxe (also offered as a station wagon), the confusingly named Coronet 440, which despite its name, never came with a 440 cubic inch engine, and the Coronet 500. The 500 was the Dodge version of the Satellite and could be had as either a hardtop or convertible.

At 117 inches, the Coronet rode on a wheelbase an inch longer than the Plymouth, and in fact, throughout the muscle car years the wheelbases of the more upscale Dodge muscle car models were an inch longer than those of their counterparts from Plymouth. Dodge might have built cheap cars, but Plymouth built cheaper ones, though the Plymouth sported that hood ornament that the Dodge lacked, for what that is worth.

Visually the '65 Coronet resembled the Belvedere, but with sculpted flanks and stainless brightwork that ran the length of the car. It shared the same roofline as its Plymouth cousin, and the tail panel featured full length molding and bright housing for the taillights. Coronets came standard with bench seating, but could be ordered with buckets, as well as air conditioning, power steering and brakes, and a line of other options.

Under the hood, the Coronet 500 offered a full range of V-8 engine options, including 273, 318, and 361 offerings. Like the Satellite, however, the performance began with the 383 cubic inch engine producing 330 horses. The transmission options were identical as well—3-speed manual, 4-speed manual or 3-speed Torque-Flite automatic. As with the Plymouth, manually shifted transmissions were shifted by inferior equipment.

Names like "Belvedere," "Coronet" or even "Satellite" were unlikely to intimidate anyone on the streets—Plymouth's full-sized Fury is scarier, namewise—despite

The Plymouth Satellite's Dodge cousin, the 1965 Coronet (courtesy Vanguard Motor Sales, Plymouth, MI).

the fact that the 330 horse 383 allowed it to slug it out on equal footing with the engines powering the GTO, Gran Sport and 4-4-2. While image was an integral part of a muscle car, and the early Mopar B-bodies decidedly did not have any—it was the power plant that was the heart and soul of the muscle car, and in 1965 the 426 S option was brought back for an encore in both the Satellite and the Coronet 500. Again producing 365 horses, the 426 powered B-bodies could demolish any of GM's garden variety offerings.

The early Chrysler mid-sized performance cars had to be special ordered with all the right performance options in order to present as capable adversaries of GM's midsized cars. In 1965 neither Dodge nor Plymouth offered a complete performance package like the GTO, the 4-4-2, Gran Sport or the SS Malibu. Because of this, they ended up being more expensive for comparably equipped vehicles. It was a bitter irony for Chrysler that the mid-sized performance Dodges and budget minded Plymouths rivaled the cost of considerably plusher Buicks and Oldsmobiles. Few were willing to pay Oldsmobile premiums for a Plymouth, and this coupled with styling generally seen as less attractive than the GM cars hindered the sales of the twin offerings from Mopar. Plymouth sold just over 25,000 Satellites in '65, including 1,561 426 Belvederes and Satellites. Dodge sold another 7,322 383-powered Coronets of all models, and another 2,117 426-powered Coronets. These numbers were a far cry from the number of GTOs Pontiac was pushing out the door.

\* \* \*

**Hood ornaments are not generally considered intimidating, but exceptions do exist (courtesy Gateway Classic Cars, St. Louis, MO).**

The car maker still lagging behind in the mid-sized muscle car market, while basking in the immense popularity of its Mustang, was Ford. Ford trotted its redesigned full-sized Galaxie out once again, this time armed with optional 390 and big 427 cube engines under the hood, but the Galaxie was Ford's equivalent of the coelacanth—a prehistoric beast that didn't know it should be extinct.

Once again, Ford's intermediate offering in 1965 was its Fairlane, substantially unchanged from the previous model year. The Fairlane 500 and Sports Coupe were the top offering and the Fairlane at least appeared to be moving in the right direction in 1965. While a 6 cylinder was available on base Fairlanes, it now featured a 2 barrel 289 as the entry level V-8, with the 260 having been jettisoned. As with the Mopars, savvy buyers could step up to a substantially better performing V-8; unlike Mopar with its 383 offering, Ford apparently learned absolutely nothing from the GTO in 1964 and the Fairlane's utter inability to compete with it, as once again, the most powerful V-8 available was the little 289 small-block valiantly dragging the intermediate Fairlane with its 271 horsepower. The Hi-Po 289 featured dual exhaust and 4 barrel carburation, and could be mated to a 3 or 4-speed manual transmission or the 3-speed Cruise-O-Matic automatic. However, with the GM and Mopar engines producing more horses than the Ford had cubes, in a car roughly of the same curb weight, the Fairlane once again just wasn't in the same class. Ford still sold just over 64,000 hardtop Fairlane 500s and Sport Coupes, but as with '64, this number includes all engine types.

**1965 Ford Fairlane owned by Scott Nickett of Doylestown, PA (photo by owner).**

**1965 Mercury Comet (courtesy Gateway Classic Cars, St. Louis, MO).**

Mercury again offered its Cyclone as the top of the Comet line. Like its Ford cousin, the Cyclone was offered with the 225 horse 289 cubic inch engine standard, but could be optioned up to the 271 horse HiPo offered in the hottest Fairlanes. The Cyclone also came standard with a 4-speed manual transmission, with the 3-speed Merc-O-Matic automatic as an option. All Cyclones fitted with the 271 horse 289 received Ford's heavy-duty "top loader" 4-speed tranny as the only option. All Cyclones got upgraded heavy-duty brakes and suspensions. Bucket seating was standard, and the Cyclone had unique stainless trim and badging.

Mercury didn't build many '65 Cyclones—only an estimated 400, and only about 90 built with the HiPo 289, according to Ford. Like the Ford, the 289 powered Cyclones were simply not capable of running with the large cubic inch powered offerings from Chrysler or GM.

*  *  *

The newest niche in the performance car market—the pony car market, initiated by Plymouth and then promptly commandeered by Ford's Mustang, was where Ford was concentrating most of its efforts. For Ford, the mid-sized muscle car market was simply an afterthought, a distraction to be participated in out of some sense of obligation. What Ford really concentrated on was selling hundreds of thousands of Mustangs and beating the hell out of Plymouth's Barracuda.

The Mustang for 1965 was very similar to that of the previous model year, with Ford seeing no real reason to change much about the most popular car of its era, and the runaway winner of *Motor Trend*'s Car of the Year award. The most impactful change was the availability of a new body style, the fastback, which joined the hardtop and convertible body styles and featured C-pillars that sloped gently toward the decklid. The fastback body style, while found on various cars over the following years, is nearly synonymous with the Mustang, and it was fastback Mustangs that would form the basis of the muscle car variants of Ford's little pony car.

There were other, more subtle changes as well. The base engine, a 170 cubic inch 6 cylinder, gave way to a 200-cube slant 6 later in the model year. As with the Fairlane, the 260 cid V-8 engine option was replaced by the same 2 barrel 289 that powered the mid-sized Fords. Also as with the Fairlane, the most potent Mustang engine offering was the 271 horse 289 Hi-Po K-Code. Mustangs featured standard bucket seating, AM radio and floor shifting of either the 3 or 4-speed manual or the Cruise-O-Matic 3-speed automatic transmissions. An interesting interior option was the famous "Pony Interior," which featured seat covers replete with rampaging horses, wood grain accents and upgraded instrumentation.

A late model year introduction to the Mustang family was the GT option. The GT was the high-performance version of the Mustang, and featured the 4-barrel 289 or K-Code 289, dual exhaust and choice of 4-speed manual or Cruise-O-Matic 3-speed automatic. Upgraded handling and front disc brakes, practically unheard of in 1965, and GT striping were options. The GT also featured a special grille housing fog lamps and special GT badging. The GT was still small-block powered and no real threat to the GTO or any of the other mid-sized muscle cars, but the emergence of the GT model was a significant step in the development of the Mustang and what it would eventually become—a pint sized, big-block powered muscle car, still bearing the GT badging.

The diminutive '65 Mustang, like the '64 model, was no muscle car. Regardless, all traditional mid-sized muscle cars combined were only a fraction of the Mustang's sales, with Ford building an incredible number of them—559,451 in fact.

As if the popularity of the Mustang weren't enough to cement the nameplate in the historical consciousness of the American public, there were the specially built,

**The new-for-1965 fastback Mustang (courtesy Vanguard Motor Sales, Plymouth, MI).**

Mustang-based performance cars produced by former chicken farmer and race car driver Carroll Shelby.

Best known in 1965 for building the earlier, two-seat, Ford powered Cobra, Carrol Shelby used the Mustang as his starting point to building high-performance road racing cars, working over the 289 and enhancing the Mustang's steering, suspension and brakes. The Shelby Mustang, dubbed the GT-350, would become an icon of the muscle car era, and by 1967 there was a large cube powered Shelby Mustang called the GT-500. Due to their low production numbers and high price, the Shelby Mustang were never in the mainstream of the automobile world of 1965, but they were iconic and important automobiles. The Shelby name would ride a Mustang through the 1970 model year (though the 1970 models were simply leftover 1969s) and the Shelbys are among the most popular and valuable Mustangs today.

\* \* \*

Once again, Plymouth offered a feeble defense to the marauding Mustangs dominating the pony car landscape with its beleaguered Barracuda. The little Plymouth seemed to be cursed again in '65. The Barracuda was released before the Mustang in '64, only to have the Ford steal the show a mere two weeks later. The big news on the pony car front was the Mustang's new fastback; the Plymouth had always been a fastback.

Like the Mustang, the 1965 Barracuda was little changed from the '64 model. Unlike Ford, Plymouth had plenty of reason to change it. Compared to the sleek, sporty Mustang, the Barracuda can only be described as awkward, with its huge back glass and ruler-straight lines. Re-tooling a car line takes years of design time and substantial investment, both of which Chrysler had to invest in the Barracuda to make it competitive with the Mustang, and the aggressively named Plymouth continued to be more baitfish than Mustang hunter.

Despite this, and but for the inevitable comparisons to its Ford nemesis, the Barracuda might have experienced a better fate. The little car featured bucket seating, AM radio and rear fold down seats for a true 2+2 form like the fastback Mustangs. It offered comparable cabin room inside, despite riding on a wheelbase 2 inches shorter. Additionally, the huge back glass could be used as a solarium, if one so chose. The Mustang was entirely unsuited for use as a solarium. The engine offerings were comparable as well—the base 170 cube slant six from the previous year was replaced by a bigger 225-inch slant 6, an indestructible workhorse of an engine that would power economy Chryslers well into the '70s and known in Mopar lore as the "leaning tower of power." Up from that was the 273 V-8 outfitted with two-barrel carb and producing 180 horsepower. The most powerful engine option for the Barracuda was the 273 Commando, featuring 10.5:1 compression, 4-barrel carb, more radical camshaft and dual exhaust, all of which combined for 235 horsepower.

The most competitive Barracuda however, was dubbed the "Formula S" incarnation, aimed squarely at the top end, sporty Mustangs, like the GT. The Formula S featured the Commando 273, but also sported accents such as upgraded suspension, special badging, a tachometer and larger wheels and tires. Keeping up with the Mustang GT, factory air and front disc brakes were available.

The refinements Plymouth applied to the Barracuda, particularly the Formula S, as well as the full model year, led to the sale of 64,596 Barracudas. The good news, or actually great news for a Chrysler division unused to anything remotely like

**1965 Plymouth Barracuda (courtesy Gateway Classic Cars, St. Louis, MO).**

**1965 Barracuda badgework (courtesy Gateway Classic Cars, St. Louis, MO).**

good news in the early 1960s, was that this number represented a nearly three-fold increase in Barracuda sales. The bad news, which Chrysler was much more used to hearing, was that the number was less than 9 percent of Mustang sales. It was a remarkable fact that of every 100 pony cars sold in 1965, nearly 92 wore the Blue Oval.

\* \* \*

The 1965 model year was the last of the first phase of the muscle car era. There were still plenty of full-sized performance cars being sold before their virtual extinction in the near term, and the growing list of mid-sized, more affordable performance models squeezed them out. The mid-sized muscle cars that did exist were either option packages on more mundane models, like the GM offerings, or had to be special ordered at considerable expense, like the Sport Satellite. Ford didn't even make a serious attempt at the mid-sized performance niche, relying instead on its legions of pony cars to carry its banner. Those early muscle cars of 1964 and 1965, while not having the flash and brute power of what would come later, represent an interesting time of the greater muscle car epoch. These proto-muscle cars represent a bridge between the full-sized, large cube sleeper behemoths prowling the streets of the late 1950s and early 1960s and the audacious cars powered by obscene amounts of horsepower that would follow in just a few short years.

Interestingly, the 1964–65 model years in a way paralleled American society as a whole. While amazing cars in their day, the muscle cars of those years represent a sort of conservative innocence compared to the upheaval, change and turmoil that would come later in the decade in both the automotive world and wider American society.

# 5

# The Other Escalation of 1966

## Chevrolet Awakens and the Coming of the Hemi

In many ways, 1966 was the pivotal year of the 1960s. It was a year of transition, and one that saw the beginnings of the events and images of what we now identify, decades later, as "The '60s." The war in Southeast Asia was rapidly becoming the defining event of the decade as it transitioned from a nuisance brushfire in a faraway country few Americans had ever heard of and began to take its place in the forefront of the American consciousness. This year saw what is now known as the "escalation," the '60s analogue to George W. Bush's more successful "surge" in a later war. By the end of 1966, there were more than 385,000 U.S. troops in Vietnam, more than double the number of the previous year. The United States Air Force conducted vicious strikes on targets throughout the North but specifically the North Vietnamese capital of Hanoi and the port city of Haiphong. The image of American B-52s with endless ordnance falling out of their bomb bays is one of the iconic images of the 1960s.

The reaction to Johnson's escalation provided other iconic images of the times—the emerging war protests. The popularity of Barry Sandler's "Ballad of the Green Berets," an ode to America's elite fighting force in Vietnam, illustrates the relative popularity of the effort in Vietnam in 1966, and the protests weren't nearly what they would become in later years, but the nascent protest movement would signal what would come later in the decade. The protests were more acute in Vietnam itself, highlighted by images of a red-robed Buddhist monk setting himself alight in front of the American consulate in Hue to protest American support of an unpopular, Catholic dominated government.

Race relations were transforming as well and still played a predominant role in the American consciousness, as the non-violent protests in the Martin Luther King, Jr., mold of the early '60s were growing more angry and violent. There were race riots in distinctively non–Southern American cities such as Watts, a suburb of Los Angeles, Chicago, Lansing, and, of all places, Omaha, shattering the arrogant notion that race issues were confined to the "backward" South. The National Guard was called to duty to deal with the rioting and looting in Omaha and Chicago; fortunately, those Guardsmen handled things better than their compatriots in Ohio would four years later. Stokely Carmichael founded the Black Power movement, and the Black Panther Party came into existence. There were highlights on the racial front, however, as the Texas Western (now University of Texas–El Paso) men's basketball team, a predominantly black team, defeated the lily-white Kentucky in the NCAA national championship game, opening the door to black recruiting nationwide.

The story of Julian Bond is an example of the currents of the 1960s that sometimes flowed together, standing as he did at the intersection of the struggle for civil rights and opposition to the Vietnam War. Bond was a founder of the civil rights group the Student Nonviolent Coordinating Committee and was duly elected to the Georgia House of Representatives following the passage of the Voting Rights Act, which finally gave blacks the franchise in the recalcitrant Deep South. Due to Bond's opposition to the Vietnam War—and definitely not because he was black, as Georgia assured everyone—he was denied his seat in Atlanta, and it took a ruling from the U.S. Supreme Court to allow him in the doors at the statehouse.

America's taste in popular music was evolving as well. The Beatles were as popular as ever, though they were pelted with rotten fruit at a concert in Memphis. The lesson learned by the Fab Four was that making favorable reference to one's own popularity in relation to Jesus Christ prior to performing in Tennessee is not wise. Matching the national mood, the feel-good sound and topics of the early 60s, songs focused on things like high school loves, surfing and cars, began to give way to darker, psychedelic sound. English acts were still popular, such as the Rolling Stones and the acid-rock act Cream. The San Francisco sound was beginning to emerge with the Grateful Dead at the van. The Mamas and Papas reached number one with *Monday, Monday,* and the Doors were gaining momentum. Janis Joplin and Jimi Hendrix made their debut performances in 1966. Most of these acts would suffer tragedy, victims of their drug fueled, psychedelic times. Hendrix, a left-handed guitarist who played a right-handed axe upside down because as a child he couldn't afford a proper one, died of an overdose of sleeping tablets in 1970. Janis Joplin, who once beat the Doors' Jim Morrison senseless with a bottle of Southern Comfort, OD'd three weeks later. Morrison died of an overdose a year after that. Ironically, it was the Dead who managed to stay more or less alive beyond the decade, until frontman Jerry Garcia died in 1995—of a heart attack—at the age of 53. Most principal members of the Rolling Stones are inexplicably still with us.

Despite Kennedy's confident proclamation that the U.S. would put a man on the moon by the end of the decade, in 1966 the U.S. was trailing the Soviet Union in the race to do so. The Soviets accomplished an important first: the first ever man-made object to reach another planet, when *Venere 3* was intentionally crashed onto the surface of Venus. Early in the year, the Soviets' *Luna 9* conducted humanity's first soft landing on the surface of the moon, and *Luna 10* reached and maintained lunar orbit, demonstrating that the U.S. was still lagging behind in the Space Race. The U.S. managed to accomplish both feats later in the year, but 1966 saw U.S. failings in its space program. *Gemini 8* was launched into Earth's orbit, but the mission was aborted early and the astronauts successfully recovered. A second U.S. lunar mission to attempt a landing on the moon was a failure of sorts; it crashed into the moon's surface when it was supposed to perform a soft landing. Perhaps America's biggest space related accomplishment took place in Hollywood with the launch of the sci-fi series *Star Trek*. The starship *Enterprise* may have failed in its stated five-year mission "to explore strange new worlds, to seek out new life and new civilizations, to boldly go where no man has gone before" (it was cancelled after three seasons), but *Star Trek* nerds and Space Race observers fueled a surge in interest in mathematics and engineering careers that would transform the U.S. aerospace industry into the world's leader it is today.

There were other transformational happenings on the American stage as well. In sports, the American Football League and the National Football League merged to become the modern NFL. Cigarettes now came with warnings to alert people that intentionally putting smoke in their lungs *could be* bad for them. Americans began their annual love-hate relationship with the Grinch in 1966. The Supreme Court mandated the requirement of *Miranda* warnings. Ground was broken for the World Trade Center—the future tomb of nearly 3,000 Americans. Ronald Reagan got his first major job in politics by winning the California governorship. Reagan quickly outlawed LSD. San Francisco might or might not have received that news.

President Johnson's federal government continued its push to occupy more and more of the field of American society in 1966. Following on the heels of the Civil Rights Act and the Voting Rights Act, and as a part of his "Great Society" program, Medicare came into effect. Congress quietly passed the National Traffic and Motor Vehicle Act, a seemingly benign body of legislation that led to the establishment of the U.S. Department of Transportation, which would have a profound effect on the American automobile, shipping and transportation industry.

Culturally, 1966 was certainly transformational. In that year, the muscle car world was evolving as well.

* * *

As it was for American society as a whole, 1966 was a transitional year for the American muscle car, and a year of change for a large portion of muscle car models. Convinced of the popularity of the performance intermediate, car makers began to build them as stand-alone models rather than simply option packages on more mundane vehicles. Simply put, the muscle car was growing up and coming into its own. Ford got more serious about challenging the General's intermediate super car dominance, while Chrysler, cautious due to a lesser margin for financial error, continued to take small steps toward a full-blown effort in the muscle car wars. However, it was Chrysler, timid as it was, that released the most potent engine of 1966. Like Lyndon Johnson in Southeast Asia, Chrysler began the first serious escalation in the horsepower wars that would define the remainder of the muscle car era.

In the 1960s, car lines were generally treated to frequent restyles. A lifespan of two to three years was generally the shelf life for a particular body shape, after which it was redesigned to give the car a fresh, new look. The regular restyles would hopefully generate continued public interest on the theory that no one would buy a new car if the one already owned was in otherwise good shape and looked just like the newest model. Sometimes the power trains and engine options were changed as well, but the body style is what was regularly transformed.

For 1966 GM's entire mid-sized A-body line, the platform on which the GTO, 4-4-2, Gran Sport and Malibu were built, received a complete restyle. From Chevy at the bottom of the price range to Buick at the top, all A-bodies received a make-over. Gone were the straight but popular lines of the 1964–65 body styles. Instead, the A-bodies were treated to a new, "Coke-bottle" design, more sculpted and with a pinch just aft of the doors. All A-bodies received a semi-fastback "flying buttress" C-pillar with recessed back glass providing a shared roofline. Fenders and quarter panels, though similar, were unique to each manufacturer, but doors were shared. Each make's design team had full artistic freedom with the front and rear ends. This was the template from which the various GM divisions built their muscle cars.

In 1966, Pontiac still led the way, riding on the momentum and reputation of the previous two model years. In terms of performance, the days of the GTO's unquestioned dominance were rapidly coming to an end. The GTO had reached adulthood as a stand-alone model, rather than a high-performance option on the lowly Tempest, but by 1966, there were plenty of cars that could kick a base GTO to the curb. The mechanical offerings from Pontiac were essentially the same as the previous year: a base 335 horsepower 389 engine with a 3-speed manual transmission standard and a 4-speed manual and two-speed Powerglide automatic as options. An optional Tri-power carburation system of three two-barrel carburetors boosted the horse-power to 360, as would an optional Ram Air cold air induction system.

The cosmetic changes, however, were what caught the attention of the public. The 1966 version of the Goat had gigantic shoes to fill given the popularity of the beautiful '65 model. Judging by sales numbers, Pontiac hit the mark and then some. The A-body restyle gave the GTO a more streamlined, elegant look, which was accented by the front end that carried the Pontiac staple stacked headlamps and split grille from the '65 model. The blacked-out grilles, borrowed from the GTO's larger cousin the Grand Prix, incorporated amber colored driving lamps and the now famous white block letter "GTO" in the left hand grille. The power bulge hood was carried over from the '65. The rear end was highlighted by some of the most distinctive taillights of any muscle car, featuring louvered covers to give them a slotted appearance.

On the inside, the GTO was well equipped with standard features and could be equipped like a Grand Prix if one so chose. Air conditioning, power windows and AM/FM radio with rear speaker were optional, as was "reverberation," which delayed the sound slightly to the rear speaker to provide an unusual effect. Bucket seats were standard, and a console was available with either the floor mounted automatic or manual transmissions. A real wood applique adorned the instrument panel, which could be upgraded to rally gauges. Power brakes, including power front disc brakes, were available, as were power steering and a power, quarter panel mounted antenna. The result was a substantial departure from the earlier Goats in terms of appearance that made the car seem much longer and more luxurious, but in reality it was no bigger or heavier than the '65 model.

The muscle car buying public approved of Pontiac's efforts to restyle the GTO, and it voted with its dollars. In fact, by the raw sales numbers, the 1966 Pontiac GTO was the most popular mid-sized muscle car of the entire muscle car era; Pontiac sold nearly 100,000 copies of the little GTO. Today, the 1966 model is consistently over-looked in favor of its '65 and '67 siblings, and '66 GTOs are seen less frequently today, despite the much higher production (and much cooler taillights).

**The unusual and stylish louvered taillights of the 1966 Pontiac GTO (courtesy Vanguard Motor Sales, Plymouth, MI).**

By 1966, the GTO was obviously still popular, in part due to its carefully crafted image and street reputation, but this would change. GTO production numbers would steadily decline over the rest of its lifespan, due in part to Pontiac's sister divisions cannibalizing it, but also from the mass of performance mid-sized models that would be built and released in the over the next two years.

At Oldsmobile, the 4-4-2 remained the intermediate performance car though, unlike the GTO, the 4-4-2 was still an option package on the F-85 or more upscale Cutlass A-body. Oldsmobile's 4-4-2 got an external facelift, using the same "Coke bottle" styling that spanned the GM A-body line. The front fenders received faux vents behind the front wheels, and the headlamps were quad horizontal units flanking a narrow grille, with a tri-color 4-4-2 emblem set low on the left hand side. Matching emblems graced the quarter panels and the deck lid.

The biggest news for the 4-4-2 was the addition of two new engine options. The first was dubbed the L69 and essentially mirrored Pontiac's Tripower—three two-barrel carbs sitting atop Olds' 400 block and producing 360 horses—the same rating as the Tripower Pontiac. Also making its timid debut was what would grow into one of the most feared engines of the era, the mighty W-30. The W-30 was essentially a cold air inducted L69. Oldsmobile probably lied when they rated the W-30 at 360 horsepower. A 3-speed manual transmission was standard, with a 4-speed manual or two-speed Jetaway automatic transmission optional. The L69 was only available with either of the manual transmissions. If one opted against either of these high-performance engines, the standard engine was still formidable—a 400 cubic inch block producing a rated 350 horses, or 15 more than the base 389 in the Pontiac, as well as more torque. As with the hotter engines, transmission choices were the standard 3-speed manual or optional 4-speed manual. The two-speed Jetaway automatic was available as well, but only shifted on the column—unusual for the more upscale Oldsmobile. Limited slip rear ends were available as well, and the standard heavy-duty, police inspired suspension assured that 4-4-2 was one of the best handling muscle cars of the model year. Standard braking was manual drums all around, though power assist was optional.

4-4-2 interiors were luxurious but sporty, in the tradition of Oldsmobile. Bucket seating was standard, with full vinyl, pleated seat covers. Consoles were standard as well with manual transmission cars. Instrumentation was housed in twin pods set in a brushed aluminum housing. Creature comforts available included air conditioning, power windows, power steering and a tachometer.

The 4-4-2 was certainly a worthy competitor for its Pontiac cousin, but the 4-4-2 did not enjoy the sales surge the GTO did. In fact, the 1966 4-4-2 production actually slumped to just under 22,000 units, including 151 W-30 cars. This is probably due to the reality that Olds simply wasn't seen by the public as a builder of performance cars, having drifted away from that niche since the Rocket 88 of the late '40s. Through the '50s, Oldsmobiles rivaled Buick and Cadillac in terms of GM luxury. The 4-4-2 was facing stiff headwinds, particularly with the popularity of the GTO. Where the GTO made up nearly a third of Pontiac's A-body sales, 4-4-2 made up only 10 percent of Oldsmobile's A-bodies sold.

Buick's muscle car entry for 1966 was again the Skylark based Gran Sport, which became its own model rather than an option on the Skylark. The Gran Sport received the same restyle as the rest of GM's A-body line, but Buick was Buick, and as such, the Gran Sport had to have a little added panache that would set it apart from its cousins at Pontiac, Olds and Chevrolet. The Buick, available in hardtop, pillared coupe or convertible form, featured a crease that ran the length of the car's body about two-thirds of the way up, and bright trim at the rockers. It also featured faux vents, sufficing for Buick's trademark "ventiports" behind the front wheels, and the wheel openings themselves were adorned with stainless trim. The hood featured twin, rear facing non-functional hood scoops, sans hood ornament for 1966. The front end featured a blacked-out grille divided both horizontally and vertically by bright trim, and horizontally set headlights. A Gran Sport emblem was set low in the grille on the driver's side, and both Skylark and GS badging were located on the quarter panels.

The base engine for the Buick was again the 401 cubic inch Wildcat power plant producing 325 cubic inches. Optional upgrades included a 340 horse 401 and an ultra-rare 332 horse, 11:1 compression 401. Only a rumored fifty or so of the latter were produced. The standard transmission was a 3-speed manual with which no Buick buyer would ever live; indeed, the vast majority of '66 Gran Sports were ordered with a two-speed Super Turbine 300 automatic. A 4-speed manual was also available. The Gran Sport featured a heavy-duty suspension and, as in '65, utilized the heavy convertible boxed frame to help assure a ride that the discriminating Buick buyer would recognize in a Buick.

Unusual for Buick, standard seating was a notchback bench with a fold-down

**1966 Buick Skylark Gran Sport convertible (courtesy Fast Lane Classic Cars, St. Charles, MO).**

center armrest. However, seating was full vinyl and, of course, buckets and a center console were optional. Power seating was an option, as were power steering, brakes, antenna and windows. AM/FM radio and tilt steering were available as well.

The Gran Sport was caught in the same perfect storm of factors as the 4-4-2. The near 100,000 GTOs Pontiac sold sucked a lot of oxygen out of the GM A-body performance car market. In terms of performance, the heavy Gran Sport was outclassed by the GTO, the 4-4-2 and especially the new A-body offerings from Chevrolet. Finally, Buick was simply Buick. Buick had no widespread reputation for performance. It had a reputation, unfair in light of the Gran Sport, of building cars perfectly suited for hauling executives to business meetings and old people to church. When people thought of performance in 1966, they did not typically think of Buick. All of this added up to a significant sales slump compared to the '65 model; Buick sold only 3,816 units.

What people did think of when pondering GM performance was the Chevrolet Chevelle SS 396. Initially released in small numbers in the '65 model year, Chevrolet's 396 would gain notoriety as one of the most famous power plants of the muscle car era and would help establish Chevrolet's performance A-body, now badged as the SS Chevelle, as a legend in American automotive history.

The Chevelle SS 396, known simply as the SS 396, got the same basic restyle as the rest of the A-bodies, but, like its corporate cousins, with Chevy specific styling. The hood was adorned with two sideward facing faux scoops set in the middle of the hood. The grille, simply styled with minimal brightwork, was unique among GM A-bodies in that it wrapped around to the front edges of the fenders and featured

**1966 SS 396 Chevelle hardtop (courtesy Fast Lane Classic Cars, St. Charles, MO).**

a simple SS badge with engine callout in the center. The quarter panels—slightly shorter than those of its cousins—were graced with simple block letter "Super Sport" emblems. While sharing a wheelbase with the other GM A-bodies, this shorter rear deck gave it a smaller, more agile appearance than other A-bodies. The tail panel was as simply styled as the rest of the car, with simple taillights and "CHEVELLE" spelled out in block letters and a small SS 396 badge of warning on the right side. While the A-body offerings from Pontiac, Olds and Buick were designed to offer as much style as they did performance, the SS Chevelle didn't bother much with elegance. The SS, simply styled and all business, had an aura of unadulterated aggression. With the unique wrap-around grilles, the car even appeared to be leaning forward.

This air of aggression was ably backed up by the 396 cubic inch engine, now widely available. The base 396 was a 325 horsepower unit; while it rated less horsepower than its competitors, it was more than a match in the lightweight Chevelle body. Up from that 325-horse engine was the L34 396 featuring a more aggressive cam and more efficient carburation for 360 horsepower. Finally, the rarest of them all was a 375-horse version of the 396, known as the L78, with 11:1 compression, high flow carb and heads taken from the Corvette's 427 cubic inch block. The 375-horse 396 marked the most powerful engine available in a GM A-body for 1966. Ram Air GTOs and W-30 4-4-2s, indeed.

Transmission choices were standard GM corporate fare: 3-speed manual as standard, but with two different 4-speeds optional, as well as the two-speed Powerglide. Automatic equipped cars were shifted on the column, in keeping with Chevy's budget mindedness, but could be shifted on the floor when the optional console was ordered.

The L78 could only be had with a heavy-duty 4-speed manual; positive traction rear end was mandatory as well with the L78 and was optional on all others. Heavy-duty suspension with sway bars was standard as well, as was manual drum brakes. Power assist was optional.

The interior of the '66 SS was as understated as the exterior. A bench seat was standard, though buckets were optional. Buckets coupled with the Powerglide also likely meant that a console was a mandatory option; there are no known '66 SS Chevelles with buckets and a column mounted shifter. A tachometer was standard equipment. Tinted windows, power windows, power seating, air conditioning, AM/FM, tilt steering column and power steering were among the options; the economical Chevelle SS could be dressed up like a Buick, should one choose. The SS 396, however, was a muscle car with a singular purpose, and few opted for such power-draining frivolities.

Chevrolet was GM's volume division, as well as its historical performance one, and it was the only division to compete with the astronomical sales numbers of the GTO. Though the SS 396 was a car that could destroy the Pontiac on the street, sales numbers fell short of its Tin Indian rival. However, Chevy did sell a respectable 72,272 SS Chevelles in one version or another. Though Pontiac-Chevy warfare would continue unabated for the remainder of the muscle car era, 1966 saw the waning of

With its widespread release in 1966, the Chevrolet's 396 finally gave the Bowtie Division a performance engine capable of taking on rival Pontiac's GTO and taking its rightful place atop of GM's performance divisions (courtesy Gateway Classics Cars, St. Louis, MO).

Pontiac's dominance, and the SS 396 would eclipse the Pontiac going forward. Chevrolet was set to reclaim its rightful place, at least in the minds of Chevy people, as GM's performance flagship. After 1967, the other GM divisions would build some truly legendary muscle cars, but it would be Chevrolet that would carry the banner in the war against GM's mid-sized performance rivals from Chrysler and especially despised Ford.

* * *

Through the 1966 model year, the mid-sized performance market was almost exclusively the domain of General Motors. In previous years, Ford had made half-hearted attempts to play in GM's sandbox with the 289 powered Fairlanes and Mercury Comets, but these were no match for the large cube offerings from the GM divisions. Through 1965, Ford seemed content to rest on the laurels of the galloping success of the Mustang. They couldn't be blamed, with Ford execs wallpapering their offices with dollar bills generated by Mustang profits. By 1966, the Blue Oval, having witnessed the runaway success of the GTO and to a lesser extent other mid-sized performance mid-size cars, decided that Ford might be able to elbow its way into the mid-sized performance car market. At the very least, Ford needed to appear to be making an effort.

Ford was reluctant to let any car maker—particularly Chevrolet—have something that went unanswered and in 1966 finally got serious about a performance mid-size car to compete with the rampaging GM offerings. If Ford entered the muscle car wars somewhat reluctantly and seemingly out of a sense of obligation, once the engineers at the Blue Oval set to work, they did it right. All those SS Chevelles needed to be dealt with, after all.

Ford again based its mid-sized competitor on the unexciting Fairlane. With cars bearing cool, youth friendly badges such as GTO, SS, 4-4-2 and Gran Sport, a car named for Henry Ford's estate was hardly one to stir one's blood. Be that as it may, Ford did the 1966 Fairlane right, afterthought though it was.

Keeping pace with the GM A-bodies, the Fairlane was redesigned for 1966, in such a way that it resembled a smaller version of the still-popular-but-fading-as-a-performance-car full-sized Galaxie. The car was stretched out by half an inch and for 1966 rode on a 116-inch wheelbase, making it an inch longer than the GM A-bodies. The car featured a thin C-pillar with a raked back glass and a redesigned grille. The Fairlane line did a lot of Ford's heavy lifting, coming in a dizzying array of models, from basic transportation to station wagons to personal luxury cars to the performance options, dubbed the Fairlane GT and GTA, differing only by transmission. The "A" in GTA obviously stood for "automatic." The performance Fairlanes featured a hood with non-functional side facing scoops similar to those found on its arch-nemesis, the SS Chevelle. The stacked headlamps were offset with the upper lights set farther forward, and the grille bit back into the fender, again, reminiscent of the Chevelle. This combined with the raked back glass and aggressive stance gave the impression the car was leaning forward, straining to be set loose. Rocker panel molding with "GT" or "GTA" badging adorned so optioned cars.

While the car certainly looked the part of a muscle car, it still had to perform

**The 427 powered, R-code 1966 Ford Fairlane (courtesy Streetside Classics, Charlotte, NC).**

as one. The wide range of the utilitarian Fairlane line necessitated several engine options. Two different 390s were yanked out of the by-then fat and happy Thunderbird and stuffed into the engine bays of Fairlane 500 and 500 XL models—a two-barrel producing 270 horses and a four-barrel making a more robust 315. Fairlane GT/A models, however, got a 390 Thunderbird Special 390, producing 335 horses and dressed up with performance appearing chrome bits. Transmission choices were a standard 3-speed manual or heavy-duty "Top-loader" 4-speed on the GT, and a 3-speed "Sports Shift" automatic for the GTA. The automatic could be operated as a traditional automatic or the gears could be worked manually; Ford advertised it as "a manual for him and an automatic for her," a bit of naive sexism that surely angered the newly formed National Organization for Women.

The suspension was redesigned as well for 1966, and the GT/As came with the heavy-duty variety, as well as manual drum brakes all the way around, with power and/or front discs as options. Limited slip rear ends in various gear ratios were also optional.

The interior of the GT/A was lifted nearly completely from the upscale Fairlane XL, save specific bits of trim and other GT/A specific items. Standard features included bucket seating with full vinyl seat coverings, padded dash pad, and a console. Power steering and wood grained steering wheel, as well as air conditioning were among the list of optional creature comforts.

For those for whom a 335 horse 390 was not enough car, a few—very few—

Fairlanes were built with Ford's fire breathing 425 horse 427, equipped with dual four-barrel carbs. Interestingly, 427s were not available in the GT or GTA Fairlane, but only in the base model, the Fairlane 500 or Fairlane 500XL. These were made specifically for NASCAR and IHRA super stock drag racing. NASCAR required that car manufacturers build a certain number of the same cars they wanted to run on the track for the buying public. This was called homologation, and it was to ensure that the "stock" cars used in stock car racing were indeed "stock." As the 1960s wore on, the homologation rules would provide some of the most interesting, if limited production, cars of the era. Only 57 of these cars were built and are among the most valuable muscle cars in existence today.

With the introduction of the Thunderbird Special engine into the midsized, lightweight Fairlane, Ford finally had a true mid-sized muscle car capable of competing with the offerings from GM. The 375-horse SS Chevy would make tiny bits of metal out of the Fairlane GT/A, but it would do the same to most anything else. The law of averages dictated that the Ford was far more likely to square off against a base SS or, even more likely, a 335-horse GTO. This was not missed by Ford's advertising department. A prominent Fairlane GT/A ad from the era showed a Fairlane with the tail of a tiger ("tiger" was one of the many names by which the GTO was known) hanging out from under the hood with the caption "how to cook a tiger." While Chevrolet was never far from Ford's mind, the ad guys knew exactly which car was still at the top in 1966. Despite the advertising images of GT/As literally eating

1966 Ford Fairlane badgework (courtesy Gateway Classic Cars, St. Louis, MO).

GTOs, the GT/A didn't sell in the numbers the SS or the GTO did. It was, however, a moderately popular model with the buying public. Perhaps suffering some from dedicated Ford people buying Mustangs, Ford was still able convince 37,342 people to forgo the little pony car and try the Fairlane GT/A.

Ford's upscale division, Mercury, followed the mothership and offered its own mid-sized muscle car as alternative to those buyers who appreciated Ford but wanted something a little more upscale. Thus, while the Ford Fairlane GT/A was aimed at the Chevys and Pontiacs at the lower end of the GM ladder, the Mercury Comet Cyclone GT was built to take on the 4-4-2 and Gran Sport at the upper end.

For all practical purposes, the Mercury was identical to its Ford cousin. Like the Ford, the Comet Cyclone was lengthened for 1966 to an identical 116 inches. Like the Fairlane, Comets came in a range of styles, and were identical to the Fairlane. The Cyclone and Cyclone GT set themselves apart from the Ford with a grille divided horizontally by a body color header panel, checkered flag badging and unique tail panel. The Cyclone GT added dual exhaust, a unique hood featuring twin non-functional scoops, GT striping, heavy-duty suspension and, unique among mid-sized muscle cars in 1966, standard front disc brakes, with or without power assist. As the performance model of the Comet, the Cyclone itself was offered in an array of engine choices, including a 200 horse 289, or a 265 or 275 horse version of the 390 found in the Ford. The GT, however, stepped up to the 335-horse engine found powering the Fairlane GT/A. Transmission choices mirrored the Fairlane GT/A, except that Mercury's sexist automatic was called the "Merc-O-Matic."

The 1966 Mercury Comet Cyclone GT (courtesy Gateway Classic Cars, St. Louis, MO).

**Tail badging of the Fairlane's upscale cousin, the Mercury Cyclone (courtesy Gateway Classic Cars, St. Louis, MO).**

On the inside, the Cyclone GT was plusher than the Ford. It offered richer interior accouterments, such as a standard console and five-instrument cluster. Power steering and air conditioning were optional. All of this opulence pushed the base price of the Cyclone GT up by about 100 bucks over that of a like-equipped Fairlane GT/A. Like the Fairlane, the Cyclone came in convertible or hardtop body styles.

Mercury didn't sell many Cyclone GTs in 1966, presumably because the average performance car buyer cared little for the creature comforts offered in the Mercury over the Ford, and saw little point in paying for what was essentially a more expensive Fairlane GT/A. There were, however, 13,812 buyers who did care about the amenities offered by Mercury and another 2,158 who wanted the option of dropping the top on their GT.

1966 saw Ford finally, if reluctantly, join the mid-sized muscle car wars and build a car that could compete with the hordes of GM built cars roaming the boulevards. While this was big news, perhaps the biggest news of the 1966 model year was the escalation of hostilities committed by Chrysler.

\* \* \*

If Ford had to be dragged into the mid-sized performance car competition, finally jumping in with both feet in 1966, Chrysler was more willing, and took small, cautious steps. The previous year saw the 383 put into Coronets and Belvederes, and these were perfectly capable, if relatively unknown, as performance cars. Chrysler did not offer any model or option package equivalent to the GTO or 4-4-2; each option had to be checked off one by one to arrive at the same place as the GTO simply by being a GTO.

If Chrysler was slow to build mid-sized performance cars either as option packages on existing models or as stand-alone models, the Pentastar dropped a performance bombshell in 1966 when it released a detuned street version of its mighty 426 "Hemi" race engine to the public. With this, Chrysler set loose one of the most legendary engines in the history of the American automobile.

Terrifying competitors on professional drag strips since the 1950s, Chrysler engines with hemispherical combustion chamber design—hence, "Hemi"—finally matured in its 426 displacement incarnation. Chrysler's decision to make available the 426 "street Hemi" was an attempt to satisfy NASCAR to make the race Hemi eligible again for NASCAR races. The 426 race Hemi had been banned after the 1964 season after entirely demolishing the field and winning twenty-six races, and in order to be allowed out of time-out, it had to be available in sufficient numbers to the buying public. And so, the 426 "street" Hemi was born, with its dual four-barrel—yes, two, four-barrel—carbs producing a massive 425 horsepower, widely believed to be underrated by the Pinocchios at Mopar. For the mathematically declined, the rated horsepower of the 426 Hemi was a full 50 horsepower over the top of the line GM offering, the 375 horsepower SS 396. On paper, that was the end of that competition, but the real life equalizer was that the Hemi was notoriously unreliable and hard to keep in tune, thereby giving its competitors some cause for hope. Regardless of its tendency to throw a temper tantrum, the mighty 426 Hemi would power the most deadly Chrysler performance cars until the very end of the muscle car era.

For 1966, Dodge again trotted out the B-body Coronet as its mid-sized offering. Like the intermediate lines of the other manufacturers, the Coronet pulled a lot of varied duties. There were four-door cars and wagons bearing the Coronet badge, as well as economical kid haulers. As in 1965, the top of the line Coronet was again the Coronet 500, available only in hardtop or convertible form.

The 117-inch Coronet line was slightly revamped for 1966, and offered clean, straight lines in stark contrast to the sculpted Coke-bottle designs of the GM A-bodies or the smooth Fords. The front end featured a split grille, and Coronet badging adorned the leading edge of the fenders. There was a slight pinch just aft of the doors, under which was decorative molding in the shape of three horizontal bars. The C pillar, reminiscent of the '64 Ford Galaxie, was angled sharply and straight down to the linear lines of the quarter panels. The car sported decorative rocker panel molding between the wheels. The tail panel featured tail lamps in the form of truncated triangles turned on their side and block "DODGE" lettering across the length of the tail in between. All in all, the '66 Coronet was an attractive car but was overshadowed by the dynamic changes of the GM A-bodies.

Powering the reskinned Coronets was a wide range of engines, and practically any engine, up to and including the Hemi, was available on nearly any 2-door trim level Coronet. The 500 was available with several lesser engines, but the real performance started with the 325 horsepower, four-barrel 383. Up from that was the mighty Hemi. Transmission options included a 3-speed manual, but this could be swapped for a heavy-duty 4-speed or 3-speed TorqueFlite automatic. Hemi equipped cars received heavy-duty radiator and brakes, beefed up suspension and either the 4-speed or the automatic. Hemi equipped cars were necessarily a different kind of

**1966 Hemi Coronet 500 (courtesy Gateway Classic Cars, St. Louis, MO).**

beast from their little brothers, requiring beefed up components to handle the power and massive torque the engine produced.

As the 500 was the top of the Coronet line, the interior of the car was plush. Bucket seating with a console was standard, but a full range of options was available, including power steering and brakes, power windows, rear speaker and air conditioning. However, Dodge served up a mesmerizing list of possible Coronet trim level and engine combinations. This was a double-edged sword for Dodge: while buyers could tailor their Coronet nearly any way they wanted to, they had to pay for each one of those options. Or they could head to a GM or Ford dealership and buy a "pre-packaged" muscle car model.

Dodge sold a very healthy number its Coronet models across the whole line. Including all body styles and trim levels, there were 250,842 Coronets sent to new homes. Of these, 11,236 were powered by the 383 Magnum engine, and another 365 had Hemis stuffed between the fenders.

In addition to its Coronet line, Dodge offered a new model midway through the 1966 model year, a name badge that would adorn Dodge products for decades to come, and one of the few that have survived to our own modern era. Announced to the world during the Rose Bowl on January 1, 1967, that new model was the Dodge Charger.

Technically, the Charger nameplate first appeared as a special performance option on the compact 1965 Dart. The reborn 117-inch wheelbase 1966 Charger was its own, stand-alone model and was the result of an intersection of several competing wishes within Dodge. For some reason, Dodge dealers were clamoring for a Dodge badged version of the Plymouth Barracuda, which Chrysler brass did not want to build. They reckoned a Dodge Barracuda twin would only add further competition for the little Plymouth already being hammered by Ford's Mustang. At the same time, Chrysler witnessed the modest popularity of the Marlin, a car built by Rambler, a car company completely devoid of any performance reputation.

**1965 Rambler Marlin, owned by Stan Kelly of Porterville, CA (photo by John Spangler, San Jose, CA).**

The Rambler Marlin is an automobile generally forgotten by automotive history, coming as it did in such a dynamic period for the industry and having the misfortune of being built by Rambler. This is unfortunate, as the Marlin is a unique vehicle that deserves better, regardless of how it was perceived in its time. For example, the '65 Marlin was one of the few cars to come with standard front disc brakes. The Marlin was unusual among American cars for its fastback body style. While fastbacks were not unknown—the Barracuda had always been a fastback and the Mustang adopted the body style for 1965—the Marlin was not a pony car, riding on a 112-inch wheelbase, and fastbacks of that size were practically unknown in the market at the time. The Marlin was AMC's attempt to cash in on the emerging youth market identified by Pontiac and Ford, and AMC built the Marlin to compete with Plymouth's Barracuda. Judging by the sales numbers, it did not do this very well. By just about any measure, the Marlin was unappreciated, even by Rambler standards.

Chrysler, the smallest of the Big 3 and perpetually on the brink of oblivion, was not above poaching ideas from tiny, hapless Rambler. Chrysler aimed to suck out of the room what oxygen there was in the Marlin's market and to compete in a segment of the market dubbed the "personal performance" market, whatever that might have meant. That segment slotted somewhere on the market spectrum between the sporty Mustang and Ford's Thunderbird, and examples included Pontiac's Grand Prix, Buick's Riviera and Oldsmobile's new Toronado.

Built on the Coronet platform, the '66 Charger bore a substantial—perhaps

**1966 Dodge Charger 383 with the optional "hide-away" headlamps (courtesy Vanguard Motor Sales, Plymouth, MI).**

even litigious—resemblance to the smaller Marlin; the Charger was built with a fast-back design made popular by the Barracuda and especially the Mustang. In keeping with Dodge's desire to showcase the sportiness of the Charger, the slant six and even the 273 engine, the engine that powered the hottest Barracudas, were not available. Engine options started with the 318 and 361, but muscular versions were equipped with the 325 horse, 4-barrel, dual exhaust 383 Magnum and the 426 Hemi was optional. A 3-speed manual transmission shifted on the column was standard, but the car could be had with a 4-speed manual or a 3-speed automatic. The car came standard with bucket seats in front and rear, as well as a console that ran the length of the interior. The interior included top of the line features, such as deluxe door panels, courtesy lights and vinyl trim.

If one were observant enough, it was readily apparent that the Charger was simply a Coronet body with a fastback roof welded on. The grille was clearly lifted from the Coronet. Dodge, however, offered vacuum operated "hide-away" headlamps as an option, and hideaways would become synonymous with the Charger for the rest of the muscle car era. When this option was chosen, the Charger had one of the most distinctive front ends of its time, dubbed the "electric shaver" grille that ran the width of the front end. There was likewise a full length taillight panel with chromed CHARGER lettering.

The unique design was popular, selling 37,344 units, including 12,328 383-powered cars and an impressive 468 with the Hemi. The car successfully vanquished the Marlin to the scrap heap of automotive history and was the progenitor to one of the most notorious name plates of the entire muscle car era.

Near the bottom of the economy scale among the car makers was Plymouth, and the budget friendly car maker offered its own performance B-body, again from the Belvedere line. Though they were very similar to the Coronet, there were substantial differences that set the Belvedere family apart from their Dodge cousins. Like the Dodge, the Belvedere line got a restyle for '66 and featured a longitudinal body line that ran along the upper part of the car's flank from stem to stern and featured an opposite recessed line lower on the body. The grille was revised and incorporated amber driving lamps set beside the single headlamps. The Belvedere rode a 116-inch wheelbase which was an inch shorter—and therefore cheaper—than the Coronet. The "Belvie" featured the same angular tapering C-pillar as the Coronet, and like the Dodge, it came in pillared coupe, hardtop and convertible body styles, as well as a wagon.

The non-wagon Belvedere line came in three trim options starting with the basic Belvedere I, powered by a standard six-cylinder and backed by a 3-speed manual transmission. The Belvie I was the only model available in the lightweight pillared sedan. Up from that, naturally enough, was the more upscale Belvedere II, which shared the same base engine and transmission as the Belvedere I, but featured more amenities such as rear seatbelts and a padded dash pad as standard equipment. Finally, as in '65, the Satellite occupied the top of the Belvedere line. The Satellite was Plymouth's only viable answer to the GTO. It was similarly equipped with standard bucket seating, padded dash pad, seatbelts, accent lighting and full carpeting. The Satellite's base power plant was not in the same universe as those offered on the GM muscle car offerings, being the 273 V-8.

Like the Coronet, however, Plymouth allowed a wide range of engine offerings in the Belvedere line, even down to the base Belvie I. The most serious of these were the same four-barrel 383 Magnum, producing 325 horsepower, or the mighty 426 Hemi. Standard 3-speed trannies could be upgraded to 4-speed manuals or the TorqueFlite 3-speed automatic, and the Hemi equipped cars received either of the latter, as the lightweight 3-speed manual could not handle the ferocity of the Hemi. The Hemi equipped cars also received heavy-duty radiators, brakes and suspensions.

The reskinned Plymouths hit the ground running in 1966, on the strength of a remarkably successful and highly visible NASCAR campaign. Belvederes won 12 of 49 races that year, the most significant of which was Richard Petty's win at Daytona. On the strength of this, epitomizing the "Win on Sunday, Sell on Monday" phenomenon, the Belvedere line was a strong seller in 1966. Plymouth sold 86,685 2-door models across the line in all body styles. As a nearly $900 option, Hemi production was very limited, but interestingly far more of the expensive Hemis were stuffed into the cheaper Belvederes than into the Coronets. There were 136 Belvedere I's equipped with the Hemi, and another 541 Belvedere IIs. Another 844 Satellites were so equipped.

Most assuredly, the 1966 Chrysler B-bodies, equipped with even the 383, surprised a lot of competitors on the street. It was a fine example of the "sleeper" car. There was no flash, such as the hood scoops adorning the GTO or the Chevelle, and the Plymouth still sported a hood ornament. Even Buick had dropped that bit of un-coolness by 1966. The only revelation the cars allowed that might warn that they

**1966 Plymouth Hemi Satellite (courtesy Vanguard Motor Sales, Plymouth, MI).**

were something more than a grandmother's basic transportation was a small, unassuming badge on the fender with an engine callout, easily overlooked. The 383 cars were competitive with the offerings from Ford and GM, but the 426 Hemi cars were truly fearsome.

Fortunately for mortal GTOs, 4-4-2s, Fairlanes, SS Chevelles and Gran Sports, the prohibitive price of the optional Hemi engine kept them from being too prevalent on the street, and the cantankerous nature of the engine made those that were prowling around less effective than they otherwise might have been. When running right, however, there was simply nothing on the street in 1966 in stock form that could keep up with a Hemi powered Mopar. Though released early in the muscle car wars, the 426 Hemi was the peak Mopar engine, and served as Chrysler's top of the line performance engine, relatively unchanged, throughout the remainder of the muscle car era. Today, due to their rarity and legendary status, Hemi powered cars are among the most sought-after muscle cars, with their value multiplying literally thousands of times above original sticker price.

While Dodge and Plymouth offered mid-sized cars that could be built with high-performance options such as big-block performance engines, heavy-duty suspensions and high-performance transmissions and rear ends, they did not offer an off-the-showroom-floor muscle car like the GTO, 4-4-2 or Fairlane GT/A. Coronets, Belvederes, Satellites, and even Chargers and Barracudas came standard with decidedly low performance six-cylinders or 273 cubic inch blocks. Once these midsized Mopars had been "spec'd" out with options that put them in the same class as the GM and Ford muscle cars, they were generally more expensive. Not many saw the

**Chrysler's legendary 426 Hemi (courtesy Streetside Classics, Charlotte, NC).**

wisdom in paying more for a Chrysler than for a similarly capable GM or Ford intermediate performance car, and with less flair at that. Chrysler products earned, and in some ways still carry, a reputation for poor quality. In the '60s, it was earned. Windows didn't seal properly, there were creative gaps of differing widths between body panels, interior parts inexplicably fell off, and leaky engine and transmission seals allowed Chrysler cars to "mark their territory" with fluids. Indeed, Chrysler cars seemed to be the domain of many gremlins. Chryslers might have been equipped with bulletproof drivelines, but the rest of the car might fall apart around that driveline, and the cars generally had the feel that they'd been constructed in a high school shop class. As a result, Chrysler products simply were not as popular as their GM and Ford competitors. While Chrysler sold a healthy number of competitive, muscular Coronets and Belvederes in 1966, few customers agonized over whether to buy a Buick or a Plymouth.

\* \* \*

For one more year, there was a clear line of demarcation between the pony car class and the larger wheelbase performance intermediates, the "muscle cars." For one more year, the hottest Mustangs and Barracudas came equipped with small block engines, and for one more year they had the pony car market entirely to themselves. For one more year, the pony car market was a bit clenched firmly in the teeth of the Mustang.

1966 Mustang convertible (courtesy Gateway Classic Cars, St. Louis, MO).

Visually, there was little different between the 1965 and 1966 Mustang, which meant there was very little difference between the 1964 and 1966 Mustang. The first-generation body style was getting a little long in the tooth in an era when car makers regularly redesigned car lines. Ford could barely produce Mustangs fast enough to keep pace with demand, and there were major changes planned for the '67 model year, so the Blue Oval just drove on, refusing to fix what wasn't broken for the 1966 model year. The grille was slightly restyled, with the iconic pony emblem surrounded by a new chrome "corral." The faux vents aft of the doors were restyled as well, and the little pony was again offered in hardtop, convertible and the popular fastback introduced in 1965.

Ford offered a 200 cubic inch six-cylinder as the standard Mustang engine, with three versions of Ford's famous 289 available to bring the Mustang into the realm of a performance car. The first was a two-barrel version producing 200 horses. Next up from that was a version topped with a four-barrel and producing 225 horsepower. The true performer was again the 271 horse 289 HiPo. All engines save the HiPo 289 came with a 3-speed manual tranny standard, with Cruise-O-Matic 3-speed automatic and a 4-speed manual as options. Should one choose the HiPo, the purchaser was limited to only the 4-speed manual, a choice reminiscent of Henry Ford's Model T, which at one time he proclaimed could be bought in any color the customer wanted as long as it was black.

**1966 Mustang fastback (courtesy Gateway Classic Cars, St. Louis, MO).**

On the inside, the Mustang was ho-hum, unless the optional "pony" interior, carried over from 1965, was ordered. An interior décor group was also optional, which included full instrumentation—no idiot lights—in a five-gauge cluster, bright pedals, a wood steering wheel and matching wood grained glove box and appliques on the instrument panel.

The GT package was offered again in 1966. The 271 HP engine was standard, and it also included a host of visual and performance enhancements such as manual front disc brakes, grille mounted fog lamps, GT stripes and gas cap, side identifiers, and exhaust tips.

Ford continued to frantically build Mustangs as fast as it could, to the tune of more than 600,000 of its little ponies being set loose in 1966. By contrast, the '66 Mustang's contemporary, the 1966 GTO, the most popular muscle ever car built in terms of production, didn't even hit the 100,000 mark. In light of that, to get one's mind around Ford's level of Mustang production is difficult.

\* \* \*

Once again for 1966, Chrysler offered the only competition, feeble though it was, to the stampeding Mustangs, unless one counted the 1966 Marlin, and there were very few Marlins produced to count. This again came in the form of Plymouth's Barracuda. As with the Mustang, there was little to separate the '66 Barracuda from its earlier vintages, but significant changes lay in store for the upcoming

'67 model year. The Barracuda retained the fastback designed with the exceptionally large back glass. Again based on the dull Valiant model (and, as in '65, with no Valiant badging to admit it), the Barracuda did get some minor restyles to the front sheet metal, grille and taillights. It also featured larger bumpers. The Barracuda got updates on the inside as well, with a new instrument cluster featuring gauges for oil pressure and a tachometer. A center console was an option for the first time.

Unfortunately for the little Plymouth, the restyles stopped there. Engine and transmission offerings were the same—225 cube six-cylinder, a two-barrel 273 cube block producing 180 horsepower and the top of the line 273 four-barrel producing 235 horses. The standard transmission was a 3-speed manual, with a 4-speed manual and the 3-speed TorqueFlite automatic as options.

To counter Ford's Mustang GT, Plymouth again offered the Formula S package on the Barracuda. This package included an upgraded, stiffer suspension, larger wheels and tires, tachometer and special emblems. Air conditioning and front disc brakes were offered as options.

The Barracuda was a capable car, but compared to the exciting Mustang, it was simply dull. Where Ford was offering things like GTs with aggressive stripes, luxurious interiors with running horses, fog lamps and the like, Plymouth had no answer. The Mustang could be had in a variety of body styles, where the Barracuda was offered in only one. In short, Plymouth did little to inspire people to buy a Barracuda. Ford did an excellent job separating the Mustang from its roots as a spicy version of

The Chrysler Corporation's gold Pentastar emblem ensured the world knew who built the 426 Hemi (courtesy Gateway Classic Cars, St. Louis, MO).

the sleepy Falcon. In the mind of most of the car buying public, the Barracuda was simply a rebadged Valiant, and no one in the market for a performance car was going to consider a Valiant. As a result, Plymouth built only 38,029 Barracudas for 1966, which includes 21,523 V-8 versions. Of these, 5,316 were Formula S models.

\* \* \*

The 1966 model year was a transition year for the American muscle car. Up until that year, the cars retained many characteristics of cars from the late '50s and early '60s. They were small, and one had to know where to look for them, but they were there. For example, the 1966 GTO still used pot metal for its interior knobs, bezels, and switches, while the 1967 model would go to lower quality—and cheaper—plastic. The '66 had a real wood veneer surrounding the instrument panel, while the '67 went to vinyl fake wood. Perhaps more importantly, the '66 was the last of the 389 equipped GTOs, the same engine that had powered big Pontiacs since the late 1950s. The '66 GTO was still a mid-sized car with a big car engine. Late in '65, Chevrolet released its 396, designed specifically as a performance engine. Same for Mopar's Street Hemi. Pontiac, Buick and Olds would do so for 1967, with the various new 400 cube blocks.

The 1966 model year saw, for all practical purposes, the end of the original muscle car concept of stuffing a big-car engine into a cheaper, smaller car to produce a super car for the masses. That concept would be revisited later in the era, but, after 1966, like the war in Vietnam, the muscle car wars between the various car makers would continue to spiral out of control through the remainder of the decade.

# 6

# Summer of Love

### *The American Muscle Car Comes of Age*

With 1967 came the beginning of the end of American innocence. The definitive end would come a year later, but the events of 1966—the escalation of the war in Vietnam and the protests it inspired, the race riots, and the general souring of the national mood—threw tinder onto the brush pile of 1967, waiting for the ignition of 1968. Today, 1967 is fondly remembered as the Summer of Love, with pictures of peace-loving girls wearing floral coronas solemnly stuffing flowers into the rifle barrels of soldiers. Hippies gathered at the corner of Haight and Ashbury in San Francisco to commiserate about the evils of capitalism, the bloodthirstiness of Lyndon Johnson and the human condition, in general. They came to turn on, tune in and drop out, dreaming of the better world that would dawn with the Age of Aquarius.

The historical truth of 1967 is much different. Across the United States, the social pressure continued to mount. Southerners, tired of Yankee hypocrisy on issues of race, must have felt vindicated as self-righteous Yankees suffered continued racial unrest with Northern cities such as Detroit and Newark in the flames of race riots. The non-violence of Martin Luther King, Jr. was increasingly sidelined in favor of a more militant brand of activism championed by Malcolm X and the Black Panther Party. On the plus side, Thurgood Marshall, the first black Supreme Court justice, was sworn in.

Troop levels in Vietnam continued to escalate, reaching 475,000 by year's end. More and more of those troops were coming home draped in the flag. There was no end to the conflict in sight. War protests grew proportionally across the country. An increasingly frustrated General William Westmoreland, Johnson's steward over the mess in Southeast Asia, exhibited the cracks in the American façade about the war by implying that the protests were emboldening the Vietnamese communists to continue to resist in order to force the U.S. public, unwilling to bear the cost in blood and treasure, into an untenable position politically. It was a remarkably prescient observation. To help accelerate the growing public distaste with the war, President Johnson asked Americans to do their part by asking for a 6 percent increase in taxes, as if sacrificing thousands of their sons on the altar of a war that was increasingly seen as unwinnable was somehow not doing enough. Carl Wilson of the Beach Boys refused to be inducted into the Army and was indicted for draft dodging. Wilson offered to perform with the Beach Boys in lieu of military service, which was magnanimous since that is what he would have spent his time doing anyway. That didn't fly, and he was convicted after failing to perform any community service at all. Boxing's heavy-weight champion Muhammad Ali refused his trip to Vietnam as well, and he was also convicted of draft dodging. Ali at least he had the good sense not to arrogantly offer to fight in lieu of service.

The year was not all bad. San Francisco had 20,000 people attend a "Human Be-In," whatever that was, and the first "teach-in" was held on the campus of the University of Michigan. The California city of Monterrey saw the first of the music festivals for which the '60s would be remembered, with Jimi Hendrix, Janis Joplin, the Who, and the Grateful Dead being the headliners. Grace Slick of the Jefferson Airplane protested the hypocrisy of reading fantasy tales such as *Alice's Adventures in Wonderland* to children and being surprised when people tried to live it for real through the use of LSD. Paul Newman starred in the iconic movie *Cool Hand Luke*. The first Super Bowl, the beginning of an annual event seemingly as big as Valentine's Day (and certainly more enjoyed by American men), was played, with the Green Bay Packers defeating the Kansas City Chiefs.

The United States began to catch up with the Soviets in the Space Race, but at a substantial cost. The crew of *Apollo I*, the program that would eventually claim victory in the race to the moon, was killed when their capsule caught fire and burnt up during a launch rehearsal. *Surveyor IV*, the unmanned lunar observation vehicle, exploded on its approach to the moon. However, 1967 did see the successful launch of the gigantic *Saturn V* rockets that would carry men to the moon and the testing of the re-entry vehicle meant to bring them back.

At the end of the Summer of Love, the pacifists and counter-culturists in the Haight-Ashbury district of San Francisco held a mock funeral for "Hippie," representing them all. For them, by year's end it became clear that Aquarius would not arrive in 1967. In fact, on the brink of 1968, that mythical and hopeful age seemed even further away.

\* \* \*

For all the domestic happenings in 1967, an ominous international event in a far-away land would eventually provide one of the nails in the coffin of the American muscle car. The cars were blissfully unaware. Like fish living in little pools after the tide's retreat, the muscle cars and their happily ignorant makers and owners were unaware of what was going on out in the greater sea.

The event was what we now call the Six-Day War. After years of simmering tension between the Arab world and the Jewish state of Israel over issues of sufficient complexity to comprise a separate work, the Middle East exploded into open warfare in June of 1967. Egypt built a coalition of Arab states, with the primary members being Syria and Jordan, both of which, along with Egypt, shared a border with Israel. The open goal of this coalition was the destruction of Israel as a political entity. Israel, however, enjoyed the staunch support of Europe and, in particular, the United States, while the Arab states were backed by the Soviet Union. The war started with a pre-emptive strike by the American equipped and trained Israeli forces, and when the smoke cleared a mere six days later, Israel had not only destroyed the forces of the Arab states, but also occupied significant chunks of Egypt and Syria. More importantly, Israel had wrested the ancient city of Jerusalem, holy to Jews and Arabs, as well as Christians, from Jordanian control and promptly named it the capital of the Jewish state.

The humiliation of the defeat caused widespread animosity against not only Israel, but also her western and American backers. That the now-infuriated nations of the Middle East controlled a significant portion of the world's known oil reserves was an accident of geology—abundant, exportable oil the United States had long since been discovered to be cheaper to import than to produce domestically. Cheap Arab oil fueled not only the muscle cars, but also the Vietnam War effort. Before long, the Arab states realized the weapon that fate had placed in their hand and would later prove to be an effective tool to express their displeasure with the U.S.' stubborn support of the Jewish state. The average 1967 price of a gallon of the gasoline feeding the insatiable American muscle cars was 33 cents, but it wouldn't stay that way if the Arab states shut off the spigots. The Six-Day War represented the warning wisps of a cloud forecasting a coming storm—a warning that could only be appreciated in hindsight.

* * *

The 1967 model year was a landmark for the American performance car industry. It wouldn't be the last, and that there would seem to be one landmark year after another in the short history of the muscle car indicates the frantic pace of the escalation of the muscle car wars. By 1967, the muscle car had fully come of age, and the battles between the car makers for street and, more importantly, sales supremacy were in full swing.

The entire GM midsized line, the platforms on which the muscle cars were built, would remain substantially the same for the second year after the redesign of 1966. The Coke-bottle styling remained for one more year, in anticipation of a major re-style in 1968. The A-bodies retained the subtly dangerous stance and tried to make the cars elegant, and indeed, the 1967 models are generally more popular than their siblings from 1966.

That popularity is not without justification. Generally speaking, the GM A-body muscle cars were better performers than those of 1966. The muscle versions of the A-bodies were now equipped with power plants intentionally built as performance engines. The days of the 389 Pontiac and 401 Buick engines intended for a Bonneville or Wildcat, only to be hammered into a GTO or Gran Sport, were gone. The smaller GM divisions of Pontiac, Buick and Oldsmobile, in an attempt to compete with the field that suddenly included purpose-built engines like Chevy's 396 and Chrysler's 426 Hemi, amped up the performance output of their muscle car engines, specifically designed for performance. GM muscle car power trains were no longer simply big car engines shoehorned into the smaller A-bodies. They were built to run.

GM didn't stop the performance upgrades at the engine. The old two-speed automatic transmission—a GM staple since the '50s—was replaced by a more performance friendly 3-speed. Suspensions were upgraded as well, and people realized that a muscle car hurtling down the road and weighing in the neighborhood of a ton and a half was a hell of a load to stop. Hence, upgrades in braking systems and disc brakes became more common. Other safety upgrades across the entire A-body line were a collapsible steering column and a dual circuit master brake cylinder. Sadly, multiple carburation was banned by GM for the 1967 model year with the exception of the Corvette, and an era of Tri-power Pontiacs and Oldsmobiles came to an end.

The GM muscle cars were finally universally stand-alone models, though still sharing the bodies of a particular line. The GTO still looked like a Tempest, the 4-4-2 like a Cutlass, a Gran Sport like a Skylark and an SS Chevelle like a Malibu, but things had definitely changed at General Motors.

The dominance of Pontiac's GTO had waned by 1967, but in the minds of the American public, it was still revered, a first among equals. The Goat received a newly designed 400 cubic inch engine, and, as in years past, the base GTO produced 335 horsepower. This number was likely underrated, as the new engine was redesigned from stem to stern with an eye on performance, and it was topped with a new Rochester carb, all of which were considerable upgrades over the old 389. However, what we remember today as the "base" GTO actually wasn't. Few remember that for some reason, Pontiac saw fit to offer a two-barrel version of the 400 in GTOs, sort of a dirty little secret among fans of Pontiac's super car. Little time need be spent on that, a true sheep in wolf's (or tiger's) clothing. The base four-barrel GTO, topped with the Rochester Quadrajet, produced 335 horses, identical to 1966, but the top factory engine option for 1967 was a high output 400, or H.O., producing 360 horses and replacing the legendary Tri-power. Atop the H.O. engine, the Q-jet offered performance on par with the Tri-power without the difficulties of keeping three carburetors in tune together. Finally, Pontiac offered the first of its legendary cold air induction Ram Air engines as a dealer installed option, also producing 360 horses. Transmission choices were upgraded from 1966 as well, with the 3-speed manual with Hurst shifter standard and one of two 4-speed manuals, also shifted by Hurst, as an option. The old, underwhelming two-speed Powerglide automatic transmission was mercifully jettisoned in favor of a new performance 3-speed automatic called the Turbo-Hydromatic.

Aesthetically, the '67 GTO looked very similar to its predecessor from 1966. The blacked-out egg crate grilles were replaced with pewter colored plastic apparently designed to look like thick wiring patterned into diamonds. The design was much more attractive than it sounds. The louvered taillights were replaced by slotted lamps integrated into the tail panel. Thicker brightwork adorned the rocker panels and incorporated the GTO crest, moved from the fender on the '66 models. A new hood mounted tachometer option mounted in a pod directly in front of the driver allowed the driver to monitor engine revolutions while racing without the inconvenience of glancing down at the dash panel. Eyes on the road safety, '60s style, and the hood tach would probably violate some safety regulation today.

Inside were standard full vinyl bucket seating and carpeting. A console was a popular option, as were air conditioning and power steering and brakes. Automatic transmission equipped cars could be had with column shift, but these were rare. If a buyer opted for a console, automatic transmission cars received a unique feature—a Hurst built shifter called the dual gate "His and Hers" shifter. This gear selector allowed "her" to select gears as normal—park, reverse, drive, etc.—but allowed "him" to work "his" way through the gears manually. Sexism in the car industry and its marketing was, obviously, rampant during the 1960s.

1967 Pontiac GTO (courtesy Vanguard Motor Sales, Plymouth, MI).

Pontiac's hood tach (courtesy Gateway Classic Cars, St. Louis, MO).

**1967 Oldsmobile 4-4-2 (courtesy Fast Lane Classic Cars, St. Charles, MO).**

The 1966 and 1967 GTOs were very similar, but they were not the same. Up through 1966, Pontiac essentially dominated the muscle car field; as a result of the wild success of the 1964 model and an aggressive advertising campaign, the GTO was the best known performance intermediate car on the market. Despite the sales numbers of the '66 model, Chevrolet punched Pontiac in the gut with its SS 396 Chevelle, and the mechanically redesigned '67 GTO was the result of the effort to keep pace. Regardless, in terms of sales, the GTO was falling back into the pack. Sales were down nearly 20 percent, to just under 82,000 units. However, the fact that today 1967 GTOs are far more common than the '66 is a testament to its enduring popularity. Due to the similarity between the '66 and '67 models, many of those 100,000 1966 GTOs built have sacrificed themselves to people restoring 1967s.

Oldsmobile's 1967 version of its 4-4-2, like the GTO, offered little difference from the previous model in terms of style. The 4-4-2 was now the top option for the Cutlass line; the 4-4-2 option on the F-85 was dropped. The front end was slightly redesigned with new grilles, while still using the horizontal layout of the quad headlamps, now separated by a running light. The faux fender vents of the '66 were replaced by colorful 4-4-2 emblems, the last year they were used. The tail lamps were redesigned, and the hood received functional louvers in lieu of the plain hood.

Under the hood, Olds equipped its street fighter with a pair of 400 cubic inch options: the base L78 400 topped with a four-barrel carb producing 350 horses and the cold air breathing W-30 that produced the same 360 horses as the hottest GTO. Fortunately, Olds wisely declined to offer a two-barrel 4-4-2. The basic GM fare was offered with regard to transmissions: 3-speed manual was standard, now with Hurst built linkages. A 4-speed manual was optional, as was the old Jetaway two-speed automatic, abandoned by Pontiac, shifted on the column or through a floor mounted console. W-30 cars were equipped with either the 4-speed manual or a 3-speed Turbo Hydromatic automatic. Inside was typical Olds style—bucket seating was standard, as was carpeting. Gauging was a two pod arrangement surrounded by brushed aluminum, and Rally Pac gauging was again offered.

The '67 4-4-2 was a very attractive car, combining subtle pugnacity with Olds refinement, and was a stylistic upgrade over the '66 model. Despite this, sales were sluggish compared to the GTO and SS Chevelle, with just shy of 25,000 copies being built. Olds was having trouble finding any elbow room in the market with the GTO's reputation and Chevrolet's 396, not to mention the increasing offerings from other car makers.

Again for 1967 Buick offered its Skylark based Gran Sport, now simply dubbed "GS," as its intermediate performance car entrant, aiming at the muscle car driver with discriminating tastes, not to mention more disposable income. Like its corporate cousins, the 1967 GS models looked an awful lot like the 1966 models. The GS for '67 sported twin simulated hood scoop bulges and restyled front and rear ends. Skylark badging was gone, as the GS had finally grown into its own line, rather than simply an option on the Skylark. The '67 version of Buick's muscle car finally looked the part.

Departing from its corporate siblings, Buick offered two versions of the Gran Sport. The entry level Buick muscle car was the GS 340, a hardtop-only offering equipped with, appropriately enough, a 340 cubic inch power plant producing 260 horses. The GS 340 package looked the part and included red rally stripes and matching painted hood scoops, an aggressive look that risked writing checks its driveline couldn't cash. In keeping with the budget theme, interior choices were limited to a black bench seat. Transmission choices were the standard 3-speed manual or a Super Turbine 300 two-speed automatic.

The GS 340 was Buick's answer to Pontiac's two-barrel GTO—a car that looked more dangerous than it was but could be had at a lower sticker price and insurance premiums as the latter were slowly ascending for muscle car models. Taking the long view of the muscle car era, Buick was actually forward thinking with the GS 340; in later years, as sales for muscle car models plummeted due, in part, to rising insurance premiums, car makers began offering "junior muscle cars" in the vein of the Buick GS 340. Built on intermediate platforms sporting the look of true muscle cars, these mini-muscle cars came equipped with smaller engines and thus could be insured more cheaply—essentially what the GS340 was in 1967. An interesting variation on the GS 340 was the California GS, which was a GS 340 produced in limited numbers and marketed in, logically enough, California. The car was based on the Skylark's pillared coupe and equipped with California specific smog equipment and special badging.

The top GS offering was the GS 400. Like Pontiac, Buick outfitted its street gladiator with a newly redesigned 400 cubic inch engine that was a significant performance upgrade over the previous year's 401. It shared the same rally stripes and hood scoops as the little GS 340, and its 340 horsepower rated higher than the base Pontiac

**1967 Buick GS 400 (courtesy Gateway Classic Cars, St. Louis, MO).**

and Oldsmobile. Buick, however, didn't offer an option to compete with Pontiac's HO or Olds' W-30 360 horsepower cars. With Buick being Buick, a full line of heavy luxury options came standard; the added weight of those options came standard, at no cost. The GS 400 arguably needed the extra 5 HP just to compete with the lighter Pontiacs and Oldsmobiles. Transmission choices paralleled those of Pontiac and Olds: 3-speed manual standard, upgradable to a 4-speed manual, or 3-speed Super Turbine 400 automatic. A range of rear end gearing was available, as was a limited slip rear end. Buick continued to outfit all GS cars with the stronger, boxed frame typically found on convertibles.

On the inside, it was all Buick. Though bench seating was standard, it was far more common for Buick buyers to fork over a few bucks for full vinyl buckets and a center console. The dashboard was trimmed in brushed metal, with knobs operating all the important functions. A horizontal sweep speedometer dominated the instrument cluster.

With competition increasing, and without a solid reputation for building muscle cars, Buick sold fewer than 14,000 GS 400s. The 1967 Buick Gran Sport was a very good looking, stylish car, but Buick buyers were far more likely to buy a Riviera than a muscle car. The muscle car market was, by definition, a youth driven market, and one of first-time car buyers. Buick didn't sell a lot of cars of any badge to those demographics. Buicks were sold to many people who really wanted Cadillacs, and kids and first-time car buyers didn't really want Cadillacs. Or apparently Buicks.

While Pontiac still held the edge in sales of its GTO over the SS 396 in 1967, Chevrolet's midsized performance offering had closed the gap in terms of performance in 1966 and was rapidly closing it in sales as well. It might have been inevitable; Chevy was GM's performance flagship marque, and Pontiac, not to mention

**Aft callouts of Buick's elegant GS 400 (photo by author).**

Buick and Olds, had always lived in the long shadow of the Bowtie in terms of volume and performance.

As with the rest of the A-body line, there wasn't a lot to differentiate the '67 SS from the '66. Most visibly, the front end lost the wraparound element of 1966, the tail panel was restyled with new wraparound taillamps, and the faux hood scoops were revised. The 396 was the only engine available in the SS Chevelle, but it came in different flavors. The base power plant for the SS Chevelle was again a 325-horse version, topped with a Rochester four-barrel carb. Up from that was the L34 option 396 breathing through a Holley carb. Chevy rated the L34 at 350 horsepower, which was a decline from the 360 offered in 1966 and, at least in terms of rated horsepower, was behind the hottest Pontiacs and Oldsmobiles.

The story goes that this reduction in rated horsepower was the result of an effort on the part of GM to protect the Corvette, perhaps because the explosion of performance intermediate offerings, generally cheaper than the Corvette, was poaching some of the two-seater's sales. GM mandated that no car but the Corvette would have an advertised horsepower to curb weight ratio of more than 1:10. An application of simple math would illustrate that, at 360 horses, the lightweight SS Chevelle was in violation, while the heavier Pontiacs, Oldsmobiles and Buicks were not. Regardless, the folks at Chevy were liars; the L34 likely produced more than 360 horses. Mathematics dictated that this restriction did not apply to the heavier, 360 horse Pontiacs or Oldsmobiles.

The most potent 396 was one that wasn't even advertised by Chevrolet and took the right connections knowing the right palms to grease in order to even obtain, and that was the formidable L78, producing 375 horses. This is essentially the same engine offered in the '65 Corvette, even bearing the same L78 code, which produced 325 horsepower, so people can draw their own conclusions on the actual horsepower produced by this creature. There was plenty of incentive to lie—if the much tamer L34 violated the horsepower-to-weight mandate, the L78 certainly would.

Like the other GM divisions, transmission choices were a standard 3-speed manual or a choice of two 4-speed options. The Turbo Hydromatic 3-speed auto was optional on all SS 396 cars save the L78, which could only be had with a manual transmission. Automatics were shifted on the steering column unless the floor mounted console was opted for; manual transmissions were shifted on the floor, with or without the console. A wide range of rear end gear ratios and positive traction were available as well.

Standard seating was in line with Chevrolet frugality: bench seating, but at least it was in full vinyl trim. Buckets were optional, and Chevy offered a wide range of optional appointments, such as power steering, power disc brakes, air conditioning and so forth, to allow potential buyers across the spectrum to get into an SS.

Chevrolet sent 63,000 SS Chevelles of all stripes home with new owners, including 612 L78 cars, which was a decrease from 1966. The general excuses of more intermediate performance offerings being available and sales fratricide applied, but perhaps the most impactful reason for the decline in SS Chevelle sales can be blamed on, of all things, Chevrolet itself, as 1967 saw the introduction of yet another performance car to stand alongside the SS Chevelle and the Corvette.

\* \* \*

Having fully joined the intermediate performance fray in 1966 with its redesigned Fairlane GT/A, Ford kept at it again in 1967, though the really big news out of Dearborn was in the pony car arena. Even in '66, with the new performance Fairlanes, it always felt as if Ford's participation in the mid-size performance car market was grudging or out of a sense of obligation and a disinclination to let GM and Chrysler occupy the field. Nothing much changed for '67, either in the GT/A Fairlanes, the feeling that Ford was a reluctant contributor or the Blue Oval's emphasis on the Mustang.

The Fairlane GT/A was again what Ford offered as its champion to battle GM's hordes and the emerging threat from Chrysler. Again, the only difference between the GT and the GTA cars was the transmission, and they were available in either hardtop or convertible form; no pillared coupe was available. The GT/A cars got some cosmetic changes from the 1966 model, but like the offerings from General Motors, the 1967 Fairlane looked nearly identical to the 1966. The biggest changes from '66 were a revised aluminum grille and revamped taillights.

In 1966, the only engine option for the Fairlane GT/A was the S-code Thunderbird Special 390 four-barrel producing 335 horses. While this was still the top option for the GT/A cars again in '67 (Ford's monster 427 was not available in the Fairlane GT/A), the option books were opened to the GT/A cars, offering Ford's entire V-8 inventory, except for the 427. Consequently, a variety of 289s and 390s could be found in the line, with the base engine being a 289 small block. Transmission options were determined to some extent by engine. All GT/A cars came standard

**1967 Ford Fairlane GTA (courtesy Gateway Classic Cars, St. Louis, MO).**

with a 3-speed manual transmission; 289 powered cars could be had with a C-4 automatic; and all GT/A cars could be had with a 4-speed "Toploader" manual or heavier duty C-6 3-speed automatic.

Like its competitors, the Fairlane GT/A met new government mandated safety requirements, such as a collapsible steering column and dual circuit brake master cylinder. Unique among muscle cars of any year, the Fairlane GT and GTA offered front disc brakes, with or without power assist, as standard equipment.

On the inside, the GT/A shared the same interior as the posh Fairlane XL, with only slight alteration to trim. This included full carpeting and full vinyl adorning the seating and door panels. A console was an option for floor mounted shifters or even for column mounted automatics.

Though the 427 was conspicuously missing from the engine lineup available in Ford's mass-produced intermediate muscle car, that isn't to say 427 powered Fairlanes didn't exist. In fact, they did. Though the 427 wasn't offered in the GT/A, as in 1966 it could be had in extremely limited numbers in a Fairlane 500. The high-rise intake manifold was gone for 1967, as was the "teardrop" fiberglass hood that it necessitated. All were 4-speed manual transmission cars, and all were sold specifically for race purposes. A 427 lurking under the hood of a Fairlane 500 usually reserved for transporting blue haired old ladies to church was the very definition of a sleeper. With very little in the way of exterior indicators to warn rivals of just what they were dealing with, the awesome 427 Fairlane surprised a lot of base GTOs or Gran Sports and could easily handle Hemi powered Mopars and 375 horse SS 396 Chevys.

Ford had hoped to capitalize on the momentum generated from the relatively strong sales that resulted from the efforts of the '66 GT/A cars, but it was not to be. In fact, sales fell by nearly half, with only 18,670 hardtops and 2,117 convertibles sold in 1967, despite the wider range of engine and transmission availability. Ford built 229 427-powered Fairlanes as well, which represented an increase of nearly 400 percent. The GT/A, like all other intermediate models, suffered from an influx of competition in 1967, as well as from Ford's palpable lack of enthusiasm in the intermediate performance car market.

Mercury's marketing campaign for 1967 was heavy on the sexism—Mercury advertised itself as the "man's car." Mercury advertising mentioned man's this and man's that, and it would be interesting to contemplate such a campaign were it launched today.

Upscale Mercury again had its analogue to the Fairlane GT/A, and again it came in the form of the Cyclone. Like the GT/A cars, there was only a slight restyling to the exterior of the car to differentiate it from the '67 model, with only a redesigned grille and tail panel serving as the difference. The Cyclone GT cars featured special striping, a twin scoop hood, and GT badging and engine brightwork to set them apart from the standard Cyclone. The Cyclone and Cyclone GT were only offered in hardtop and convertible body styles.

The Cyclone name badge covered the lower end of the performance scale of the GT/A, as it was outfitted with the 289 standard. The Cyclone GT picked up at the upper end of the GT/A scale; there was no 289 available in the Cyclone, only the "Marauder" 390, Mercury's version of the Thunderbird 390 from Ford, rated at 320 horsepower. Unlike Ford, Mercury did not differentiate between transmission

1967 427 Mercury Cyclone (courtesy Steven Anastos of Red Hills Rods and Classics, St. George, UT).

choices in its badging; the Cyclone GT could be had with either the standard 3-speed manual transmission, or the upgraded 4-speed "Toploader" or "Merc-O-Matic" 3-speed automatic transmission. As with the GT/A, the 427 was not available on the Cyclone GT but was available on lesser Mercury intermediate cars of the Comet line, such as the 202, the Caliente and the Cyclone.

The Cyclone and Cyclone GT shared the same safety features as the Ford, including the standard front disc brakes. On the inside, the Cyclone featured standard bucket seating with full vinyl coverings, as well as full vinyl door panels. A wood steering wheel was standard, and a console was an option, as were air conditioning and a full range of creature comforts befitting a Mercury.

Mercury's once and future problem, and one that would lead to the marque's eventual demise in 2010, was that there was very little to differentiate it from what were essentially the same, lower priced cars offered by Ford. This "me, too" image of Mercury always hampered sales, particularly of performance models, a niche in which Mercury had always struggled. Consequently, Cyclone GT sales were anemic in 1967, with only 3,519 hardtops and another 378 convertibles sold. Sixty 427 cars across the Comet line were also built.

* * *

If Ford reluctantly entered the intermediate performance car market, finally offering an off-the-shelf muscle car package in the Fairlane GT/A and Cyclone GT, Chrysler practically had to be dragged to the show. By 1967, Chrysler had the most terrifying engine commonly available to the public in its 426 Hemi and a long history of building heavy-duty suspension and drive train components owing to Chrysler owning the lion's share of the police car market. Most of the pieces were there to build great muscle cars. What Chrysler lacked was a reputation for building cool cars. Nameplates like Coronet 500, Belvedere and even Satellite just didn't inspire people like GTO or SS did. There were plenty of mid-sized Dodges and Plymouths running around that were perfectly capable of running with the muscle car offerings from Ford and GM, but these lacked the flair of those competitors. Thus, Chrysler's biggest handicap coming into 1967 was it lacked a performance intermediate car equipped with the performance driveline and, most importantly, wrapped in a package that would provide the flash and panache it needed to appeal to the younger, mostly male muscle car market.

For 1967, Dodge upped its game, again using the venerable Coronet model as its starting point. It developed new badging with an eye to copying the youth friendly trend of a simple letter sequence to denote performance, in the spirit of GTO, SS or GT/A, and came up with the "R/T." R/T indicated the performance Dodges that wore the badge were capable of work both on the track and on the road as well, as it stood for "Road and Track." With that, Dodge created what is arguably the most iconic Chrysler emblem of the muscle car era, and one that would adorn performance Dodges well into the 1970s, only to be resurrected again in the 2000s.

The first in a long line of performance Dodges to wear the R/T badge was the Coronet, which rode a 117-inch wheelbase and was available only in hardtop and convertible body styles. Dodge didn't screw around with trifling engine options in its

Coronet R/T as Pontiac did with its two-barrel GTO or even Chevy with its 325-horse 396. No, Chrysler figured if it were going to leap into the performance intermediate market it might as well go full speed ahead. The base engine for the Coronet R/T was an old Mopar staple, a 440 cubic inch monstrosity more commonly found in Dodge trucks, but redesigned with an eye on performance with new heads, exhaust manifolds, camshaft and carb to produce 375 horsepower. For those keeping score, the 375 horsepower of the redesigned 440 was the highest base horsepower, by far, of any commonly available muscle car offering of the time. To further underscore the seriousness with which Dodge was taking things, it only offered one optional engine—the Hemi. Transmission choices were a standard TorqueFlite 3-speed automatic, shifted on the column unless the floor mounted console was opted for, or a 4-speed A-833 manual as a no-cost option. The differential was determined by engine and transmission choice, and positive traction was available on all rear ends. Stopping was handled by manual drum brakes all around, though power assist was available, as was front disc braking.

The hood was adorned with a set of louvers centered and set back toward the windshield instead of a true hood scoop. The flanks were adorned with faux vents just aft of the doors. The grille featured full length brightwork of vertical bars, and the tail panel matched, incorporating vertically louvered tail lamps. R/T badging was incorporated in the driver's side of the grille and passenger's side of the tail, as well as on the quarter panels behind the faux vents.

On the inside, the Coronet R/T traded some of the plushness of the Coronet 500 for the performance but was still in the same ballpark as the market measuring stick, the GTO. Bucket seating in full vinyl covering was standard, as was a 150 MPH speedometer. The car was fully carpeted, and air conditioning and power steering were optional, as were power windows and remote driver's side mirror.

With the Coronet R/T, Dodge finally had an off-the-showroom-floor performance model in the class of the offerings from GM and Ford. Dodge performance buyers no longer needed the perseverance to go through the option sheets to create their performance car—it was all neatly wrapped up in the R/T package, and with more base horsepower to boot. The Coronet R/T may have lacked the reputation and the mystique of the GTO or the SS Chevy, and the resultant sales were modest in the maiden model of the Coronet R/T, as Dodge only sold 10,109 units, including 628 convertibles and 238 Hemis. Sales were modest to say the least, and perhaps even disappointing, but with the Coronet R/T, Dodge sheepishly entered the roiling muscle car market fray with both feet. It was a foothold from which Dodge would make much more noise as the era rolled along.

For those Mopar aficionados who did prefer something that stood out from the rest of the B-body field, Dodge brought back its big fastback, the Charger, for an encore in 1967.

Again built on the 117-inch Coronet platform, there was not a whole lot different from 1966 in the final year of the first generation Charger. It was again all Coronet from the beltline down, including the faux vents behind the doors. The roofline was the same fastback as the previous year, as was the unusual seating arrangement of four bucket seats and a full length console. The car still featured the full width grille,

**1967 Dodge Charger (courtesy Vanguard Motor Sales, Plymouth, TN).**

with or without hide-away headlamps, and a full width tail light across the tail panel. In fact, about the only thing distinguishing the '66 and '67 Charger was the addition of fender mounted turn signal indicators, which came standard in '67.

Engine choices started with the base 318 producing 230 horses. The 361 offered in 1966 was retired and in its stead was a two-barrel version of the 383, which produced 270 horses. Genuine performance started with the four-barrel 383, producing the same 325 horsepower as it did in 1966. The same 440 as was available in the Coronet R/T was added to the list of engine choices, and the awesome 426 Hemi was still available. A column shifted 3-speed manual was standard fare on 318-equipped cars. All other Charger buyers had to choose between either the TorqueFlite 3-speed automatic and the A-833 4-speed manual. A variety of rear ends were available, as determined by engine and transmission choices, and positive traction was optional. Standard four wheel manual drum brakes stopped the car, with front wheel discs and power assist optional.

Inside, Dodge spared no effort in accenting the car's sporty intentions. Gauging was housed in four round clusters, and there was plenty of brushed metal trim. A full length console was optional and was usually opted for. The standard wood steering wheel of 1966 was made optional for '67, and a front bench seat was for some reason available as well. Power everything, including windows, steering and locks, was optional, as was air conditioning.

After modest success in the sales department in 1966, Dodge had high hopes for its Charger coming into 1967, but it was not to be. The novelty of a fastback intermediate car had definitely worn off. The Charger, Dodge's entry into the NASCAR circuit, showed well despite having an aerodynamic profile roughly equivalent to a brick thrown into a hurricane. The Charger had the added issue of lacking a true identity. Was the car a mid-sized muscle car, facing competition not only from its corporate stablemates, but from across the entire car building spectrum? Or was it a sport-luxury model aiming at the market share owned by the Ford Thunderbird, Pontiac Grand Prix, Buick Riviera and Olds Toronado? Dodge appeared to be attempting to make the Charger both, and it did neither very well. This maelstrom of issues caused sales to plummet catastrophically by nearly sixty percent when compared to 1966. The Charger name plate was definitely in trouble heading into the 1968 model year.

While Dodge handled the upper end of Chrysler's muscle car market share, Plymouth, builder of taxicabs, police cars and other of the most basic forms of transportation, had its entry into the muscle car sweepstakes. In a blatant rip-off of Pontiac, Plymouth offered the GTX, and in keeping with the male dominated marketing of the times, Plymouth referred to the GTX as "the gentleman's hot rod."

The GTX was the performance version of the otherwise unexciting Belvedere line and Plymouth's version of the Coronet R/T. Unlike the offerings from Ford— the Fairlane GT/A and the Cyclone—the GTX was not a twin. There were discernable differences, at least on the exterior. The Plymouth rode a 116-inch wheelbase; the Dodge was built on a 117-inch platform. The Plymouth sported a hood adorned with twin scoops, as opposed to the Dodge's louvered hood. The quad headlamps were incorporated into the grille that was adorned with a single, bright horizontal bar between them, and the tail was likewise understated, with tail lamps slightly recessed and with PLYMOUTH spelled out between them. The molded flanks lacking the louvers of the Dodge gave the GTX a more refined look, with subtle GTX callouts only on the deck lid and the forward edge of the fender. Unfortunately, Plymouth saw fit to remind people of the GTX's heritage, as the fender badging included the word "Belvedere" above GTX.

The business part of the GTX, the power train, was identical to the Dodge. The 375 horse warmed-up 440 Super Commando was standard, with the Hemi as the

**1967 Plymouth GTX (courtesy Gateway Classic Cars, St. Louis, MO).**

**The fender callout of Plymouth's new-for-67 GTX, revealing its humble Belvedere heritage (courtesy Gateway Classic Cars, St. Louis, MO).**

only option. Transmission choices were identical as well—3-speed TorqueFlite auto was standard, shifted on the column unless the console was ordered, or the optional 4-speed manual. Braking was the same as well, with manual drums standard, with or without power assist, and front discs were available. Positive traction rear ends, which were determined by engine and transmission choice, were optional.

The interior was stolen from the top-of-the-line Satellite and featured standard, full vinyl bucket seating and full vinyl door panels, with an available chrome console. A 150 MPH speedo dominated the clunky instrument cluster. Headrests, power windows and locks, remote mirror and wood grained steering wheel were also available options.

The GTX was the second of the dual threat offered by Chrysler in 1967, and while it never really scared Pontiac or the other GM divisions as a threat to their muscle car dominance, it was a perfectly capable car and one of the storied badges of the era. The GTX was the pinnacle of Plymouth's style and luxury in the performance car market and was in that sense an anomaly of sorts for Plymouth, which was much more used to satisfying the need for basic transportation. In fact, the GTX outsold its Dodge counterpart, with 12,010 hardtops and another 680 convertibles sold.

\* \* \*

Today, when people look back on the muscle car era, the term "muscle car" has expanded to include many cars that do not fit the traditional definition of what a "muscle car" was. There is substantial argument over the proper definition of "muscle car," but if one accepts the definition as "an intermediate car equipped with a large cubic inch displacement performance engine," a lot of cars would be excluded, and some of them very, very capable performers. For example, all Corvettes would be out, as would the awesome 350-horsepower 327 Novas, as neither of these were intermediates. Most Corvettes were small blocks. This definition would also rule out early '60s 421 Pontiacs, 413 Mopars and 406 powered Galaxies, as these were full-sized cars, and all Chevrolet Novas, as they were smaller cars. For the same reason, it would also rule out late '60s 427 powered Impalas, great performers all, but for one reason or another, not included in the traditional muscle car definition. It also excluded other cars that were never intended to be true performance cars but that were necessarily equipped with big engines, like Ford's Thunderbird or Pontiac's Grand Prix.

How that definition is perhaps too exclusive, however, is with the pony cars. Up through 1966, there is truly no objective way a Ford Mustang or Plymouth Barracuda could conceivably be considered in the same class as the intermediate performance offerings from the Big 3. They were much smaller cars and came equipped exclusively with small block engines. That isn't to say that the 271 powered Formula S Plymouth or the HiPo 289 Mustangs weren't good performers, but they were not in the same universe as a 400 powered GM A-body. Today, however, the muscle car definition used by most has justifiably expanded to include what had been considered pony cars. 1967 provided the reason why.

\* \* \*

Coming into 1967 the Ford Mustang was everywhere. Songs were sung about it. Bedtime stories were told, and the bards worldwide played harmonious homage to it. Carroll Shelby used the Mustang as the base for his high-profile road racing operation and developed the GT 350. Though Plymouth's Barracuda valiantly carried out its lonely battle against the Mustang, the Ford simply obliterated the little Plymouth. Ford sold nearly 681,000 Mustangs in 1964 and 1965, while Plymouth sold fewer than 103,000 Barracudas in the same period. In 1966 the flogging was worse with well over 600,000 Mustangs sold in comparison to 38,000 Barracudas. To put that in perspective, there were 1,666 Mustangs galloping around to every Barracuda.

By 1967, the Mustang in its original incarnation was getting a little stale, and for that model year, it got a makeover. The car was similar to the previous models but was made slightly longer, wider, and taller, and this gave the car a more muscular stance. The added dimensions were necessary because for the first time, Ford offered big-block power in the little Mustang. The Mustang was initially conceived as a blank slate with an endless list of options, allowing buyers to create virtually any type of car, from economical grocery getter to tight handling road car, and the 1967 Mustang stayed true to these roots. The addition of big-block engines simply expanded the capabilities of the Mustang into muscle car territory.

The '67 Mustang was available in hardtop, fastback or convertible body styles. The fastback slope continued to the edge of the deck lid for 1967, where in previous years it had stopped short. The '67 model had the ubiquitous Mustang faux vents aft of the doors, as all Mustangs had before it. The new dimensions coupled with a redesigned, deeper set grille gave the car a much more aggressive appearance. Adding to this appearance were twin faux scoops molded into the hood. The tail panel was reworked as well, featuring three vertical taillight lenses in a recessed panel.

The muscular version of the '67 Mustang was the GT/A, complete with GT

**1967 Mustang GT in fastback form (courtesy Vanguard Motor Sales, Plymouth, MI).**

badging and rocker panel striping. The GT/A could be had with small block power, but the newly available 390 cubic inch Thunderbird Special engine rated at 320 horses turned the Mustang into something completely different. The 390 was essentially the same engine that powered the GT/A Fairlanes and the Cyclone GT and could be backed by the 4-speed Toploader manual transmission or a 3-speed automatic. Dual exhaust was standard on the GT model, and an array of rear ends, with or without positive traction, was available as well. Power front disc brakes were standard on the GT, as were an upgraded suspension and limited slip rear end.

Inside, Ford continued to offer its long, long list of options to personalize the Mustang, even to make it a miniature Thunderbird, if one wished. Bucket seating was standard, and options included power windows, locks, and steering, sport steering wheel, console and air conditioning. Cruise control was also optional.

For 1967, Mustang sales plummeted to just over 472,000 cars. This is still a remarkable number of cars when compared to the sales numbers of its competitors, but the days of the Mustang having the entire pony car pasture essentially to itself were over. It may have taken Ford's competitors three years to finally build a competitor to the Mustang, but in 1967, the Ford found itself fending off more than just the Barracuda it had dominated in years past. In 1967, the pony car market broke out into open warfare.

Some of the Mustang's newfound competition came from within, in the form of Mercury's Cougar. As opposed to the Cyclone line, the Cougar, while substantially based on the Mustang, was no mere clone of the Ford. In fact, the Cougar would become nearly synonymous with Mercury and would be heavily used in Mercury

**1967 Mustang GT front fender with emblem (courtesy Vanguard Motor Sales, Plymouth, MI).**

advertising, so much so that Mercury reminded the buying public that its car lines could be found "at the sign of the cat."

At its inception, Mercury was conceived as a brand to fill the gap between the Ford line and the much more upscale Lincoln line in the Blue Oval's lineup. True to that, Ford executives envisioned the Cougar as a filling a niche of a personal luxo-sports car between the Mustang and the plush Thunderbird, a niche similar to that which the Charger was trying, and failing, to fill. Because of its place in the Ford line, it rode a wheelbase three inches longer at 111 inches. Unlike the Cyclone, the Cougar was no dressed up Mustang and had little in common on the exterior, though their mechanicals were essentially the same. The Cougar, even in base form, was decidedly more luxurious and more powerful than the Mustang. No six-cylinder was available in the Cougar; its base engine was the 200 HP 289. Unlike the Mustang, the Cougar could not be had in any body style save hardtop. The 1967 Cougar's "electric shaver" grille of vertical louvers with hide-away headlamps made the 1967 Cougar one of the most distinctive cars of the era. The tail panel matched with vertical louvering and incorporated sequential tail lamps scavenged from the Thunderbird's parts bins. Sequential taillights would make an appearance again in Mustangs of the 2010s.

The Cougar was designed to emulate the touring sports cars of Europe, and to that end Mercury offered the XR-7 package. This popular option offered leather bucket seating, an automatic transmission, power steering and brakes, and a simulated walnut dash panel and steering wheel. It offered a plethora of lights and map cases, like European cars, and even an optional overhead console containing various warning lights. For the performance minded, however, there was the Cougar GT.

The Cougar GT was a performance package for the base Cougar or it could be combined with the XR-7, and the heart of the GT package was the installation of the same 320 horse 390 that powered the GT Mustangs, though in Mercury parlance it was referred to as the 390 Marauder engine. Standard transmission was a heavy-duty 3-speed; the "Toploader" 4-speed manual and 3-speed Merc-O-Matic automatic were optional, as were limited slip differentials. The GT package netted a heavier suspension and upgraded braking, with power assisted front discs standard. An additional option package was the Dan Gurney Special package, to celebrate the success of Gurney and the 1967 Cougar on the Trans Am road racing circuit. The package essentially consisted of unique decals, engine brightwork, special wheel covers, and not much else.

The 1967 Cougar was an impressive car and not simply a dressed-up Mustang. It was the rare Mercury that had its own identity, and the list of standard and available options made the Cougar substantially more upscale than a Mustang. As a result, the automotive press was duly impressed; the Cougar was named *Motor Trend*'s Car of the Year. While *Motor Trend* named the entire Ford line its car of the year in 1964, and in that year the Mustang was the flagship of the Ford lineup, the Cougar's 1967 *Motor Trend* trophy was the first time a muscle car or pony car had won the award outright. Not even the GTO or the legendary Mustang had pulled off that feat.

The Cougar and its badge made its debut in 1967, and the Cougar would highlight Mercury's "At the Sign of the Cat" advertising campaign for years to follow (courtesy Gateway Classic Cars, St. Louis, MO).

Sadly for Mercury, 1967 was the high water mark for the brand during the muscle car era. The Cougar helped move Mercury out the long shadow of Ford, at least for a time. The Cougar wasn't going to match the Mustang in terms of sales, but it acquitted itself very, very well, with nearly 151,000 units sold, including 8,464 GT/ As. Not too bad for a brand generally treated as an unwanted stepchild by Dearborn.

* * *

Despite the overall success of the debut Cougar, it never put the Mustang's dominance in any real jeopardy. It is unlikely that Ford executives would have let that happen in any case. A much more serious threat to the Ford emerged in 1967, when GM finally roused itself out of its pony car slumber and launched an assault on the little Ford. Naturally, Ford's longtime nemesis Chevrolet would lead the attack and would be flanked by a Pontiac. Oldsmobile was not happy that it didn't get a pony car entry instead of Pontiac, but then, neither Pontiac nor Chevy got an equivalent car to Oldsmobile's revolutionary front wheel drive Toronado. The twin attack would be two of the more storied cars of American automotive history: Pontiac's Firebird and Chevrolet's Camaro, both built on a 108-inch wheelbase and classed as "F-bodies" in GM vernacular.

Like the Mustang, the Camaro was aimed at the youth market and was designed to be available with a wide range of engine and interior options, allowing the buyer to customize the car in just about any configuration imaginable yet be seen in a sporty body style. Chevrolet further copied the pony car formula with the long hood/short deck style and made it available in either hardtop or convertible form.

The standard engine was a 140 HP six-cylinder, but the performance minded opted for more potent power plants. The first rung on the performance ladder was a 210 HP version of Chevy's infinitely upgradable 327, but the real Camaro muscle performance began with either of two options wed to the SS package. The first of these was a 295 horse 350 cubic inch mill that was exclusive to the Camaro, and the second was the mighty 396 borrowed from the SS Chevelle.

As with the SS Chevelle, the 396 available in the Camaro came in multiple configurations. The first was the same 325 horse version found in base Chevelles, and the second was the 375 horse version found in the Camaro's larger sibling. Those 375 horses instantly made Camaros so equipped the top dog in the pony car class with respect to performance, and due to the smaller size of the Camaro, allowed it to compete with the larger mid-sized cars offered at the time. A 3-speed automatic transmission was offered alongside the standard 3-speed manual, as well as a 4-speed manual. A full range of interior and power options were available, and the Camaro, with or without the SS package, could be had with an RS package, for Rally Sport. Where the SS package was more performance geared, the RS was an appearance package that included hideaway headlamps and special badging, as well as other niceties.

For those with the right connections, Chevy offered a special option package known as option code "Z/28," which equipped the car strictly for road racing on the small block Trans American circuit. Homologation required the Z/28 be offered in small quantities to the buying public, and the option gave the car a 302 small block required by Trans Am racing, which limited engine displacements to no more than 305 cubic inches. The little 302 was wildly underrated at 295 horses. The Z/28 option came standard with power front disc brakes behind beefier 15 inch tires and wheels and heavy-duty suspension, all of which came in handy on the Trans Am road courses. Factory headers helped free up the escape of exhaust, and the car featured a spoiler and special hood vents to feed huge carbs. Illustrating the seriousness with which Chevrolet was taking Trans Am racing and the effort to challenge the Shelby Mustangs and Cougars being run by Ford, the Z/28 went on to claim wins in 18 of 25 Trans Am events in 1967. Today, '67 Camaros with the Z/28 package are among the most desirable of Camaros of any year.

The Trans Am wins gave Chevy what it needed to comply with the "win on Sunday, sell on Monday" rule of 1960s marketing, and that exposure coupled with the styling home run of the Camaro gave Chevrolet an instant hit and set the stage for literally decades of Camaro popularity. The Camaro was hot, new, and offered an amazing range of options as well a much more powerful engine option than the Mustang, which, despite the 1967 restyle, was growing a little stale. Consequently, Chevrolet sold 221,000 Camaros to jubilant fans of the Bowtie. Of these, 34,410 wore the fabled SS badge. While those aren't Mustang sales numbers, they were enough to get the attention of Ford and for Dearborn to look at the Camaro as a serious threat to the Mustang. In fact, simple math illustrates that the total of Camaros and Mustangs sold in 1967 roughly equals the sales totals for the 1966 Mustang. One need look no further than that to see the threat the Camaro posed.

Six months later, Pontiac followed in the footsteps of Chevy and joined the pony car fray with its Firebird, built on the same 108 wheelbase F-body platform as the Camaro. Like the Camaro, it was available in hardtop or convertible form. Though it shared the same long hood/short deck and overall form of the Camaro, the Firebird was no clone of the Chevy. With the DNA of the GTO available to it, Pontiac's pony car was all Pontiac.

To put further distance between the Firebird and the Camaro, Pontiac offered the Firebird in five distinct option packages and marketed them as five distinct models, which they called the "Magnificent Five." The least magnificent of the five was the base six-cylinder, followed by a marginally more magnificent Firebird powered by Pontiac's innovative overhead cam six-cylinder. The base V-8 offering was a two-barrel 326 producing 250 horsepower. Next up from that was the "HO" or "high output" 326, equipped with four-barrel carburation and producing 280 horsepower, comparable to Chevy's 327, though much less famous.

Power came in the form of one of two 400-cubic-inch engines: the base 400 that produced 325 horses, or the Ram Air 400, deceitfully rated at the same 325 horsepower but featuring cold air induction breathing through small twin hood scoops. These engines were exactly the same as those installed in GTOs. The GTOs were rated at considerably more horsepower, however, because GM mandates at the time restricted horsepower output to no more than 1 horsepower per 10 pounds of car. The curb weight of a Firebird was 3,250 pounds, hence 325 horsepower, allegedly achieved by a modified carb linkage that limited the secondary barrels from opening fully. Why the 375 horse 396 SS Camaro was not so limited is not clear. Pontiac

**1967 SS 350 Camaro Pace Car. This limited edition Camaro commemorated the 1967 Indy 500, where it served as pace car (courtesy Gateway Classic Cars, St. Louis, MO).**

people might say it was simply because of the preferential treatment always afforded Chevrolet, which allowed them to get away with things other divisions could not; perhaps they should remember back to 1964 and consider DeLorean's skullduggery and how the original GTO came about.

The standard transmission for the Firebird 400 represented a bit of heresy for GM; it was a heavy-duty 3-speed manual build by the Ford Motor Company. An optional Muncie 4-speed was available on the Firebird 400s, as well as the 326 powered 'Birds, replacing a 3-speed Saginaw unit. The Turbo-Hydromatic 3-speed automatic transmission was also optional on all Firebirds, regardless of engine. A wide range of rear end ratios were available and could be had in limited slip configuration. Manual drum brakes at all four corners were standard; front discs and/ or power assist were optional.

Differentiating the Firebird from the Camaro were Pontiac's iconic split grille, quarter panel molding and taillights similar to those of the GTO. Also borrowed from the GTO was the optional hood tachometer. Engine callouts were located on the outer sides of the hood scoops, as well as on the right-hand side of the deck lid. Pontiac inexplicably included its arrowhead emblem on the center of the front bumper on 400-equipped cars only. In true pony car fashion, a wide range of options allowed for nearly limitless customization. Air conditioning, power steering, power windows, power locks, and console were all optional. Standard seating was full vinyl covered buckets.

1967 Pontiac Firebird 400 (courtesy Vanguard Classic Cars, Plymouth, MI).

Fender badging gracing the 1967 Firebird (courtesy Streetside Classics, Charlotte, NC).

Pontiac didn't offer cool packages with the ever popular abbreviations-as-names, like the SS or RS options offered on the Camaro or the GT/A on the Mustang. It lacked the stripes and graphics of its competitors as well. Pontiac also had no analog to the Z/28, as Pontiac didn't participate in the Trans Am road racing series. This may or may not have hurt overall sales with Pontiac selling just under 83,000, including 18,636 with 400s. These are strong numbers for intermediate muscle cars, but the little Pontiac didn't come close to the still-strong popularity of the Mustang or even the Camaro. What the 1967 Firebird did do, however, was mark the debut of a car that would become the performance flagship of the division for the next 30-plus years, long after its bigger brother the GTO had faded into history.

* * *

Amid the swirling storm that suddenly was the pony car market, there was still Plymouth's stalwart little Barracuda, the little car that had spent the past three model years tied to Ford's whipping post. But Plymouth persevered in the market that was suddenly gaining steam, hoping to cash in on the pony car phenomenon. Plymouth realized the first generation Barracuda was abjectly failing as a competitor to the Mustang and suddenly found itself in competition with Pontiac and Chevrolet for the market's scraps left by the Mustang. To meet the competition in the pony car market, Plymouth restyled the Barracuda for 1967. Compared to previous models, the results were spectacular.

The Barracuda was offered in hardtop ("notchback"), fastback, and convertible body styles, breaking away from the Valiant body style. Thankfully, the Barracuda also lost the monstrous back glass of the 1964–66 models. The '67 Barracuda got on the Coke-bottle body bandwagon, sported minimum exterior trim, and departed from the traditional long-hood, short deck pony car formula. A revised, split grille incorporating single headlamps and driving lights dominated the front end.

The 225 cubic inch slant six was standard, as were a two and four-barrel version of the old 273 that had always powered the hottest Barracudas. The two-barrel version produced 260 horses, while the four-barrel produced 235. With the redesign of the Barracuda, however, the engineers at Plymouth got their slide rules out and widened the engine bay by two inches in anticipation of wedging in Chrysler's 383 to better compete with the 390s offered by the Ford products and the 396 and 400s available in the GM ponies.

Arriving a couple of months late in the model year, the 383 was available and could only be had with the Formula S. The four-barrel 273 was also an option with the Formula S. The Formula S package also netted a heavy-duty suspension, tachometer, rally gauges and special emblems and trim. Because things didn't fit quite right into the crowded engine compartment of the little Plymouth, more restrictive exhaust manifolds had to be used, and this reduced the horsepower output of the 383 engine to 320. Standard transmission for the Barracuda was a 3-speed manual with a 3-speed TorqueFlite auto as well as the A-833 4-speed manual optional. Plymouth had to make some concessions to offer the 383 in its Barracuda.

Unlike other pony car offerings, the list of available options was relatively short. Coating the engine in butter and jamming it into the barely-big-enough engine

*This page and opposite:* The three body styles of the 1967 Plymouth Barracuda—traditional fastback Formula S, convertible and the new-for-'67 "notchback" body style (courtesy of Vanguard Motor Sales, Plymouth, MI).

compartment left no space for air conditioning or power steering as options. Braking featured standard drums all around, but these were upgradable to power assisted drums or front disc/rear drum, with or without power assist.

Inside, split bench seating was standard, unlike other pony cars which offered buckets standard. Bucket seating was available, as was a console. Power windows and locks were also available, and air conditioning and power steering were available as long as the 383 wasn't insisted upon.

The Barracuda's reskin proved popular. Plymouth found new homes for more than 62,500 Barracudas in 1967, just shy of twice those sold in the previous model year. Of these, 7,193 were Formula S models, and 1,841 were equipped with the 383. As with the Firebird, these were solid sales numbers, only tarnished when compared to the Camaro and Mustang against which the Barracuda was competing. Barracuda sales were dinged somewhat by a big-block compact offering from Dodge, the 383-powered Dart GTS, though it was more of a powerful compact in the tradition of Chevy's Nova than a true pony car.

\* \* \*

The muscle car wars were gaining momentum as the 1967 model year drew to a close. The old stalwarts—the GTO, the 4-4-2, and such—were suddenly facing pressure from new adversaries, most notably from Chrysler in the form of the GTX and the Coronet R/T. The little pony cars were finally given big-block power at the expense of their traditional nimbleness, but this transformation brought the pony cars so equipped squarely into the muscle car arena.

As the counterculture out in San Fran was lamenting the death of "hippie" and

**Chevrolet left no doubt which car maker built the superb 1967 Camaro (photo by Davies Vanpool, Ketchum, OK).**

the shortening days at the end of the Summer of Love, the performance car buyers looked ahead with anticipation to see how Detroit could possibly top what went on in 1967.

They would not be disappointed.

1964 GTO convertible, owned by Larry Crider of Sapulpa, OK (photo by Darla Willhite).

The 1964½ Ford Mustang, the first in the line of what would become the most popular American car ever built (courtesy Vanguard Motor Sales, Plymouth, MI).

1965 Buick Skylark Gran Sport, owned by Mark Ascher of St. Paul, MN (photo by owner).

**1965 Plymouth Satellite (courtesy Vanguard Motor Sales, Plymouth, MI).**

**1966 GTO (courtesy Vanguard Motor Sales, Plymouth, MI).**

**1966 Oldsmobile 4-4-2 (courtesy Vanguard Motor Sales, Plymouth, MI).**

1966 Plymouth Barracuda, owned by Davis Maas of Grosse Pointe Woods, MI (photo by Karen Fontanive).

1967 Chevrolet Super Sport 396 Chevelle (courtesy Fast Lane Classic Cars, St. Charles, MO).

1967 Dodge Coronet R/T (courtesy Vanguard Motor Sales, Plymouth, MI).

1967 Mercury Cougar GT (courtesy Vanguard Motor Sales, Plymouth, MI).

1967 Chevrolet SS 350 Convertible Camaro (courtesy Vanguard Motor Sales, Plymouth, MI).

The car that changed the trajectory of the muscle car wars, Plymouth's 1968 Road Runner (courtesy Vanguard Motor Sales, Plymouth, MI).

*Above and middle:* The magnificent, sinister 1968 Dodge Charger R/T (courtesy Vanguard Motor Sales, Plymouth, MI).

The 1968 Ford Torino GT (courtesy Vanguard Motor Sales, Plymouth, MI).

The 1968 AMC Mark Donohue Javelin SST, with 390 cubic inch engine and the Go-Package (courtesy Gateway Classic Cars, St. Louis, MO).

Pontiac's 1969 GTO Judge (courtesy Fast Lane Classic Cars, St. Charles, MO).

Ford's budget supercar answer to the Plymouth Road Runner, the 1969 Torino Cobra. Owned and photographed by Chuck Knudson, Bloomington, IL.

1969 A12 440 "Six Pack" Super Bee (courtesy Fast Lane Classic Cars, St. Charles, MO).

1970 Plymouth Superbird (courtesy Fast Lane Classic Cars, St. Charles, MO).

**1969 Ford Mustang Mach 1 (courtesy Gateway Classic Cars, St. Louis, MO).**

**1969 Camaro Z/28 (courtesy Gateway Classic Cars, St. Louis, MO).**

**1969 Pontiac Trans Am (courtesy Rocky Rotella).**

1970 Chevrolet Chevelle SS 396 owned by Joseph and Shelia Salvo of Newport Beach, California (photo by Wesley Allison).

1970 Dodge Coronet R/T (courtesy Fast Lane Classic Cars, St. Charles, MO).

1970 Ford Torino Cobra (courtesy Vanguard Motor Sales, Plymouth, MI).

Mercury's 1970 Cyclone (courtesy Vanguard Motor Sales, Plymouth, MI).

American Motors' 1970 Rebel Machine, in early model year red, white and blue trim (courtesy Diego Rosenberg).

1970 Ford Mustang Boss 302 (courtesy Vanguard Motor Sales, Plymouth, MI).

1970 Mercury Cougar Eliminator (courtesy Vanguard Motor Sales, Plymouth, MI).

1970 Plymouth 'Cuda (courtesy Gateway Classic Cars, St. Louis, MO).

Pontiac's 1971 GTO Judge (courtesy Fast Lane Classic Cars, St. Charles, MO).

1971 Buick GS (courtesy Gateway Classic Cars, St. Louis, MO).

1971 Plymouth Road Runner 340 (courtesy Vanguard Motor Sales, Plymouth, MI).

Ford's redesigned 1971 Mustang Mach 1 (courtesy Vanguard Motor Sales, Plymouth, MI).

**1971 Chevrolet Camaro Z/28 (courtesy Gateway Classic Cars, St. Louis, MO).**

**1971 Plymouth 'Cuda (courtesy Fast Lane Classic Cars, St. Charles, MO).**

**1972 Ford Gran Torino (courtesy Gateway Classic Cars, St. Louis, MO).**

1972 Chevrolet Camaro Z/28 (courtesy Vanguard Motor Sales, Plymouth, MI).

1972 Oldsmobile Cutlass 4-4-2 (courtesy Gateway Classic Cars, St. Louis, MO).

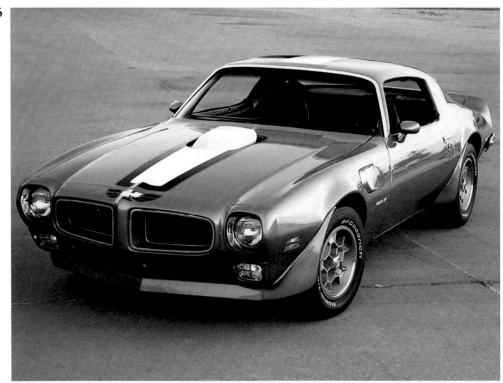

1972 Pontiac Trans Am (courtesy Rocky Rotella).

The author and his 1966 GTO (photo by Darla Willhite).

# 7

# Revolution

## *America Burns and Plymouth Goes Back to Basics*

In the broad sweep of American history, there are several pivotal years—arbitrary measurements of time, really, in which climactic events took place that shaped, or scarred, the face of the national consciousness in both the long and the near term. For the United States, those years might be 1609 and the founding of Jamestown, or, of course, 1776. More important to the ideals of 1776 might be 1783 and the end of the American Revolution. The fabric of the nation was torn in 1860 and forced back together again in 1865. Of course, 1941 and the attack on Pearl Harbor come to mind, and our recent memories are scarred by 2001.

To that list 1968 must be added. In 1968, the tempest that had been gathering for years, if not decades, finally broke loose in a perfect storm of events—social, economic, political and military—that continue to shape the nation today.

Early in 1968, the center began to collapse, and things fell apart. In January, the forces of the North Vietnamese Army and the Viet Cong guerrillas launched the Tet Offensive, which is arguably the crucial event of the war in Vietnam. It was certainly the turning point of the war for the American public. Public support for the war had teetered uneasily on a knife's edge for years; Tet finally pushed it off. Though Tet resulted in a resounding defeat for the Vietnamese Communists, the American public learned that the military and President Johnson had been less than forthright about how splendidly the war was progressing. Iconic newsman Walter Cronkite, America's anchorman, declared the war was unwinnable, and public support for the war in Vietnam plummeted. In a democracy, unpopular wars are by definition unwinnable.

This political and military unhappiness coincided with an election year, and the '68 presidential election proved to be perhaps the most tempestuous in modern American political history. In March, President Johnson had a dismal showing in New Hampshire's democratic primary, after which Robert Kennedy, brother of the slain president, announced his own candidacy. Lyndon Johnson, always adept at reading political tea leaves, then shocked the world by withdrawing from the presidential race, his presidency devoured by the monster he created in Vietnam. Civil rights icon Martin Luther King, Jr., champion of non-violent protest, was murdered in Memphis in April. Two months later, Robert Kennedy was himself gunned down after winning the California democratic primary. Race riots and anti-war protests grew, and the Democratic Party limped into its convention in Chicago, where there was obscene violence in protest of just about everything. A divided Democratic presidential field jockeyed for the right to be heir to Johnson's smoldering throne, with Vice President Hubert Humphrey, darling of the Democrats' liberal wing, securing the nomination. Alabama governor George "Segregation Now, Segregation Tomorrow, Segregation Forever" Wallace ran a third party campaign, prying from Humphrey the Democratic Deep South. As it turns out, the flight of the Deep South to the Republican Party would be permanent, or at least has been to date. With the country seemingly coming apart, Republican Richard Nixon, after having promised us all he would disappear in 1960, emerged as president by promising to restore the order so many desperately wanted.

The assassination of King sparked race riots across the nation, and again in 1968, American inner cities burned. At Columbia University, students protesting the war in Vietnam locked themselves into several buildings on campus, and the siege lasted nearly a week. In August, Soviet forces effectively invaded Czechoslovakia, a Communist bloc ally of the Soviet Union suddenly in revolt. The U.S., paralyzed by the festering wound in Vietnam, was unwilling to aid the aspiring Czechs. African American medalists Tommie Smith and John Carlos raised their fists, a gesture of black power, during the playing of the "Star Spangled Banner," a precursor to symbolic protests by black NFL athletes fifty years later.

No one, right or left, was happy in 1968. The deaths of Kennedy and King alarmed liberals and the November election of Nixon truly terrified them. Conservatives were concerned about the progress in the war in Vietnam, the racial violence, and what they saw as the general breakdown of American society. While they were thrilled that eight years of Kennedy and Johnson—mostly Johnson—were over, they suddenly realized the trade-off was that Richard Nixon was now running things.

It was a bad year indeed.

* * *

If revolution and violence raged on the college campuses and in the inner cities, they did as well in the muscle car world. Just as 1968 was a revolutionary year in the broader scope of American history, it was as well on the streets and strips around the nation as the great powers of the automotive world entered a new phase—the greatest phase—of the muscle car wars that had been rapidly escalating since 1964. If the Cold War was measured in terms of ballistic missile throw weights, warheads counts, and mutually assured destruction, the muscle car wars were measured in cubic inches, horsepower and torque, and in 1968, these measurements reached new heights.

By 1968, however, dark clouds were gathering on the horizon for the American muscle car, though they weren't recognized as such at the time. Insurance companies were more and more coming to the realization that powerful cars designed to go very fast with marginally effective safety features were a high risk, and premiums began to creep northward. In 1968 more safety mandates from the federal government took effect. In '67, they included dual circuit master brake cylinders and collapsible steering columns; by 1968, the only thing standing between the public and the extinction of the human race seemed to be whether or not American cars were equipped with side marker lights. As innocuous as the required-for-1968 side marker lights were, they were but a harbinger of government's efforts to protect us all from ourselves, which would only accelerate as time would go on.

The earlier years of the muscle car wars were characterized by the relative dominance of the GM machines—the early GTOs and the later SS Chevys, ably supported by Buick's Gran Sports and Olds 4-4-2. Ford was busy owning the pony car market, and mid-sized muscle cars seemed but an afterthought. Chrysler's factory-built supercar packages were late to the game with the 1967 Dodge Coronet R/T and Plymouth GTX, but they were the forerunners of what Chrysler would unleash in 1968. The era of General Motors dominance was waning. This year Mopar took the offensive in the muscle car wars, stunning General Motors and Ford with the unexpected success of its midsized performance offerings.

\* \* \*

A successful muscle car had two prerequisites—performance and style. Performance from Chrysler was never a problem. Back to the 1950s and up through 1968, Chrysler had always been known for bulletproof drivelines. Where Chrysler had fallen short was in the area of style. Chrysler never seemed to put much effort into designing attractive cars that would appeal to a large swath of the car buying public. There was also the marketing aspect, and Chrysler had—and has since—always had its issues in this area as well. As a result, Chrysler has historically run a distant 3rd in sales behind GM and Ford. It was hoped that a redesign, coupled with a renewed effort on marketing, would boost 1968 sales.

For 1968, the entire B-body Mopar line received a complete cosmetic re-design. Gone were the marginally popular straight lines and sharp angles that had characterized Plymouth's Belvedere and Dodge's Coronet lines in 1966 and 1967. It was as if the Chrysler brass took all the straight edges the design team had used to make long, straight body lines and hard angles and replaced them with compasses and protractors to soften the lines of the B-body lines. Either that or they fired everyone. Regardless, the flared quarter panels, Coke-bottle profiles and soaring rooflines gracing Mopar's B-body offerings introduced in 1968 represent the pinnacle of Chrysler's mid-size styling.

Chrysler maintained its previous intermediate performance offerings in Dodge's Coronet R/T and its ailing Charger, and Plymouth brought back the GTX as well. Plymouth's little Barracuda soldiered on, now battling Camaros, Cougars and Firebirds as well as its ancient nemesis the Mustang in the pony car market. But it was Plymouth, by going back to the future, so to speak, that seized battlefield initiative.

\* \* \*

The Plymouth division had always lived near the lowest rungs on the ladder of American cars. Plymouth was known for building cheap, sensible transportation that many times felt like they may have been built in Yugoslavia. Plymouth had had its moments—the underrated Barracuda, wedge powered Savoys and Belvederes of the early '60s and GTO-fighting performance Satellites—but no one really noticed. Plymouth was known for no-frills, entry level vehicles that were the first car of countless newlyweds and new parents aspiring to one day own a Dodge or—dare to dream—an Imperial.

In 1968, Plymouth gambled that there was still a youth performance market and further reckoned that by 1968 this market, the same one that fueled the '64 GTO's sales, was largely abandoned. By and large, the muscle car was getting a bit porky by 1968. The Ronny and the Daytona's "Little GTO" of 1964 wasn't so little anymore. Muscle cars began putting on weight in the form of an ever increasing list of standard equipment. Light bench seats became "no cost options" in favor of bucket seating, which contained twice the heavy metal framing of a bench. Consoles became standard. Heavy power steering pumps, air conditioners, and power brake boosters were becoming more prevalent. In addition to adding weight while simultaneously sapping engine power, these items caused the cost of the base muscle car to steadily rise. For example, the base 1964 GTO weighed about 3,000 pounds and had a cost of a little over $2,800. By 1968, the fat Goat tipped the scales at a robust 3,500 pounds and cost over $3,100. This was a common trend across the intermediate performance spectrum. Performance purists could always save weight by deleting standard equipment—even heaters and radios—but "no cost options" were just that—they were no cost. They didn't lower the price of the car any. The buyer still paid for the car as if the bucket seating wasn't replaced by the cheaper bench seat, for example. In short, muscle cars were beginning to price themselves out of the youth market.

The market that went nuts for the 1964 GTO as twenty-somethings had figured out by 1968 that air conditioning made the air cooler, power steering didn't tear your rotator cuffs and cars with power brakes didn't have to be stopped with both feet on the brake pedal, knuckles white from gripping the steering wheel in sheer terror. Plymouth, however, believed there was still a market for young, mostly male buyers who would buy a cheap super car with few of these options, a market that didn't care about air conditioning or power brakes. So Plymouth—the great builder of taxi cabs, police cars and the like—played to its strength of building cheap cars. Plymouth tore pages from John DeLorean's playbook and recreated 1964 all over again, aiming for that forgotten youth market. In '64, Pontiac, even with the GTO aimed at young buyers, struggled with the idea that the car could not be *too* cheap—Pontiac had an image to maintain, after all. Plymouth had no such qualms.

Plymouth set out with the goal of building intermediate muscle car short on equipment and long on performance that could run the quarter mile in less than fifteen seconds for under $3,000. The legendary car that was the result was for some reason to be called the La Mancha before Plymouth came to their senses and paid Warner Brothers handsomely for the right to call the new Belvedere based car "Road Runner," after the uncatchable Saturday morning cartoon nemesis of Wile E. Coyote.

Partnering with Warner Brothers for the Road Runner name was a marketing coup. The cartoon graphics appealed to the youth market, who grew up watching the starving coyote chase the little bird through the cartoon desert southwest. There may not have been a more perfect name for a car built to, well, quickly run down the road.

To ensure that the performance backed up the graphic silliness of a cartoon sticker on the doors (and a special horn designed to imitate the cartoon bird's "beep beep"), Chrysler pilloried its parts bins. At the time, Chrysler had cornered the market on vehicles provided to law enforcement entities nationwide, and as a result, those bins were chock full of pre-designed heavy-duty components suitable for a boulevard bruiser, with very little cost in research and development. The workhorse 383 cubic inch engine was heated up with heads borrowed from the 440 and a hotter camshaft for an underrated 335 horsepower. The fire breathing Hemi was the only optional power plant. The Road Runner was outfitted with a hood featuring side facing non-functional scoops, though they could be made functional with the optional "Coyote Duster" cold air induction system. Weight and cost were kept to a minimum by offering next to nothing in the way of standard equipment. Instrumentation was a Belvedere station wagon's bar speedometer with idiot lights instead of more expensive gauges to monitor engine functions. The A-833 4-speed manual transmission was standard, shifted with a cheap, craptastic Inland shifter that was like shifting gears with a rope.

Bench seats with cloth and vinyl covers were standard. The car rolled around on simple stamped steel wheels adorned with stainless steel "poverty caps." Initially, the only body style was a pillared coupe (though a hardtop was offered later in the model year) with pop-out quarter windows because the roller mechanisms were both heavy and expensive. A radio even cost extra. Carpet wasn't even standard; instead one got a rubber floor mat. Though power steering and brakes, bucket seating and the like were optional, Plymouth endowed a base Road Runner with all the opulence of a forklift.

The car tipped the scales at less than 3,400 pounds, and road tests proved the car would run the quarter in under fifteen seconds. The cost was under $2,900 for a Road Runner coupe. The Hemi option significantly raised the price, but the 1968 Hemi Road Runner is among a very few cars that can legitimately claim the mantle of the most potent muscle car ever built.

Plymouth set out to remake its image in 1968, hiring a new ad agency and bringing Petula Clark, of the song "Downtown" fame, to help push Plymouths out the doors. However, no one was more shocked by the success of the '68 Road Runner than Plymouth; sales were expected to maybe hit 20,000, but buyers came in droves. As a result, Plymouth set nearly 45,000 Road Runners loose on the world to hunt unsuspecting GTOs, Fairlanes and Chevelles. Plymouth had finally found its muscle car hit, and other car builders were forced to recognize that Plymouth had not only truly arrived on the muscle car scene, but re-defined it.

Flanking the Flintstonian Road Runner, Plymouth continued to offer its GTX as a more luxurious alternative to its stripped down supercar. An upscale supercar certainly wasn't Plymouth's forte, and it was essentially offered simply so as not to entirely abandon that section of the market share. As a part of the Belvedere line, the GTX was restyled for 1968 and unlike the Road Runner, it was offered in hardtop and convertible form; there was no coupe option. The GTX included a different and considerably less cheap-looking grille than that of the Road Runner, as well as a more stylish rear end. It featured the same hood as the Road Runner, though it did have bright wheel well moldings and twin stripes along its lower flanks, just forward of "GTX" callouts.

Engine options for the GTX remained the same as the previous model year:

**In keeping with the budget friendly nature of the 1968 Road Runner, Plymouth went with decals rather than more expensive metal badging for the cartoon figure. Plymouth didn't even spring for color on the decals in 1968 (courtesy Fast Lane Classic Cars, St. Charles, MO).**

375 horse 440 four-barrel standard, with the mighty 426 Hemi as the only option. Alongside the new Road Runner, the Plymouth performance offerings included the restyled Belvedere based GTX as its luxury-muscle offering. As in 1967, the GTX came standard with the 375 horse 440 power plant, with the 426 Hemi optional. The 3-speed TorqueFlite automatic transmission was standard, though the heavy-duty A-833 4-speed manual was one of those "no cost" options. A variety of rear ends, with or without positive traction, could be had.

Though a GTX and a Road Runner were very similar on the outside, they were worlds apart on the inside. For starters, the GTX came standard with carpet. It also had the heavy sound deadening underneath that carpet that the Road Runner lacked. Bucket seating with a console was standard, as was faux wood graining on the dash. Revealing its Plymouth heritage, however, was the Belvedere's cheap bar speedometer with idiot lights that was included on even the lowliest Plymouths. Power steering, brakes, windows and doors were optional, as well as air conditioning and AM/FM radio.

The 1968 GTX, with its restyle, was an attractive car, but it was a car without a home. For a car positioned as an alternative to the likes of the GTO, 4-4-2, its fraternal cousin the Coronet R/T and others, the "Plymouth" emblem, prominently displayed on the driver's side of the hood worked against it. Plymouth simply wasn't known for building luxury muscle cars, and even die hard Mopar fans first thought of Dodge when they went shopping for something more upscale. The Road Runner was

1968 Plymouth GTX (courtesy Gateway Classic Cars, St. Louis, MO).

Quarter panel callouts graced the flanks of the 1968 Plymouth GTX (courtesy Gateway Classic Cars, St. Louis, MO).

much more what people thought of when they thought of Plymouth, and the Road Runner's success hurt the GTX, as sales were down significantly from 1967 to 18,940 GTXs of all types being sold.

Filling a niche somewhere between the stripped Road Runner and the plush GTX was the Sport Satellite. While more plush than sport and lacking high-performance gear like sway bars, sculpted hood, heavy-duty suspensions, brakes, and radiators, the Sport Satellite could be had with a respectable 330 horsepower version of the 383, an engine that, until Chrysler spiced it up for the Road Runner, was considered a very capable performer, powering the vast majority of Plymouth Satellites and Dodge Coronets that had challenged GTOs in the early battles of muscle car wars. The Sport Satellite is almost criminally underrated by posterity, and was a much more potent vehicle than history remembers it being, living as it did in the shadows of the Road Runner and GTX.

Naturally, the folks at Dodge began to scream for their own stripped down super car. What they got was the Super Bee, Dodge's version of the stripped down Road Runner and another late '60s Mopar destined to automotive greatness. The Super Bee (as in "super B-body") was a product of the Coronet line, and while it rode on a 117-inch wheelbase an inch longer, it copied the Road Runner in just about every other aspect, right down to the silly graphics. Dodge preferred to save cost and to design its goofy graphic in house, and a hard charging, helmeted bumble bee was the result.

As with the Road Runner, the Super Bee was initially available only as a pillared coupe, though a hardtop was offered later in the model year. The Super Bee featured a blacked-out flush grille incorporating quad headlamps and with "DODGE" spelled out across it, all of which sat under a power bulge hood. It had the same molded quarter panels of the Coronet line, in place of the fender and quarter panel crease of its Plymouth counterpart. The taillights were teardrop-shaped, turned on their sides and set wide across the tail panel also adorned with "DODGE." Optional was a twin set of "bumble bee" stripes that wrapped around the tail and incorporated the gear grinding bumble bee emblem.

As with the Road Runner, the warmed up 383 was standard, with the 426 Hemi as the only option. The standard transmission was the heavy-duty A-833 with the 3-speed TorqueFlite automatic an option. Dodge figured out much earlier than Plymouth that the standard Inland shifter on manual equipped cars was trash and wisely switched to something made by George Hurst midway through the model year. Heavy-duty rear ends in a multitude of gear ratios were available, with or without positive traction. Standard braking was a manual drum system at all corners, with power assist available; front discs were available as well. Heavy-duty suspension was standard.

The Super Bee was a Dodge, and not a cheap Plymouth, so it got the same rally instrumentation as the Coronet R/T and full vinyl interior trim, though bench seating was standard. It also came with carpet. Bucket seating, power steering and a console were popular options, and the Super Bee could be outfitted to near Coronet 500 trim levels with the addition of light packages, power windows and locks, air conditioning and AM/FM radio.

The Dodge was a little bigger, a little heavier, a little more expensive, and sported different body accents, but it was essentially the same car as the Road Runner. The Super Bee was released later in the year, in response to the popularity of the Plymouth, so it had some ground to make up on its cousin. Consequently, Dodge sold only 7,844 Super Bees in 1968.

**1968 Dodge Super Bee coupe, owned by Jim Sams of Sapulpa, OK (courtesy Barbara Sams).**

The release of the Road Runner/Super Bee one-two punch from Mopar redefined the rules of engagement, so to speak, of the muscle car wars. There had been budget muscle cars before, but these two cars were different in that their performance hearts were wrapped in exterior buffoonery of cartoon images and gimmicky horns. There were both serious and decidedly unserious at the same time—much like the late 1960s themselves. The Road Runner and Super Bee marked the beginning of an upward spiral of audaciousness and buck wildness in terms of marketing, graphics and performance. The 1968 Road Runner and Super Bee were the first arrivals at the wild party that would be the coming years of the muscle car era. After 1968, Chrysler made sure whimsical was in style.

Once again for 1968, Dodge offered the Coronet R/T as its counterpart to the GTX. As in 1967, the GTX and the Coronet R/T were essentially fraternal twins. The Dodge rode on a wheelbase an inch longer at 117 inches, and like the GTX was only available in hardtop and convertible form. As the top of the Coronet line in terms of performance and luxury, the Coronet R/T differed little externally from the Super Bee. It even shared the same "bumble bee" stripe—still called a "bumble bee" stripe, though there wasn't anything bee-like about the Coronet R/T.

As in 1967, the 375 horse 440-cube engine was standard, mated to a TorqueFlite 3-speed automatic transmission. The bulletproof A-833 4-speed was optional, as was the mighty 426 Hemi. All the heavy-duty gear that accompanied the performance B-bodies was found on the Coronet R/T as well—heavy-duty manual drum brakes,

Dodge's gear-grinding bumble bee adoring the tails of Super Bees equipped with the optional "bumble bee" stripe was created in-house, saving Dodge the outlay Plymouth paid to Warner Brothers for the use of the Road Runner (courtesy Gateway Classic Cars, St. Louis, MO).

heavy-duty suspensions and rear ends, etc. Power and/or disc brakes were optional, as were positive traction rear Sure-Grip" rear ends in a variety of gear ratios.

The Coronet R/T, as an upscale alternative to the Super Bee, came standard with bucket seating, faux wood grained interior surfaces, rally gauging, and a console. Like the 4-speed tranny, a bench seat was available, if for some reason someone wanted one, as a "no cost" option. Luxury options such as air conditioning and power steering were much more common in the Coronet R/T, given its status as a "gentleman's" muscle car.

The Coronet R/T was positioned to directly compete with the upscale offerings from GM and Ford, such as the Olds 4-4-2, Buick's GS and Mercury's Cyclone, as well as its GTX kin. As a Chrysler product, it was ill positioned to do so. In the 1960s, and chronically over a longer period, Chrysler products were seen as inherently inferior. Consequently, sales of the remade Coronet R/T were a somewhat disappointing 10,849 units.

Part of the cause of what was ailing the sales of the Coronet R/T could easily be found by taking a look across the lot at any Dodge dealership, because in addition to the Super Bee, the big news in Dodge camp was the completely redesigned Charger and its muscle variant, the Charger R/T.

The 1968 Dodge Charger is quite simply one of the most eye-pleasing cars ever

**1968 Dodge Coronet R/T (courtesy Streetside Classics, Charlotte, NC).**

designed by the American automotive industry. The car is a beautiful creation, rivaling even the 1965 GTO in terms of aesthetic beauty. A famed antagonist's role in the 1968 classic Steve McQueen film "Bullitt" illustrated, however, that the car possessed a darkly sinister look as well. Very few cars can capture the design schizophrenia of both refined elegance and raw brutality better than the 1968 Dodge Charger.

A radical departure from the failed Coronet based fastback effort of the 1966–67 Chargers, the 1968 model featured a gaping maw of a grille, unbroken by any molding, that stretched across the entire front of the vehicle, hiding the headlights, and was reminiscent of the huge air intakes on jet aircraft. The car featured molded hood and doors with recessed areas, belying its Coronet heritage, and the flared quarter panels on all 1968 B-bodies provided a powerful, aggressive stance. Wedged between the quarters was a semi-fastback flying buttress roofline with sunken back glass mimicking the 1966–67 GM A-bodies. Complementing the jet intake grille were two pair or round taillights on each side of the tail panel that resembled the exhaust cones of the Atlas rockets powering the then climaxing Apollo space program.

The '68 Charger gained in beautiful brutality over its previous incarnations. In R/T form, it also gained weight. Where the Road Runner and Super Bee strived to save weight, the Charger fully embraced its voluptuousness. Dodge still saw the Charger as a "personal luxury" vehicle, and built it to rival the Ford Thunderbird, Pontiac Grand Prix and the like, though the Charger was built on a smaller 117-inch B-body wheelbase.

Heavy bucket seating was standard, as was a console. The dash was equipped with high-end gauging, including an optional tachometer. Air conditioning was optional, as were power windows and door locks. These options were common; few shopping for stripper cars bought Chargers when Road Runners and Super Bees were available.

As the top of the Charger line, the Charger R/T came with a full complement of standard interior comforts. While lesser engines would be had in lower scale Chargers, the muscular R/T variant came standard with the 375 horse, 440 Magnum engine. The 426 Hemi was the only option for the R/T. Typical Mopar fare was offered as transmission choices in the R/T: 3-speed TorqueFlite automatic or a "no cost," heavy-duty 4-speed manual. A range of rear ends, with or without limited slip, were available. The big Dodge was brought to a stop by manual drum brakes at all four corners, though power assist and disc braking were available, as was power steering.

As a result of all of this comfy goodness, a base '68 Charger R/T tipped the scales at just under 3,600 pounds, making it among the heaviest of the intermediate muscle cars. In fact, the Charger R/T was nearly equal in weight to a full-sized Chevy Impala of the same model year.

As with the entire Mopar B-body line for 1968, the public seemed thrilled with the '68 Charger, and it was the first of a series of Chargers with a design and performance that have withstood the test of time. With the 1968 incarnation of the Charger, Dodge saved the car from destruction following the disaster of the 1967 model. Sales of the new and improved Charger eclipsed 96,000—a 600 percent increase over 1967—including 17,582 R/Ts.

Slipping under the radar and decidedly overshadowed by the new Mopar offerings of 1968 were some unheralded but capable offerings from Chrysler. They are the non–R/T version of the Dodge Charger, Plymouth Satellite and Sport Satellite, and the Dodge Coronet 440 and Coronet 500 (the "440" and "500" were the unhelpful designations Dodge gave to trim levels, not to engine displacements, which has caused decades of confusion). These cars were not recognized as true muscle cars in their day and were not marketed as such. They did, however, hail from the same lineage as the supercars Chrysler was building—the Satellites from the same mid-size Belvedere line as the Road Runner and GTX, and the Coronets from that of the Super Bee and Coronet R/T. These cars lacked the performance features found on their muscle car brethren, such as bumble bee stripes, performance hoods, heavy-duty suspensions or performance rear ends, but they could be had with a surprisingly strong 330 horsepower 383 cubic inch engine. While it was not the heated up 383 that was found in the Road Runner or Super Bee, it was essentially the same engine that had powered earlier Belvederes, Satellites, Coronets and Chargers that had capably fought base model muscle intermediates from Ford and GM. If one couldn't afford a true muscle car but wanted a weekend cruiser that wouldn't embarrass itself, one could do a lot worse than one of these cars. And today, while the prices of true muscle cars are soaring, someone wanting to break into the hobby can get into a Sport Satellite or 383 Charger for a fraction of the cost of a Road Runner or Charger R/T.

By 1968, Mother Mopar had fully deployed all of its forces in the muscle car wars. The introduction of the Road Runner and Super Bee completed the order of battle for Chrysler for the remainder of the muscle car era as the last intermediate muscle car models it offered. The lightweight 383-powered Road Runners and Super Bees provided the mass of Chrysler's street soldiers, but always patrolling the darkened

The grille of the 1968 Dodge Charger R/T, hiding the standard 375 horse 440 or optional 426 Hemi behind it (courtesy Vanguard Motor Sales, Plymouth, MI).

boulevards were the battlecruisers—the 440- and Hemi-powered Dodges and Plymouths that represented the heaviest of Chrysler's firepower. In 1968, few things were scarier for the unwary GTO, Gran Sport or 4-4-2 pilot than stumbling across a lurking Hemi Road Runner or dreadnaught Charger R/T.

\* \* \*

General Motors, unaware of the emerging danger posed by the new or redesigned intermediate offerings from Chrysler, came into the 1968 model year on a hopeful note. In 1967 sales were down across the entire performance intermediate A-body line, but this drop in sales was correctly attributed to the expanding options from which people could choose. Back in 1966, for example, the only real options for a factory built muscle car package were the GTO and the SS Chevelle. The 4-4-2 and GS were built in smaller numbers; Ford was putting most of its effort into the Mustang and gave only passing concern to its Fairlane, and Chrysler's angular and awkward bodies could be outfitted as bona fide muscle cars, but they had to be specifically built that way. By 1967, GM's divisions were competing not only with one another, but also with the revamped intermediates Ford introduced a year earlier as well as the Coronet R/T and GTX from Chrysler. Some buyers who might have purchased a midsized performance GM opted to buy one of the ever-expanding options in the pony car market.

The fight for market share would get even more intense in 1968. In 1966, performance car buyers had the option of the GTO, SS Chevelle, Fairlane and Mustang, with the 4-4-2, Dodge Charger and Gran Sport taking a limited part of the market. By 1968, buyers could choose from Pontiac's GTO or Firebird, Chevy's SS Chevelle or Camaro, the Olds 4-4-2, Buick's Gran Sport, the new Ford Torino or Mercury Cyclone, the Mustang or Mercury Cougar, Dodge's Charger, Coronet R/T or Super Bee, or Plymouth's Road Runner, GTX, or Barracuda. Additionally, American Motors entered the fray, and this doesn't even consider the Corvette. Sales were bound to be down.

Despite this, GM entered the 1968 model year with optimism that wasn't unfounded. Sales in 1967 were still strong, and following the pattern of redesigning the A-body every two years, the entire GM line was restyled in 1968. Gone were the long, slab sides and pinched-behind-the-door Coke-bottle design of the 1966–1967 models. Instead, the GM intermediates were treated to a radical revamping, in which the wheelbase was shortened by 3 inches to 112 inches and the lines were more rounded, more curvaceous and flowing. The old pillared coupe was retired, and instead the new A-body performance offerings could only be had in a hardtop or convertible. The new semi-fastback design was more aerodynamic in appearance and simply looked powerful. The 1968 restyle represents a point of departure for the GM A-bodies, and serves to divide the era of the "early" GM muscle cars from the "late" models. While the classy and refined 1966–1967 styles have proven themselves to have lasting popularity, they retained undertones of the early 1960s full-sized GMs. There are legions of fans of each era, but there isn't a lot of overlap. The 1968 GM redesign oozed masculinity and power and proved to be an immediate hit that has transcended the decades since.

Chevrolet, which had reclaimed its rightful place as GM's performance division in 1966 with the SS 396 Chevelle and its popular 1967 Camaro, counted once again on the Malibu line and its SS Chevelle as its flagship intermediate performer. The 1968 SS became a stand-alone model in the Malibu line and was no longer an option on the Chevelle. The grille housed two sets of twin horizontal headlamps and wrapped around and into the fender, reminiscent of the 1966 front end. The SS Chevelle featured a hood with subtle twin domes that ran from midway down the hood back toward the windshield, capped with chrome molding. The tail panel was simple—just a black panel above the bumper with simple rectangular taillights that wrapped around into the quarter panel to double as the mandated-for-'68 side marker lights.

The twin domes of the hood concealed one of three of Chevy's now-famous 396 cubic inch engines: the 325 horse L35 base engine, the 350 horse L34 and a pair of awesome 375 horse versions, the L78 and L79. The differences between the L78 and L79 were found in the heads and valve structure. All SS 396 engines came with chrome valve covers, and the two higher horsepower engines also had chrome, open element air cleaners. The 325 horse engine and all engines mated to the 3-speed Turbo-Hydromatic automatic transmission also received a black snorkel type air cleaner. In addition to the automatic, the standard 3-speed manual transmission could be upgraded to one of two heavy-duty 4-speed manual transmissions, depending on engine choice. Suspensions were of the heavy-duty variety. As was standard

**1968 Chevrolet SS 396 Chevelle (courtesy Gateway Classic Cars, St. Louis, MO).**

across the industry, braking was manual drums all around, with power and front discs optional. Disc brake equipped cars received power assist automatically. Limited slip rear ends in a variety of gear ratios were also available.

Bench seating was standard, though buckets and a console were available as options. Other options included air conditioning, tach, and power windows and locks. Cruise control was also optional, as were several radios as upgrade over the basic AM set that was standard. Tilt steering column and sport steering wheel were also optional.

The buying public was kind to the Chevelle line, as it was to Chevrolet in general, as sales across the board were up over 1967. Chevy sold 417,844 versions of the Chevelle line of all body styles. Of these, 57,595 SS Chevelles were sold, including 2,286 convertibles. While this was a bit off the pace from 1967, those were strong numbers, given the wild increase in competition for market share that emerged in 1968.

Pontiac's GTO for 1968 offered the same basic styling changes as the rest of GM's A-body line, but John DeLorean was still with Pontiac, now elevated to division head, and he was loath to have his GTO appear to simply be a clone of the Chevrolet, or anything else for that matter. Consequently, the GTO sported important differences to set it apart from the rest of the A-body line.

First was the introduction of a bumper made of rubberized plastic, called "Endura," rather than a classic steel, chrome plated bumper. Pontiac stressed the toughness and energy absorption qualities of the Endura bumper, and to drive the point home, a commercial was developed in which a guy beat the hell out of the front end of a GTO with a metal rod, to seemingly no ill effect. The revolutionary bumper set the GTO apart from its GM intermediate cousins, though early in the model year

**The 1968 Pontiac GTO (courtesy Vanguard Motor Sales, Plymouth, MI).**

there were production and fit problems with the Endura, so traditional chrome was available and is occasionally seen on a GTO; such GTOs are commonly accused of being clones, as the Endura bumper was exclusive to the GTO and all other cars of the LeMans line received chrome. Secondly, the GTO offered optional vacuum operated "hide-a-way" headlamp doors that turned downward when the headlamps were activated and hid the headlamps in Pontiac's ubiquitous split grille. The tail lamps, while reworked with the rest of the car, bore a resemblance to the 1967 lamps. The long, molded hood incorporated two subtle non-functional hood scoops in the middle and could again be had with a tach. The 1968 GTO would still wear the GTO 6.5 liter crest, though that venerable icon would be retired after the model year. The lack of brightwork up front and the hide-away headlamps certainly set the GTO apart from the rest of the A-body crowd, just as DeLorean wanted it.

The GTO was equipped with a base 400 engine, slightly reworked from 1967 and producing a rated 350 horsepower—more than the base SS Chevelle. Up from that were two options, each reaching a rated 360 horsepower. The first was the H.O. 400, and the second was the Ram Air 400, which featured functional hood scoops and a foam seal from the hood to allow the carbs to suck cold air through the hood. Each of these horsepower ratings, particularly for the Ram Air 400, was looked at with some skepticism. A final engine offered late in the model year was the Ram Air II, which had reworked internals to produce a rated 366 horsepower. Pontiac may have believed rating it with an odd 366 horsepower rating would appear more honest than a standard rating in some multiple of 5, but everyone saw right through that. The Ram Air II engine is a legendary Pontiac engine, and the 366 horse rating fooled no

**Early production 1968 GTOs had the chrome bumper from the LeMans due to production difficulties with the Endura bumper (courtesy Gateway Classic Cars, St. Louis, MO).**

one. For some reason, Pontiac saw fit to again offer the two-barrel 400 version of the GTO, with a rated horsepower of 265.

Transmission choices included a standard 3-speed manual or one of two optional heavy-duty 4-speeds. People who didn't feel like shifting themselves could opt for the Turbo-Hydramatic 3-speed automatic transmission. Two-barrel GTO owners had to live with only the automatic.

Bucket seating in full vinyl was standard in the GTO, as it always had been, though a bench could be substituted for no cost. AM radio came standard as well, as did a padded dash pad and carpet. Popular interior options included power steering, air conditioning and tilt steering column. The instrument cluster was revised for '68, featuring a three pod arrangement. Rally gauges were optional and included a choice of dash or hood mounted tachometer. Power windows, locks and radio upgrades were available as well.

The motor press was duly impressed with the 1968 GTO, to such an extent that it was named by *Motor Trend* magazine as its car of the year. The car was popular in the real world with the purchasing public as well. Sales were strong, up from 1967 on the strength of the new restyle and the GTO's already legendary status. Though they could not match the level of the 1966 model—no performance intermediate ever reached that level again—DeLorean and Pontiac had to have been pleased to have beaten the SS Chevelle in sales, with over 87,684 units sold.

With the A-body redesign, many consider the 1968 4-4-2 to be the most attractive car to ever wear the nameplate. This is arguable, as Oldsmobile simply didn't

1968 Olds 4-4-2 (courtesy Gateway Classic Cars).

build an unattractive vehicle in the muscle car era. Oldsmobile finally made the 4-4-2 its own line, rather than an option on the Cutlass; Pontiac blessed the GTO with the same dispensation in 1966. Due to the GM-wide A-body restyle, the 4-4-2 got the same basic design as its corporate siblings, but with enough creative license given to the Olds designers to set the car apart. The front end featured a relatively small grille flanked by two sets of dual headlamps set horizontally, each pair separated by a driving light. The hood featured a subtle bulge adored with chrome ribbed faux hood scoops. Subtle 4-4-2 badging adorned the grille, fenders and deck lid; the old tricolor emblem of 1964–1967 was retired in favor of block numbers.

The base 4-4-2 was equipped with a 400 cubic inch engine rated at 350 horsepower with a 3-speed manual transmission topped with a shifter made by Hurst. Olds' heavy-duty suspension that had always made the 4-4-2 among the best handling of muscle cars was standard as well, with front and rear sway bars. Upgrading to an optional 4-speed, still with Hurst shifter, netted an identical 350 horses, but the optional 3-speed automatic transmission lowered the rating to 325. Opting for the W-30 package provided cold air induction through intakes hidden neatly under the bumper, so the hood still had Oldsmobile style, without gaudy hood scoops. The W-30 package also came with low rear end ratio, 4-speed manual transmission or 3-speed automatic and special striping.

Oldsmobile offered another performance engine option for the 1968 F-85/Cutlass line, the W-31 "Ram Rod 350." The Ram Rod was Oldsmobile's answer to Buick's GS 350 "junior" muscle car and was powered by a 350 cubic inch engine producing a very respectable 325 horses mated to a mandatory manual transmission and

**Oldsmobile's 1968 W-31 "Ram Rod" Cutlass (courtesy Vanguard Motor Sales, Plymouth, MI).**

manual brakes. It came with special "Ram Rod 350" identification on the air cleaner and fenders and breathed through the same cold air induction setup as the W-30.

Once the powertrain options were figured out, Olds buyers, as they were wont to do, could begin piling on options. Bucket seating in full vinyl was standard, though philistine Olds buyers could have a bench. From there, the common list of creature comforts available on most cars could be added on—power steering and brakes, power windows and doors, air conditioning, radio upgrades, etc.

In 1968 Oldsmobile began a long relationship with George Hurst of Hurst shifter fame to build the first of the Hurst/Olds line. Though GM mandated that horsepower in intermediate cars be limited to no more than one horsepower per 10 pounds of car, Hurst/Olds or "H/O" cars had as their heart a 390 horse 455 cubic inch Oldsmobile engine. The GM mandate was circumvented, perhaps with a wink and a nod, because the 4-4-2s on which the H/O cars were based were actually born with the standard 400 cubic inch block. These were swapped out at Hurst for the 455s; as far as Olds was concerned, they had 400s when they left the factory and Olds could not be held accountable for what happened to them after that. The H/O cars were equipped with a heavy-duty 4-speed and Hurst shifter. Optional was the 3-speed automatic, with gears selected by a Hurst dual gate "His and Hers" shifter. The H/O was only available in Peruvian silver with black stripes and white pinstripes and featured special Hurst badging, bucket seats, disc brakes and heavy-duty cooling system.

Compared to the GTO and SS Chevelle, sales of the attractive 4-4-2 were sluggish. However, the more than 33,500 4-4-2s, combined with the Hurst cars,

**1968 Hurst/Olds (courtesy Steven Anastos of Red Hills Rods and Classics, St. George, UT).**

represented a substantial increase over the 24,883 units sold in 1967, a testament to the popularity of the A-body restyle. Olds sold an additional 742 W-31 "Ram Rod" cars in 1969.

In 1968, Buick asked America if it wouldn't really rather have a Buick. Compared to 1967, a few more people actually did, at least with respect to Buick's 1968 GS offerings.

Buick's A-body muscle cars came in two varieties again in 1968. The first was the GS 350, which in previous years was the GS 340, but with a new, higher displacement 350 cubic inch engine; the second was the GS 400. The Skylark line, which included the GS, differed from the rest of GM's A-body stable in that the Buick featured a sweeping, curved crease in the sheet metal that began at the front of the fender and arced down to the rocker panel just forward of the rear wheel well. The hood had a recessed section running the length of its center and trimmed in stainless steel molding that culminated in an understated scoop at the leading edge of the cowl. This recess was matched on the deck lid, ending at the bumper, with "BUICK" spelled out on the lower edge of the deck lid. Like its corporate cousins, the GS line, which finally did become its own line in 1967, did not include a pillared coupe, and while the GS 400 could be had in either convertible or hardtop, the GS 350 only came as a hardtop. The 350 powered GS California was offered again in the Golden State and was the only GS available as a post coupe. The wheel wells were surrounded by bright moldings. In the rear, the quarter panels were formed as to give the wheel wells a very Buick like skirted look unusual in a muscle car.

In 1968, the GS cars were intentionally designed to look more like Buick's big cars, and sales increased that year across the Buick line, which says a lot about what buyers of Buick muscle cars were looking for.

The sedate 350 cubic inch engine, backed by an automatic transmission, produced 280 horsepower, which wasn't a lot of horsepower to push around a lot of Buick. Buick buyers were still Buick buyers, and most GS 350 cars were laden with

**Fender emblem of Oldsmobile's Ram Rod (courtesy Vanguard Motor Sales, Plymouth, MI).**

heavy and/or power sapping options; take the "GS" badging from the car and what was left was only marginally more muscular than a Skylark. The GS 400, however, produced a very respectable 340 horsepower. A 3-speed manual transmission was standard, but the majority of Buick GS cars came with a 4-speed manual or a 3-speed Super Turbine automatic, which is the same automatic tranny available in every other GM A-body, just called something more Buick-like. Positive traction rear ends were available, though true performance rear gearing wasn't available with the optional-but-frequently-chosen air conditioning. Drum brakes, with lightweight aluminum drums up front, were the standard braking system, though power assist was available, and was usually opted for. Front disc brakes were also available.

On the inside, it was all Buick extravagance: Bucket seating wrapped in full vinyl, wood grained dash, console, air conditioning, power windows and doors all were available. These options were common on GS cars. Bench seating was available if the buyer preferred it.

The GS 400, still riding on its boxed frame, gained quite a bit of weight for 1968, and it was never a lightweight to begin. The GS 400 wasn't in the same class as the Ram Air GTOs or the hottest 396 Chevys, but it could respectably go up against just about any of the base level muscle cars of 1968.

Buick performance didn't end with the GS 400, however, and the inclusion of a new dealer installed engine option made the GS a dangerous car to deal with, even for the hottest or cars of 1968. This engine package, offered by the most unlikely of car makers, was destined to be a legend of the muscle car era, and was called the Stage 1. The "Stage 1" name may not mean a lot today, but it did in 1968. Stage 1 referred

1968 Buick GS 400 (courtesy Gateway Classic Cars, St. Louis, MO).

**Buick's GS Stage 1 badging, named for the multi-stage liftoff of the Saturn rockets propelling the Space Race in the late 1960s (courtesy Streetside Classics, Charlotte, NC).**

the first stage of the fiery, spectacular launches of the multi-stage Atlas rockets used by the Apollo program that literally everyone knew about.

The Stage 1 featured a hotter camshaft, cold air induction, and 11:1 compression ratio. The package also included a modified four-barrel carb, heavy-duty suspension and power disc brakes. The 1968 Stage 1 was rare, but it reportedly knocked a full second off the heavy Buick's quarter mile elapsed time and added 5 MPH of speed, making it a bona fide performer capable of taking on anything on the street. Even the most vicious W-30, Hemi or SS car attempting to prey upon what appeared to be a sedate, run of the mill GS 400 would have been shocked when the Stage 1 turned the predator into prey.

Buick sold over 26,343 Gran Sports in 1968. This number includes 4,831 California GS cars, 8,317 GS 350s and 13,197 GS 400s. This marked a substantial increase over 1967's 17,505 units. The impressive 8,000 plus GS 350 cars is interesting in that it revealed an emerging market for the smaller displacement "junior" muscle cars, which were easier to keep off the radar of the insurance companies and their ever-rising rates for large engine displacement performance cars. Buick's strong GS sales, like those of Oldsmobile, offered evidence that Buick's patrician place on the affluence scale protected it from the sales blight Chrysler's cheap cars inflicted on the lower end of GM's divisions.

\* \* \*

The dramatic changes 1968 brought to GM and Chrysler, with the revamping of both car makers' intermediate car lines and with the additions to the Mopar lineup, were mirrored in Dearborn. Ford belatedly began to rouse itself from its sluggish, "everyone-else-is-doing-it-so-I-guess-we-should-too" approach to building intermediate performance cars. Through 1967, Ford never seemed to give the attention to the mid-sized muscle car market and instead focused on dominating the pony car market. Fairlanes and Cyclones equipped with 390 cubic inch power plants valiantly took on the phalanxes of GM's offerings, but the Ford products never quite captured the mystique of the GTO, SS, 4-4-2 or even the GS cars. By 1968, Lee Iacocca had decided it was time for a change.

That change came in the form of a total cosmetic restyle of Ford's intermediate line. The Fairlane was retired as Ford's performance mid-size option, and in its place was "Ford's newest bright idea," the all-new Torino. In reality, the Torino was still a part of the faithful old Fairlane line, representing its performance model and based on the upscale Fairlane 500. It was also Ford's tacit recognition that the "Fairlane" badge was equal to skinny dipping with old people on the excitement scale; "Torino" was thought to be more exciting. Ford trotted out no fewer than 14 different Fairlane based intermediates in 1968, with all two door models sharing a 116-inch wheelbase. The Torino could be had in convertible or hardtop, and the Torino GT had a fastback form dubbed "sportsroof" as an additional body style option. While built on the same wheelbase as years prior, the Torino was a larger car than the previous years' Fairlane GT/GTAs, with four inches of additional length.

Performance began with the Torino GT. The Torino trim level netted special emblems and moldings to set it apart from the Fairlane 500, and the GT got special wheel covers calling out "GT," GT exterior trim and lights in the door panels. The GT came standard with a two-barrel 302 engine producing 210 horsepower, but labor difficulties forced Ford to go with a two-barrel 289 engine later in the model year. Regardless, either could be optioned away in favor of the heroic old 390, trotted out for another go-around. The 390 could be had with either a two- or four-barrel carb; obviously the four-barrel was the muscle car, and it produced 325 horsepower with dual exhaust. Transmission choices included a standard 3-speed manual, which could be upgraded to the "Toploader" 4-speed manual or 3-speed "Cruise-O-Matic" automatic. Rear ends were available in many different gear ratios, and limited slip "Traction-Lok" rear ends were optional. Manual drum brakes were standard, though power assist and front discs were optional.

The GT Torinos were intended to come standard with bucket seats, but again, a labor strike at the factory put the kibosh on that; buckets could be had, but a bench was standard. Special badging and a redesigned, sportier instrument panel were featured in the GT. Console, power steering, power windows and locks and air conditioning were options, though the availability of air conditioning was dependent on the engine choice.

All this luxurious goodness pushed the Ford to a curb weight of over 3,200 pounds. Road tests from the time record a fastback GT with a 390 four-barrel and automatic transmission having run the quarter at 15.8 seconds at 90 miles per hour. A W-30 Oldsmobile or Ram Air GTO, the 390 Torino was not.

This would begin to change, however, late in the model year with the introduction of one of Ford's legendary engines of the era, the 428 Cobra Jet, or "CJ." The Cobra Jet conjured images of Carroll Shelby and his fabled two-seat Cobra and caused immediate excitement among the Ford faithful. In truth, the 428 Cobra Jet saved Ford in terms of muscle car credibility. While the 390 Fairlanes of earlier years were attractive, competent cars, the 390 wasn't a true performer in the vein of the contemporary offerings from GM and Chrysler. The 428 CJ changed all of that, and provided Ford with a bona fide performance engine. The mid-year introduction of the Cobra Jet, or "CJ," not only provided the limited number of '68 cars so equipped with an engine capable of competing with anything on the street, but set the stage for later models to come in greater numbers.

Ford rated the CJ at a hilarious 335 horses, about the same base horsepower as the 383 offered in base Road Runners and Super Bees; Ford lied about this, and Ford lied magnificently. True horsepower for the 428 CJ, sucking in oxygen through cold air induction, was estimated to be closer to 410 horsepower. *Car and Driver* road tested a CJ Torino with an automatic in 1968 and turned a 14.2 quarter time at 98.9 mph. Five more horses than the 390 indeed. While extremely rare due to its late introduction, the CJ's unknown-but-certainly-more-than-335 horsepower put the Torino squarely in the class of the hottest cars of the model year, and finally gave the Ford faithful something on par with the SS 396 from despised Chevrolet.

Ford's restyle of its intermediate line proved successful. The Blue Oval built more than 371,000 intermediates across all body styles; 103,384 of them were Torino GTs. Due to the general state of confusion as to what engine was available when, thanks to the auto workers union, there do not seem to be any hard production numbers, but it is safe to assume that the majority of those 100,000 GTs were of the small block 289/302 variety.

Mercury, of course, had its own sister ship to the Torino GT, the more upscale Mercury Cyclone GT. The Cyclone name began life as Mercury's answer to the Ford Falcon in the mid-'60s, and then became Mercury's Fairlane GT/A clone in 1966.

**Mercury's 1968 Cyclone (courtesy Gateway Classic Cars, St. Louis, MO).**

With the 1968 restyling of the Ford mid-sized line, the Cyclone evolved as well, separating itself from the Comet and becoming its own model in the Mercury mid-sized lineup. For 1968, the Cyclone was only available in coupe and fastback form; there was no convertible.

As in the past for the unhappy Mercury intermediate performance models, the Cyclone GT was essentially a glorified Torino, offering the same body styles and engine and transmission options. The Cyclone got a 302 standard, while the Cyclone GT got the 390, intimidatingly called the "Marauder" engine by Mercury, and, like the Torino, the Cyclone GT received the 428 Cobra Jet option mid-year. The Mercury being a Mercury, the Cyclone GT offered more plush accouterments such as bucket seats wrapped entirely in upscale Comfort-Weave vinyl, special wheel covers and body striping, and a special heavy-duty handling package.

The Cyclone GT got some positive exposure, as a 428 CJ powered Cyclone running at Daytona was named the fastest car of the year, setting a new speed record at 189.22 MPH. Turning that exposure to sales on the theory of "win on Sunday, sell on Monday" exposed good news and bad news for the 1968 incarnation of the Cyclone GT. The good news was that twice as many people in 1968 opted to purchase a Cyclone GT as did in 1967. The bad news was that 1967 sales were awful, and awful multiplied by two is still awful. Mercury sold just over 6,400 of the restyled GT Cyclones in 1968, making a 1968 428 Cyclone GT one of the rarest of all muscle cars.

\* \* \*

For the intermediate performance car market, 1968 was a revolutionary year. All three of the major car builders reworked their intermediate car lines, and Chrysler and Ford released new models. It was the unleashing of the budget Road Runner and Super Bee that would cause the most apprehension in the board rooms of GM

**Ford's 428 badging on Torino. Mercury's Cyclone carried a similar warning (courtesy Gateway Classic Cars, St. Louis, MO).**

and Ford. The Torino, GTO and the SS Chevelle, with lower base price points, were more affected by the release of the cheap offerings from Chrysler than were the Olds 4-4-2, Buick GS and Mercury Cyclone. Those who might have been attracted to a base SS Chevy or Torino GT would have been attracted to a Road Runner or Super Bee instead, while the class of buyer that would typically buy a 4-4-2 or Gran Sport was unlikely to have even noticed a Plymouth dealership, much less ever stopped to shop at one. The 4-4-2 and GS cars were therefore insulated somewhat by the introduction of the cheap B-body Chryslers. In fact, Buick, Mercury and Oldsmobile saw modest increases in the sales of their performance mid-sized models for 1969.

This left the car makers scrambling to answer the new threat to their market share posed by the cheap Mopars, and for 1969, the car buying public would benefit from the efforts to match Chrysler. In the long term, automotive history itself would be the benefactor.

* * *

Mirroring the rapidly expanding battle in the intermediate market was the warfare taking place in miniature among the pony cars. Last year had seen the first large cube engines installed in the Mustang and Barracuda, as well as the introduction of new pony car models from Chevrolet, Pontiac and Mercury, which all had large engine displacement options. By 1968, these smaller, lighter, and cheaper cars were blurring the lines between the pony car and the mid-size muscle cars. Indeed, by 1968, about all that separated them was wheelbase. The year also saw the introduction of two new small performance models, one of which was classified as a pony car meant to engage the Mustang and its ilk. The other, no one really knew how to classify.

The progenitor of the class was becoming decidedly more muscular by 1968, primarily due to the new engine options available. The car also grew slightly in weight, a trend that would continue through the end of the muscle car era and ending with the introduction of the Mustang II in 1974. As always, the Mustang was offered in hardtop, fastback, and convertible forms.

The GT option was still the top horse in the stable, and while a host of lesser engines were available in the Mustang, the GT started with a new 302 cubic inch mill that was bound for greatness in later years. The 302 topped with a four-barrel producing 235 horsepower replaced the venerable old 289 that had powered Mustangs since 1964. The Mustang gained true muscle car credibility with the 390 cubic inch Thunderbird Special, rated at 325 horsepower, which was essentially the same engine as was offered in 1967. Up from that was the same 428 Cobra Jet that was found in the new Torino, carrying the same ludicrously understated 335 horsepower rating. Rumor had it (as did Ford's promotional publications) that the mighty 390 horse 427 cubic inch engine was also available, though it is generally accepted that a 427 equipped Mustang was never built in 1968. The 302 came standard with a 3-speed manual transmission, while the 390 was standard with the heavy-duty "Toploader" 4-speed manual. Three-speed automatic options were also available. Positive traction rear ends were available in a variety of gearing. Standard brakes for the GT were manual drum brakes all around, though the 390 and 428, and presumably the 427, required front discs. Power assist was available as well.

A Mustang with the GT package was as aggressive on the outside as it was under the hood. The GT package provided for fog lamps set in the grille, special GT badging and striping. It also featured a "flip-open, quick action" gas cap with "GT" emblazoned on its surface. The GT package also featured special wheels and a heavy-duty suspension and mandatory dual exhaust. The usual Mustang interior options were available, such as consoles, power steering, air conditioning and the like, and the GT featured special GT badging on the interior.

Ford's Mustang continued to dominate the market named for it, selling an unfathomable 317,404 units of all engine displacements. The 390 option for 1967 was a step in the right direction for the Mustang, but the 390, even in a Mustang, was not in the same class as the intermediate offerings from GM and Chrysler and certainly could not withstand a 396 or Ram Air powered Camaro or Firebird. The inclusion of the 428 Cobra Jet in the Mustang allowed Ford's pony to compete with anything on the street.

After the surprising 1967 success of the Cougar, Mercury's upscale pony car, the Cat returned with little to differentiate the 1968 Cougar from the previous year, aside from the addition of the government mandated side marker lights and minor changes in trim. From the outside, the 1968 Cougar was essentially the same attractive car it had been in 1967. The electric shaver grille and sequential tail lamps were

**1968 Mustang GT (courtesy Gateway Classic Cars, St. Louis, MO).**

carried over from 1967, and styling wise, the Merc was arguably more attractive than the Mustang.

The Cougar featured the same V-8 engine updates over the previous year as were found in the Mustang. In fact, the engines Mercury was offering were more exciting even than those offered in its Ford cousin. This is because, just as in 1967, no six-cylinder was offered in the Cougar, keeping in line with its classier-than-a-common-Mustang persona. Base engine was the same 302, but performance came again in the Cougar GT, powered by the same Marauder 390 four-barrel engine as in 1967, producing 320 horsepower. Beyond the 390-powered GT were two more performance options for Cougar buyers wanting even more. Those were the GT-E and the XR7-G.

If the Plymouth Road Runner represented the bottom end of the 1968 performance car price ladder, the Cougar GT-E was the top. The Cougar's GT-E package itself cost half what a base Road Runner did. For that money, however, one got the top of the line in Ford performance. The heart of the GT-E package was Ford's fire breathing 427 cubic inch engine, wildly underrated at 390 horsepower, growling under a subtly scooped hood. Heavy-duty suspension was standard, as were power front disc brakes. Transmission options were limited to the standard 3-speed Merc-O-Matic automatic or no-cost option 4-speed manual. Special wheels and special identification badges completed the package. Late in the model year, the 427 was replaced with the same 335 horse 428 Cobra Jet that was available in the Ford cars.

The Cougar XR7-G was for those with more discriminating tastes. The XR7-G was a high-performance version of the Cougar's XR7 trim package and was named, like the Dan Gurney Special trim package offered in 1967 and again in 1968, for road racing legend and Mercury pilot Dan Gurney. Where the Dan Gurney Special was essentially a dress-up package, the XR7-G was something more, combining the luxury of the XR7 with substantially more performance.

The XR7-G, being based on the XR7, was available with the engines available on

**1968 Mercury Cougar (courtesy Fort Pitt Classic Cars, Sharpsburg, PA).**

that option, meaning that the base XR7-G engines were either a two- or four-barrel 302, producing 210 and 235 horsepower, respectively. There were few XR7-Gs built with these engines, however—231, to be relatively exact—as most XR7-G buyers preferred one of two 390s. The weaker of the two was a two-barrel version, exhaling through single exhaust and producing 280 horses. Only 62 of these were built. The second 390 option was far more popular, as it was where true performance began with the G cars. This 390 was identical to that found in its Mustang cousin, a four-barrel, dual exhaust power plant producing 320 horses. Just 310 XR7-G cars so equipped were built. Finally, while the potent 427 was reserved for the GT-E, the 428 Cobra Jet was available in the XR7-G. This was the same four-barrel, dual exhaust, cold air inducted 428 found in the hottest Fords, producing the same dishonest 335 horsepower. Only 14 of these were built. Transmission choices were typical Ford fare, dependent on engine selection: 3-speed manual as the base transmission for the low-end engines, with the C4 3-speed automatic as options. Heavier duty 4-speed "Toploader" manuals and C6 3-speed automatics were options on the higher performance engines. With the XR7-G cars being Mercs, manuals were seldom selected.

Based as it was on the XR7 trim package, the XR7-G was plush on the inside and aggressive on the outside. The hood featured chrome hood pins and a scooped hood, functional on 428 equipped cars. Race-inspired bullet-shaped mirrors and fog lamps completed the exterior, as did special C-pillar badging. Leather trimmed bucket seats were standard, as was full gauging to include a tach, oil pressure, and a trip odometer. A roof mounted console housed trendy toggle switches for fog lamps, and the steering wheel was vinyl wrapped.

**Ford's intimidating Cobra Jet shaker hood scoop (courtesy Gateway Classic Cars, St. Louis, MO).**

XR7-G owners like to call the cars "Mercury's Shelbys." This is a leap of imagination, as about all G cars share with the Shelbys is that they were built in the same plant. To be a Shelby car, Carroll Shelby's interaction with it is required, by definition, and the great Texan didn't have anything to do with the Cougar. That said, Mercury fans are very protective of the Cougar, and rightly so. Few and far between are the instances where the performance offerings from Mercury differentiate much from their Ford cousins. This is particularly true in the muscle car era; pot metal badging and nicer seat covers are about all the difference between a Cyclone and Fairlane. The Cougar, however, was different. With its unique front and rear ends, Euro-car styling, and exceptional trim packages, the Cougar was no higher priced Mustang. Mercury built 113,741 Cougars in 1968, and while these were not anywhere near Mustang numbers, they were very strong for Ford's bastard stepchild division. Of these, 2,800 were 390 equipped GTs, 357 were 427 powered GT-Es, and another 37 were late model year 428 E cars. Also included in this number are 619 XR7-Gs.

* * *

While Ford may have dominated the pony car class, it was taking body blows from GM's twin pony car offerings, the Camaro and the Firebird.

Following the tried and true pony car formula, Chevy offered a wide spectrum of Camaro offerings, in terms of options and trim and performance packages. Like

**1968 SS 396 Camaro (courtesy Vanguard Motor Sales, Plymouth, MI).**

the Mustang, it could be had in hardtop or convertible form and with a wide range of engine options, from a pair of six-cylinders up through four different 396 options.

True Camaro performance again began with the SS option. The SS package netted Chevy's 295 horse, four-barrel 350 cubic inch engine. Four 396 options were offered on the SS Camaro. First up was the 325 horse L35, followed by a new for '68 350 horse L34. Following that were a pair of 375 horse options: the awesome 375 horsepower L78 and the L89, featuring aluminum heads. All 396 offerings featured four-barrel carburation and dual exhaust and could be had with heavy-duty 4-speed transmissions or 3-speed Turbo-Hydromatic automatics, though 3-speed manuals were standard. They also featured heavy-duty suspension and drum brakes, with power and/or front discs as options. The SS package came with appropriate badging and striping, as well as a special hood featuring faux vents. The addition of the Rally Sport trim package made the ultimate SS Camaro for 1968 and added a blacked-out grille, gauging on the console, and other trim upgrades and badging.

The Z/28 package gained in popularity in 1968 on the strength of its successful 1967 Trans Am racing campaign which saw Z/28 cars win 10 of 13 races. The Z/28 was again powered by the small block 302 producing 290 horsepower, and it was a pure racer; heavy-duty suspension, disc brakes, and the lack of air conditioning or automatic transmission bespoke of its racing heritage.

Aside from the Z/28, the SS Camaro offered the typical options of the era: air conditioning, power steering, power brakes, power windows and locks, a variety of radios and the like. Chevrolet made sure Camaro buyers could customize their cars as extensively as they wished.

All told, 30,695 Camaros wore SS badging in 1968, most of which were one variety or another of the 396. While that number represented a drop from the Camaro's maiden model year of 1967, performance Camaro sales were still strong, and even Ford had to notice the more than 235,000 Camaros of all varieties sold in 1968.

Pontiac's analog to the Camaro, the Firebird, was also tasked with eating into Ford's Mustang sales. The '68 Firebird wasn't much changed from the Firebird's maiden model and was again offered in convertible and hardtop forms. Subtle differences were the deletion of vent windows and the addition of side marker lamps and wraparound parking lenses. The non-functional hood remained the same (unless Ram Air was optioned for), as were the front and rear ends.

Pontiac again offered the Firebird in five different versions, from basic six-cylinders up through the hot Firebird 400, and with additional 400 offerings—the 400 H.O. and the Ram Air 400. The base 400 was rated at 330 horsepower, 5 more than in 1967, indicating that the Firebird gained some weight in its sophomore year. The H.O. 400 was rated at 335 horses, using different heads and camshaft. Selecting the Ram Air option boosted this number to 335 horses, though that number is believed to be considerably underrated. The boost in power was attributed to the opening of the nostrils on the hood and using low restriction exhaust manifolds taken from the 428. The Ram Air 400 in the Firebird is exactly the same setup that produced 360 horses in the GTO, but Pontiac modified the throttle linkage on the four-barrel Quadrajet carb to retard the horsepower output—the GM power-to-weight mandate had to be given due deference, but this was an easy fix for the enterprising Firebird owner seeking the engine's full potential.

The higher performance Firebirds—the 400, H.O. 400 and the Ram Air 400—used a heavy-duty 3-speed manual transmission bought with two different Muncie manual transmissions as options. People who didn't want to put forth the effort to shift gears themselves could opt for Pontiac's 3-speed Turbo Hydra-Matic 400. As

**1968 Pontiac Firebird 400 (courtesy Gateway Classic Cars, St. Louis, MO).**

usual, rear end options came in a variety of gear ratios, and "Positrac" limited slip rear ends were optional. Brakes were manual drum brakes all around, but front discs and power were optional.

The interior was standard pony car fare: a nearly endless choice of options to allow the purchaser to customize his or her Firebird as was seen fit. Bucket seating in full vinyl was standard, and consoles, a variety of radio and speaker options, and light packages were optional. Power steering was optional as well, as were power windows, power door locks and air conditioning.

Compared to the Camaro, the Firebird was understated. It did not come adorned with striping or an equivalent to Chevy's big SS or RS badges. A simple "400" emblem on the hood scoops and the deck lid was as flamboyant as the Firebird got. Despite this, the Firebird proved a popular car again in 1968 and put a substantial dent in the Mustang's market to the tune of more than 107,000 units. Of these, 21,336 were Firebird 400s, including 523 Ram Air variants.

* * *

By 1968, the pony car class had become a swirling maelstrom of performance warfare, with the newer and rapidly improving offerings battling each other on the streets and strips across the nation. In the middle of it all, desperately trying to hold its ground and protect Chrysler's feeble foothold of market share, was again Plymouth's little stalwart, the Barracuda, now in the second year of its redesign. Despite Plymouth's best efforts—redesigns, improved engine offerings, and the abandonment of the giant back glass of the first generation Barracuda—the car just didn't catch fire in the market. To be sure, the first and second generation Barracuda had, and still has, its fans, but in 1968, the Plymouth faced the double-edged sword of the exciting new pony car offerings flooding the market as well as the misfortune of having been a product of the Chrysler Corporation. That Chrysler heritage, however, provided the little Plymouth with the Pentastar's bulletproof drivelines. In fairness, the Barracuda never really suffered from a serious performance deficit in its class; the 273 offered in earlier models could stand up to any of the small block Mustangs. The introduction of the 383 as an option on the Formula S Barracuda allowed it to easily compete with the 390 Mustangs and all but the very hottest Firebirds and SS Camaros. Despite all of this, people just didn't like Barracuda very well, and it was never in the same universe as the Ford in terms of sales. In 1967, the Cougar, Firebird and Camaro all blew past it as well.

The 1968 version of the Barracuda saw little change in the area of exterior design. The most significant changes were revisions to the grille and the government mandated side marker lights. Also new were an optional chrome fuel door and a redesigned rear end. Three body styles—notchback, fastback and convertible—were still offered on the Barracuda.

Plymouth spent a substantial amount of effort to revamp the Barracuda's performance image in order to keep pace with the GM and Ford ponies. Part of this was upgrading the Formula S option on the Barracuda, casting off the old 273 cubic inch base engine on the Formula car, and replacing it with a new 340 cubic inch, 275 horse small block that has proven to be one of Chrysler's best engines of the era. For those

**1968 Barracuda Formula S (courtesy Vanguard Motor Sales, Plymouth, MI).**

who couldn't live without a big block, and who could live with the woeful handling and stopping of the front-heavy cars, the 383 cubic inch engine was still available, a less potent version than that offered in the Road Runner and Super Bee, but still producing a very respectable 300 horsepower. Plymouth did it right in transmission choices as there were only two: the heavy-duty A-833 4-speed manual and the TorqueFlite 3-speed automatic. Several rear end gear ratios were available, depending on transmission choice, and limited slip was optional. Manual drum brakes were standard, with front discs optional, but due to the size of the 383 block, a power steering pump could not be wedged into the tiny engine compartment and was only available on 340 powered cars. The Formula S package also netted a heavy-duty suspension, sport stripes and special 340 or 383 callouts in the faux hood scoops.

For the truly adventurous, and perhaps those with no real reason to live, Plymouth offered a very small number of Barracudas equipped with the gigantic 426 Hemi. This car was strictly limited to professional drag racers, and, thankfully, was not generally available to the public. If the 383 was hard to handle in the tiny Barracuda, one can only imagine the terror involved in trying to pilot a Hemi powered car.

On the inside, bucket seats were standard only on the convertible; it was bench seating for the notchback and the fastback, though the rear seats did fold down in the fastback. A décor group was available that included bucket seating, revised basket weave rear seats, map pouches in the doors, rear ashtrays and wood graining on the door and quarter trim panel. The optional rally gauge cluster featured a 150 MPH speedometer, trip odometer and wood grained dash panel.

Try as it did, Plymouth just couldn't sell many 1968 Barracudas; the car just couldn't gain any traction in the highly competitive pony car market. Plymouth only sold 45,412 Barracudas. Formula S production was equally terrible, with only 5,196 built in total, including 3,917 340s and just 1,279 equipped with the 383. Though no one knew it at the time, the Barracuda, with its new engine offerings, was at the base of a J-curve that would ascend rapidly over the next three model years. Its best days were ahead of it.

* * *

Lost in the long shadow cast by the Big Three automakers was little American Motors Corporation, or AMC, which by and large had sat out the horsepower wars of the 1960s. American Motors, always an afterthought in American performance cars, indeed if it were thought of at all, formed in 1954 with the merger of two smaller car makers and became best known for a line of cars called Rambler. In fact, AMC was colloquially called "Rambler" well after the company itself had abandoned the name; old timers today still refer to AMC cars as Ramblers. American Motors was not only the smallest of the major American car makers, but it was the smallest by a wide margin and was eventually swallowed up by Chrysler in 1987. The legacy of AMC survives today with Chrysler's Jeep line, which had been owned by AMC since 1970.

AMC, or Rambler, or whatever one wanted to call it had a history of building cars that can only be charitably described as solid, but decidedly unexciting. The reputation of AMC was of building basic, no-frills, economical transportation: sensible cars for sensible buyers at sensible prices. No gimmicky horns or flashy stripes or cars called trendy acronyms or named after option codes.

This was largely an economic decision. In the big scheme of things, performance cars are somewhat of a niche category, whether intermediate or pony car. They served primarily to showcase the car maker, to establish reputation and to bolster the car maker's entire family of product. In terms of bang for the buck, they were luxuries. The highest selling muscle car of the era was the 1966 GTO, with just under 100,000 units sold. At the same time, Pontiac sold 359,092 of its entire Tempest line, which included the GTO. In that same year, Chevrolet sold 447,364 units of its Chevelle line, and only 72,272 were SS models. These numbers don't even take into account other models, such as Pontiac's Bonneville and Grand Prix or Chevy's Impala or Chevy II. Performance cars, even the best-selling ones, represented but a fraction of a car maker's overall production. AMC simply didn't have the research and design budget for such luxuries, nor the production facilities. In short, AMC was too small and too poor to invest in low return performance cars. In 1968, however, American Motors decided to gamble, and to try to cash in, proportionally speaking, on the '60s performance craze. In 1968, tiny AMC marched to war against the giants.

AMC waded into the pony car wars with its new Javelin, a 109-inch wheelbase vehicle built on the Rambler American's pre-existing platform, in order to save on production costs. History has been unfairly unkind to the Javelin, standing as it did in the long shadow cast by the Mustang, Camaro and Firebird. This is unfair, as the Javelin offered features not found on its contemporaries, such as standard front disc brakes and more interior room. The car featured standard bucket seating and full carpeting, as well as the usual array of interior options, such as power steering and brakes, power windows and locks, and air conditioning. On the outside, the Javelin followed the standard pony car template of long hood/short deck and a semi-fastback design. The Javelin was only available in hardtop and featured a wide, deeply set, split front grille. The hood had subtle twin scoops mounted out front, and the flush door handles added to the sporty look of the car.

AMC did what it could do to set its Javelin apart from the pony car pack. One of the more interesting color schemes of the entire muscle car era could be found on the Javelin SST Mark Donohue package, designed to celebrate the famed driver's association with AMC and the Javelin on the Trans Am racing circuit. In addition to the features of the SST, the Mark Donohue edition came wrapped in a patriotic red, white and blue color combination that can only be described as outrageous, even for the wild late '60s. Additionally, in January of 1969, AMC unveiled its wild "Big Bad" color options, including Big Bad Orange, Big Bad Red and Big Bad Blue. The Big Bad paint even covered the bumpers, much like the Pontiac Endura bumpers. Chrysler receives a lot of retrospective credit for the association of its wild High Impact colors and the wild automotive styling of the late 1960s, but Chrysler had nothing on AMC for exterior outrageousness, and AMC would top even itself in the coming years.

The Javelin's base engine was a 232 ci six-cylinder, but the sportier Javelin SST netted the choice of two 343 cubic inch blocks, the most powerful of which was a four-barrel version producing 280 horsepower. The SST also included interior upgrades such as sport steering wheel, simulated wood grain door paneling and reclining seats.

Finally hitting its stride mid-year, and perhaps in response to the surprising popularity of the "Jav," AMC made a 315 horse 390 cubic inch available with the "Go Package" as an alternative to the four-barrel 343. The Go Package also included heavy-duty suspension, sway bars and power front disc brakes. Transmission choices were the standard 3-speed manual, a heavy-duty 4-speed manual or the 3-speed "Shift Command" automatic. Rear ends could be had with positive traction, called "Twin-Grip" in the AMC vernacular (standard on Go Package cars) in a variety of gear ratios.

AMC made a surprising splash in the pony car battle, as it sold more than 56,400 Javelins in its maiden year. These numbers are nowhere close to the otherworldly sales of the Mustang, or indeed even of the Camaro, but proportionally speaking, AMC caught lightning in a bottle with the Jav, even if AMC's bottle wasn't very big. The Javelin not only held its own, but in a magnificent coup, actually outsold Plymouth's Barracuda, causing considerable consternation at Plymouth over the future of its struggling pony car. Today, while the market for first generation Camaros, Firebirds, and big-block powered Mustangs is going through the roof, Go Pack Javelins command a much more reasonable price and represent an outstanding value to anyone wishing to enter the '60s performance car market.

AMC offered a second performance car option for 1968, one of the most unusual cars of the era. Following the trend of acronyms-as-names so popular in the era, it was called the AMX.

The AMX was an unusual car that is difficult to categorize. Coming only in hardtop form, the AMX was essentially a Javelin with 12 inches of wheelbase lopped off

**1968 AMC AMX (courtesy Vanguard Motor Sales, Plymouth, MI).**

to 97 inches, giving it the shortest wheelbase of cars now lumped into the muscle car category. Saving on fabricating costs, the Javelin and the AMX shared body panels. The short wheelbase and small size of the AMX wasn't the only thing distinguishing it from true muscle cars because it was known as "American's other two seater." The AMX was a genuine two seater, like the Corvette, and not simply a 2+2 with fold down rear seating like some of the Mustangs and Barracudas of the time. As a short wheelbase two seater, the AMX was not a muscle car, or even a pony car, and it certainly was no roadster like the Corvette. The AMX was truly a categorical bastard, but it was equally truly a very cool car.

Where the Javelin's engine options started with a sedate six-cylinder, American Motors didn't mess around with the AMX. It was intended to be a performance car and really nothing else. AMC only offered V-8 power in the AMX, and while the base engine was the relatively unexciting 235 horse 290, at least it was a four-barrel with dual exhaust. The 280 horse, four-barrel 343 was up next, and the top of the ladder was AMC's underappreciated 315 horse, four-barrel 390. The base transmission was a heavy-duty 4-speed made by Borg-Warner, and after January of 1969, the 4-speed was shifted by an industry gold standard Hurst shifter. The Shift Command 3-speed automatic was the only tranny option. The AMX was standard with heavy-duty suspension with sway bars. Standard rear end was an open model, but the Twin Grip limited slip rear end was optional, and standard with the Go Package, available on the AMX as well as the Javelin. The Go Pack also netted a heavy-duty radiator.

Like the Javelin, it could be had in Big Bad color schemes and came adorned with racing stripes if the Go Package was ordered. The interior was much like the

Javelin's, only with half as much of it. Bucket seating was standard, and instrumentation was identical to the Jav as well.

AMC was rightly proud of its little AMX, which sold 6,725 copies in 1968 and has a virulently loyal following today.

It was said that Ford's Edsel—a disaster of such epic proportions that Henry Ford II was extremely hesitant to get on board with Lee Iacocca's gamble the Mustang—was a car in search of a market, and hence its abject failure. In a way, AMC did the same thing with the AMX. In a time when performance intermediates and pony car sales were still strong, AMC developed a two seat, short wheelbase V-8 powered non-roadster that was a car in a class by itself. The difference, however, between Ford and AMC is that American Motors had to find new niches in the market in order to sell cars, compete, and stay afloat. The AMX represented an attempt to find a niche in which AMC could fit. By any standard, 6,000 copies of a car isn't very many. Many automotive historians claim that the new road AMC began to travel in 1968— away from solid, practical cars and into performance and niche cars like the Javelin, AMX, and, later, the SC/Rambler, The Machine, SC/Hornet, Gremlin and even the weird Pacer—set AMC on a collision course with the Big Three that it could not survive. Indeed, AMC was eventually swallowed up by Chrysler in 1987. That sad tale

Fender badging just aft of the front wheels on AMC's entry into the pony car wars, the Javelin (courtesy Gateway Classic Cars, St. Louis, MO).

was years away, however. In 1968, AMC burst onto the scene with an excitement not known from the tiny company building cars in Wisconsin. In 1968, the performance world took notice of American Motors.

\* \* \*

The events of 1968 forever changed the cultural and political landscape of the country. The fabric of the nation was altered drastically, and we are still feeling the effects of the momentous events of those years. While there hasn't been an assassination on the scale of the King and Kennedy slayings (though John Hinckley Junior gave it a shot in 1981), the Deep South is still solidly Republican after Nixon's transformations. The prodigies of the counterculture, in full stride in 1968, are still influencing the American landscape, though now as gray headed grandparents still hoping to see the coming of Aquarius before the sand empties from the top of their hourglasses; at least they can take some satisfaction in having lived long enough to see the legalization of pot in some states.

The trajectory of the muscle car world also changed in 1968. The solid success of the cheap Plymouth cars would spark a new battle for the lower end of the muscle car market, and by the end of the 1968 model year the order of battle for all car makers was essentially complete; American Motors still had a couple of nasty surprises to spring on the market, and Dodge had one more late entry, but by and large, all of the models known today as "muscle cars" had made their appearance on the battlefield. Sales of the intermediate performance cars, however, with some exceptions, continued the slow descent that started in 1967, the victim of higher insurance rates and rising prices due to ever-lengthening lists of standard equipment and government safety mandates. An additional reason for the slow decline of the performance intermediate—the traditional "muscle car"—was the cannibalism of the pony car. As the performance arc of the pony car continued to ascend, with the same engine options as those of the intermediates becoming more and more available, many people who might have bought an SS 396 Chevelle bought a cheaper and lighter SS 396 Camaro instead. 4-4-2 buyers opted for Firebirds. The astronomical rise in 1968 pony car sales, despite the introduction of new models and improvements in existing ones from 1964, embarrassed even the most popular intermediate performance car numbers of 1968. Like the small mammals that would come to dominate the earth scurrying at the feet of dinosaurs, the rise of the pony cars was an indication of one of the factors that would be the doom of the muscle car, as they themselves had once sounded the death knell for the big SS Impalas, 406 Galaxies and Pontiac 2+2 Catalinas of an earlier age. Although 1968 was not the end of the muscle car era by any means, the clouds of that end gathered on the distant horizon. The muscle car genre still had plenty of life, and the crescendo began to build even further in 1969.

\* \* \*

No one who lived through the momentous year of 1968 shed any tears with its departure. The political killing of Kennedy and the racial slaying of King were the lowlights of a year with plenty from which to choose. Tet and the deterioration of the military situation in Vietnam, race riots, and the absurdity of the Democratic

National Convention created a sense of dread and caused people to cast their forlorn glances to the future, led by a president who likely wouldn't be, had Kennedy lived. There was reason for hope, at least symbolically, as the first ever pictures of an "earth-rise," taken by American astronauts from lunar orbit, were broadcast to the world on Christmas Eve, 1968, a poetic and peaceful end to one of the most tumultuous years in American history.

# 8

# Moon Shot

## *The Acceleration of the Muscle Car Wars*

Following the incredible political, social and military turmoil of 1968, people of the United States wearily stared into an uncertain future as the calendar flipped to 1969, apprehensive of what could possibly come next. For the first time in eight years, a Republican, the same Republican the nation had passed on in 1960, occupied the White House. A wave of anxiety, particularly in the Deep South, swept Richard Nixon into office. Nixon promised to restore order at home and an "honorable end to the war in Vietnam." After the national upheavals of 1968, few Americans looked toward the New Year with any confidence of either.

As it turned out, 1969 was relatively calm. There were still the ubiquitous war protests, and participants numbering in the millions in Vietnam Moratorium Day and related marches marched on Washington, D.C. Racial unrest was equally ubiquitous, with riots taking place in Springfield, Massachusetts, and Jacksonville, Florida. Police and the National Guard were called to quell race rioting in Cairo, Illinois, and Baton Rouge, Louisiana. Few minorities believed that a Republican president would continue the progress in racial justice that had taken place under Kennedy and Johnson. Police in New York City raided the Stonewall Club, a gay hotspot, ostensibly for serving liquor without a license. The short term result was a day of rioting, and the long-term result was that Stonewall became the genesis of the gay and lesbian movement in the United States. President Barack Obama named the Stonewall Inn a national monument in 2016.

The Kennedy family was in the news again, as the youngest brother Teddy pled guilty to leaving the scene of an accident in Chappaquiddick, Massachusetts—a fatal accident in which Kennedy plunged an Oldsmobile off a bridge and into a pond. His passenger, Mary Jo Kopechne, drowned, and Kennedy didn't report the accident for over ten hours. With the Kennedys being the Kennedys in Massachusetts, that was the end of that, though the incident undercut Teddy's presidential aspirations. At least he wasn't assassinated.

In St. Louis, a man in St. Louis known as "Robert R" died of a mysterious disease that no one could put their finger on. Not until 1984 was it determined that Robert R. was in fact America's first victim of the scourge that would ravage the country two decades later, which would come to be known as AIDS. America was introduced to its most notorious serial killer, a charismatic sociopath named Charlie Manson, when his followers slaughtered seven people in California, including model, actress and mother-to-be Sharon Tate. In Libya, an obscure colonel named Muammar al-Kaddafi led a coup and seized control of the country. The U.S. public would get more acquainted with Kaddafi two decades later when the Libyan government was implicated in the involvement of a fatal terrorist attack in a German disco and, more spectacularly, the bombing of Pan Am flight 103 over Lockerbie, Scotland.

Richard Nixon was inaugurated in January, and the American Left shuddered at the prospect of the disaster they knew was coming; they were right, of course. Nixon, however, did in fact keep his promise to wind down the Vietnam War. Nixon announced the "Vietnamization" of the war in Southeast Asia, a new direction in which the U.S. would turn the war effort over to the South Vietnamese and begin a drawdown of U.S. troops. Commensurate with that, Nixon in fact did withdraw 25,000 troops, even as he expanded B-52 strikes into Cambodia. Perhaps nothing better exemplified the futility of the Vietnam conflict than the battle over Hill #937, better known as Hamburger Hill, in which seventy-two U.S. service members died, only to abandon the hill less than a month later.

Further compounding the souring of public opinion of the Vietnam War was the release by the Cleveland *Plain Dealer* of photographs from a forgotten backwater of a Vietnamese village called My Lai. The photos depicted the result of a massacre of hundreds of South Vietnamese civilians suspected of Communist sympathies. William Calley, the Army officer deemed responsible for the massacre, was formally charged with war crimes.

The year had its triumphs too. Two of the world's great and iconic commercial aircraft, the Boeing 747 and the Concorde, took their maiden flights. The Arkansas business started by Sam Walton and now known as Walmart was incorporated, and Led Zeppelin released its eponymous first album. Hundreds of thousands of music fans gathered for a music festival in upstate New York near the town of Woodstock, the pinnacle of the '60s music festival trend. The Supreme Court in its *Alexander v. Holmes County Board of Education* decision put a stop to the Deep South's fifteen year post–*Brown v. Board of Education* foot-dragging and ordered public schools desegregated "at once."

The Soviet Union put its *Venera 5* lander on the surface of Venus, and as incredible as that was, that event was the consolation prize to 1969's most notable achievement, the U.S. victory in the Race to the Moon and the landing of American astronauts on the lunar surface. This unparalleled scientific achievement fulfilled President Kennedy's 1960 challenge to do so by the end of the 1960s and ended millennia of mankind's inquisitiveness about Earth's cosmic fellow traveler.

\* \* \*

In the war between the American car builders, a conflict now raging into its sixth model year, the rapid escalation of horsepower continued unabated. Weaponized intermediates and pony cars were equipped with the armament of ever increasing engine displacements, horsepower and torque, and were wrapped in more and more outrageous graphics and paint schemes.

The atmosphere in which this battle raged, however, was becoming more and more toxic to performance cars and there were ill omens of which no one seemed to take note. In 1968, the government mandated side marker lights and seat belts. In 1969, the mandate was headrests. Each new mandate the car makers were volun-told to include increased both weight and price. The weight depressed performance, and the engineering dollars that went into finding ways to meet the government's mandates were naturally passed on to the consumer, creating a de facto tax on new cars. Further, insurers were beginning to take notice that young people hurling themselves around in 3,000 pound machines at 100 miles per hour with poor brakes and handling might be inherently dangerous. This realization was beginning to manifest in steadily rising insurance premiums on performance vehicles. If this weren't enough, the average cost of a gallon of gas was up from 17 cents a gallon 1964 to 34 cents in 1969. These changes would take some time to influence the performance car market, but they were there—a slow developing poison that would eventually and profoundly affect the American performance car market.

Yet in 1969, the car makers hardly seemed to notice—perhaps it was willful blindness as they waged war with a previously unmatched intensity. The 1969 model year would see the muscle car era approach its zenith and begin arguably the greatest two year stretch in the history of the American performance car.

* * *

Plymouth's introduction of the Road Runner in 1968 and its effect on the mindset of Chrysler's rival car makers cannot be overstated. The Road Runner, and to a lesser extent, its sibling the Super Bee, changed the game. The car builders—General Motors, in particular—were stunned by the success of the cheap, lightweight Mopar B-bodies as they ran rampant over all but the hottest, high horsepower competition. Like Wile E. Coyote—knife and fork in hand—General Motors and Ford joined a desperate attempt to catch Plymouth's little bird.

Pontiac, the original creator of the low-priced budget supercar built for the youth market, was the car builder that took the Road Runner the most seriously. Pontiac's GTO was the progenitor of the reasonably priced super car for the masses, but by 1969, the GTO was suffering a sales trend that was generally downward from its high water mark in 1966. With the Road Runner, Plymouth was encroaching on Pontiac's territory, and the Tin Indians were struggling to halt the slow erosion of Pontiac's piece of what market share remained.

Plymouth had tried to play in the same sandbox as the GTO and its upscale cousins the 4-4-2 and GS Buicks with its GTX. The GTX was a viable alternative to the GTO, but Pontiac never really viewed the GTX as true competition to the GTO, and indeed it wasn't. Plymouth was punching above its weight trying to build upscale performance. The Road Runner, however, was right in Plymouth's wheelhouse—cheap, bare-knuckles power, built around Chrysler's bombproof drivelines—and Pontiac planners viewed the threat the Road Runner posed with pants-wetting terror. Staring into their crystal balls, Pontiac bosses predicted that the Road Runner's sales would not only increase in 1969, but would increase substantially. Pontiac brass and planners, as well as marketing wizard Jim Wangers, held several hand-wringing meetings to figure out how to best respond to the Road Runner. What would eventually come of Pontiac's efforts to catch the Road Runner would be one of the most iconic performance cars of the late muscle car era. Building on the by-1969 legendary reputation of the GTO, Pontiac offered a performance package on their venerable but aging performer, a package Pontiac called The Judge.

The Judge came about after many fits and starts. Conceptually, the new Pontiac budget performer was supposed to be a lightweight, cheap muscle car based on the Pontiac A-body platform, precisely built on the Road Runner/Super Bee model. As austere as Pontiac was willing to go, the new car would come with a base 350 cube high output engine, manual transmission, bench seating and not much else, not even power steering or brakes. Various names were suggested, such as "H.O." or "Mini-G," which is a perfectly good name for a diminutive hip-hop artist or perhaps a donut, but hardly the name for a muscle car intended to deal with other budget muscle cars with names the Chrysler products were sporting. Wangers worried that the budget Poncho would defeat the purpose of protecting the GTO sales and would in fact be seen as a cheap alternative to the GTO, further eroding the GTO's diminishing sales. Sensitive to this concern, the decision was made to make the new car an option on the GTO, an attempt to harness the glory of the name and transfer it to the new model. John DeLorean, *El Jefe* at Pontiac, then vehemently declared no GTO would ever have an engine of smaller displacement than 400 cubic inches as long as the world was spinning on its axis. With that, 350 was out, and a 400 cubic inch engine was in. The end product of these deliberations would be a 400 cubic inch powered GTO option named for a punchline from a comedic variety show popular with the youth called *Laugh-In*: "Here come da Judge."

By the time the good idea fairies at Pontiac finished destroying the original concept for The Judge, what they had created was, in fact, the very opposite of the Road Runner. Where the Road Runner was light and cheap, the Judge ended up being the most expensive and heaviest GTO to date. Regardless, the 1969 Judge is considered by many to be the high water mark for the GTO. Clothed in the bright, retina-damaging colors and psychedelic graphics that were 100 percent late '60s styling, the Judge was certainly an attention grabber. Pontiac may have failed in building a budget alternative to the Road Runner, but it stumbled into building an icon of the era.

Architecturally the 1969 GTO and its Judge option were little different than the 1968, aside from GM's deletion of wing windows across the A-body line, a change made to its Firebird and Camaro the year previous. As in 1968, the '69 GTO was only available in hardtop or convertible form. Gone was the original GTO crest that had adorned every GTO since 1964, and in its stead was a pot metal GTO badge on the lower fender just aft of the front wheel well. The GTO crest lived on, however, in the shape of the quarter panel mounted clearance lights. The 1969 retained the Endura bumper and optional hide-away headlamps from 1968. The split grills were divided horizontally by a bright bar, and the GTO badge still adorned the driver's side grille. The Judge package included a rear spoiler, hood mounted tachometer, blacked-out grilles and T-handled Hurst shifter on manual transmission cars. Early Judges were available only in bright Carousel Red, which was Pontiac's interesting name for "orange." Later, Judges could be had in any color available on the standard GTO. Interestingly, the Judge package also netted Rally II wheels without trim rings, a chintzy vestige of the budget muscle car the Judge was originally to be.

Standard offering for the '69 GTO was a base 350 horse 400 cubic inch engine with a four-barrel Rochester carb and 3-speed manual transmission. Most GTO buyers opted to upgrade the tranny to either a 4-speed manual or 3-speed Turbo-Hydromatic automatic. Optional on all GTOs and standard on The Judge was the 366 horsepower Ram Air III engine that breathed cold air through functional hood scoops that could be opened or closed by pulling a knob in the cabin. The ultimate engine offering in the GTO was the Ram Air IV, conservatively rated at 370 horsepower and considered by many to be the greatest Pontiac engine of the era. Contemporary road tests showed the Ram Air IV GTO could hurl itself through the traps in under fourteen seconds and would reduce all but the hottest lightweight Plymouths to clouds of brightly colored feathers. The interests of completeness mandate mention that the 265 horse, low compression 400 topped with a two-barrel carb was inexplicably still available for 1969. Manual drum brakes were standard, but discs and power assist were available, as was a limited slip differential in varying gear ratios.

Interior and comfort options essentially remained what they had been through the years. Air conditioning was becoming more and more popular, as was power steering. Power windows and doors were available as well.

The '69 GTO remains one of the most popular of the GTO models, but the bump in 1968 sales proved to be an outlier. Even the audacity of the Judge and the exciting engine offerings could not prevent the continued downward trend in GTO sales, a trend which would continue through the end of the muscle car era. Regardless, Pontiac managed to sell 72,287 GTOs in 1969, including 6,833 Judges. This sales number

1969 Pontiac GTO convertible (courtesy Vanguard Motor Sales, Plymouth, MI).

represented a precipitous fall of more than 15,000 units from 1968 numbers. More importantly, it marked the sad end of the GTO's reign on the muscle car throne. For the first time since the inception of the muscle car era in 1964, the GTO was outsold. For the first time in its life, The Great One was suffering.

The car that was outselling the GTO and was busily hammering nails into the Goat's coffin was the SS Chevelle. Unlike Pontiac, Chevrolet didn't seem to panic over the cheap Chryslers, and in 1969, Chevrolet didn't build a car specifically to compete with them. Chevrolet chose instead to simply ignore them. Chevrolet stood in the breach, confidently taking on Chrysler's onslaught with what it had on hand.

Chevy's confidence came from the fact that what it had on hand was formidable, as it still had its range of 396 engines. Chevy dropped the SS 396 as its own model in the Chevelle line and made the SS a performance package on the entire Chevelle line. The SS package could now be had on the basic Chevelle 300 or the more upscale Malibu, and even the car/truck hybrid El Camino. Theoretically, one could get an SS 396 Chevelle station wagon, and for the good of the SS legend all should hope that never happened. The SS package again included 396 cube engines in a range of horsepower production that were essentially the same as 1968. Late in the model year, the 396 was bored out to 402 cubes; Chevy left the legendary 396 badging in place. Engine choices, whether 396 or 402 cubic inches, began with the base 325 horse L35, the 350 horse L34, the 375 horse L78 and L89, the latter equipped with aluminum heads. Transmission choices for the SS Chevelle included the base, heavy-duty 3-speed manual for the shift-it-yourselfers. Two heavy-duty 4-speeds were optional, as was the TH400 3-speed automatic. Chevrolet even saw fit to include a safety switch that prevented the car from starting if the clutch pedal was not depressed, and the government didn't even have to tell them to. Standard braking was manual drums all the way around, and, as usual, power assist for manual brakes and power discs were options. A range of rear end gear ratios was available, as was positive traction.

Stylistically, not much changed for the SS Chevelles. Essentially, redesigned tail lamps were the only significant change from the '68 model. Bench seating was standard, with buckets optional. The standard fare was optional on the inside, including lighting packages, tilt steering wheel and, for those who felt a real need for such things, a tissue dispenser.

With the SS package and its range of 396 engine options available to the entire Chevelle line, and with Chevrolet's entry level price point, savvy Chevy fans had options to custom build their very own lightweight, budget supercar. A base Chevelle 300 with the L35 equipped SS package undercut even the cheapest Road Runner, commanding a sticker price of under $2800. The Chevelle 300 didn't have the panache of the higher end of the Chevelle line, and therefore, despite their basement level price, lagged behind other SS Chevelle possibilities in price; the heavier and more expensive Malibu based SS package remained more popular with buyers.

Beyond the excellent 375 horse 396 offerings of the SS package Chevrolet offered in limited numbers the ultimate '69 Chevelle, known as COPO (for Central Office Production Order). COPO Chevelles were only offered to a small group of

**The 1969 SS Chevelle (courtesy Vanguard Motor Sales, Plymouth, MI).**

dealerships and individuals. The COPO Chevelles came armed with Chevrolet's goliath 425 horsepower L72 427, Chevrolet's most powerful engine to date. Today, the COPO cars are easily the rarest and most sought after Chevelles of the entire muscle car era, with only a little over 300 COPO Chevelles produced. Considering that they were built specifically to have the hell beaten out of them on the street or track, there are far fewer than 300 left today.

Chevrolet sold 86,307 SS Chevelles in 1969, with one 396/402 or another. This is an increase of over 20,000 from 1968 and is remarkable in the highly competitive 1969 performance arena, with its myriad of differing choices. In a year where sales of most intermediate performance models were trending the other direction, the SS Chevelle seemed to have rockets for tail pipes in terms of sales. This is a strong testament to the popularity of Chevrolet and the division's emphasis on no-nonsense cars designed for the everyday man or woman. Chevrolet's 375 horse 396 outgunned the GTO beginning in 1965, and by 1969 it had done so in sales. The Pontiac, Olds and Buick may not have liked it, but in 1969, Chevrolet was the king of GM performance. *Plus ça change, plus c'est le meme change.*

GM's more patrician divisions—Buick and Oldsmobile—essentially ignored the budget muscle car market in 1969. Building cheap cars is just not something these divisions did, and they weren't going to start. Frankly, while Oldsmobile had more of a performance legacy and took the intermediate performance car market seriously, the 4-4-2 and the GS weren't what kept the lights on at these two divisions. Instead they concentrated on what did to pay the bills and what they did best—building luxury barges and catering to an older and more affluent market. That said, Olds and

**Hood emblem on the 1969 Chevrolet Chevelle (courtesy Gateway Classic Cars, St. Louis, MO).**

Buick continued to turn out the 4-4-2 and GS, and by 1969, both Buick and Oldsmobile were hitting their stride in mid-size performance.

The 4-4-2 for 1969 was relatively unchanged from the 1968 model. The car received an altered grille treatment, with the horizontal quad headlamps no longer separated by parking lights. The grilles were separated by a downward extension of the hood which met a similar chrome upward molding of the bumper, adorned with a 4-4-2 badge. The tail lamps were also slightly redesigned. A new hood featured dual bulges running the length of the hood; conservative Olds still refused to offer scoops. Striping ran the length of the bulges if the W-30 package was opted for.

The base four-barrel, 400 cubic inch engine produced 350 horsepower as long as it was mated to the optional heavy-duty 4-speed manual transmission. If backed by the Turbo-Hydromatic 3-speed automatic, a different cam was used, reducing horsepower to 325. The optional W-30 400 cubic inch engine increased horsepower to 360 through the use of cold air induction—the air inlets inconspicuously hidden in the grille, of course. While the W-30 is the Olds engine history remembers best, there was the less known W-32, a slightly detuned version of the cold air inducted W-30 producing 350 horsepower. A heavy-duty 3-speed manual transmission was standard, but a close or wide ratio 4-speed was optional, as was the Turbo-Hydromatic 400 3-speed automatic. The TH400 was the only tranny available with the rare W-32. Drum braking was standard, in manual form, though front discs were optional. Power assist was not available with the W-30, though it was with the lower horsepower W-32. Limited slip rear ends were optional as well.

**1969 Oldsmobile 4-4-2 (courtesy Vanguard Motor Sales, Plymouth, MI).**

Oldsmobile's relationship with Hurst continued, and in 1969, the Hurst-Olds models came draped in what would become the H/O's characteristic gold on white paint scheme. The H/O also featured odd "mailbox" hood scoops, a rear spoiler, bright H/O badging, and more importantly, a 380 HP 455 engine taken from the Olds full size car line and installed again by Hurst to ensure Oldsmobile was not offending any GM corporate mandates on horsepower-to-weight.

Oldsmobile offered small block performance for its F-85 Club Coupe and Cutlass line. Called the W-31, the engine featured a small block 350 cubic inch engine fed by cold air induction of the same set up as the 4-4-2. The 350 produced a very respectable 325 horsepower, and for 1969 was available with a Turbo-Hydromatic 350 3-speed transmission, in addition to the 3- or 4-speed manuals that were mandatory on 1968's Ram Rod 350, the car the W-31 replaced. The smaller W-machine was as close as Olds got to a budget supercar, and for 1969, it put 913 of these junior muscle cars on the road.

Oldsmobile mandated standard bucket seating in its intermediate performance cars, though a rare bench was optional at no cost. A center console was optional, as were air conditioning, power steering, and power windows and locks. The interior was adorned with faux wood finish and a padded dash pad.

In what was becoming a trend, sales for the 1969 4-4-2 fell from the 1968 numbers to just over 26,358 and 914 Hurst/Olds models. Thankfully for Olds, intermediate muscle wasn't what kept its lights on.

Even stodgy Buick, GM's last outpost on the price point ladder before Cadillac, couldn't resist being swept up into the tornado that was the late 1960s performance

1969 Hurst/Olds, owned by Rusty Small (photo by Diego Rosenberg).

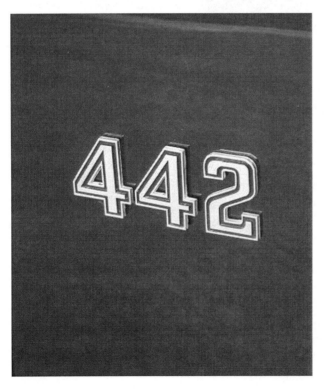

market. Up to 1969, Buick's Gran Sport/GS cars felt like afterthoughts from a division used to providing cars to funeral homes, even after the introduction of the dealer installed Stage 1 package in 1968. For 1969, however, Buick gave the GS a slight but more aggressive restyle and spent more effort promoting its performance credentials.

The major restyle for the '69 GS cars, both the GS 350, offered again in 1969, and the GS 400, was a new hood featuring centrally mounted,

By 1968, Oldsmobile had settled on large block numbers for its 4-4-2 badging (courtesy Gateway Classic Cars, St. Louis, MO).

**1969 Buick GS 400 convertible (courtesy Gateway Classic Cars, St. Louis, MO).**

functional hood scoops. That the scoops were functional is saying quite a bit about the tone normally conservative Buick wanted to set for its GS cars; in all other GM performance intermediates, hood scoops were non-functional, if they were there at all. Buick deleted the twin chrome strips on the deck lid for 1969, and aside from these changes, the '69 GS was nearly identical to the '68 model.

Engine options were the same as well, and though Buick didn't advertise any increase in horsepower now that they breathed cold air through the new-for-'69 induction system, it is widely accepted that the official ratings understated horsepower. The GS 350 produced 280 horsepower, and while a 3-speed manual transmission was standard on the GS 350, a 4-speed manual with Hurst shifter was optional. Also optional on the GS 350 was the Turbo-Hydromatic 350 3-speed automatic.

The base GS 400 produced 340 horsepower, again an underrated number for the purposes of the bean counters at the insurance companies. As with the GS 350, a 3-speed manual was standard but could be upgraded to a heavy-duty Hurst stirred 4-speed manual. Buick replaced the Super Turbine 400 with the Turbo-Hydromatic 400 3-speed manual—essentially a name swap.

For 1969, the Stage 1 option was given official sanction by Buick and was made a standard option on the 400, rather than being an over-the-counter dealer upgrade. Buick was indeed serious about performance. The Stage 1 package included special performance items: camshaft, valve springs, and carb, among other components. Buick claimed the Stage 1 package boosted horsepower to only 350 horses; this was a lie.

If there were a Stage 1, then it logically follows that there would be a Stage 2, and indeed there was. The rare, barely streetable Stage 2 was not available to the public; Stage 2 components were only available through dealers, and even then sales of the Stage 2 package were highly regulated. The Stage 2 package included 11:1 compression pistons, an aggressive camshaft, headers, and high flow Holley carb. Buick claimed all of this added up to another five horsepower to 355, though those in the know peg the increase at closer to an additional 100 horses.

Rear ends were standard GM fare—open differential in a range of gear ratios. Stage 1 and Stage 2 cars mandated a limited slip differential. Drum brakes were standard on all GS cars, though Buick continued to use lightweight and rapid cooling aluminum drums on the front. Power assist was available, as were front discs.

Interior plushness was a trademark of Buick, so the standard full vinyl bench seat was a little surprising, particularly considering that Olds mandated buckets in its 4-4-2. Vinyl covered bucket seating was optional. Faux wood and stainless trim adorned the interior, and of course carpeting was standard. Air conditioning, power steering and power brakes were so common in GS cars that they might have been standard equipment; power windows and locks were also popular options. The heavy GS 400 might have been a hell of a lot slower than the lighter stripped-down cars, but then the Buick was a hell of a lot more comfortable going home from the track.

In contrast to the 1968 sales spike for the GS models, sales dropped precipitously in 1969. Buick sold just 7,910 GS 400s, and, interestingly, another 9,879 of the little GS 350, in both convertible and hardtop form, plus 1,468 Stage 1's. Buick did itself no favors by offering no special edition of its GS cars. There were no stripped down, budget Buicks on the Road Runner model; Buick's brass likely couldn't have stood the thought of that even being contemplated. There was no special edition Buick like the Hurst/Olds, and there was no Buick equivalent to the Judge. Buick simply trotted out the GS 400 and junior GS 350, checked the mid-sized performance car off the list, and returned to concentrating on building cars with much more profit

The psychedelic decals adorning the three-year run of Pontiac's GTO Judge option (courtesy Fast Lane Classic Cars, St. Charles, MO).

margin, like the LeSabre and Electra, universally enjoyed by moneyed, blue-haired church-going old ladies.

Buick and Olds sales might have suffered from a reality as true today as it was rapidly becoming in the late '60s: that a customer might be able to afford a performance car itself only to realize that the insurance premiums put the entire, actual cost of operating the car—payment, fuel and insurance—far beyond the budget. When buying a Buick, getting past the first hurdle—affording the car itself—was tough, and no performance intermediate of the muscle car era was good on gas. Then there were the insurance premiums after that. This might explain the larger sales of the GS 350, as to buy it was less expensive and its far lower horsepower rating avoided the notice of the insurance companies. That also might explain the falling sales of Pontiac's, Buick's and Oldsmobile's intermediate performance models, while cheaper Mopars and Chevys saw sales increases in 1969. Perhaps buyers otherwise willing to buy a Buick or Olds were willing to skimp on plushness and buy a cheaper Plymouth or Chevy to offset insurance costs. Buick and Olds sales may also have been drawn off by the redesigned Dodge Charger. Regardless, the Buicks and Oldsmobile performance intermediates exited the 1969 model year as listing ships in terms of sales.

\* \* \*

Ford reinvigorated itself and its intermediate performance fan base with the late '68 release of the thundering 428 Cobra Jet, immediately giving the Blue Oval a level of street cred impossible for the 390 to fill. Wishing to avoid screwing up 1968's good thing, Ford changed little for the 1969 version of their performance intermediate, the Torino GT.

In terms of styling, the 1969 version of the Torino was practically identical to the 1968 model. It was again offered in three forms—hardtop, fastback, and convertible. The major points of tinkering were a new grille and taillight treatment. Under the hood, however, were some major changes in the middle section of the GT's engine lineup.

Gone for good was the 289 cubic inch engine, finally and fully replaced by the 302. While a Ford engine of that displacement would gain legendary status in 1969 in a limited edition Mustang, the 302 powering base level Torino GTs was decidedly not the same engine. To be absolutely clear, Ford did not put a Boss specification 302 in a Torino in 1969. The 302 Ford did put in the Torino GT shared little but a name with its more famous cousin, produced an anemic 220 horses and exhaled through single exhaust. Stepping up from that waste of effort was a pair of new-for-'69 351 cubic inch Windsor offerings, the most intimidating of which was a four-barrel producing 290 horses with dual exhaust. Ford would have had more luck catching the Road Runner using engines made by Acme.

Beyond the 351s, Ford offered big-block power by again trotting out the rapidly-going-stale, 320 horse, four-barrel 390 and two versions of the 428 cubic inch engine, either of which was simply awesome. The difference between the two 428s was that the J-code version utilized cold air induction breathing though a functional shaker hood scoop and producing a horsepower rating of 360 horses. This was the Super Cobra Jet. The non-ram air Cobra Jet produced the same 335 rating as it did in

**1969 Ford Torino GT (courtesy Vanguard Motor Sales, Plymouth, MI).**

1968. Both ratings were pure fiction, arrived at entirely for the benefit of the buyers when they went to visit their insurance agent.

All big-block GTs came standard with Ford's indestructible "Toploader" 4-speed manual, in close or wide ratio. Ford's C6 3-speed automatic could be had behind any big block. Rear ends came in a variety of ratios, and all could be had with "Traction-Lok" limited slip. The two lowest geared rear ends mandated limited slip, revealing their intent to be used as racers, and were only available with the 428. Stopping the heavy Ford fell to manual drum brakes standard equipped, but power and/ or discs were optional.

Interior choices were standard fare for the era, and little changed from 1968. Power steering, locks and windows were options, as was a console. Air conditioning was as well, though Ford literature claimed it was not available with 428 powered cars. Bench seating was again standard, though buckets were optional, as was a center console.

While history remembers Pontiac's Judge as the market's response to the Road Runner, fans of the Blue Oval would take issue, as the GTO wasn't the only car to join Wile E. Coyote in his pursuit of the Road Runner. Ford's bare-bones budget super car was a stripped-down version of the Fairlane/Torino line called, creatively enough, the "Cobra," named after the standard 428 cubic inch engine.

Following Plymouth's model, the Cobra was offered in basement level Fairlane trim in an effort to keep the sticker price down—cloth and vinyl covered bench seating and cheap door panels. A heavy-duty suspension, standard 4-speed and cheap wheels completed the base Cobra. For those of more discriminating tastes, it could be opted up to Torino GT trim, with its full complement of standard and optional features. The Cobra could be had in hardtop or fastback rooflines; no convertible Cobra was offered. Under the hood, the Cobra was all business—the only engine choice to be made was whether to spring for the Super Cobra Jet version or the standard Cobra Jet 428. The Cobras featured chrome hood pins and a blacked-out grille and snake emblems on the lower fenders.

Contemporary road tests put the cold air inducted Cobra at 14.2 through the quarter, which was substantially quicker than the base Road Runner or Super Bee. The fact that the lightest Cobra, the hardtop, tipped the scales at more than 3,600 pounds—200 pounds heavier than a base Road Runner—subtly revealed Ford's creative horsepower ratings for the 428.

Advertisements for the Cobra left no question as to what the car was intended to compete with. A minute long commercial depicts a wheeled cartoon snake speeding through a desert environ and over a hill, followed by a weak "beep beep" and a cloud of brightly colored feathers, while the pitch man declares that the Cobra "eats birds for breakfast."

Ford sold a lot of Torino GTs of all engine varieties, nearly 82,000 units. Despite the savagery of the 428, in either form, sales of the Cobra were relatively stagnant at 14,885. Those numbers were nowhere near those of the Road Runner, or even of the rarer Super Bee; not only was the Cobra heavier, its average base cost was more than $200 more than the Plymouth, and in 1969, 200 bucks was a chunk of change.

Mercury, of course, had its performance intermediate model for 1969, but Mercury's Cyclone for the new model year was substantially different than it was in 1968. While the Cyclone was still based on the Montego line, which paralleled Ford's Fairlane line, it was only available in "sportsroof" fastback configuration. The Cyclone GT as an independent model died with the Johnson Administration but for 1969 became an appearance package on the Cyclone. The GT package consisted of bucket seats, upgraded steering wheel, body striping, racing mirror on the driver's side, special wheels and appropriate badges. The GT package did not include any engine options. The same engine options as were available on the Torino GT were available on any Montego, including the Cyclone: 302, two or four-barrel 351, 390, or the big 428. Transmission and rear end choices mirrored those of the Ford as well, and par for the course for Mercury, interior accouterments were plusher than those found on the Ford.

Though people typically did not connect "budget" with "Mercury," Ford's upscale division got into the budget muscle car game in 1969 as well. Mercury's cheapo muscle car was simply called the Cyclone CJ, and it was essentially a Cobra clone.

Calling the car "CJ" painted Mercury into a corner in terms of engine choices. As with the Cobra, buyers didn't have to agonize over the choice, as there were only two: 428 Cobra Jet or 428 Super Cobra Jet, with the only difference being the inclusion of cold air induction and functional hood scoops on the SCJ. Transmission options were identical to the Ford, with the only appreciable difference being that the Mercury automatic was called the "Merc-O-Matic." Low gear ratio rear ends were only available with the Super Cobra Jet, and "Traction-Lok" was available.

**1969 Mercury Cyclone CJ (courtesy Vanguard Motor Sales, Plymouth, MI).**

Manual drum brakes were standard, though front discs and power assist were options.

Ram air versions of the 428 got hood pins on the leading edge of the hood. A heavy-duty suspension, blacked-out grille and special "CJ" callouts on the lower fender and rear quarter panel completed the CJ package. Departing somewhat from Mercury's interior standards in accordance with the CJ's concept as a budget racer, it came standard with a bench seat and basic steering wheel. Buckets were optional. Mercury was only willing to go so far, however; sporty rally gauges and simulated wood trim gave the car a more affluent feel. A "Sports Appearance Group" package was available, which essentially put GT accents on the CJ: sport mirror, turbine wheel covers and "rim-blow" steering wheel. Air conditioning was a rare option and was only available on cars equipped with an automatic transmission and the 3.00:1 Traction-Lok rear axle. Aside from this, the typical Ford interior options were available.

Mercury's efforts to convince folks to buy its budget racer may have been a bit of a fool's errand, as Mercury simply wasn't known for such things. Mercury asked its dealers to stress that the Cyclone CJ, starting at over $3,200, was significantly less expensive than Dodge's Charger R/T. The obvious flaw in this logic is that, in concept, the Cyclone CJ wasn't built to compete with the R/T. It was a budget racer, or was supposed to be; Mercury couldn't have it both ways and expect buyers to pay R/T Charger premiums for Super Bee baseness, and the CJ was significantly more expensive than a Super Bee. Math matters, and as a consequence, Mercury only moved 2,175 CJ Cyclones in 1969.

\* \* \*

The Ford Motor Company, along with its Mercury division, helped in accelerating a sub-trend within the muscle car era, one remembered now as the "aero" cars, which were a group of cars built from 1969 and 1970 specifically to compete on the NASCAR oval tracks.

By 1969, automotive racing—whether sanctioned drag racing or the NASCAR and Trans Am series—was very popular. In an era without the Internet, 500 television channels or social media, racing of all types was closely watched by car people. Unlike other professional sports, people could more closely mimic what professional racers were doing, only as amateurs. Obviously, there were no amateur NASCAR tracks available to the "weekend warriors," but there were plenty of road courses and especially drag strips scattered around the country on which everyday people could mimic their Sunday afternoon heroes. The sales adage of the day was "win on Sunday, sell on Monday," meaning that a direct line could be drawn from success at the track to sales at the dealerships. And after all, despite the glamor of the performance cars of the 1960s and the residual nostalgia they inspire today, all the car makers really cared about was profit, however it was generated. If six-cylinder tricycles were profitable, the car makers would have made them. Thankfully, they weren't, and Sunday's track victories paved the path to showroom profit.

NASCAR rules mandated "homologation" of vehicles that raced on its ovals. This means that a given number of track versions of the cars that would be run on the NASCAR circuit had to be produced and offered to the public. In 1969, the rules mandated that at least 500 track versions of the cars be offered to the buying public. Today, this notion is absurd; the cars run on the NASCAR circuit bear no resemblance to the production cars bearing the same name, outside of a basic shape and nameplate. In 1969, however, the cars on the track and those on which they were based for public consumption shared a great deal in common, though the racers benefited from the ability of the professional pit crews compared to the everyday shade tree mechanic.

Late in 1968, Dodge put a modified version of its Charger on the NASCAR circuit, a wind cheating version of the 1969 Charger called the Charger 500, and the new Mopar was a threat to the Blue Oval. However, in 1968, Ford discovered its restyled intermediate fastback cars were pretty fast, primarily due to their own sleek, wind cheating design. Indeed, a Mercury Cyclone GT recorded 1968's fastest time at Daytona. For 1969, Ford built upon that discovery and offered special, homologized versions of its Torino and Cyclone to the buying public in an effort to battle the Charger 500.

Both of FoMoCo's homologized cars were essentially the same. Ford's offering was the Ford Torino Talladega, named for the Alabama high bank racetrack that debuted in 1969. Mercury called theirs the Cyclone Spoiler, ostensibly because the car featured a rear air foil not found on the regular production Cyclone. Mercury also had a Spoiler II, which featured an extended, and even more aerodynamic, nose. The Talladega had a similar modified nose. Naturally, both the Talladega and the Spoiler were based on the Torino/Cyclone fastback sportsroof and in addition to the modified front ends, the cars featured substantial modifications to increase performance

**1969 Ford Talladega, owned by Richard Fleener of Murfreesboro, TN (courtesy Richard Fleener).**

and lessen drag at high speeds. These included a flush grille and headlamps and redesigned rocker panels that lowered the car's center of gravity by allowing it to sit lower to the ground. The Talladega was powered by the 428, while the Mercury had to make do with the higher revving four-barrel 351. Aside from the modifications to their bodies, both the Ford and the Mercury cars were distinctively clothed. The Talladega came in only white, maroon or blue and sported bench seats. The Spoiler came in two trim versions, each paying homage to the racing team piloting them: a red and white clad "Cale Yarborough Special" and a blue-on-white "Dan Gurney Special."

The Ford cars were extremely successful during the first part of the 1969–1970 season. Mercury cars won eight races and the Talladega won twenty-nine. The wind-friendly Ford products hammered the Dodge and dominated the circuit until Chrysler went back to work to even further reduce wind resistance, upping its game significantly. The Ford NASCAR editions were one-year outliers and are highly sought after today. After the 1969–1970 season, Ford dropped its corporate sponsorship of racing of any kind, though Ford cars continued on the track by teams without factory sponsorship. The final tally for production of the two models was an estimated 745 Talladegas built and 353 Spoiler IIs.

\* \* \*

*Top and above:* 1969 Cyclone Spoiler II (top) and Spoiler (bottom), in Dan Gurney and Cale Yarborough trim respectively. Both are owned by Richard Fleener of Murfreesboro, TN (courtesy of the owner).

**Quarter panel callouts of Mercury's 1969 Cyclone CJ (courtesy Vanguard Motor Sales, Plymouth, MI).**

The 1968 restyle of the Chrysler B-body line, which is generally considered to be the golden age of 1960s Pentastar styling, immediately made Dodge and Plymouth a very real player in an intermediate performance car market that up to then had been dominated by General Motors. As a consequence, Chrysler's B-bodies came into the 1969 model year riding a wave of popularity uncommon for the Pentastar; the stars aligned in 1968 in terms of performance—which Chrysler had always had in abundance—and style, which it most decidedly had not.

In terms of sales, Plymouth's Road Runner was popular beyond the division's wildest dreams. Plymouth had caught lightning in a bottle, and other divisions were predicting not only an increase in sales for the cheap Plymouth, but a significant increase. They were right.

Externally, the Road Runner was largely unchanged from 1968. The pillared coupe and the hardtop offered in mid–1968 were brought back as body style options, and, somewhat remarkably, the hardtop was actually cheaper in '69 than the year before. An expensive convertible joined the lineup, an early indication that the Road Runner was destined to gravitate away from its budget supercar roots in the years to come. The grille was cleaned up, deleting the cheap appearing series of horizontal squares with a horizontal bar construction, subtly split in the middle. The taillights were changed as well, and the cheap, black and white, unexciting Road Runner door decals were replaced with cheap, more exciting, full color decals featuring Warner Brothers' bird at full speed. The hood remained essentially the same, with recessed, side facing simulated scoops with engine callouts replaced with upward facing

The 1969 Plymouth Road Runner (courtesy Gateway Classic Cars, St. Louis, MO).

scoops with engine callouts still on the side. Performance paint was changed from a blacked-out block in the middle to two wide stripes and side marker lights went from round to rectangular.

Under the hood, Plymouth saw little reason to mess with the success of 1968, and initially at least, the engine options for 1969 differed even less than the exterior changes. The exact same 335 horse Road Runner/Super Bee specific 383 was mated to the A-833 4-speed manual as the standard transmission, though it was now mercifully shifted by a Hurst shifter, rather than the crappy Inland shillelagh used in 1968. The TorqueFlite 3-speed automatic was the only optional transmission. Likewise, there was only one engine option as well, the elephant 426 Hemi again mated to either the 4-speed or the TorqueFlite. Cold air "Air Grabber" induction was available and was barely kept from suffocation by sucking air through the top of hood scoops awkwardly designed for cold air induction. Chrysler offered several rear end options of varying ratios, and positive traction was available; it was standard on the ultra-heavy-duty Dana rear ends. Braking was the standard, marginally effective fare of the day—manual drums all around, but with power and/or front discs as options.

A mid-year option on the Road Runner was a new engine offering known in the Plymouth world as the 440 "Six Barrel" as a high-performance alternative to the 426 Hemi. The solid lifter Hemi is one of the greatest engines of the muscle car era, and history has rightly bestowed legendary status upon it. However, the 426 Hemi was barely streetable. It was a cantankerous and petulant engine, and while when running in top trim the 426 was very nearly unbeatable, it was very difficult to keep running in top trim. For those willing to sacrifice the 35 horsepower for more reliability, Chrysler weaponized its 375 horse 440 cubic inch engine by re-engineering it and topping it with three two-barrel Holley carburetors to produce 390 horsepower.

**1969 Plymouth Road Runner with the A12 440 "Six Barrel" option (courtesy Vanguard Motors, Plymouth, MI).**

Importantly, torque output—considered by some to be a better gauge of engine performance than even horsepower—was on par with the Hemi at lower RPMs.

The 440 Six Barrel, available only on the Road Runner's pillared coupe and hardtop, featured a black, fiberglass lift-off hood secured to the car with hood pins at every corner. In contrast to the playful cartoon character adorning the Road Runner, the Six Barrel cars had a malevolent look that left no question that they were intended for nothing but destroying pretenders to their boulevard thrones. Their black 15-inch wheels even came sans trim rings; as regulations at most drag strips required the removal of trim rings and hubcaps, Plymouth saved owners the trouble and removed them at the factory, adding to the car's primitively savage persona.

The inside of the 1969 Road Runner was still pretty Spartan, but in a giant step in Buick's direction, the Plymouth offered standard carpeting. Bench seating was standard, and the cheapest coupes still used a vinyl and cloth covering. The standard optional goodies like consoles, air conditioning, power steering and upgraded steering wheels and radios were available of course, at added cost, and opulent Road Runners were still rare in 1969; buying one and loading it up with GTX options defeated the purpose.

While the addition of standard carpeting was likely not the reason, *Motor Trend* chose the 1969 Road Runner as its Car of the Year, edging out a very good car in Pontiac's new downsized Grand Prix. The attention from *Motor Trend*, the stir it caused in 1968, and the addition of the convertible propelled Road Runner sales sharply upward. The Road Runner nearly doubled its sales from 1968 with 79,693 units sold;

**"Plymouth" emblem found on the hood of the 1969 Road Runner (courtesy Hankster's Hot Rods, Indiana, PA).**

nonetheless the SS Chevelle succeeded where Wile E. Coyote failed as it finally caught the Road Runner, at least in terms of sales, with a margin of 6,614 units.

Plymouth's civilized counterpart to the Road Runner was again the GTX, the top end of Plymouth's Belvedere-based B-body line. Marketed as Plymouth's "business man's muscle car," GTX shared the main restyles of the Road Runner, though with more refinement. For example, the restyled tail lamps were a bit deeper and brighter and the grille a shade more opulent. Rather than the stripes adorning the lower fenders and doors of 1968, the '69 model featured a wide band of flat black on the lower rockers, accented by a red or white stripe.

As in years past, the GTX was offered in either convertible or hardtop body styles and came standard with the 375 horse four-barrel 440 engine, with the mighty 426 Hemi as the only option. The TorqueFlite 3-speed transmission was standard, but one could opt down for the A-833 4-speed manual with Hurst shifter. As with practically everything else in those days, manual drum brakes were standard, but power assist or power discs were optional. The available rear end gearing was increased for 1969, with or without positive traction.

For Plymouth's upscale offering, comfortable things came standard, such as plush bucket seating in full vinyl covering. Consoles were popular options, as were air conditioning and power steering. Faux wood graining adorned the dash. The GTX was a nice, refined muscle car. However, an upscale personal luxury performance intermediate was out of Plymouth's wheelhouse and was never a terribly popular or good selling car. By 1969, the GTX was suffering stout competition in the upper end of the muscle car market. This competition was not only from the high-end Oldsmobiles, Buicks and Mercurys, but also from inside its own family, primarily from the restyled, resurgent Dodge Charger R/T. The GTX was trying to be what the R/T

**1969 Plymouth GTX (courtesy Gateway Classic Cars, St. Louis, MO).**

Charger was, and the Charger was much better at it. Plymouth lost whatever grip it had on the luxury muscle car market, and it sold only 14,614 GTXs in 1969.

For 1969, Dodge again offered three distinct performance intermediates, and the flagship, after its skyrocketing 1968 sales, was the Charger. In fact, the 1969 Charger has provided Americana with one of its most iconic vehicles of popular culture, though mention of it today is considered somewhat taboo. That car is *The General Lee*, from the CBS television series *The Dukes of Hazzard,* which ran from 1979 to 1985, and the 2005 movie of the same name. *The General Lee* was the vehicle driven by the Duke Boys, two ornery cousins from Georgia who spent the majority of their time befuddling local law enforcement and running all over fictional Hazzard County doing good deeds. What makes the vehicle so offensive, aside from its namesake, is the Confederate regalia adorning the big B-body, including a Confederate battle flag painted on the roof. Apparently, the car is so offensive that it should not be viewed by anyone, ever, without proper and ample trigger warnings. Thus, that particular politically insensitive '69 Charger is *automobilia non grata*; thankfully for western civilization the filming resulted in the destruction of over 300 of the hateful things. Luckily for more politically correct '69 Chargers and their owners, the taint of the General Lee has not yet spread so far that all '69 Chargers are unmentionable.

The R/T was again the performance version of the Charger, and the 1969 encore to the wildly popular '68 model was just as stunning, even while sporting some significant differences. The wide maw of a grille of '68 was replaced by one divided vertically in the middle, though the vacuum operated hide-away headlamps were still there. The twin round tail lamp pods were replaced by two long rectangular units that stretched across the tail panel. The molded doors and subtle spoiler effect to the deck lid remained. The R/T tail stripe was optional.

**The 1969 Dodge Charger R/T (courtesy Vanguard Motor Sales, Plymouth, MI).**

Engine options for the R/T were the same as in 1968 as well. The available engines were again the 375 horsepower, four-barrel 440 or the 425 horse 426 Hemi. The standard transmission was the A-833 4-speed but the TorqueFlite 3-speed automatic was a very popular option. Heavy-duty rear ends in a variety of gearing options was available, including the Dana, and positive traction was available as well. Chrysler standard drum brakes were standard, and power braking was optional as well. Optional as well were power front disc brakes.

The interior continued to offer a full range of plush standard features, including simulated wood grain, bucket seats and rally gauges. A console had to be opted out of, and map pockets adorned the full vinyl door panels. A new interior package, the Special Edition or "SE" package, was optional for 1969, adding bucket seats trimmed in leather and vinyl, a wood grained instrument panel, and a sport steering wheel. Air conditioning and power steering were popular options for the upscale Charger. The Charger, already a bit portly in 1968, packed on a few more pounds for 1969, as it corpulent frame grew by an average of 100-plus pounds in curb weight. Fat didn't come free; the average price went up by nearly 100 bucks, too.

Dodge put more than 18,776 of the big R/Ts on the road in 1969, and due to the wild popularity of the second generation Chargers, a good percentage of those managed to survive the Duke Boys' shenanigans and are still on the road today. Finding one that isn't painted in bright orange and with symbols of Southern heritage on the roof is a welcome breath of fresh air.

Flanking and competing with the Charger at the top of Dodge's intermediate performance offerings was again the Coronet R/T. The Coronet was the top of

Dodge's line of the same name, representing a personal luxury performance vehicle—exactly the same niche the Charger was ably filling. It was, in essence, what it always had been: Dodge's counterpart to the GTX. Regardless, it didn't take a lot of effort or fabrication dollars to up a base Coronet to a Coronet R/T, so Dodge figured "why not?" and drove on with the stumbling Coronet R/T.

The Coronet R/T was an attractive car in its own right, coming as it did from Chrysler's B-body line. The car's front end featured horizontal headlamps housed in two pods separated by a long, thin, blacked-out grille with the "R/T" badge neatly tucked on the driver's side. The flanks were clean, with bright rocker panel molding and wheel well opening trim. Large faux air scoops were optional on the quarter panel just behind the doors, as were twin stripes banding the back end of the quarter panels and deck lid. The standard hood featured a non-functional power bulge. The tail panel housed long tail lamps reminiscent of the Charger's but housed in such a way as to appear to be three distinct lenses on each side.

Engine options for the Coronet R/T continued as they had been since the car was introduced in 1967 and matched those of the Charger R/T and the GTX: base 375 horse, four-barrel 440 or the 426 Hemi. Cold air induction was an option—and standard on Hemi equipped cars—called "Ramcharger" on Dodges. When the Ramcharger option was checked, the non-functional base power bulge hood was replaced with a completely different one with twin scoops set wide on the front edge of the hood. Transmissions were the same as well, with the TorqueFlite 3-speed manual coming standard and the 4-speed manual as a "no-cost" option. The Coronet R/T wasn't treated any more specially than any other Mopar intermediate when it came to stopping, as it fell to manual drum brakes to try to stop the car. Power-assist and power front discs were optional for those worried about such trivialities as stopping.

The inside featured all the creature comforts one would expect from a high end personal luxury car. Bucket seating in full vinyl was standard. The horizontal 150 MPH speedometer could be replaced by an optional Rally Instrument Cluster, which featured a full complement of rally gauges. Air conditioning, power steering, power windows and doors and a range of radios were all optional.

Like the GTX, the Coronet R/T was a sad car in 1969. Its performance and looks were certainly not the issue, however. The cars simply weren't able to compete in the market that had been redefined by its own divisions. Additionally, there were simply too many other options for purchasers, and the Coronet R/T was particularly vulnerable to the impressive Charger R/T. By 1969, both the GTX and the Coronet R/T were dying creatures of an earlier age, though that age was a mere two model years previous.

Dodge's final performance intermediate was more in line with the contours of the market as it was in 1969, a market it had itself helped to shape. Dodge again offered the Super Bee as its budget counterpart to Plymouth's Road Runner, and the Super Bee did its part to help Chrysler maintain its stranglehold on the world of the cheap supercar.

Just as the Road Runner was only slightly changed for 1969, so too was the Super Bee. In fact, there is very little differentiating the budget Bee from its relative in the Coronet line, the Coronet R/T. A hardtop Super Bee was available for 1969, though

**1969 Dodge Coronet R/T (courtesy Gateway Classic Cars, St. Louis, MO).**

no convertible was. The Super Bee lacked the brightwork on the rockers and around the wheel well openings. The taillights were revised, and the long thin lamps were the same as those found on base Coronets and resembled those of the Charger. The grille was identical to the Coronet R/T; the speed-freak bumble bee emblem replaced the R/T badge. The Coronet's Ramcharger hood was standard but was made functional when the Ramcharger cold air induction option was chosen. A "bumble bee" stripe belting the quarters and deck lid was optional, and it integrated the Super Bee emblem. The Coronet R/T's faux quarter scoops were also an option.

The engine and transmission options mirrored those of the Road Runner, with the 335 horse, four-barrel 383 standard or the 426 Hemi mated to either the A-833 4-speed manual or TorqueFlite 3-speed automatic. Ramcharger was mandatory on the Hemi. Rear end options were identical as well. Braking was the usual insufficient crap found on most everything else in 1969, and was identical to all other performance B-bodies—manual drum brakes, with power assist and/or front discs as options.

The inside was sparse but not quite the cave man level of that found in the Road Runner, primarily due to the rally instrument panel stolen from the Charger's parts bins. That said, cloth and vinyl covered bench seating was standard, though buckets and consoles were popular options. The full range of typical options were available as well, such as air conditioning, power steering and the like, but with roughly 1000 bucks separating the base Super Bee from the Coronet R/T, adding too many options

**Dodge's 1969 Super Bee hardtop, with Ram Charger hood and optional faux quarter panel vents (courtesy Vanguard Motor Sales, Plymouth, MI).**

would blur the lines between the two models and defeat the purpose of Dodge's budget racer.

The 1969 model year may well be the pinnacle for the Super Bee. Though 1968's sales were negatively impacted by the Super Bee's mid-year release, sales for 1969 skyrocketed by comparison, from 7,844 to 24,087. The Road Runner was still the leader in the budget performance intermediate market, but the suits and ties at Chrysler were pleased with the Super Bee's supporting effort.

In mid-model year, Chrysler saw fit to grant Dodge the same dispensation it did Plymouth, in the form of the same triple-carb, 390 horse 440-cube engine that Road Runners were using to blister drag strips around the country. Dodge's Super Bee with the A12 package (it was the A12 package at Plymouth as well) was identical to the Six Barrel Road Runner, the heart of which, obviously was the engine, tabbed with the much cooler name of "Six Pack" by Dodge. In fact, the Six Pack moniker was so popular that it has survived through the subsequent decades and occupies a seat on automotive Olympus alongside the Hemi, whether referring to a Dodge or a Plymouth, while the Six Barrel name has faded from consciousness; today, 440 six-barrel Road Runners are incorrectly called "Six Pack" cars, though no one cares. The point is the same. Regardless, the Six Pack Bees are identical to the Road Runners beyond the engine—lift-off fiberglass hood, black 15-inch wheels, transmission and rear end choices, etc., with the only major difference being the extra inch of wheelbase of the Dodge. Dodge even managed to sell more A12 cars than Plymouth did, with 1,907 Six Pack Super Bees sold.

For the Six Pack Dodges and Plymouths of 1969, beauty, grace and style went out the window, sacrificed for performance functionality and brutality. Of the muscle cars of the era, most of which attempted to meld performance and style into some kind of harmony, no cars perfected the look of a bare-knuckle street combatant better than the Six Pack Mopars of 1969.

As previously mentioned, Ford's major competitor in the war-within-a-war world of the aero cars of the NASCAR circuit was Mopar. The back and forth, cause and effect escalation of aerodynamic one-upsmanship between the two car building giants played out in a relatively short amount of time, from the late 1968 entry of the strange 1969 Charger 500 to the withdrawal of Ford from the field after the 1969–70 racing season.

The 1967 Mopars—Coronet based Chargers from Dodge and Plymouth Belvederes—performed ably but unspectacularly on the NASCAR circuit that Chrysler knew it had to do something or quit trying. Not willing to abandon the field to Ford, Chrysler's first clumsy attempt at helping a 3,500-pound car roughly shaped like a brick efficiently cut through the atmosphere was the Charger 500, so named for the number of copies that had to be offered to the public to satisfy NASCAR's homologation standards.

The Charger 500 was theoretically a more aerodynamic version of the 1969 Dodge Charger. The wind trapping recessed grille and hideaway headlamps of the Charger were removed in favor a flush grille snatched from the 1968 Coronet line and placed in an extended nose, the attractive flying buttress back glass was made flush. The result was one hell of an ugly Charger-ish thing looking like the bastard child of an attractive 1969 Charger R/T and a homely back door companion base Coronet. The Charger 500 came with either the 375 horse 440 or, more rarely, the 426 Hemi, both mated to the TorqueFlite 3-speed automatic transmission. Aerodynamically speaking, the Charger 500 was marginally less wind resistant than the 1968 Chargers and Road Runners that Dodge and Plymouth had been trotting out to the NASCAR speedways prior, but the 500 was still like trying to throw a brick into a hurricane. The car provoked Ford into producing its own slippery Torino and Cyclone based Talladegas and Cyclone Spoilers, and Chrysler was back to taking a beating by the Ford products. It was back to the drawing board for Chrysler.

Effort 2.0 was a car that not only upped the ante in the aero wars, but effectively put an end to them and was so successful it drove Ford from stock car racing altogether. The car was the 1969 Dodge Charger Daytona, and simply put, it was the most outrageously built car of the muscle car era, if not the entire history of the American automotive industry. While not built in large numbers, better than any other car of the era, the Daytona has come to stand for the out-of-control styling ridiculousness that characterized the later years of the muscle car era.

The Daytona was equipped with Chrysler's standard performance engines of the day—the 375 horse four-barrel 440 or the 425 horse 426 Hemi, backed by either the bulletproof A-833 4-speed or the 727 TorqueFlite automatic. It was the appearance of the Daytona, however, that made it downright alien.

The Daytona was built on the Charger's 117-inch wheelbase and was outfitted with a wind slipping, bullet shaped nose cone that greatly extended the overall length of the car. The nose cone contained hide-away headlights and front air dams to force

**1969 Dodge Charger 500 (courtesy Vanguard Motor Sales, Plymouth, MI).**

the front end of the car down onto the track to provide better stability. The front edge of the special hood was pinned down to assure it rode flush and did not create drag at speed. The car's most unusual feature was the rear spoiler, towering nearly two feet above the deck lid and stretching up into the car's slipstream to create rear downforce to compensate for the front spoilers, pinning the car to the track and preventing the rear end from riding up.

Ace Plymouth pilot Richard "The King" Petty requested to drive a Daytona. He was denied, and he immediately defected to Ford, only to be lured back when Plymouth released its own "Winged Warrior," the 1970 Road Runner–based, 116-inch wheelbase Superbird, which was essentially the same car as the Daytona.

Armed with the cars known today as the "Winged Warriors," Chrysler returned fire on Ford on the NASCAR circuit. Daytonas and Superbirds shattered speed records on the super speedways, collecting thirteen wins in the 1969–70 season. Ten of the top fifteen finishers at Daytona in 1970 were Mopars. A Daytona broke the 200 MPH barrier at Talladega. They were essentially in a class of their own.

The winged cars would continue to dominate until Ford pouted long enough that NASCAR rules were modified to outlaw the mammoth Chrysler engines offered in the winged cars. Engine displacements were limited to no more than 305 cubic inches, for which, as luck would have it, the new Ford Boss 302 was perfect. Federal safety rules also helped kill the winged cars, as the cone shaped front ends could not meet coming bumper impact requirements, so the winged cars faded away.

To satisfy NASCAR's homologation requirements, the winged cars had to be offered to the public in sufficient numbers, in substantially the same form as those

**Dodge's answer to the Ford aero cars, the 1969 Charger Daytona, owned by Richard Fleener of Murfreesboro, TN (courtesy the owner).**

being run on the NASCAR super speedways. Hilariously except for the danger, these 200 MPH capable cars came standard with manual drum brakes. Chrysler itself doesn't even know how many winged cars it built, but the best guess is that Dodge built 503 1969 Daytonas. Plymouth built far more Superbirds in 1970, as NASCAR changed the homologation rules, raising the minimum from 500 to 1000 units or one unit for every two dealerships nationwide, whichever was greater. Therefore, Plymouth had to build 1,935 Superbirds, or thereabouts. Ironically, given prices for winged cars reaching deeply into six and sometimes seven figure territory, the cars sold extremely poorly, owing to their impracticality and outrageous design. Production examples sat on dealer lots for months and months, with dealers unable to get another unit of something desirable until they sold. They seemingly could not be given away.

The winged cars are the thing of legend today. The 2006 hit animated movie *Cars* resurrected a Superbird, aptly named King, complete with Richard Petty's light blue regalia and number 43. The car was voiced by none other than The King Richard Petty himself.

\* \* \*

The 1969 model year was a powerful encore for Chrysler's Plymouth and Dodge performance intermediates. Though sales of the GTX and Coronet R/T were stumbling, those falters came in large part through the success of the other Chrysler products, primarily the Charger R/T, which followed up the brutally beautiful '68 model with an even more popular '69 version. Plymouth is rarely ever second to Chevrolet in anything, but the Road Runner continued to defy even Plymouth's expectations and was just edged out by the SS Chevelle for the top selling performance intermediate. The Super Bee took advantage of a complete model year to triple its sales.

It was a marketing truism that positive public exposure of high-visibility vehicles bolstered sales across a car maker's entire line of cars. In 1969, Dodge and Plymouth enjoyed the positive image by-product of success after success of the B-body line.

Everyone knew the Hemi, and had for years, and while it was feared, its mechanical petulance gave it a considerable Achilles' heel. The Six Pack cars not only offered a worthy, reliable alternative, but a high profile one. Anyone who saw an A12 car on the showroom or the track was unlikely to forget it. Making further impact in the public's eye—pardoning the pun—were Chrysler's "High Impact" colors, released in 1969. In an era when earth tones were very popular on even performance cars, the borderline obnoxious, visible-from-space colors draping Dodge and Plymouth cars are what come to mind when one thinks of late '60s muscle cars. Like the A12 cars, no one can forget the High Impact color schemes—colors like Plum Crazy, Vitamin C Orange, Panther Pink, Lime Light or the maybe politically incorrect Green Go. People remember seared retinas. Standing above all the other success for the Chrysler B-body lines from Dodge and Plymouth were, of course, the winged Daytonas and Superbirds. Week after week, race after race, the readers settled in with their morning

Dodge's "Six Pack" air cleaner found on its awesome A-12 Super Bees (courtesy Gateway Classic Cars, St. Louis, MO).

coffee and a Monday paper and saw news of yet another strong performance of a winged car at some southern superspeedway.

The positive exposure of the B-body line combined with attractive styling unlike anything ever offered by Chrysler created an alchemy that undoubtedly influenced thousands to spend an evening or a Saturday afternoon at a Dodge or Plymouth dealership appraising a new B-body car.

* * *

Just as things were escalating in the intermediate performance market, so too were they in the pony car field. The prior two model years had seen the smaller wheelbase pony cars begin to edge more and more into the domain of the performance intermediates, and indeed, it was the rising popularity of the pony cars, with their smaller price tag and larger engine options, that was eroding the overall popularity of the mid-sized performance models. For the open-minded performance car buyer, it made little sense to pay more for a heavier car with the same power train, and thus pony car sales continued to surge.

Ford's Mustang would continue to own the performance pony car market, and in fact the Mustang's performance offerings expanded for 1969. Ford's grip was slipping, however, as rival models introduced in the previous couple of model years began to hit their stride and offer for the first time a serious challenge to the Blue Oval's dominance.

The youth-friendly, hip and whimsical trend that started with the Road Runner in 1968 and continued with cars such as the Super Bee and Cobra was not lost on the Mustang's planners. Since its introduction in 1964, the Mustang had steadily grown—literally and figuratively. The Mustang grew in size and weight while still riding on its 108-inch wheelbase. By 1969, it had grown nearly four inches in length and gained an inch in width. The Mustang had also grown into a full-fledged performance car, capable of competing with just about anything on the street; while the venerable old 390 that powered earlier GT models may not have been the most capable performance engine Ford ever built, the inclusion of the 428 changed the game.

Ford, however, recognized that the Mustang was getting a bit stale. One could gaze upon a 1968 Mustang and still see a strong resemblance to the introductory model. The Mustang needed a bit of freshening up and some new, exciting life breathed into it. A substantial redesign for 1969 attempted to capture the performance bona fides the Mustang had earned with its GT offerings while appealing to the youth market with a catchy name and graphics. In an era when jet aircraft exceeding the speed of sound still commanded some reverence, an era much closer in time to Chuck Yeager's 1947 feat of exceeding the speed of sound—achieving *mach*, in aeronautical terms—Ford created one of the iconic performance pony cars of the era—the Mustang Mach 1.

Aside from the limited production performance Mustang variants Ford offered in 1969, the Mach 1 was the top of the line. Offered only in the fastback "sportsroof" configuration, the Mach 1 featured quad headlamps, with each side of the front end adorned with one set wide and the other set inside the blacked-out grille. The grille, lacking the chrome Mustang emblem or "corral" framing it found on earlier

Mustangs, gave the front end a clean appearance, which was enhanced by the standard hood pins. Two different scoops could be found on the '69 Mach 1's hood, an integrated bulge or a shaker style scoop depending on engine choice. The "sportsroof" of 1969 differed from the fastback of previous years in that the angle of the roof ended with a slight upturn at the end of the deck lid, creating a small ducktail spoiler. The C pillar was decorated with a Mustang medallion, and below that, just aft of the doors, was a faux scoop reminiscent of the Shelby cars. Low gloss paint adorned the hood and cowl, and reflective stripes with "Mach 1" callouts were applied from the front wheel opening back through the quarter panels and trunk panel. Late in the model year, front and rear spoilers and rear window louvers were available as dealer installed options. Not to be outdone by the red-white-and-blue color schemes of American Motors or the High Impact colors from Chrysler, Ford released its own blinding palette of optional paints known as the "Grabber" colors—bright blue, yellow, orange and green.

Ford offered six different engine options on the Mach 1. The lowest rung on the ladder was a 351 Windsor that was more sizzle than steak, equipped as it was with a two barrel; this was the only Mach 1 which exhaled through single exhaust. With 250 horses, this engine choice sadly reduced the Mach 1 to little more than an appearance package. Thankfully, most Mach 1 buyers scoffed at this and opted instead for the four-barrel 351 Windsor, offering 290 horses and blowing its pollution through dual pipes. Next up was the venerable old 390, soldiering on again to produce 320 horses. All of these options included a non-functional hood scoop, though an optional "shaker" hood was available.

From there, the Mach 1 got serious. As with the Torino and Cobra, two 428 Cobra Jets were available, either with or without Ram Air and rated at the same 335 horsepower as those offered in the intermediate muscle cars. The cold air induction version offered a functional shaker scoop while the standard 428 did not, though it was optional.

The last engine option—one kept on the down-low by Ford—was the Super Cobra Jet. Still rated at 335 horsepower, the SCJ 428 came as a part of the $155.45 "Drag Pack" option package, which also got the buyer a performance oil cooler, functional shaker scoop, unique internal engine components, and either a 3.91 or 4.30 "Traction-Lok" limited slip rear end. Clearly, the SCJ Drag Pak cars were built for the track. Transmissions varied by engine displacement. The 3-speed manual was the base tranny for the 351 cars. Either a wide or close ratio version of Ford's famous "Toploader" for speed manual was optional for all Mach 1's. For those too lazy to shift for themselves Ford offered its C4 3-speed automatic for 351 equipped cars, with the 390 and 428 cars receiving heavier C6 3-speed automatic.

Though completely eclipsed by the Mach 1, Ford still offered the GT package on its Mustang. For all practical purposes, the GT was a Mach 1 without the Mach 1 identifiers. It was only available in the sportsroof, engine and transmission options were identical, etc. The only exterior identifiers to the GT were a special GT gas cap and GT specific wheels.

Responsibility for stopping the performance Mustangs, whether Mach 1 or GT, fell to manual drum brakes all the way around, though power assist was an option.

Front disc brakes were optional as well, and power was mandatory with discs. Rear ends were available in a wide range of gear ratios, with "Traction-Lok" optional; 3:91 and 4:30 geared cars mandated Traction-Lok."

Finally feeling the effects of the competition in the intense pony car market, Mustang sales across the spectrum slipped to 299,824, of which 10,080 were 428 Cobra Jet powered cars, and another 3,181 were Super Cobra Jets. The Mach 1 was a resounding success, with 72,458 sold, comprising 24 percent of all Mustang sales. The success of the Mach 1 effectively killed the Mustang GT; with only 5,396 units sold, it was not brought back for 1970, though it would be resurrected in 1982 and still exists today.

The Mach 1 and the GT weren't the only performance versions of the Mustang Ford offered in '69. Ford offered two others, and these have eclipsed even the Mach 1 in terms of its mythology: The Boss Mustangs.

The most well-known was the Boss 302, so named for the 302 cubic inch small block intended for the Trans Am road racing series that was gaining popularity in the late '60s. Stressing handling and road-worthiness, the Boss 302 was Ford's answer to Chevy's Z-28, which had been beating the hell out of Ford's 289–based Trans Am cars.

Continuing a pattern of dishonesty even a politician would envy, Ford rated

Ford's magnificent Boss 302 Mustang (courtesy Gateway Classic Cars, St. Louis, MO).

the Boss 302 at 290 horses. A 4-speed manual and front disc brakes were standard. The Boss 302 came standard with chin and rear deck spoilers and blacked-out hood, as well as rear window louvers. Like Pontiac's Judge, the Boss 302 confidently announced itself in a limited number of colors: Bright Yellow, Calypso Coral, Acapulco Blue and Wimbledon White, accented by a black, reverse "C" stripe that began aft of the wheels and ended just below the C-pillar on the quarters. The Boss 302 was available only as a fastback, but setting itself apart from its fastback brethren, the Boss 302 lacked the simulated scoops on the quarters and the medallion on the C-pillars.

The other Boss in the Ford lineup was the Boss 429, so named for the mammoth 429 cubic inch engine Ford somehow wedged between the little Mustang's shock towers. The Boss 429 was built for the sole reason of satisfying NASCAR's homologation requirements; the Boss 429 was actually a part of the ongoing war between Ford and Chrysler on the superspeedways. At the time of its development, NASCAR only required 500 copies built and sold to the public and put no restrictions on cars or engine combinations. In hopes that the Mustang's lighter body would offset its clunky aerodynamics, the fiery Mustang went to work on the high banks of NASCAR. The Mustangs that housed the 429 had to be heavily modified to take on the massive 429 block; each copy of the Boss 429 was hand built by outside contractor Kar-Kraft, in order to modify the suspension to accommodate the engine's mammoth size.

Like the Mach 1 and its smaller sibling the Boss 302, the Boss 429 was only available in the sportsroof body style. Aesthetically, the Boss 429 resembled the Mach 1 or GT, as it sported the same grille and faux scoops on the quarter panels. An oversized hood scoop gave away what lay beneath, and fenders flared to make room for the reconfigured front suspension carried understated "Boss 429" callouts just behind the front wheel cutouts.

The four-barrel 429 was rated at 375 horsepower, but everyone knew that was crap. The standard transmission was Ford's "Toploader" 4-speed manual, as was a low geared "Traction-Lok" rear end. The Boss was available only in five colors, and there was only one interior choice—black high bucket vinyl covered seats without the folding rear seats found in all other sportsroofs due to the battery necessarily being located in the trunk because there was no room left for it under the hood.

The Boss cars were magnificent in either configuration; the Boss 302 is widely considered to be a better car due to its nimbleness with the lighter 302 up front, without the unwieldly imbalance of the heavy 429 in the modestly sized car. Unfortunately for posterity while luckily for those competing with street versions on the cruise routes, they were limited production vehicles. Ford built 1,628 of its Boss 302s in 1969 and only 859 Boss 429s.

While Ford's fighting retreat in the pony car market was led by the Mach 1 and the Boss cars, Mercury again contributed to Ford's war effort with its upscale pony car, the Cougar. While similar to the two previous versions of the Cougar, the 1969 version was a bit longer and a bit heavier. The hideaway headlamps and novel sequential taillights were retained, though the grille now sported horizontal barring, rather than the "electric shaver" look of previous years. As a result, the 1969 Cougar was

**1969 Mustang Boss 429 (courtesy Gateway Classic Cars, St. Louis, MO).**

substantially heavier than the Ford counterparts, weighing nearly as much as the base versions of the larger mid-sized muscle cars.

The GT, XR7-G and the GT-E versions of the Cougar were gone for 1969. For the new model year the Cougar featured engine choices identical to the Mach 1: two-barrel single exhaust 351, four-barrel, dual exhaust 351, 390, or the 428, with or without cold air induction. Each of these engines was available on the base Cougar or the higher end XR-7. Horsepower ratings were identical, as were transmission and rear end choices. A special hood adorned 428 powered cars, complete with hood striping.

A convertible body style joined the lineup for 1969, and the Cougar continued to fill the gap between the Mustang and the Thunderbird. Bucket seats, wood paneling and all the other comfy goodies were standard, with many more like air conditioning and power steering optional. The XR-7 package continued to be offered as an upscale trim package for those just not satisfied with the base Cougar.

The most exciting Cougar offering for 1969 was a special, low production version, unveiled late in the model year, tabbed with the threatening name of "Eliminator." The Eliminator was positioned to kill two birds with one stone, as it was simultaneously Mercury's counterpart to both the Mach 1 and the Boss cars.

Like the Mach 1, the Eliminator was available in a limited number of colors. A scooped hood rested above a blacked-out grille with hideaway headlamps. A stripe ran from the leading edge of the fender back to the quarter panel just behind the door, and ended with block lettering "ELIMINATOR" forward of the rear wheel well.

Also syncing with the Mach 1, the Eliminator was offered with the same engine choices, with the exception of the two-barrel 351; it may not have been up to the challenge of propelling the hefty cat. The Eliminator also offered either of the two 428 Cobra Jet engines, with or without cold air induction. Standing in as Mercury's

**1969 Mercury Cougar GT 390 (courtesy Gateway Classic Cars, St. Louis, MO).**

**1969 Mercury Eliminator (courtesy Vanguard Motor Sales, Plymouth, MI).**

Boss Mustang equivalent, the Boss 302 engine was made available for homologation purposes to allow the Eliminator to compete in Trans Am racing. Like the 302s, the Eliminators were equipped with chin and deck lid spoilers and rocker panel molding taken from the XR-7. Completing its role as Boss Mustang analog, there were even two Eliminators built housing the awesome Boss 429 engine.

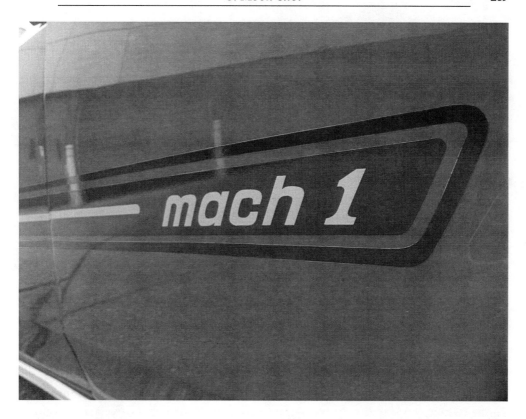

**Callouts for Ford's new performance Mustang option, the Mach 1 (courtesy Gateway Classic Cars, St. Louis, MO).**

Though there were similarities between the 1969 version and the two previous, popular models, sales remained strong for the Cougar. Mercury sold 100,069 Cougars of all configurations in 1969, down slightly from 113,741 the previous year. This number includes 2,250 Eliminators. The Cougar continued to stand out in the Mercury lineup. Though it shared a lot of its DNA with the Mustang, it wasn't simply a clone of the Ford, as many other models in the Mercury lineup were. In fact, the Cougar became so synonymous with Mercury that for much of the following decade, Mercury advertisement directed potential buyers to Mercury dealers found "at the sign of the cat."

As 1969 drew to a close, the pony car market still belonged to Ford, though the chokehold it had maintained on it since 1964 was being wrenched loose. The new offerings from Chevy, Pontiac, and even American Motors and Plymouth were eroding Ford's market share. The Mach 1 and Eliminator packages were efforts to reinforce the defenses and to shore up the bulwark in an effort to maintain the lead. For the 1970 model year, things for Ford would just get tougher.

* * *

By 1969, Ford's rivals were inflicting damage to the Blue Oval's dominance of the pony car market, as sales of the Mustang were faltering, if 299,000 copies can be considered "faltering" in any sense of the word. That's still an amazing number of cars being sold, so a little perspective helps: in 1965, the first full model year of the Mustang, Ford pushed more than 550,000 Mustangs out the door. By 1969, there were more options in the pony car field, and the car maker making life the most miserable for the Mustang was Ford's most ancient antagonist, Chevrolet, with its magnificent 1969 Camaro.

The Camaro has a long history, spanning three decades, and still marches on in the Chevrolet lineup, remaining very true to the original concept of the pony car—great styling, affordable performance, and a long list of option packages for personal customization—and modern Camaros still wear the RS and SS badges of their forebears. In that long lineage of Camaros, most regard the 1969 model as the pinnacle of Camaro styling. If imitation is the sincerest form of flattery, the 1969 model is indeed highly regarded, as it was this ancient warrior on which Chevrolet modeled the latest generation of Camaros when it resurrected the nameplate in 2010, after an eight-year hiatus.

By 1969, the Camaro hit its stride, growing from simply a Chevrolet copy of Ford's original pony car, and the 1969 model exuded a menacing confidence. The Coke-bottle styling of the previous two models was muted, and Chevy sculpted a character line running back from the tops of the wheel openings, making the car appear longer, lower and decidedly more aggressive. Faux vents ahead of the rear wheels were added, and the grille was restyled, with single, round headlamps shifted slightly inboard. Adding the Rally Sport option provided hideaway headlamp covers.

The Camaro was available with a six-cylinder engine for those who wanted big engine Camaro style without big engine Camaro insurance rates; even six-cylinder Camaros could be outfitted with the sporty Rally Sport appearance, further enhancing the performance image, if not the performance itself. The standard V-8 offering in the Camaro was Chevrolet's famed 327 cubic inch engine.

As with the two previous model years, actual Camaro performance began with the SS models. The base engine on the SS package was again a 350 cubic inch engine inhaling through a four-barrel carb and polluting the atmosphere through dual exhaust. For 1969, the 350 produced a very respectable 300 horsepower, up five from 1968. Up from that were Chevy's famous 396s, all with four-barrel carburation and dual exhaust. These were the same 396s available on the SS Chevelles: the 325 horse L35, 350 horse L34, the 375 horse L78 and aluminum headed, 375 horse L89. The base transmission in 350 equipped cars was a heavy-duty 4-speed; optional on the 350s was either a close or wide ratio 4-speed that was standard on SS cars with the 396. One of two 3-speed automatics was available as well, differing only with choice of 350 or 396 engine. The heavy-duty Turbo-Hydramatic 400 3-speed was added to the transmission choices for the 375 horse 396s; in 1968, the high horse 396s could only be had with a 4-speed manual. Brakes were manual drum brakes all the way around, though power assist and power discs were optional. A variety of rear ends were available, with or without positive traction.

SS cars had several differences that set them apart from their more timid brethren. The stock hood was the same as in 1968, with center mounted, non-functional ornamentation designed to resemble velocity stacks. Optional on SS cars was a cowl induction hood which has become iconic and perhaps the most identifiable feature of

**Chevrolet's 1969 SS 396 Camaro (courtesy Gateway Classic Cars, St. Louis, MO).**

the 1969 Camaro; much like the 1967-only Stinger hood on the Corvette being found on all models of mid-year Corvettes, the cowl induction hood is one of the most common hoods found today on all first-generation Camaros, even on those on which it was not available from the factory. The blue Chevy "bowtie" emblem on the grille and tail panel was replaced by SS emblems, and "hockey stripes" adorned the SS flanks from the leading edge of the fender and ending at the doors, just ahead of the quarter panels.

Other than an SS emblem in the steering wheel, there was nothing on the inside to differentiate the SS Camaro from any other. Bucket seating was standard, and the houndstooth pattern returned from 1968. Instrumentation could be upgraded and a console was available, which neatly housed auxiliary gauges. Interior package upgrades included items like glovebox lights, bright trim around the pedals, and wood accented instrument panels. Power steering was optional, as were air conditioning, power windows and power door locks. A range of radio options were available as well.

The Trans Am inspired Z-28 was available again, powered by the 302 cubic inch engine, producing a rated 290 horses; Chevy was no more honest than anyone else, as true horsepower production is pegged at closer to 350. The Z-28 featured heavy-duty suspension, front and rear spoilers and standard front disc brakes.

Beyond the SS and Z-28 cars, Chevrolet went above and beyond for special dealers and racers, duplicating the Central Office Production Order, or COPO, effort and offering COPO Camaros as well as Chevelles. Like the COPO Chevelles, the smaller Camaro was outfitted with Chevy's 425 horsepower 427 cubic inch monster; one of those 427s was an all-aluminum block unheard of in the era. COPO Camaros could be had with either the heavy-duty 4-speed manual or the heavy-duty Turbo-Hydromatic 400 3-speed automatic. COPO Camaros were essentially stripped down vehicles built for a singular purpose—attempted suicide on a drag strip.

The penultimate first generation Camaro was immensely popular, selling 277,453 copies of all types, and approaching the Mustang's level of sales. Among these were 34,932 SS Camaros, and 20,302 Z-28s. Chevrolet built a scant 69 COPO Camaros, and sadly given their purpose in their short lives, few have survived the brutality to which they were subjected.

The 1969 model year was the high point of Camaro styling in the muscle car era. Chevrolet had committed to a redesign of its little F-body pony for 1970, and while the next generation of Camaros was handsome and has legions of fans, it didn't and doesn't command the reverence of the first generation cars highlighted by the beautiful 1969 model.

Over at Pontiac, the Firebird was again offered as GM's second alternative to the Mustang. Pontiac, ever seeking to avoid Mercury's fate and intensely defensive of its independence of Chevrolet, ensured that its F-body was no rebadged Camaro.

Despite this, many of the changes to the Firebird tracked those of the Camaro. The '69 Firebird appeared lower, longer and more pugnacious than earlier models. The split grille was deeply recessed and surrounded by brightwork and flanked by horizontally set quad headlamps. A body color Endura front end encased the grille, and the hood with twin nostrils set in the middle was retained from the '68 model, complete with engine callouts. Accenting the fenders were a set of faux vents just behind the wheel well openings. On the back end, the car features a wrap-around chrome bumper with block "PONTIAC" lettering and a Firebird emblem set just above. The fuel cap was placed behind a hinged door, and 400-equipped cars had a small "400" callout on the deck lid. While Camaro's lines were revealed in the Firebird's profile, Pontiac's engineers ensured it was substantially set apart from the Chevy.

Under the hood, Pontiac offered the Firebird with two different six-cylinders and a two-barrel 326 cubic inch V-8. True performance began with a four-barrel, dual exhaust High Output 350 producing 325 horses. After the 350 was a trio of 400 cubic inch offerings, and for 1969, they had the carb restrictions removed, so they produced identical horsepower ratings as those offered in the GTO. The first produced 350 horses and next up was either the Ram Air III (with Ram Air) or the 400 HO (non–Ram Air). Either way, it was rated at 360 horses. The top of the line was the Ram Air IV, rated at 366 horsepower. A heavy-duty 3-speed manual was standard for all Firebird V-8s, but heavy-duty 4-speeds and the Turbo-Hydromatic 3-speed automatics were optional. As was standard for the day, manual drum brakes were found all around, but these could be upgraded with power or front discs. Rear ends could be had in varying gear ratios and with or without limited slip.

Pontiac did not offer an alternative to the 302 powered Z-28; Pontiac never developed a true small block performance engine in the muscle car era, and it sure as hell wasn't going to use Chevy's 302. Therefore, Pontiac did not compete in Trans Am racing. Regardless, Pontiac wanted a special Firebird to rival the Z/28 in sales, if not on the track. Not a car maker to let trivialities stand in the way, Pontiac appropriated the spirit of the Trans Am circuit and built a special, Firebird based, low production model that would become the flagship of the brand for decades, called, appropriately enough, the Pontiac Trans Am.

The Trans Am option was released with little fanfare late in the 1969 model year, at the same time the Judge option was unveiled on the GTO. The Trans Am had as standard equipment the Ram Air III, with the Ram Air IV as the only option. The

1969 Pontiac Firebird 400 (courtesy Vanguard Motor Sales, Plymouth, MI).

Fender badging for what many consider to be the ultimate first-generation Camaro, the 1969 Z/28 (courtesy Gateway Classic Cars, St. Louis, MO).

same transmission choices offered on the 400 Firebirds were offered on the Trans Am, or TA, and a heavy-duty suspension and mandatory limited slip differential were found beneath. Power assisted front disc brakes were standard, with drums in the rear.

While the Z-28 was only available in hardtop form due to its racing heritage, Pontiac had more freedom and offered the TA in hardtop or convertible form. Only in white with twin stripes running along the top of the hood and deck, the TA featured a special hood with functional scoops placed far forward. The TA came equipped with chin and deck spoilers.

While the 1969 Trans Am was nothing particularly special in terms of performance, it certainly stood out from run of the mill Firebirds and was visually more attention grabbing than the Z-28; the Z-28 and the Trans Am would battle each other within the GM stable for the next 30 years.

Cars in the final year of a body style's generations generally do not fare well in terms of sales, and GM let the world know that the Camaro and Firebird F-body line would be radically reworked in 1970. While Chevy's Camaro defied reality, Pontiac's Firebird did not. Sales of the 1969 Firebird dropped precipitously from over 117,000 in 1968 to 87,708 for 1969. Pontiac built only 689 Trans Ams and only eight ultra-rare convertibles.

* * *

Plymouth was nothing if it wasn't persistent. While the sales numbers for Mustangs, Camaros, and Firebirds were still stratospheric, the faithful little Barracuda was once again Chrysler's entry into the pony car sweepstakes.

For 1969, the Barracuda wore its same basic shape that it had since the first redesign back in 1967; by 1969, it was getting a little stale. There were only minor changes to the base Barracuda, such as a switch to rectangular marker lights and slightly revised taillights. For 1969, however, Plymouth substantially upped the performance of the Barracuda by introducing a new performance package that not only relegated the old Formula S to the back burner, but introduced a name plate instantly recognizable by fans of the muscle car era even today—the 'Cuda.

Barracudas had been colloquially referred to as "'Cudas" for years, but in 1969 Plymouth officially embraced the moniker. The 'Cuda package, only offered on notchback and fastback body styles, upped the Formula S by offering non-functional hood scoops, racing stripes, and heavy-duty suspension and brakes. 'Cudas could be had in small block, four-barrel 340 cubic inch form, producing 270 horses. Standard big-block power for the 'Cuda was again the 383 offered in the Formula S, but it now produced 330 horses.

For the serious 1969 Mopar pony car enthusiast, of which there were not many, Plymouth would grease up a 375 horse 440—the same engine powering the GTX, Coronet R/T and Charger R/T—and force it into 'Cuda, presumably by having assembly line workers jump up and down on it. That much weight in the front end of the little A-body must have made it the automotive equivalent of *Mr. Toad's Wild Ride*, but it sent the signal to the rest of the pony car world that Plymouth was getting serious about competing with the more popular Ford and GM cars.

**1969 Plymouth Barracuda 440 (courtesy Vanguard Motor Sales, Plymouth, MI).**

The standard transmission for the 'Cuda was a 3-speed manual, but those are rare, as most buyers opted to upgrade things to a 4-speed A-833 manual or the TorqueFlite 3-speed automatic. Brakes were mandated power front discs with rear drums.

Plymouth still offered the Formula S package on all three body styles, including the convertible. The Formula S was essentially the 'Cuda without the standard disc brakes, hood scoops or striping. Engine options were limited to the 340 or the 383, there was no 440 offered on the Formula S.

'Cudas came standard with a vinyl covered bench seat, while the Formula S had buckets standard. Buckets were available on the 'Cuda, and were mandatory, along with a console and automatic transmission, if the 383 was ordered. As usual, there was a long list of the options available, including an interior décor package, power steering, a range of radios and the like. For 1969, power steering was available on 383 cars, unlike in 1968.

Despite all of this, Plymouth simply could not sell Barracudas, or 'Cudas, or Formula S's or however Plymouth wanted to badge its little pony. Sales of Barracudas across the line dropped by 25 percent for 1969 to just over 32,000 units, including 1,467 'Cudas of all varieties and another 2,557 Formula S cars. Luckily, plans were in the works to breathe new life into the Barracuda line, with the introduction of a car entirely rebuilt from the ground up in 1970.

\* \* \*

After the surprising success AMC found in 1968, the little car company that obviously could came into 1969 riding a wave of confidence it rarely enjoyed; it was even rarer that that success came in the arena of performance cars. American Motors was not the first thought people had when thinking of performance vehicles. Be that as it may, American Motors had some attractive and successful performance vehicles. To some extent, AMC had to find small and unusual niche vehicles to compete, but the point was, AMC was competing and intended to continue to do so in 1969.

The flagship performance vehicle in the AMC stable was again the 109-inch wheelbase Javelin. Not wanting to mess with success, AMC didn't change much for 1969; changes were expensive to engineer, and AMC couldn't afford to change much had it wanted to do so. The major changes were a redesigned grille and optional side striping, which could be had on the base Javelin or with the more upscale SST trim package. An interesting mid-year offering was known as the "mod-Javelin." This option featured a unique roof-mounted spoiler and well as rocker trim that mimicked exhaust side pipes, à la the Corvette. On the inside, the 1969 Javelin received restyled door panels and carpeting and retained the buckets-only seating. A tachometer was standard. The usual list of typical interior options was available—air conditioning, power steering and the like.

Perhaps the biggest news to the Javelin's appearance for 1969 was the dramatic encore to the wildly patriotic red, white and blue special edition Javelins—the "Big Bad" colors. The Big Bad colors were AMC's mid-year answer to Mopar's High Impact palette. Big Bad Blue was a light blue very similar to Ford's Grabber Blue. Big Bad Orange and Big Bad Green looked a lot like Dodge's Go Mango orange or Plymouth's Lime Light green. Big Bad color packages also included matching, painted front and rear bumpers and lower front valance.

While there were tamer Javelins available, performance Javelins were equipped with the "Go Package." The Go Package was both an appearance and performance

1969 AMC Javelin (CZmarlin/Christopher Ziemnowicz, Wikimedia Commons).

**1969 American Motors 390 equipped AMX (courtesy Gateway Classic Cars, St. Louis, MO).**

package. The hood sported twin hood scoops set far forward and wide apart. The package also included disc brakes, heavy-duty, sway bar equipped suspension and "Twin-Grip" limited slip rear end. Engine options were either the 280 horse, four-barrel 343 cubic inch power plant or the 315 horse 390 engine. Transmission choices were either a 4-speed manual, which came equipped with a Hurst shifter mid-year or a 3-speed Shift-Command automatic.

The Javelin surged forward for 1969, with more than 45,000 units sold in the model year. Selling 45,000 of *anything* was significant for tiny American Motors, but 45,000 cars competing in the arena of the Mustang was downright impressive. In fact, the Javelin managed to humiliate one of the Big Three, as it outsold Plymouth's Barracuda, a car used to sales humiliation. As significant a victory as that was for AMC, it perhaps says as much about the Barracuda as the Javelin.

While the 1968 version of the AMX didn't see the same popularity as the Javelin, the strange little niche car was brought back for 1969. Very little changed between the two years, as it was again essentially a Javelin without the rear seats. There were no major body style changes, and the engine lineup remained essentially the same as the previous model year—a 235 horse 290, a 280 horse 343 and the 315 horse 390 cubic engine. The two-barrel 390 was dropped for 1969. Transmission choices were the base 4-speed manual or the Shift-Command 3-speed automatic. The Go-Package was available on the AMX and included the same features as the package on the Javelin. The interior was exactly the same as the Javelin as well, save the rear seats.

The little AMX sold well, relatively speaking, for AMC. Where the Javelin was punching above its weight somewhat, the AMX was selling in more traditional American Motors numbers with 8,293 AMXs finding new homes for 1969, resting comfortably in its little niche, somewhere in the Twilight Zone between Corvette and pony car.

The final performance car in the American Motors lineup was as unusual as the AMX. This was the SC/Rambler, the result of an unlikely partnership with the Hurst Company.

The SC/Rambler was one of the most traffic stopping vehicles of the entire era, visually topping even its Big Bad brethren and High Impact Mopars. Built on the 106-inch wheelbase of AMC's compact Rogue, the SC/Rambler was too small to be considered a traditional, intermediate sized muscle car, or even a pony car. It was more in the vein of Chevrolet's Nova or the Dodge Dart, but regardless, it was an interesting outlier of the muscle car era that deserves ample attention for both its appearance and its performance.

American Motors advertised the SC/ Rambler as a car that "could make life miserable for any GTO, Roadrunner, Cobra Jet or Mach 1," and it was probably true. The tiny car was substantially lighter than the typical intermediate or even pony car. Powering the little car was only one option—the four-barrel, 315 horse 390 found in the hottest Javelins and AMXs. That was it. No other options. The 390 breathed cold air through a functional, but decidedly strange, hood scoop. The list of transmission options was no greater, as the car only came with a 4-speed manual worked with, naturally, a Hurst built shifter. A 3:54 geared Twin-Grip limited slip rear end was the only option out back. Thrush, a premier exhaust company of the era, provided the exhalation of the big 390. The car came with front disc brakes, sway bars and heavy-duty suspension.

As wild as this all was for a normally harmless little Rogue, the exterior was coated in one of the most spectacular paint schemes of the era. Of course spectacular can be a positive or a negative, and many saw the SC/Rambler both ways. The car came in two paint schemes: a red and blue stripe running along the rockers over white, or an even more outlandish broad red stripe covering most of the bodysides with a huge blue arrow on the hood pointing to a large functional scoop and "390 CU. IN." embossed in the arrow. The scoop, pointing drunkenly at an upward angle, had large red lettering spelling out "AIR," as if there was any question as to the purpose of the scoop. Thinking of everything, AMC even saw fit to paint the car's usually attractive Magnum 500 wheels blue.

Inside, it was only a bench seat covered in charcoal colored vinyl, with red, white and blue headrests. The car didn't even come with a radio, though one could be opted for. A Sun tachometer was standard. That was about it for creature comforts for the SC/Rambler. Air conditioning wasn't an option.

The SC/Rambler was built entirely for the strip, and there were only 1,512 of them made, making it one of the rarer cars of the era. The 106-inch wheelbase put the little Rambler in the same class as the compacts like the Chevrolet Nova, but it was a decidedly athletic compact. Contemporary road tests put the little AMC through the quarter in 14.44 seconds at 104 MPH, which is plenty to embarrass base Road Runners, GTOs or Mach 1's, just as the advertisements promised. Though the SC/ Rambler was not made in significant numbers, the fact that the car and its outlandish paint scheme are remembered today is a testament to the attention it brought to AMC and is indicative of the hyperactive wildness of car styling in the late 1960s.

\* \* \*

1969 American Motors SC/Rambler (Christopher Ziemnowicz, Wikimedia Commons).

If 1969 was a year of triumphs, perhaps the biggest of those was that it was not 1968 anymore. Aside from millions of Americans being able to flip the calendar, however, there were other triumphs: the moon landing, the drawdown in Vietnam, and Woodstock come to mind.

In the world of the American performance car, 1969 was the most exciting model year of the muscle car era to that point. From the 1968 model year to 1969, there was a substantial escalation in the war between the cars' makers, as they not only ratcheted up the horsepower,

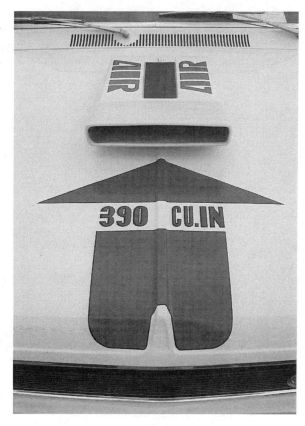

AMC ensured there were no questions as to the nature of its 1969 SC/Rambler (CZmarlin/Christopher Ziemnowicz, Wikimedia Commons).

torque and performance, but tried to one-up the others with outlandish styling to attract the attention of the diminishing pool of young buyers. It is said that the past is prologue; little did anyone know that 1969 was just a prelude—a warmup—for what was to come in 1970. By comparison, in terms of automotive performance and styling, 1970—the final year of a tumultuous decade—made 1969 appear very tame indeed.

# 9

# Wild Life

## *The Zenith of the American Muscle Car*

The fading of the decade of the 1960s saw, appropriately enough, the corresponding fading away of many of the iconic institutions that defined that tumultuous decade. In 1970 the withdrawal from South Vietnam and the "Vietnamization" of the war accelerated. Nixon announced the withdrawal of another 40,000 U.S. troops, scheduled to be home by Christmas. The Vietnam War was drawing to a close, though the American boys drafted in 1970 may not have noticed. The countries of Laos and Cambodia didn't notice, either, as U.S. airstrikes and ground incursions into these two neighbors of Vietnam represented a widening of the war, even as the U.S. drew back. In a bit of rare good news from Southeast Asia, for the first time since 1965, November saw a complete week with zero American deaths.

After the triumph of 1969, NASA began winding down the Apollo program. Among those final missions was the ill-fated Apollo 13 mission, which was crippled after an oxygen tank explosion. The safe return of the Apollo 13 astronauts, relying on 1970 technology and equipment built by the lowest bidder, was arguably as great a technological achievement as putting a man on the moon. Things were less fortunate for the football teams at Wichita State University and Marshall University, as aircraft carrying their teams and supporters each crashed in 1970. Marshall eventually returned to the gridiron, but Wichita State never has.

Political violence continued in the U.S. Terror bombings seemed to be particularly popular, the most spectacular of which was the Black Panther bombing of a police station in San Francisco. The overenthusiastic Weathermen accidentally bombed themselves in New York, which fortunately prevented them from striking their intended target, a dance for non-commissioned officers from nearby Fort Dix. When student protesters at Kent State University in Ohio threw rocks at armed Ohio National Guard soldiers sent to keep the peace, the confrontation turned tragic as the Guardsmen, who apparently would have rather been doing something else on their drill weekend, overreacted and opened fire, killing four. Never a group to miss an opportunity to take a jab at "The Man," Crosby, Stills, Nash and Young put the blame squarely on Nixon and immortalized the event in song. Eleven days after the Kent State incident, a barrage of police gunfire at a dormitory at Jackson State University in Mississippi, following violent protests by black students, killed two students and wounded 12.

With the fading of the decade, some of its icons faded as well. The Beatles released their final album before the Fab Four degenerated into opposing litigants in a lawsuit filed in Britain. Guitar god Jimi Hendrix died after a drug overdose. Less than a month later, Southern crooner and hard partier Janis Joplin checked out as well when she overdosed on heroin.

While some of the cultural icons of the '60s were literally dying out, the final year of the decade saw some debuts that would become cultural mainstays in their own right. Monday Night Football debuted in September with a Cleveland Browns victory—a historical anomaly in and of itself—and, for better or worse, Howard Cosell was a regular attendee in living rooms across the nation. Susan Lucci began a career of futility on the long-running soap opera *All My Children*. The first Earth Day was celebrated, naturally, in San Francisco, and Casey Kasem began his long career on *American Top 40*. Rodgers and Hammerstein's *Oklahoma* made its TV debut on Thanksgiving, and the North Tower of the World Trade Center was completed, making it the tallest building in the world.

The political turmoil of the late '60s gave birth to the satirical comic strip *Doonesbury,* which helped to bring the buffoonery of our elected officials more clearly into the national consciousness. Jimmy Carter left the peanut farm in Plains, Georgia, and was sworn in as that state's governor the same year that his future nemesis, Ronald Reagan, was elected to a second term in California. In an important political milestone, on the premise that if young men were old enough to be drafted, they ought to have a say in the person drafting them, the voting age was lowered to 18 for federal elections, though it would take the ratification of the Twenty-Sixth Amendment to the U.S. Constitution in 1971 to make the change effective for state and local elections nationwide.

Of more relevance to the American automobile, President Nixon established the Environmental Protection Agency. The impact of this new federal agency over all aspects of American life, including cars, would be and still is profound. The EPA was put in charge of enforcing the Clean Air Act of 1970, an ominous piece of legislation for the less-than-efficient performance cars of the era. This act establishing emissions standards in automobiles would, as much as any single piece of legislation, most negatively impact the high-performance muscle cars. Also during 1970 came an unfortunate glimpse of what was to come with the introduction of the Ford Pinto, a sort of a self-propelled Molotov cocktail, as well as the Chevy Vega and the AMC Gremlin. For performance enthusiasts, it was not a good omen.

\* \* \*

By any measure, 1970 was the high tide of the muscle car wars, and indeed, many would contend that it was indeed the high point of the American performance car industry to date. While there have certainly been better performing cars since that time, 1970 was witness to the most vulgar display of styling audacity and brute force performance ever seen. The model year saw the widest variety of muscle nameplates available, wrapped in retina-scorching colors and powered by the widest range of max cube engines. This year, with scant exception, every car maker had its entire line of what we today call "muscle cars" available to the public. Ironically, 1970 would be the last year for some of those fantastic cars, as some would fade into history, never to be resurrected.

While 1970 was the pinnacle of the era, in truth the American muscle car was on the edge of oblivion and living on borrowed time. The American muscle car was standing on the edge of Armageddon, yet the dueling car makers continued to wage war on each other and the mechanical beasts fought blindly on.

* * *

In 1970, General Motors seemed to have finally had enough. Ironically, for a company that created some of the most iconic and revered vehicles of the muscle car era, General Motors had a strong habit of automotive conservatism that came out of a fear of the federal government and the threat of an anti-trust suit. That conservatism led GM to do otherwise inexplicable things, like refusing to participate in racing and self-imposing performance limitations that impacted its ability to compete at differing points during the muscle car era. As a consequence, GM worked very hard to tie one of its own hands behind its back. In 1964, GM limited engine displacements in mid-sized cars to 330 cubic inches. This is the mandate that forced John DeLorean to turn to Byzantine subterfuge that resulted in the GTO option on the docile LeMans. By 1967, GM had lifted this limitation, but, as if defiantly saying "we will give you this, but not a (cubic) inch more," GM limited displacements to 400 cubes. To underscore the supremacy of the GM brass, it also banned multiple carburation on any car save Chevrolet's little Corvette, so that the legendary Tri-Power GTOs and 4-4-2s suddenly became extinct after the 1966 model year. They had creative mathematical formulaic limitations on horsepower by limiting horsepower to one horse per 10 pounds of car. The list went on and on.

However, automotive engineers are creative people. In spite of these limitations, engineers built engines that performed better than their triple carbureted predecessors. By using tricks such as better flowing heads and better carburation, GM maintained its edge through the 1967 model year. In 1968, however, that edge began to dull as Chrysler built mid-sized cars with the styling that finally matched the performance offered by its premium 440 and 426 cubic inch engines, and Ford finally got off its ass and joined the muscle car game in earnest with its 428 Cobra Jet. The high-performance family of GM 396/400 cube engines performed well, and when driven right, they could easily match the higher cube competitors of Chrysler and Ford (or when these were driven wrong), but marketing had to be taken into account as well. To the average buyer seeking street cred by way of displacement bragging rights, more was better. After all, in a world of amateur drivers racing on America's neon-lit, drive-in centered boulevard scene, more cubes covered a lot of driver sins. In 1969, if a buyer visited the Pontiac dealership, his options were several 400s, albeit very good ones, but the Dodge dealership down the street was offering 440 cubes, producing more horsepower in a suddenly very good-looking car for about the same money.

By 1970, after Mopar had the audacity to put triple carbs on its huge 440 cube engine in its lightweight Road Runners and Super Bees, General Motors had finally had enough. John DeLorean, in nixing the high output 350 cubic inch engine in the Judge concept in '69, explained to his engineers that it was a 400 cubic inch world. By 1970, it was more than that. The General finally took the gloves off and struck back, blew the top off of its own cubic inch threshold and offered the biggest engines offered to date in its intermediate cars.

In 1969, Chevrolet had eclipsed the granddaddy GTO in terms of sales and coming into 1970 it led GM's counterattack with its SS Chevelle as GM's flagship performance intermediate. For 1970, GM's entire A-body platform received a bit of a styling refresh, while maintaining the basic form of the third generation redesign of 1968. For the Chevelle, major changes included reshaped quarter windows and C-pillars as well as a new front end treatment, with a horizontally split grille and quad, horizontally set headlamps. A power bulge hood graced all SS Chevelles, and optional racing stripes on the hood and rear deck were available. Also optional was a cowl induction, cold air capable hood. The rear end was also redesigned, with simple, square taillights set low in the bumper. Slightly flared fenders gave the car a more menacing appearance. As with all GM A-bodies since 1968, the SS Chevelle came in hardtop and convertible form; there was no pillared coupe available.

Under the hood, familiar SS offerings were found: the base SS Chevelle was powered by a 350 horse 396 L34; the lower horse L35 didn't make the cut for 1970. Either of the 375 horse 396s—the L78 or the aluminum headed L89—was available as well, though the L89 was put out to pasture early in the model year with only a reported 18 copies being built. The 375 horsepower engines breathed cold air through the functional cowl induction hood. Where in previous years performance stopped with the 375 horse engines, 1970 saw one more offering. The simple act of checking the Z15 option on a Chevrolet order form created one the greatest cars of the muscle car era, and one that underscored the unassuming SS fender badges with one of the most feared engine displacement callouts in American automotive history, the 454.

Chevrolet built some of the truly incredible and enduring engines of the 1960s, from its 409 in the early part of the decade, to the fearsome 396, fire breathing 427 and high-winding, hot-rodder's favorite 327. Standing out from all of these formidable power plants, however, is the 454, arguably the most recognized General Motors power plant ever made. For 1970, the 454 came in two varieties—a civilized LS5 version producing 360 horses, and the lethal LS6. The LS6 was outfitted with high compression pistons and beefed-up internal components, and it sucked cold air though the cowl induction hood, resulting in a dishonest factory rating of 450 horsepower that marked the highest rated horsepower of any engine of the entire muscle car era.

All SS Chevelles came standard with a heavy-duty Muncie 4-speed manual transmission or the reliable Turbo-Hydromantic 3-speed automatic. Those equipped with the 454 offered three choices in 4-speed transmissions, as well as the automatic. Braking was still primitive, with four drum brakes working feverishly to counteract the momentum generated by the engine. Rear ends were available in various ratios, with or without limited slip.

On the inside was standard fare for the era—air conditioning, power steering, and console were optional. A bench seat was standard, though buckets covered in full vinyl were available, as were power windows and locks.

The SS Chevelle only sold 62,372 units, including 3,773 454s of one type or another, for 1970. Sales tumbled precipitously from 1969; the victory of the SS Chevelle over its rival the GTO was, in a sense, the equivalent of a mutiny for captaincy of a sinking ship. Regardless, the LS6 Chevelle was certainly the greatest performance intermediate Chevrolet had ever built, and the car is rightly enshrined among the very few cars that can legitimately lay claim to the greatest muscle car of all time.

Backing the SS Chevelle in GM's intermediate lineup was The Great One, Pontiac's venerable GTO. Like the Chevelle, the grandfather of the muscle car got a slight restyle for 1970. Gone were the hideaway headlamps of the previous two model years. Instead, quad headlamps flanked smaller, blacked-out grille openings housing the familiar white block letter

One of the most intimidating engine callouts of the muscle car era was that of a 454 powered Chevelle. There was no outward indication as to whether the 454 within was the tamer LS5 or the uncivilized LS6. Wise would-be challengers took no chances (courtesy Gateway Classic Cars, St. Louis, MO).

"GTO" in the driver's side grille. The grille assembly was surrounded by an Endura front bumper, as in previous years. The GTO shared the slightly flared fenders that graced the flanks of the Chevelle, and the rear end received a makeover as well, with narrower taillights set in a chrome bumper beneath the deck lid. Like the rest of the GM A-body muscle car line, the GTO could be had in only hardtop and convertible configurations.

The standard engine for the GTO was the same as it was in 1969—a 350 horse 400 cubic inch four barrel. As in '69, the 366 horse Ram Air III was optional, as was the Ram Air IV, producing 370 horsepower. Mercifully, the low compression, two-barrel 400 that had somehow managed to hang around as an option since 1967 was dropped. All engines but the Ram Air IV came standard with a 3-speed manual gear box, but a heavy-duty 4-speed and the Turbo-Hydromatic 3-speed automatic were popular options.

Like Chevrolet, Pontiac took full advantage of GM's new no-holds-barred approach to the 1970 model year. Pontiac's engineers gleefully pulled the 455 cubic inch block from its Gran Prix, heated it up some and stuffed it into the GTO. Pontiac's L75 455 was underrated at 360 horsepower, with an impressive 500 foot pounds of torque. Despite this, the 455 was somewhat disappointing; contemporary track tests record a 455 GTO running the quarter slower than its Ram Air III or Ram Air IV siblings. While the L75 455 is Pontiac's version of the LS5/LS6 454 from Chevy, it wasn't on the same planet as its corporate cousin. Even among Pontiac's muscle car engines, the Ram Air IV has proven to be far more memorable than the 455. That the transmission choices for the 455 were the same as the lesser 400 equipped GTOs is telling; no 3-speed manual was offered on the Ram Air IV.

Again for 1970, Pontiac trotted out its flagship GTO, the Judge—the car that in 1969 was to be a cheap, lightweight Road Runner fighter, and turned out to be anything but. The Judge came dressed in a choice of wild colors and with redesigned

**1970 Pontiac GTO convertible (courtesy Vanguard Motor Sales, Plymouth, MI).**

tri-color "eyebrow" striping on its flanks. For those who, for whatever reason, wanted a Judge without the flair, the 1970 Judge could be ordered in any standard GTO color. The Judge came standard with the Ram Air III and with the Ram Air IV as a fire breathing option; transmission choices were the same as for the base GTO. Late in the model year, the 455 was made optional on the 1970 Judge.

Bucket seating was standard in the GTO, and the usual fare of options was available, such as air conditioning and power everything. One option as short lived and as unpopular as it was interesting was the Vacuum Operated Exhaust, or VOE. This option allowed the driver to pull a knob in the dash and essentially dump engine exhaust before it reached the mufflers. This reduced backpressure and theoretically improved performance, but it also increased engine noise. It also drew the attention of the Environmental Protection Agency, and it was quickly abandoned, with only approximately 233 GTOs so equipped. The GTO continued to gain weight in 1970; its curb weight of more than 3,600 pounds was inching close to Dodge Charger territory.

Sales for "the Humbler," as Pontiac marketed the 1970 GTO, continued to slide precipitously. Sales were down to 40,150 including 3,797 Judges, a breathtaking drop from over 72,000 in 1969. The grand old Pontiac slipped to third in mid-sized muscle car sales, behind the SS Chevelle and the Plymouth Road Runner. This was not terrible news in and of itself, but the SS and the Road Runner also saw drops in sales in 1970.

Oldsmobile took its place in the order of battle beside Pontiac and Chevrolet again with the 4-4-2. In terms of both styling and engine options, "Dr. Olds," the mad scientist from the Oldsmobile advertising campaign, really ran with things in 1970.

**1970 GTO Judge at the Pontiac-Oakland Museum in Pontiac, IL. Beyond it sit a 1971 Judge and a 1972 GTO. This car is owned and restored by Tim Dye, curator of the Pontiac-Oakland Museum (photo by owner).**

Stylistically, the '70 4-4-2 finally came of age, throwing off Oldsmobile's conservative and traditional styling. The designers at Olds went full bore into the effort to build an aggressive, malevolent looking muscle car, and by all accounts, that's what they achieved. The F-85 or Cutlass based mid-sized Olds could be had in hardtop or convertible, as well as a pillared coupe not available from its corporate cousins. The 4-4-2 got the same subtle styling changes that were found across the GM's A-body line. The car featured a redesigned front end with a 4-4-2 specific grille to set it apart from its lesser brethren in the Cutlass/F-85 line. The rear end was freshened up as well, where the single vertical taillights were replaced by two sets of twin, narrow lamps set low in the chrome bumper. For the first time, Oldsmobile offered a performance fiberglass hood, replacing the subtle cold air inlets hidden in the grilles in previous years. The new hood came complete with twin power bulges extending from

**1970 Oldsmobile 4-4-2 convertible (courtesy Fast Lane Classic Cars, St. Charles, MO).**

the cowl and culminating in twin slits just aft of the leading edge of the hood and was held down with chrome tie downs. In terms of styling, the '70 4-4-2 finally came of age, throwing off Oldsmobile's conservative and traditional styling.

That styling was backed by the 4-4-2's bombproof power plants. Oldsmobile, unlike Chevrolet and Pontiac, didn't bother offering any 400-cubic-inch mills in the 4-4-2. Perhaps Oldsmobile, knowing the class of buyer that typically bought its products, calculated that performance Olds buyers were going to pay nearly the same outrageous insurance premiums on a 455 that they would on a 400. The base engine in the 4-4-2 was a 365 horse 455 that also powered Olds' full-sized car line. This is the same engine that had powered the Hurst/Olds cars since 1968; those cars got around the GM 400-cube limit by leaving the factory with Olds 400s that were replaced by the 455s by the Hurst folks. Up from that engine, however, and the only optional engine on the 1970 4-4-2, was the W-30 455.

The W-30 option had been around since 1966; back then it was a 400 cubic inch engine fed by triple two-barrel carbs. When in 1967 GM put the kibosh on multiple carburation on anything except Chevrolet's golden child, the Corvette, the W-30 continued as the hottest Olds offering, but with a four-barrel carb. With the lifting of the GM mandate against displacements of over 400 cubic inches, Dr. Olds went nuts and grew the W-30 to 455. The 455 W-30 was rated at 370 horses and 500 ft. lbs. of torque, but anyone remotely paying attention knew that wasn't the truth. The W-30 sucked cold air through the easy breathing fiberglass hood. The car was adorned with attention-grabbing wide stripes and prominent W-30 callouts.

The standard transmission for the 4-4-2 was a heavy-duty, GM standard

3-speed manual. This transmission was not available on the W-30. Optional on base 4-4-2s, and standard on the W-30 was a heavy-duty M21 4-speed manual. The standard Turbo-Hydromatic 3-speed automatic was available on all 4-4-2s, and Hurst's "His-and-Hers" shifter housed in a console was available; Hurst shifters were standard in all manual shifted cars. Several rear ends were available, with or without limited slip, and drum brakes were standard, with or without power assist, as were front disc brakes.

The 4-4-2 was still an Oldsmobile, however. That means the car was a bit pudgy, coming as it did with standard bucket seats and a console for automatic equipped cars. As a dietary measure, the buckets could be swapped for a bench seat as a "no cost option." Olds offered a veritable cornucopia of weight-adding options such as power windows and locks, air conditioning, and power steering. Optional Rocket Rally Pac instrumentation and a Custom Sport steering wheel were offered, as well.

Dr. Olds offered another performance mid-sized option in 1970. While born of the Cutlass line, it did not have the badges or the Vehicle Identification Number of the 4-4-2 and therefore avoided the attraction of the insurance folks, who by 1970 were sniffing the performance car market with increased scrutiny.

The car was called the Cutlass SX, and it would certainly be what was known in the day as a "sleeper." The base SX did without the fiberglass hood or striping found on the 4-4-2, though these could be added as options. The SX could be had with three different versions of the 455 cubic inch engine during the model year. The first was the L33 two-barrel, dual exhaust engine producing a surprising 320 horsepower and 500 foot-pounds of torque. This engine was available until February of 1971, when the L31 455 replaced it for the remainder of the model year. The L31 retained the dual exhaust but was fed through four-barrel carburation, and this increased the horsepower rating to 365 horses.

The most exciting option in the Cutlass SX was the W-32 455, also producing 365 horsepower. The W-32 was no longer available on the 4-4-2, where it had a home in 1969 and turned the Cutlass SX into a bona fide performer allowing it to take its place among Oldsmobile's vaunted "W-machines." Where the more docile L31 utilized smaller valving and was limited to 2.56:1 rear gearing, the W-32 suffered from none of these limitations, though rear end gearing was still relatively tall at 3.08:1. Regardless of engine, all Cutlass SX cars made do with the Turbo-Hydromatic 3-speed automatic transmission, shifted on the column unless a console was ordered; no manual was offered.

The Cutlass SX was a grown-up's luxury muscle car coming with a full panoply of luxury items standard. When equipped with the W-32 455, it was for all practical purposes a very well disguised 4-4-2. The "other Olds muscle car" was intended as direct competition with the RT/SE Chargers and the new, luxury/performance offerings such as Pontiac's Grand Prix SJ and Monte Carlo SS from Chevrolet. Today the Cutlass SX is literally a forgotten muscle car and one that is criminally lost to history, coming as it did in a model year full of much higher profile offerings.

Oldsmobile reached its performance apex in 1970. The W-30 4-4-2 is one of the era's great cars, rightly ranked with the SS 454 Chevys and Hemi Mopars as among the greatest of the era. Today, 1970 W-30 powered cars command a premium, due

**1970 Olds Cutlass SX convertible (courtesy Vanguard Motor Sales, Plymouth, MI).**

to the scarcity of new ones sold in 1970. Despite the 1970 4-4-2 being honored with being chosen as the official pace car of the Indianapolis 500, the 4-4-2 suffered in terms of sales; Oldsmobile sold only 22,877 4-4-2s in 1970, including 3,100 W-30 cars. Olds also built another 7,122 Cutlass SX cars. Interestingly, Oldsmobile also built two W-30 powered Vista Cruiser station wagons, perhaps the ultimate definition of "sleeper." Down from 1969 by only around 3,400 vehicles wasn't as catastrophic as what Pontiac endured, but then, Oldsmobile never did sell a tremendous number of 4-4-2s.

Muscle cars had always seemed like an afterthought to Buick. The early Gran Sports were attractive cars, but they always retained that unquantifiable Buick "air"; Buick was, had been, and still is a marque for an older and/or more successful demographic. More so than even Olds or Mercury, Buick was overlooked when buyers thought of performance cars. The fantastic Stage 1 GS should have made more of an impact outside of Buick circles, but it would take Buick muscle literally decades to get its due, and likely that was only after the prices commanded by GTOs and SS Chevelles and even 4-4-2s made the GS cars an affordable alternative.

In 1970, Buick took advantage of the relaxation of the corporate mandates and sought to change all of that. Stodgy Buick, the conservative car maker providing sultry luxury to millions of old people and business executives—the last, lonely outpost of street credibility before Cadillac—built perhaps the most un–Buick like car it could. At least, that is, until it did it again in the 1980s.

This ultimate Buick was the GSX, and it was the perfect fusion of unprecedented performance and signature Buick luxury. Using the basic GS as the starting point—updated this year like the other A-body cars, with a reshaped C-pillar like the Chevelle's, fuller rear wheel openings and elimination of the Buick "sweepspear" contour on the bodysides—Buick abandoned its traditional conservatism in building this car and even tried its hand in the youth oriented colors-and-graphics game. For starters, the GSX was only available in bright Saturn Yellow or Apollo White, with black longitudinal striping and hood stripes, and a rear deck spoiler. It came equipped with a hood tach borrowed from Pontiac and aggressive GSX badging. The GSX appeared every bit as muscular as any competitor.

Under the hood Buick put its new-for-1970, 350 horsepower 455 cubic inch engine as the base offering in the GSX—not anywhere near the 450 horses being produced by the LS6 Chevy, though a 1970 review called Buick's horsepower rating the "understatement of the year." The Stage 1 option bumped the rating by 10 horses to 360. The incredible production for this engine, however, was not in horsepower, but in torque, which in practical terms is at least as important as horsepower. The torque produced by the 1970 455 was pegged at an incredible 510 foot-pounds, far and away the greatest of the entire muscle car era. In fact, that number would not be eclipsed for another 22 years in an American performance car, when Dodge finally managed to top it with its V-10–powered Viper; the Buick was powered by a V-8. Dodge accomplished this feat with benefit of modern technology, and not to mention two additional cylinders.

The GSX was available only with a heavy-duty 4-speed manual transmission or a 3-speed Turbo-Hydromatic automatic; Buick buyers tended to consider shifting manually to be beneath them, so the vast majority of the 678 GSXs sold were automatics. Other GSX-specific items were larger tires on chrome plated wheels, a heavy-duty suspension, 3.42:1 rear gearing with limited slip and power front disc brakes.

On the inside, it was typical Buick despite the obvious efforts at performance. Bench seating was standard, but only in black, and buckets were commonly opted for. A padded steering wheel and door panels and seating covered in high quality vinyl were standard as well. Buick's full range of options was available, including power four-way, tilt seating, air conditioning, tilt wheel, cruise control and power steering, windows and locks.

The GSX would mark the high water mark for Buick performance, not only in the muscle car era but until the mid–1980s when Buick re-emerged with its Regal based performance cars, the all-black Grand National and GNX. Contemporary tests clocked the GSX at 13.38 seconds in the quarter mile at 105 MPH. Not too bad for any car, but amazing for one that tipped the scales at a feather under 4,000 pounds.

For those 1970 buyers who wanted a more classic Buick, one less offensive to the senses of the traditional Buick purchaser, Buick offered a more run of the mill offering, devoid of absurd things like bright colors and hood tachs. For those who preferred earth tones, there was the standard GS car. Having played "Mother-may-I?" with its corporate masters, Buick upped the GS 400 from 1969 to the GS 455 for 1970. The GS engine and transmission options were exactly the same as the GSX, though a heavy-duty 3-speed manual was the standard transmission for non–GSX cars. GS 455 cars had rear end options beyond those of the GSX, and braking was standard drum brakes at all four corners with power or front discs optional.

The GS cars shared a revamped front end with the GSX, which featured a deep,

**Buick's 1970 GSX (courtesy Steven Anastos, Red Hills Rods and Classics, St. George, Utah).**

blacked-out grille divided into two sections and quad headlamps. All GS 455 cars, including the GSX, received cold air induction through redesigned twin scoops in the center of the hood. GS 455 cars had rocker panels adorned with metal trim and twin, narrow red stripes.

While history remembers the GSX—and rightly so—there wasn't much separating that flashy car from the more mundane stablemates. The 1970 GS cars, armed as they were with the torque monster 455, were more than capable performers and, like the W-30 Oldsmobiles and LS6 Chevrolet, have a place in the pantheon of the greatest muscle cars of the era.

Neither the GSX nor the GS 455 was ever going to escape the scrutiny of the insurance man, and for those few Buick buyers for whom money was indeed an object, Buick continued to offer the little GS 350. The GS 350 had always been lost as a performance car among its other contemporary intermediate performance rivals. In 1970, in a world of GM intermediates powered by 450+ engines, the GS 350 sank into obscurity.

This is unfortunate. Though the GS 350 would wilt when compared to its GM cousins, it was a capable car. The little 350 delivered a surprising 315 horsepower, breathing cold air as it did through Buick's redesigned hood. The GS 350 could be had with the base three-on-the-tree column mounted 3-speed manual or optional floor shifted 3-speed manual, heavy-duty floor mounted 4-speed manual or Turbo-Hydramatic 3-speed automatic. All the typical Buick optional goodness was available as well.

Ironically, the underpowered little GS 350, unappreciated as it is today, was more sustainable than its huge-cube contemporaries. Buick had always offered a smaller cube version of its Gran Sport/GS for those who wanted to be seen driving a GS car but without the insurance premiums. By 1970, those insurance premiums had become prohibitive to many potential performance intermediate buyers. The market responded with a nearly three-fold increase in sales for the GS 350 over 1969, and the other GM divisions finally caught onto what Buick had been doing for years.

Bucking the trend of declining sales suffered by the GS' performance intermediate cousins at Chevrolet, Olds and Pontiac, Buick actually sold more GS cars in 1970 than they did in 1969: 20,096 GS cars, compared to 19,257 the previous year. The sales tally includes 9,948 GS 350 buyers seeking shelter from the insurance premiums. Apparently, the new 455 excited Buick buyers more than it did the customers of the other GM divisions, because Buick also managed to sell more 455 powered cars than it did the GS 400 the year before, with 10,148 copies being sold, including 678 GSXs. Buick built 2697 Stage 1 455s in 1970. The 1970 Stage 1 is perhaps the most underrated of the great muscle car engines, coming as it did from bourgeois Buick and at the same time as exciting offerings from Olds, Pontiac and Chevy. In the modern market, Stage 1 Buicks, and especially GSXs, are worth their weight in gold. It may have taken 40 years, but the awesome Buick is finally getting its due.

In 1970, GM pulled no punches, having untied its hand from behind its back and fully committed to the displacement wars. In 1969, Ford and Chrysler were each offering engine displacements well in excess of the 400 cubic inches to which GM limited its divisions. Though the hottest GM 400s had no problem standing toe-to-toe with Ford's 428 and the Chrysler 440 and 426, engine displacements carried a lot of weight with the public. General Motors wanted to arrest that trend, and sought to tilt the battlefield back in its favor in 1970, sending forth phalanxes of

**1970 Buick GS Stage 1 (courtesy Gateway Classic Cars, St. Louis, MO).**

performance intermediates, armed with high displacement weaponry to battle the large cube Chryslers and Fords. While the performance of the new GM intermediates was an unqualified success, it did not translate into the increased sales as hoped.

\* \* \*

For the 1970 model year, the stylists and engineers at Dodge and Plymouth refrained from messing with the success of their B-body lines. There was a major restyle on tap for 1971, and the designers were focusing on a new E-body line for 1970. Besides, the 1968 restyle had resulted in success rarely enjoyed by Chrysler, and planners hoped that momentum would carry on into the 1970 model year. As a result, there wasn't a lot of change to the basic forms of the various B-body lines, and what changes were made were styling revisions. The High Impact color scheme continued into 1970, in a heated side competition with Ford's Grabber and AMC's Big Bad colors to blind America's drivers. Indeed, it is 1970 model Mopars for which these colors are best remembered today. Four-speed cars offered perhaps the most iconic shifter of all time—a Hurst unit with an ergonomically formed handle that allowed the driver to grip it as one would a pistol—known, appropriately enough, as the Pistol Grip shifter. Many of the Chrysler's icons of the muscle car era hail from 1970. It was the pinnacle of Chrysler's muscle car years and opposed 1968 as the bookend of what was arguably the most successful three year run in the history of the Pentastar.

Plymouth's Road Runner continued to reside at the bottom of the price point ladder among Chrysler's performance intermediate offerings. However, like the GTO before it, the 1970 Road Runner began in 1970 to drift away from its parsimonious roots, as the list of standard features, and commensurate weight, began to grow.

The 1970 Road Runner, again offered in hardtop, coupe or convertible form, retained the basic shape of the previous two models, but appeared much more refined. The cheap aluminum grilles of the 1968–69 models were replaced by a reshaped and much more attractive blacked-out arrangement of vertical bars that incorporated the quad headlamps, the bottom rising between the headlamps above an air intake slot. The front bumper incorporated two round driving lights set close toward the center. A redesigned hood featured a power bulge that culminated near the windshield and had a rear facing engine callout visible from the cabin. A wide flat black hood stripe covered the power bulge. If the "Air Grabber" option was ordered, the hood had a vacuum operated door in its center that would ominously rise to create a cold air induction scoop, with scary shark's teeth on its flanks. The tail panel was revised as well, with twin, horizontal lenses. The molded creases in the quarter panels and fenders were gone, and the flanks were smooth save for a faux vent just aft of the doors on which the Road Runner emblem was found. An optional "dust trail" stripe was a long decal of the cartoon dust trail left by the bird that ran from the faux scoop on the quarter panel, across the doors and all the way to the Road Runner decal on the leading edge of the fender. Goofy and immature? Sure, but it was a Plymouth Road Runner.

The engine offerings were identical to the two previous years, with the 335 horse 383 as the entry level engine. The only engine options were the 440 Six Barrel and the mighty 426 Hemi. Six Barrel cars did not receive a special hood as they did in 1969, and both 440 Six Barrel and Hemi cars received the Air Grabber hood as standard

**1970 Plymouth Road Runner (courtesy Fast Lane Classic Cars, St. Charles, MO).**

equipment. The standard transmission remained the 3-speed manual, but as in previous years, the A-833 4-speed manual or 727 TorqueFlite 3-speed automatic were both optional. Rear ends were available in a wide variety, including the heavy-duty Dana rear end, and limited slip was available as well. Drum brakes were standard, and power assist or front discs were optional.

On the inside, the cloth-and-fabric bench seat was still available, but bucket seats and a console were offered as options. The old, cheap horizontal bar instrument cluster was replaced by the sportier rally gauge set from the Coronet line. Power options, such as steering and brakes, were gaining popularity even in the Road Runner, and while it was still considered a frugal, budget muscle car offering it was definitely gaining weight. However, despite the restyle, the average cost of a 1970 Road Runner was essentially the same as it was in 1968.

The 1970 Road Runner was arguably the best looking of the car's first generation. The 1968 and 1969 models, while attractive, simply looked and felt "cheap" compared to the 1970; the 1970 model finally shook the taxicab look. The lineup even got its own aero-warrior for 1970 with the Superbird—similar to '69's Dodge Daytona but actually sharing no body panels. While the Superbird, like its Dodge counterpart, dominated the big oval tracks, arguably its most important contribution was wooing ace driver "The King" Richard Petty back from Ford.

Despite this, Road Runner followed the downward trend of most of its GM competitors. In fact, sales of the Plymouth were nothing short of catastrophic. In 1969, the Road Runner was second in sales among intermediate performance cars, trailing only the SS Chevelle with 79,693 total sales. In 1970, that number fell by more than half to 36,861.

These sales numbers are interesting compared to the higher priced Buick GS, which actually saw an increase in sales in 1970. This perhaps reveals something about the market and the buyers of these two respective cars; the folks who could afford a Buick to begin with were likely better positioned to also afford the insurance

**The optional 1970 "dust stripe" decal available on the 1970 Plymouth Road Runner ran from the faux quarter panel scoop to the leading edge of the fender, and perfectly represented the audacious nature of the muscle car wars by 1970 (courtesy Hankster's Hot Rods, Indiana, PA).**

premiums, whereas those who bought Road Runner were not so fortunate. Regardless, the Road Runner wasn't immune to the malaise suffered by the muscle car genre in general in 1970. The market was slowly killing the Road Runner, without the benefit of anything from Acme.

For those who wanted a little more in their Plymouth, the GTX was brought back as a more refined alternative to the Road Runner. Again a product of the Belvedere line, the GTX received styling updates like the Road Runner. In fact, the GTX was more similar to the Road Runner than it had been in the two previous model years. The GTX received the same front and rear end treatment and the same hood. About the only external differences between the two cars were the substitution of GTX emblems on the quarter panel's faux scoop and grille and the replacement of the Road Runner's dust trail striping from the fender to the quarter panel vent with twin horizontal stripes from the fender to the quarter panel vent. One important difference, however, is the availability of body styles; the convertible option was dropped for 1970, and the GTX never came in a cheap coupe, so it was a hardtop or nothing.

Engine options were the same as they had been through the life span of the GTX, the standard 375 horse 440 and the optional 426 Hemi. For 1970, however, Plymouth made the 440 Six Barrel optional as well. Transmission for the GTX excluded the 3-speed manual and made the 3-speed TorqueFlite automatic the standard tranny, though a heavy-duty A-833 4-speed was available. Braking, of course, was manual drums, though on the higher end GTX power and/or front discs were commonly opted for. Rear end options were essentially the same as for the Road Runner.

**1970 Plymouth GTX (courtesy Steven Anastos of Red Hills Rods and Classics, St. George, UT).**

While externally and mechanically the GTX and Road Runner were substantially the same car, inside they were not, at least not in base form. The GTX came standard with bucket seating covered in full vinyl, as well as full door panels and wood grain finish on the dash. Air conditioning was a popular option, as were power steering and a console.

By 1970, the GTX was essentially a glorified, re-badged Road Runner, with little to set the two cars apart other than the roughly $500 in base price. With the growing list of options available on the Road Runner, buyers soon discovered they could upgrade a Road Runner to GTX levels with less impact on the wallet. Consequently, the high end Plymouth saw a catastrophic drop in sales for 1970 with only 7,147 GTXs sold. The death spiral of the GTX was due in part to the same forces affecting muscle car sales in general, but in reality, the GTX probably had its death warrant signed in 1968 with the introduction of the Road Runner. There were only so many buyers willing to pay Oldsmobile premiums for a Plymouth, and as the Road Runner moved away from its taxi cab roots, it put additional pressure on the GTX.

As at Plymouth, things changed little over at Dodge, as Chrysler's volume division continued to do its thing. The mid-sized offerings from Dodge were the same as the previous year, though with some restyles.

The Super Bee remained Dodge's budget super car, and as Plymouth did with its Belvedere line, so Dodge did with its Coronet. As a result, the Super Bee received a cosmetic makeover. As in years past, the Super Bee was only available in hardtop or coupe form. The front end was redesigned and now featured blacked out, elliptical split grilles surrounded by large chrome loops intentionally designed to resemble insect wings. The familiar bumble bee emblem was located in the header panel between the two. The bee's wings resemblance might have been lost on buyers, but the unusual front end gave the car the appearance of wearing an angry scowl. The hood was carried over from 1969, but an optional power bulge hood featuring scoops in the middle of the bulge was available. Engine displacement callouts adorned the fenders. The familiar "bumble bee" stripe was available, or owners could opt for an updated one with a large reverse "C" shaped stripe that stretched from just behind the doors to the rear of the car and incorporated the bumble bee in its usual location. The tail panel was updated to house redesigned taillights in a stainless panel gracing the width of the tail.

Engine options paralleled those of the Bee's corporate cousin the Road Runner, with the 335 horse 383 standard. The Six Pack 440 and 426 Hemi were optional. As with the Road Runner, Dodge did away with the lift-off fiberglass hood for the Six Pack cars. The standard transmission was relegated to a 3-speed manual, but a 4-speed manual and 3-speed automatic were optional. The Ram Charger option was mandated on the Six Pack and Hemi cars, as was either the 4-speed manual or 3-speed automatic. A wide range of rear ends, including the Dana, in a variety of gearing, with or without positive traction, was optional as well. Braking was standard manual drums with power and front discs as options.

The interior reflected the Super Bee's low end status in the Coronet line. Bench seating was standard, as were carpeting and full vinyl door panels. Luxuries like a console, power steering, bucket seating, upgraded radio and steering wheels as well as air conditioning were costly options.

Today, with 1968–1970 muscle nearly worth its weight in gold, the 1970 Super Bee is among the least desirable models. Indeed, it wasn't even that popular in 1970. Enthusiasm for the 1970 Super Bee bordered on open hostility and the redesign, particularly the new front end, was roundly criticized. This is unfortunate because in reality the pissed-off looking '70 Super Bee is a very handsome car. At the time, however, the 1970 Super Bee seemed to be made of lead as sales for the car plummeted to 15,506 copies, down nearly 10,000 from the year before. With the pressures on the intermediate performance car market and the internal competition from Plymouth, Dodge planners took a long look at the future of their budget super car.

Dodge's other Coronet based performance car was again the Coronet R/T, tiredly trotted out again for the 1970 model year. Sadly for the old veteran of Dodge's street battles since 1967, for 1970 the Coronet R/T felt like Dodge was simply going through the motions and had mailed it in.

The Coronet R/T was available in hardtop or convertible; there was no pillared coupe. Externally, it shared the Super Bee's front end revisions, and where the Super Bee had quarter panel moldings in the form of a faux scoop, the R/T had a blister that further accentuated the scoop. The tail panel received a makeover but was inexplicably more austere in appearance than the Super Bee's, with two sets of three taillights separated by the block letter "DODGE" and an R/T badge underneath that seemed to be added as an afterthought. Hood choices were the same as the Super Bee's, and an R/T badge replaced the bumble bee between the grilles. The car offered a tail stripe wrapping around the rear end of the car, but there was no analogue of the attractive

**1970 Dodge Super Bee with Ram Charger hood (courtesy Vanguard Motor Sales, Plymouth, MI).**

"C" stripe as was offered on the Super Bee. All in all, the entire car simply had the feel that Dodge wasn't really trying very hard.

Under the hood, the standard engine was again the 375 horsepower 440 Magnum, and the 426 Hemi was again the top option. For 1970, Dodge offered the 440 Six Pack. Befitting the Coronet R/T's upscale image, the 727 TorqueFlite transmission was standard, but a 4-speed could be opted for. Heavy-duty suspension and brakes, though of the drum variety, were standard.

Inside, the car came standard with sumptuousness. Bucket seating in full vinyl covering was standard, as were full carpeting and wood graining on the dash and console, if one were ordered. Instrumentation was of the sporty rally variety, and the steering wheel was a premium three spoke sport wheel. Power brakes and steering were optional, as was air conditioning.

Sharing as it did the scowling front end of the 1970 Super Bee, the car was polarizing. People loved it or hated it. Judging by sales numbers, most hated it. The car suffered from friendly fire in the form of Charger sales, as both cars shared the same luxury-performance niche in the Chrysler lineup, as well as from the high-end offerings from General Motors. As such, the Coronet R/T was the sick man of the Dodge muscle lineup, and the plush Dodge had few takers, selling only 2,319 hardtops and another 296 convertibles. While it was relatively easy to turn a run-of-the-mill Coronet 500 into an R/T, Dodge could not continue to justify sales figures that low. Dodge wasn't American Motors after all, and the days of the august and dignified Coronet R/T were numbered.

Rounding out Dodge's 1970 performance intermediate lineup was again the

Charger R/T. The 1970 model shared many characteristics with the previous two iterations, such as the beautiful flying buttress roofline and hideaway headlamps. Like all Chrysler B-bodies, the Charger for 1970 received a slight facelift. The Charger retained the ubiquitous hideaway headlamps it had carried since its inaugural year in 1966. The blacked-out grille, vertically split in 1969, once again stretched unbroken across the entire front of the car. The grille was enhanced by a thin horizontal molding that served to divide it horizontally, and the entire grille assembly was surrounded by a large chrome loop. The tail panel was essentially the same as the 1969 model, with two large horizontal taillights separated by "CHARGER" in script and an R/T badge and set in a body color tail panel. The simulated louvers in the doors of the 1968–69 models were replaced by a blister creating a faux reversed scoop adorned with an R/T badge. The hood, understated in recent years, could be had with its molded scallops painted black with large engine callouts.

Engine choices for the R/T Charger were essentially the same as were available in the two previous model years—the 440 Magnum, producing 375 horses, or the 426 Hemi. A rare engine option was the 440 Six Pack, made available for 1970. The standard transmission for the R/T was the 727 TorqueFlite 3-speed automatic, but the A-833 4-speed was an option, with the legendary pistol-grip shifter. Standard braking was the industry standard four wheel drums, but power assist was available. Rear ends were available in a variety of gear ratios, and limited slip was available. Hemi powered cars automatically came with limited slip Dana rear ends, and these were optional on all R/T cars.

Inside, the car was about as luxurious as a Dodge got, as the Charger was designed as a luxury-muscle cruiser. High back bucket seating in full vinyl was standard, but for the first time, a bench seat was an option. Rally gauges came standard, and power steering was optional. Faux wood graining abounded, and opting for the "Special Edition" trim option made the car even plusher and included a console and an upgraded steering wheel.

Charger sales were still relatively strong, but, like the restyles of the Coronet and Super Bee, the changes for the 1970 model were not particularly well received. Again, like Dodge's other offerings, the 1970 model Dodge Charger has proven to be less popular than the '68 or '69 today. Sales of the big Dodge slipped again to just over 46,500 units, and of those, 10,337 were of the R/T variety.

That Plymouth offerings of a given year are more popular than those of Dodge doesn't happen often, but it was true of 1970. The Road Runner and GTX were truly beautiful cars, and were arguably the best looking models of their entire lifespan. The Dodges, on the other hand, felt like they were going through the motions. Both car makers can be forgiven to an extent for their lackluster 1970 intermediate effort, as both were distracted by another endeavor for 1970, the results of which are two of the most memorable and collectible cars of the entire muscle car era.

\* \* \*

Ford returned to the intermediate performance car wars with its Torino. Suddenly, by 1970, the Torino line was in need of a restyle, and Ford obliged it with a total makeover inspired by the supersonic fighter aircraft of the age. Available in

**1970 Dodge Charger (courtesy Vanguard Motor Sales, Plymouth, MI).**

"Sportsroof" hardtop or convertible form, the new Torino displayed a narrow Coke-bottle waist, aggressive long hood and short deck. The new Torino hit a growth spurt for 1970, riding as it did on a new 117-inch wheelbase with its overall length increasing by 5 inches. To stick the big car to the road, the car was lowered to bring its center of gravity down. Gravity, it turned out, had more of an effect on the Torino, as Ford's engineers packed at least 100 pounds of blue oval-ness into the car; it tipped the scales at well north of 3,500 pounds.

The Torino line featured 13 different models or trim levels, beginning with the base Fairlane 500, but the performance Torinos were the Torino GT and the Torino Cobra. The Torino GT came standard with a 302 cubic inch small block—not the fire breathing Boss 302, but a much more sedate two-barrel 302 producing a decidedly unmuscular 210 horses. Thankfully, those insisting on a more respectable GT Torino could skip past the pair of equally unimpressive 351 two barrels to the 351 "Cleveland" four barrel. The four-barrel Cleveland engine is one of Ford's better known and more respected engines of the era, replacing the "Windsor" 351 from 1969. The Cleveland was available with the J-code Ram Air option and produced a respectable 300 horses.

True performance buyers would have opted for one of a trio of intimidating 429 cubic inch engines, offering slightly more displacement than the biggest offerings of the previous year. The first was the "Thunderjet" 429 producing 360 horses, yanked from Ford's land yacht flagship the Thunderbird. Then there were the intimidating Cobra Jet engines—the 370 horse Cobra Jet or 375 horse Super Cobra Jet. The Cobra Jet could be had with or without Ram Air, and the Super Cobra Jet was a part of an option package known as "Drag Pak," which also provided either 3.91:1 or 4.30:1 rear

**1970 Torino GT (Vanguard Motor Sales, Plymouth, MI).**

gears and "Traction Lock" limited slip differential. Ram Air could be ordered on any 429, and all Ram Air cars featured a "shaker" hood scoop.

Torino GT transmission choices were the standard 3-speed manual transmission or an optional heavy-duty, "Toploader" 4-speed manual. The 3-speed "Cruise-O-Matic" automatic was also optional. Standard braking was manual drums all the way around, though buyers could opt for power assist or power front discs. Limited slip "Traction-Lok" was available in a variety of rear ends.

The Torino GT featured GT emblems in the grille and on the leading edge of the quarter panels, non-functional hood scoop and louvers. It also had body color racing mirrors, interior GT identifiers and rocker panel molding. The car was available in Grabber colors and could be had with hide-away headlamps and an attractive "laser stripe" running the length of the car. Bench seating was standard, but buckets were available, as was a lengthy list of options, such as air conditioning, power steering and a variety of radio choices.

For the budget minded, Ford brought back the Torino based Cobra as its frugal performer. The Cobra featured a heavy-duty suspension and meaty tires and wheels, as well as a blacked-out hood and grille to create a menacing appearance. The hood was accentuated with twist-lock hood pins, and the rear deck was adorned with a rear spoiler. The attractive laser striping of the Torino GT was an expensive luxury not available on the Cobra.

The Torino Cobra was available in only the fastback model, with the expensive convertible unavailable. The standard engine in the Torino Cobra was, confusingly enough, not a Cobra Jet engine but the 360 horse 429 Thunderjet. From there, the earth returned to its axis as the only engine options were the 429 Cobra Jet and 429 Super Cobra Jet. The heavy-duty Toploader 4-speed manual was the standard transmission, with the Cruise-O-Matic 3-speed automatic optional. Braking options mirrored those of the Torino GT.

The 1970 Torino remake spawned attractive cars, and the refined GT and the brutal Cobra were the pinnacle of that line. Though Ford was out of the NASCAR business, racing teams still drove Fords and found the 1970 to be lacking on the high banks; many teams ran 1968–69 versions. Though this damaged Ford in the "win on Sunday, sell on Monday" game, this was made up when the car snagged the coveted *Motor Trend* Car of the Year award. The Torino represented the fourth straight win for the muscle car or pony car genre, following the 1967 Cougar, 1968 GTO, and 1969 Road Runner. It would also mark the last; in a sickening preview of the cataclysm of the 1970s still to come, the 1971 award went to the Chevrolet Vega.

Bantering about the *Motor Trend* trophy was good for the Torino line as a whole, as Ford sold more than 400,000 Torinos. Like the acid induced hallucinations so popular at the time, for performance Torinos, this sales number was an illusion. The GT and Cobra models slipped in sales, mirroring the downward trend across the entire performance intermediate market. Ford sold 60,758 GT models, a number which includes the anemic 302s as well as the potent 429 cars. Cobra sales were even more distressing; only 7,675 Cobras went home with new owners.

For unhappy, upscale Mercury, it was more of the same for its Montego based Cyclone. As it always had, the unfortunate Cyclone stumbled into 1970 in the dark

The wheeled snake of the 1970 Cobra, located on the lower fender just aft of the front wheels (courtesy Vanguard Motor Sales, Plymouth, MI).

shade of the Torino in both style and performance options. Like the Ford, the Merc got a total restyle, growing to a 117-inch wheelbase. There was no convertible option; the Cyclone was only offered in a semi-fastback. Base Cyclones only featured a fender mounted engine callout as far as exterior adornment. The GT featured a prominent grille featuring standard hideaway headlamps—optional on the Torino—and a weirdly attractive gunsight molding in its center that made the 1970 Cyclone GT's front end one of the more unique of the entire era. The GT also had stainless trim separating the body color from black rockers and lower fender molding.

The Cyclones came in three different flavors, and Mercury set them up atypically. The "base" Cyclone was a car generally bereft of optional frills and exterior badging, but powered by the 360 horse Thunderjet 429. The more upscale Cyclone GT, which was ostensibly a step up from the "base" car, started with a four-barrel, 250 horse 351 Cleveland engine; no 302 was available in the more expensive Mercury as it was in the Torino GT. In the world of performance cars it may seem counterintuitive that the base car would be a more powerful car than a GT, until one considers that this is Mercury; in the Mercury world, "upscale" will always be held in higher regard than "no frills." Regardless, the Thunderjet 429 or either of the Cobra Jet 429s was available in either the "base" or GT Cyclones. Transmission choices mirrored those offered by the Torino GT: heavy-duty 3-speed manual standard, with the Toploader 4-speed manual or 3-speed automatic as options. Braking options were the same as the Torino as well, as were rear ends.

Topping the list was the Cyclone Spoiler, brought back for 1970. The Spoiler was very much a poorly disguised Torino Cobra—engine and transmission options were identical, with either the 429 Cobra Jet as the base engine or the ram air 429 Super Cobra Jet as the only engine option, mated to either the Toploader 4-speed manual or 3-speed Cruise-O-Matic automatic. Appropriately enough, the Spoiler featured front and deck lid spoilers and special graphics.

All Cyclones could be had in the eye-hurting Grabber colors, and as Mercurys, they were considerably more upscale than their Ford counterparts. Bucket seating, a console and a full complement of gauges were standard on the Mercury, and the full line of comfortable options was available as well. One such option was a Gauge-Pak, which canted the tachometer and auxiliary gauges toward the driver to create a cockpit feel. More form than function, the Gauge-Pak was one of the more distinctive instrument panels of the muscle car era

In the late '60s, Mercury's intermediate performance cars were hardly more than expensive versions of their Ford counterparts. This is unfortunate, as Mercury had proven in 1967 with the Cougar that, given some creative license and allowed to stray from Ford's leash, Mercury was capable of building unique, attractive cars that bore little resemblance to their Ford counterparts, much like the various incarnations of GM's A and F body lines. Buyers wondered why they should spend more on a Mercury when there was a nearly identical cheaper Ford—or a more unique upscale GM like Olds' 4-4-2 or Buick's GS. This coupled with the changing of the seasons with regard to intermediate performance cars inflicted a mortal wound on the Cyclone. Mercury sold only 13,496 Cyclones of all varieties, which represented a catastrophic drop of 71 percent from 1969. Less disastrous, but only by degree, was the drop in

Spoiler sales. Mercury sold 1,631 Spoilers out the doors, which was only a 50 percent drop from the year before.

Coming into 1970, it appeared the days of Mercury's intermediate performance model, the august Cyclone, were fast coming to an end.

* * *

In Kenosha, Wisconsin, tiny little American Motors was flush with pride and brimming with self-confidence, having enjoyed several successes of scale in the previous years. Last year's wild little SC/Rambler was well received despite its low production and perhaps in spite of its outlandish appearance as well. The AMX, whatever that car was, was a success as well, and in 1969, AMC embarrassed one of the Big Three when its magnificent Javelin outsold Plymouth's Barracuda. AMC had proven it could brawl with the big boys in terms of performance, if not production numbers. In October 1969, in—appropriately enough—the former Confederate state of Texas, AMC released a performance version of its intermediate Rebel, simply called "The Machine."

At 114 inches, The Machine rode a shorter wheelbase than most intermediates of the time, coming as it did from a manufacturer forced to keep a close eye on the bottom line and known more for practicality than for performance. The Machine, however, was the latest in what was a surprising line of AMC performers bearing the Rebel name badge. The Rebel first appeared in 1957 on a 4-door sedan that is rumored to be the quickest sedan built that year and second overall only to the smaller, lighter, fuel-injected Corvette. The Rebel nameplate disappeared in 1961 but was dusted off and trotted back out for 1967 before providing the base for The Machine, AMC's ultimate muscle car.

Like the S/C Rambler before it, The Machine was initially only available in a red, white and blue color scheme. This was perhaps an ode to the "American" part of AMC's name; what else would one expect from a car company named American Motors but red, white and blue? It may have been a misguided effort to tap into the fast-evaporating patriotism that was a by-product of the Vietnam War, much more prevalent in 1965 than in 1970. By 1970, that the war was lost was clear; the U.S. was enduring a humiliating withdrawal, and the public was beginning to see how the nation was treating the veterans of America's first military defeat. Enthusiasm for the war was gone, and patriotism was blasé. Whatever the thinking in Kenosha, AMC doubled down on the colors of Old Glory for initial versions of The Machine.

The Machine was another collaboration with George Hurst, just like the SC/Rambler before it. However, where the SC/Rambler was actually screwed together by Hurst, The Machine was built entirely by AMC. The aggressive grille was blacked-out and was bracketed by quad headlamps in separate nacelles. The blue hood featured a prominent functional hood scoop with an integrated hood tach that looked like it was meant to be there, as opposed to hood tachs on GM vehicles that appeared to be hastily glued on by a forgetful assembler on the way out the factory doors. The semi-fastback roofline of the hardtop-only car was vaguely reminiscent of its deceased ancestor, the Marlin, and a red stripe ran the length of the body, turning up at the rear and joined by blue and outlined white stripes to wrap across the trunk lid. The rocker panels were done in blue, and mercifully, the wheels didn't get the coat of blue paint those on the SC/Rambler did. Late in the model year, The Machine could be had in any standard AMC color, including the Big Bad colors, with a flat black hood.

Offering a wide range of engine options on a single car was an expensive proposition, and AMC avoided this by offering only one for The Machine. Wasting no effort with lesser power plants, AMC went straight to the top and offered its hottest 390 cubic inch engine. The four-barrel, dual exhaust 390 produced 340 horses and 430 foot pounds of torque. A limited slip "Twin-grip" differential was standard in either 3.54:1 or 3.91:1 gearing. A 4-speed manual transmission was standard, naturally with a Hurst shifter—the Pistol Grip no less—and the Shift-Command 3-speed automatic was the only option. The heavy-duty suspension was upgraded in the way a small company with limited resources could—raiding the parts bins of components meant for other vehicles. For instance, the rear springs came from the Rambler station wagon. Fifteen-inch wheels and a heavy-duty cooling package were standard, and power front disc brakes were optional.

On the inside, bucket seats came standard, draped in black vinyl with red, white and blue stripes on the center armrest. Instrumentation and the general layout of The Machine revealed its practical, no frills Rebel heritage, as it was relatively Spartan. The typical range of options of the era was available, such as consoles and power steering.

All in all, The Machine was an impressive car, coming as it did from AMC, a company not exactly known for cars that could be called "impressive." With its clean lines, subtle and functional hood scoops and integrated hood tach, its looks were as attractive as its performance. While the horsepower production of the 390 wasn't going to grab anyone's attention in the era of LS6 Chevys and Super Cobra Jet Fords, not as much was asked of those 340 horses; The Machine was smaller and lighter than the SS Chevy or the Torino Cobra and was capable of standing toe to toe with all but the hottest offerings from other builders.

With AMC's limited production capacity, there weren't many Machines sold. Some of this had to be attributed to the fading of the performance intermediate performance car market in 1970, but perhaps people just couldn't get their mind around the idea of a bona fide muscle car built by a company many people still called "Rambler." Whatever the reason, there weren't many Machines prowling the streets. The National American Motor Drivers and Racers Association claims that 1,936 were built, while the 1970 Rebel Machine Registry puts the number at 2,326. Despite the low sales numbers, the Rebel Machine represents the best of AMC's performance effort in the muscle car era. Like most of what AMC's performance cars of the 1960s and early 1970s, The Machine didn't get its due then and frankly, is still overlooked today.

* * *

The premium, high profile name plates weren't the only performance options available to buyers seeking intermediate performance in 1970. For those who were unwilling or unable to pay the steadily increasing costs of performance, there were alternatives.

By 1970, the insurance companies, never ones to miss an opportunity to raise

**1970 Rebel Machine in late model year solid color paint (courtesy Ron Eichler of Missouri City, TX).**

premiums, recognized that the loud-colored, graphics-heavy muscle models with ever bigger displacements and horsepower ratings were aimed at the young male market, which happened to be the market segment that posed the highest risk of accidents. They also recognized that it didn't take 450 horsepower to take the laundry to the cleaners, and that cars so equipped existed for only one reason, and that horsepower wasn't being used to pull trailers. Consequently, beginning in the late '60s, insurance premiums for performance models rose stratospherically and by 1970 were certainly nowhere near plateauing.

An age old trap in car buying, particularly among the young, excited buyer of a new performance car, is to realize with disappointment that while the car itself is affordable, when external costs such as fuel and insurance premiums are factored in, the total cost of owning the car puts it out of reach. The rising insurance rates therefore were one of the factors responsible for the steady erosion of the mid-sized performance car market that car builders suffered in the late 1960s.

Faced with this, the car builders fought back. General Motors' effort at combating the insurance companies was a class of A-body based cars retrospectively and collectively called "junior" muscle cars.

For General Motors, the concept of the junior muscle car was not a new thing. Buick, of all car makers, was way out ahead of GM's other divisions in this field with its GS 340/350 cars it had been offering for years. By 1970, Pontiac, Olds and Chevy followed suit, offering performance cars based on the A-body platform, as were GM's traditional muscle cars. Rather than being equipped with large displacement power plants, the junior muscle cars were typically offered with high performance, small displacement V-8s as base engines with large cube blocks as options. Because they did not carry nameplates or the vehicle identification numbers identifying them as performance cars such as, say, a GTO or 4-4-2, these cars avoided the scrutiny of the insurance companies. When the car was registered—and more importantly, insured—the car was simply a docile Oldsmobile Cutlass, Chevy Malibu or Pontiac Lemans. Bearing engines with smaller displacements, junior muscle cars carried a lower entry price point as well. The budget muscle car concept was a dusting off of the blueprint of the 1964 GTO or 1968 Road Runner—cheap, mid-size performance—but with the intent of staying under the radar of the insurance salesman. Essentially, the buyer traded the status of the well-known performance nameplate for affordability and practicality. In the end, the budget performance car was still a performance car.

Buick still offered its junior muscle car, the GS 350, as it had since 1967. While the GS badge might have caught the attention of the insurance man, the GS 350 wasn't even in the same universe as the GS 455 in terms of performance, but it was cheaper to insure.

Even more budget friendly—because it was not a Buick—was the Pontiac GT-37. Ironically, the GT-37 was the car Pontiac should have built in 1969 to hunt down 383 Road Runners before John DeLorean put the kibosh on the concept and its engineers and designers somehow came away with The Judge.

Introduced in the middle of the 1970, model year, and based on the cheap pillared coupe or hardtop Tempest T-37, the GT-37 came standard with sporty features such as locking hood pins, Rally II wheels, dual exhaust and special decals and stripes taken from the '69 Judge. Its base engine was an underwhelming 225 horse, two-barrel 350 cubic inch engine, but a two-barrel 400 producing 265 horses was available. True performance was obtained with the optional four-barrel that produced 330 horsepower when backed by a 3-speed automatic transmission or 345 horses with a 4-speed manual. The GT-37 lacked the body color Endura bumpers of the GTO, which kept costs down, as did the scoopless hood and standard bench seating. With dual exhaust and sporty striping and badging, however, the GT-37 nominally looked the part of a performance car.

The most important difference between the GT-37 and the GTO was that the GT-37 wasn't a GTO. While the performance of the 330 or 345 horse version of the 400 was at least in the realm of performance of the base GTO, the car was a Tempest. It carried a Tempest vehicle identification number, and it was insured as a Tempest. A little over 1,400 buyers decided that they'd rather not pay through the nose in insurance premiums, and Pontiac sold just over 1,400 copies of its little GT-37.

Chevrolet's budget entry into the junior muscle car arena drew on the ancient Malibu nameplate and was called the Malibu 400. Lesser engines could be had in the 400, but the most potent was the 325 horse, LS3 396 cubic inch engine. The LS3 was essentially the same engine as the L35 from 1969, when it represented the bottom rung on the SS Chevelle's ladder, except that it was now punched out to 402 cubic inches, as were all 396s for 1970. The horsepower rating was increased to 330 from

**Pontiac's 1970 ½ GT-37, with the rare 330 horse 400 engine, owned by Chris Smetana (courtesy the owner).**

1969's 325. The LS3 wasn't available on an SS Chevelle, but it did represent the highest horsepower output of the Malibu line. Transmission choices were either a 4-speed manual or Turbo-Hydromatic 3-speed automatic. The Malibu 400 came standard with dual exhaust, and sport striping on the hood and rear deck was an option. The car came standard with bench seating and manual steering and drum braking. The car was available in hardtop and convertible form with optional sport stripes on the hood and rear deck. It didn't have the grille or threatening cowl induction hood its bigger SS brothers did, but it was a very sporty looking car, with displacement callouts forward on the fenders.

The Malibu 400 certainly didn't carry the weight the SS cars did in 1970, but it was essentially the same car that represented the bottom rung of the SS 396 ladder just a year previously. More importantly, it was registered and insured as a docile Malibu, avoiding the premiums insurers nailed on SS cars. However, the buying public was lukewarm to the budget Chevy, with only 1,821 built, including 28 convertibles.

Oldsmobile offered not one, but two junior muscle cars for 1970—the W-31 and the interesting Rallye 350. The W-31 was introduced in 1969 as the evolution of 1968's Ram Rod 350 and was available on either the base F-85 or the more upscale Cutlass. The W-31 offered a high-performance with significant performance upgrades such as an aluminum intake manifold and low restriction air cleaner, all of which added up to 325 horsepower. The engine breathed through the same cold air induction hood as the 4-4-2, complete with chrome lockdowns. A 3-speed manual transmission was standard on the budget car, but a 4-speed was a more popular option, both of which were stirred with a Hurst shifter. A special, heavy-duty Turbo-Hydromatic 3-speed automatic was also optional. The cooling system was upgraded, and the car came with a positive traction rear end.

**Oldsmobile's Cutlass W-31 (courtesy Vanguard Motor Sales, Plymouth, MI).**

The other offering from Olds was the Rallye 350, one of the more unusual cars of the entire era, and certainly the wildest of the junior muscle cars. Aimed squarely at the youth market that was buying wild colored Mopars and Fords, the car only came in one monochrome color—retina searing bright yellow, complete with body color bumpers and even yellow wheels. It also sported a fiberglass cold air induction hood and rear deck spoiler. Youth friendly "Rallye 350" badging adorned the rear of the quarter panel. The car was available in a pillared F-85 Sport Coupe, F-85 Club coupe or Cutlass Holiday coupe, the latter of which was a hardtop without a pillar, despite Olds insisting on calling it a coupe.

A 310 horse 350 cubic inch engine powered the little Olds, and those based on the cheaper F-85 came standard with a 3-speed manual on the column; few cars, if any, were built without a transmission shifted on the floor. Cutlass based cars came with a floor mounted 3-speed manual. A 4-speed manual or 3-speed Turbo-Hydromatic 350 automatic were optional. A limited slip differential in various gearings was available, and manual drum brakes at all corners were standard. Since it was an Oldsmobile, bucket seating, air conditioning, cruise control, power doors, windows, seats and trunk release were available.

Guidance from Olds reminded its dealers that the Rallye 350 was $68 cheaper than a base Road Runner, gold standard for budget muscle cars, if "gold standard" is the appropriate term to describe cheap cars. Despite this, Olds only pushed out 3,547 Rallye 350s, perhaps indicating that Oldsmobile had strayed too far from its comfort zone with the wild color, or perhaps too far from the comfort zone of the Olds buyer. The W-31 fared even worse, with only 1,352 copies sold. While junior muscle car efforts from other divisions would continue into 1971, Oldsmobile pulled the plug on the youth friendly W-31 and Rallye 350. It was just as well. They didn't sell the inventory they built for 1970, particularly of the Rallye 350, and selling small cube performance intermediates for the youth market wasn't what Oldsmobile did anyway.

The junior muscle cars were interesting cars, and very reflective of the market realities of 1970 that gave them birth. Despite the advantages of very respectable performance, sporty looks and low price point and operating costs, the junior muscle cars just didn't sell well. People who wanted a performance car wanted a performance car; small cube power, regardless of how it was dressed up, wasn't performance in the age of 400-plus horsepower. The youth friendly well from which the original 1964 GTO and 1968 Road Runner had come had been drawn from one too many times. If it was indeed running dry—and by 1970, it appeared to be—there were dark days on the horizon for the American muscle car.

\* \* \*

While the performance intermediates across the spectrum were conducting a fighting retreat in the face of the insurance rate scourge, the battle in the pony car realm was raging with the same intensity it always had, but the performance variants of the diminutive performers were suffering from the same market pressures as their larger cousins. Pony cars as a class were better prepared for the changing times, as they had always offered more insurance-friendly performance small-blocks, and not

1970 Oldsmobile Rallye 350 (courtesy Gateway Classic Cars, St. Louis, MO).

until later in the era were the same large displacement engines powering the intermediate made available in the pony cars. Because the buying public was conditioned to the idea of a small block performance pony car, owning one didn't have the same feeling of phoniness as driving a 350 powered "performance" Tempest that, sans GTO emblems, was still a Tempest. Driving a small block pony didn't feel quite like driving a wannabe, because the idea of small block performance in a pony car was as old as the pony car itself. Though the idea of a small-block powered pony was more acceptable to the performance buyer, it was still the big displacement cars that garnered the most attention—from buyers at the time, from history, and, more importantly, from the insurers.

Enthusiasts argue about whether the pony car, as a class, reached its apex in 1969 or 1970. Those arguing the 1969 side have the 1969 Camaro and Firebird, both of which are nearly universally seen as the pinnacle of the era's design and performance for those two cars. They also have the introduction of the Boss and Mach 1 Mustangs, but these were carried over into 1970, and many consider the '70 models to be better looking, more refined cars. On the other side of the ledger was Plymouth's hapless A-body Barracuda, a car that never gained any traction in the market in the face of the Mustang and quickly fell behind the Camaro and Firebird in 1967. Even worse, in 1969 the Barracuda was outsold by a Javelin model built by AMC, a company with a tiny fraction of the production capacity of Chrysler.

On the other side of the coin, the fans of the 1970 model year have the restyle of the F-body cars from GM, which never achieved the popularity of the earlier

Fender badging on Oldsmobile's Cutlass W-31 (courtesy Vanguard Motor Sales, Plymouth, MI).

generation of Camaros and Firebirds. What proponents of this view have going for them, however, was supplied by Chrysler, with a redesigned Barracuda line and the last significant entry into the performance car market of the muscle car era, a very fashionably late entry from Dodge.

* * *

Ford's Mustang came into 1970 riding a wave of success never before seen in the history of the American automobile industry. The Mustang had thoroughly thrashed any and all competitors and showed no signs of relenting. The Mustang was the quintessential pony car—relatively cheap, sporty, sexy, and available with an inexhaustible list of performance and luxury upgrades—and Ford sold them by the hundreds of thousands. At times, Ford literally sold them as fast as they were built.

Despite some changes to its exterior and its architecture, the Mustang had never been completely overhauled; why mess with such unrelenting success? The Mustang of 1964 was built on a 106-inch Falcon's wheelbase, and while it still remained at 106 inches for 1970, the car was evolving and it had become longer and heavier over the years. Lee Iacocca may have lamented the obesity through which his mechanical prodigy was suffering as it progressed through the 1960s to accommodate Ford's gargantuan engines, but the payoff was greater performance; a 289 just wasn't going to cut it in a brave new world of 400 plus cubes.

For 1970, Ford retired two of the iconic Mustang features: the GT option, which had been thoroughly supplanted by the Mach 1, and the underwhelming 390 cubic inch engine. This left the Mach 1 package as the primary performance version of the Mustang, and for 1970 little had changed about it from the previous year. The main changes were the deletion of the faux scoops behind the doors and a return to single headlamps. This gave the car an overall cleaner appearance than the 1969 model, if not quite as brutal. The 1970 Mach 1 got rid of the lateral body striping and replaced it with wide rocker panel trim that incorporated the Mach 1 logo just aft of the front wheel well, and the logo was replicated on the edge of the deck lid. The car had a bold hood stripe framing the hood scoop, with both chin and deck lid spoilers, and was available in the full range of Ford's bright Grabber colors.

The major changes took place under the hood. The base engine for the Mach 1 was again a 351 cubic inch two barrel, but of the "Cleveland" variety rather than the "Windsor." This engine was good for 250 horsepower. The optional four-barrel 351 Cleveland with 11.0:1 compression upped that output to 290 horses. Next up were a pair of 428s: the traditionally aspirated 428 Cobra Jet and the cold air breathing 428 Super Cobra Jet. Somehow Ford didn't think cold air induction made any difference, as both engines were rated at 335 horsepower. The 428 powered cars got a shaker hood scoop standard, and this hood was optional on all Mach 1's. The base transmission was a 3-speed manual, which no one wanted; 428 cars got the heavy-duty Toploader 4-speed standard. The 4-speed manual and 3-speed Cruise-O-Matic automatic were optional. Standard braking was, as usual, drums all the way around with power assist or power front discs as options. Rear end gearing was offered in a wide range of ratios and positive traction was an option.

Inside, bucket seats were standard, wrapped in full vinyl. Interior trim featured

**1970 Ford Mach 1 (courtesy Fast Lane Classic Cars, St. Charles, MO).**

simulated wood graining, and the usual panoply of period options was available, such as power steering, choice of radio and sport steering wheels.

The Mach 1 represented the performance Mustang for the masses, produced in higher numbers and readily available for those willing to pay the premium to upgrade a fastback Mustang to something more. The ultimate in Mustang performance for 1970, however, was still found in its two Boss offerings, the Boss 302 and the Boss 429.

The Boss 302 was again sold to the public to satisfy the homologation requirements for participation in the Trans Am racing series, and the 1970 Boss 302 was essentially the same car as the 1969. The 1970 version shared the same body changes as the entire fastback Mustang line, such as the elimination of the quarter panel mounted simulated scoops and the quad headlamps. Power front disc brakes were standard, as were larger sway bars and a reinforced suspension, all necessities for the curves-and-handling heavy Trans Am road racing circuit. Ford dishonestly rated the little 302 at 280 horse, and a new-for-'70 Hurst shifter worked the standard 4-speed manual transmission through the gears as the only transmission option. Externally, the car was available in the generic Ford color palette, as well as all the Grabber colors. Exterior styling also featured a perpendicular stripe across the hood that stretched down the fenders just behind the front wheel openings, replacing the reversed C stripe of 1969.

The Boss 429, Ford's super pony, was ineligible for Trans Am racing, which required small displacement engines, and the Mustang body was banned as well on the NASCAR circuit. Essentially, Ford built the Boss 429 because it could, and it built them for neither very long nor in great numbers; Ford pulled the plug on the car in

January of 1970. The "Boss '9" naturally shared the same body as the rest of the 1970 fastback Mustang line. Aside from this the only appreciable difference between the 1969 and '70 model was that the gigantic hood scoop was painted black in 1970 where it had been body color the previous year.

The exotic 429 engine, designed for the NASCAR superspeedways, was what made the Boss 429 what it was. Its official rating of 375 horsepower was certainly an understatement. As with its smaller sibling, the only transmission available was Ford's Toploader 4-speed manual. Rear ends were likewise non-negotiable—Ford's indestructible 9 inch rear end with Traction-Lok and 3.91:1 gearing was the only choice. Like the Boss 302, the "Boss '9" was outfitted with a substantially upgraded suspension and power front disc brakes.

The Boss 429 was all seriousness and was unadorned with stripes or black trimmed panels, like those that adorned the Mach 1 and Boss 302. There was no late '60s graphics buffoonery to the Boss 429. Aside from the black hood scoop, understated callouts on the fenders and the unique growl of the solid lifter 429 were the only indications of the dangerousness of the Boss 429.

Though sales of the Mustang had fallen from the lofty number of previous years, they were still strong. Ford sold 190,727 copies of the Mustang, from little six-cylinder versions all the way up to the mammoth Boss 429. Of these, 40,970 carried the Mach 1 package. Ford built 7,013 Boss 302s and another 499 Boss 429s. These numbers revealed that the same market pressures bleeding the intermediate performance market were affecting the performance pony cars as well; Ford sold 72,458 Mach 1's in 1969, and another 5,396 Mustang GTs.

**1970 Boss 429 (courtesy Barrett-Jackson Auction Co, LLC).**

Ford's mid-level division, Mercury, decided to give it one more go in the pony car market. Even Mercury's sales slogan sounded uninspiring: "You've got to put Mercury on your list." Mercury's car lines were in trouble—particularly the Cyclone. From the view of the buying public, Mercurys were little more than dressed up, expensive copies of whatever Ford was offering.

Mercury's Cougar, however, deviated from that somewhat. The Cougar was Mercury's most recognizable line, and while it shared the Mustang's basic architecture, it differed substantially from its Mustang cousin in terms of style and luxury accouterments. For 1970, Mercury brought out what is arguably its best Cougar.

The 1970 Cougar, like those that came before it, was only available in hardtop and convertible forms. After tinkering with a grille featuring a horizontal bar design in 1969, which was not well received, Mercury went back to a grille and taillights with vertical slats for 1970, still featuring hideaway headlamp covers and sequential taillights. For 1970, the grill was split by a hood extension, itself featuring vertical barring, that extended down to the front bumper.

As befit the more upscale Cougar, the base engine was a 351, though a two-barrel—there was no 302 or six-cylinder available on a Cougar in 1970. The more muscular Cougars came equipped with the 290 horse 351 Cleveland four barrel, the same that was powering Mach 1's over at Ford. Up from that was either the 428 Cobra Jet or the 428 Super Cobra Jet, each producing an underrated 335 horsepower. If the Drag Pak option were chosen, Ram Air, Traction-Lok rear end and steeper rear end gearing were included, as well as an automatic upgrade to the Super Cobra Jet. Transmissions depended on engine—the four-barrel 351 came standard with a 3-speed, floor shifted manual, and a Hurst shifted 4-speed manual was optional, as was the Select-Shift 3-speed automatic. Cars with the 428 had the option of the Toploader 4-speed or a heavy-duty C-6 3-speed automatic.

Stopping the cat was the responsibility of 10 inch drum brakes all around, and most Cougars, being Mercurys, came with power assist. Power front disc brakes were optional as well. The Competition Handling Package was an option on the 351 cars and standard on 428 powered Cougars and included heavy-duty shocks and springs and front and rear sway bars.

The interior was what one would expect from Mercury—high-back bucket seating trimmed in full vinyl was standard, as was a faux wood grained applique around the instrument cluster. If the upscale XR-7 was opted for, the car got special emblems, wheel covers, remote mirrors and a walnut dash applique, as well as leather trimmed bucket seats.

The premier Cougar in 1970, however, was again the Eliminator. The Eliminator was the sharp end of Mercury's stick in 1970 and was all business; it was not available on the convertible body style or with the plush XR-7 package.

Offered as an alternative to both the Mach 1 and the Boss 302, the Eliminator was available with a wide range of Ford's performance engines. To match the Mach 1, the Eliminator mirrored the Ford's engine choices with the exception of the two-barrel 351 Cleveland. To answer the Boss 302, the Eliminator could also be had with that legendary Ford small block. There were only two transmission choices for the Eliminator—the Toploader 4-speed manual or C-6 3-speed automatic.

302 powered cars only got the 4-speed manual, just like the Eliminator's Boss 302 cousin.

The addition of chin and deck spoilers and a hood with a large scoop set the Eliminator apart from its lesser littermates as well. The Eliminator featured a black hood stripe that framed the hood scoop as well as lateral striping and business-like, block letter "Eliminator" callouts on the lower quarter panels. Eliminators were available in a wide range of colors, as opposed to the four offered in 1969; there are few cars of the era more striking than a 1970 Eliminator with its blacked-out grille standing in stark contrast to one of Ford's Grabber colors.

Feeling the effects of a market that continued to dwindle, Mercury sold 72,343 Cougars in 1970, representing a drop of over 25 percent. The good news was that of these 2,267 were Eliminators, which was actually an increase from the 1969 sales number. The bad news is that it was an increase of a paltry 17 units. Like the rest of Mercury's performance cars, the performance Cougar was in trouble, with sales tumbling every year since its highly lauded introduction in 1967.

Coming into 1970, Ford still owned the pony car market, but that grip was slipping. The Mustang was still the unchallenged stallion in the pony car corral, and the faltering Cougar line did its best to support. By 1970, however, the pony car market was further altered to the detriment of the Mustang, as a new challenger took to the field, yet another threat to Ford's dominance of the pony car market segment.

**Quarter panel decals identified the Eliminator option on the 1969–1970 Mercury Cougars (courtesy Streetside Classics, Charlotte, NC).**

Further, while the Mustang's old enemies still lurked, they were not the same cars the little Ford had so easily swatted away in previous years.

* * *

The same was not true for Plymouth's 1970 version of its Barracuda. After years of laboring away in the long shadow of the Mustang, playing the role of an unsuccessful David in the face of Ford's Goliath, Plymouth radically revamped the Barracuda. The Barracuda of previous years was beloved of its fans, but it never caught fire. Indeed, it barely managed to smolder. With the introduction of GM's pony car alternatives Camaro and Firebird in 1967 and AMC's Javelin in 1968, the Barracuda's suffering was only multiplied, even to the point of being outsold by the Javelin in 1969. Coming into 1970, Chrysler knew it had to take radical action to rescue the Barracuda.

This Plymouth did and did magnificently. For 1970, the Barracuda was literally a different car, sharing only a nameplate and the pony car class with its predecessor. Plymouth's 1969 attempt to stuff its largest displacement engine, the 440, into the tiny A-body Barracuda revealed an imperative need to redesign the car's architecture; like Atlas, the tiny 'Cuda valiantly tried to hold up the giant block, but simply did not have the frame to support Chrysler's biggest engines. Plymouth execs were subject to some harrowing rides in the car, and probably saw some even more harrowing product liability lawsuits on the horizon. For 1970, the whole Barracuda adventure was rethought and the phoenix-like rebirth of the Plymouth Barracuda finally put it on par with its ancient tormentor, the Mustang, in terms of style and represents the most dramatic styling turnaround of the muscle car era. Today, the performance versions of the 1970 Barracuda, the 'Cuda, command the highest premiums of any muscle car.

The Barracuda was moved off of the old A-body frame it shared with Dodge's compact Dart, shrunken by six inches and built on a new 108-inch chassis, dubbed the E-body. The E-body was not only shorter but was also wider and lower. The wider frame allowed for the greater girth of the biggest Chrysler engines, while the lower stance shifted the center of gravity and enhanced handling, particularly when the front end was weighed down by the biggest displacement engines. The car featured the short deck/long hood proportions that were a hallmark of the pony car class, but in a stark departure from the pony car playbook, there was no fastback offered.

With the new E-body, Plymouth designers went nuts exploring the new possibilities. There were no fewer than 10 different engines available across the Barracuda line, from the base Barracuda to the more luxurious Barracuda Gran Coupe to the performance 'Cuda. There was a 6 cylinder offering, as well as the workhorse old 318, but for the performance 'Cuda, the performance engine choices were both more plentiful and more interesting.

The entire stock of Mopar performance engines was available in the 'Cuda; Plymouth offered far more variety than Ford did in its performance Mustangs. The 'Cuda offerings started with the 275 horse, 340 four barrel, one of the era's most underrated engines. The 340 was considered a no-cost option against the standard engine, which was the 335 horse 383 offered in the Road Runner finally made available in the 'Cuda. Both the 375 horse four-barrel 440 and the thundering 390 horse 440 Six-Barrel were available. Then, there was the indomitable 425 horsepower 426 Hemi, which, when bolted into the new E-body, created what many consider to be the ultimate pony car.

Available in either hardtop or convertible, the 'Cuda was available with the full palette of wild Mopar's High Impact colors, as well as body striping shaped somewhat like a hockey stick, with the engine callout on the trailing edge of the quarter panel. The 383 cars got a twin scooped hood, with the "shaker" hood with subtle engine callouts optional.

Everything north of the 383, plus the 340, got the shaker hood standard. Transmission options were typical Chrysler: bulletproof A-833 manual with a shortened version of the famed "pistol grip" Hurst shifter or shifted from the column, if someone for some reason wanted to do so, or the 727 TorqueFlite 3-speed automatic. Standard brakes were heavy-duty drums all around, with or without power assist, or power disc brakes in front as an option. Rear ends were available in a wide range of gearing, with or without limited slip, and the indestructible Dana rear end was available as well.

Interiors were typically Spartan Plymouth, but there were trim packages available to make the Plymouth a little more livable, including rally gauging, optional steering wheels, power options and air conditioning. Leather seating, rare in a Plymouth, was also available and bucket seating was standard, also very non–Plymouth.

The 1970 'Cuda was vindication of sorts, both for the car itself and for Plymouth's perseverance in sticking with its little pony. Sales of the revamped Barracuda line skyrocketed when compared to 1969 sales, with 55,499 units sold; still nowhere near Mustang numbers but considering the general decline in pony car sales overall and the introduction of a new corporate competitor, this number was nothing short of remarkable for Plymouth. Of those, 14,534 were 'Cudas, including 1,784 powered by the 440 Six Barrel and, ironically, 666 copies powered by the sinister 426 Hemi. The 'Cudas are arguably more popular today than they were in 1970, with Hemi 'Cudas being considered the Holy Grail of muscle cars. The 1970 Barracuda redesign has truly stood the test of time, and while sales of the Barracuda were not on par with Ford, the long suffering Barracuda finally had its place in the sun.

For years Dodge had demanded its own pony car. Dodge was Chrysler's volume builder, and by the 1960s was seen as its performance division as well, with Plymouth handling the entry level and fleet duties. After all, how much worse could Dodge do than the Barracuda, which had always struggled to compete with the Mustang, and the later offerings from GM and AMC? The suits at Chrysler, however, denied them, not wishing to create a corporate rival to further cannibalize what share of the pony car market the Barracuda owned, which certainly wasn't much. So, Dodge made do with its A-body Dart and was told to like it.

Dodge had tried to pass off its sporty Darts, such as the GTS and Swinger, as pseudo-pony cars, but lacking a fastback that was nearly mandatory in the pony car

**The redesigned 1970 Plymouth 'Cuda could easily handle the Chrysler's biggest engines. Like a rattlesnake shaking its tail, the shaker hood scoop was a warning (courtesy Hankster's Hot Rods, Indiana, PA).**

field, the buying public didn't, well, buy it. The Darts were built by the hundreds of thousands and were meant to be basic transportation, built to battle other compacts like Chevy's Nova. More importantly, Darts were seen by the public as basic transportation and were among the favorites of mommies and librarians nationwide. What Darts were not was fun, reasonably priced mechanical sexiness, which is what pony cars were supposed to be.

By 1970, with the creation of the E-body platform, Dodge got its wish. The Barracuda moved from the A-body to the new E-body platform, and Plymouth kept the Valiant on the A-body platform. The Valiant line would include the sporty Duster variant, a model that would give the world a very good performing compact when equipped with Chrysler's potent little 275 horse 340. The Dart remained alive on the A-body platform, with a performance compact all its own called the Demon. The most important part of Chrysler's game of musical chassis was that Dodge got its own E-body counterpart to the Barracuda, known to the world as the Challenger.

The Challenger was the final model of what are now remembered as "muscle cars," arriving as late as it did in the muscle car era. The Challenger was not a cheap Plymouth, and it was aimed at a more discriminating class of pony car buyer and

**1970 Dodge Challenger R/T (courtesy Gateway Classic Cars, St. Louis, MO).**

sought to occupy the market segment from which the Cougar was retreating. Though the Challenger was classed as an E-body, it rode on a wheelbase two inches longer than its Plymouth cousin at 110 inches. Like the Barracuda line, it was available with the full range of Mopar engines, from the "leaning tower of power" Slant-6 on up to the ferocious 426 Hemi. In the long-standing (and still-standing) tradition of Dodge, the performance versions of the Challenger bore the R/T badge.

The R/T Challengers came stock with the same 383 as the 'Cuda, and like the Plymouth, upgrades included the 275 horse 340, the 375 horse 440 4 barrel, 390 horse 440 Six Pack or the cantankerous 426 Hemi. Transmission options were the same as well: the A-833 4-speed manual or 727 TorqueFlite 3-speed auto. Rear ends were performance minded, with various gearing and with optional positive traction, and the heavy-duty Dana was optional as well. Brakes, always sort of an afterthought on muscle Mopars, were manual drums all the way around, with power and/or front disks as options.

The interiors of the car were more sumptuous than the 'Cudas, trying as Dodge was to make the Challenger a Cougar. High back bucket seating was standard, as were rally gauges and a reverse indicator light on manual transmission cars. A wood grain steering wheel was standard, whereas it was optional on the Plymouth. The Special Edition package, or SE, got the buyer leather trimmed bucket seating, vinyl top, and a roof console as well as one on the floor. Body styles were identical to the Plymouth—hardtop or convertible. It was available in the wild colors Mopar was then known for, and could be had with either a full length body stripe or the iconic Dodge bumble bee stripe around the tail. The deep set grille, resembling a gaping maw, was topped with a standard R/T hood featuring twin non-functional hood scoops, with a shaker hood available.

The Challenger was a beautiful car, and the public apparently agreed. Dodge sold nearly 77,000 Challengers of all varieties, including 18,512 R/Ts. The Challenger upstaged its cousin in terms of total sales, which was to be expected from Chrysler's volume division. Sales of the R/T nudged those of the 'Cuda with 18,359 R/T cars being sold—395 with the 440 Six Pack and another 296 with the 426 Hemi. Notably, the Challenger line outsold the last iteration of the dying first generation Cougar in 1970—a rare victory of Mopar over Ford in the pony car coliseum.

The late 1960s and early 1970s were a time before there were endless entertainment options on television and an era when automobile competitions such as NASCAR, sanctioned drag racing and road racing were much more a part of the national consciousness than they are today. Back then, car makers participating in these racing circuits had to offer a limited number of versions of their competitive cars to the public in order to satisfy homologation requirements to make their cars eligible. The Camaro Z/28, Ford Torino Talladega and Dodge Charger Daytona are some examples. Other car makers, like Pontiac with its Firebird based 1969 Trans Am, didn't care to compete, but wished to capture the spirit of the Trans Am racing series in order to boost sales; indeed, Pontiac went so far as to appropriate the name of the Trans Am circuit. In 1970, both Dodge and Plymouth copied the Pontiac model and built special 340 equipped versions of their Challenger and 'Cuda that, while equipped with engines too large to allow them to compete on the circuit, attempted to capture the allure of a tight cornering road hugging racer that was at least in the spirit of the Trans Am racing series.

Plymouth's specialized 'Cuda was dubbed the "AAR," for "All American Racing." Dodge didn't seem to put much effort into coming up with a name for its version. Since Pontiac had already taken "Trans Am," Dodge simply went with "T/A" which stood for exactly the same thing and had the added benefit of having the same "ring" as Dodge's other performance acronym, the R/Ts.

The cars were very similar—the AAR's grille featured single headlamps, and the T/A had quad bulbs. The T/A had a snorkel style hood scoop while the Plymouth wore an integrated NACA style scoop, and both cars had a black hood held in place by chrome hood pins. Each featured chin and deck lid spoilers, and each had loud graphics adorning the flanks: a body length strobe stripe ending in an "AAR" shield on the quarter panel of the 'Cuda and a flowing black stripe on the Dodge with "T/A" and an engine callout on the fender. Both the Dodge and the Plymouth were motivated by the same 340 cubic inch engine, though it was topped by triple carbs to produce 290 horsepower and backed by either a 4-speed A-833 manual or 727 TorqueFlite 3-speed automatic transmission. They also had low production numbers in common—2,724 AARs and 2,400 T/As, making them, aside from Hemi powered cars, among the most sought after of all Barracudas and Challengers.

For Chrysler pony cars, 1970 was a new dawn. While the Barracuda finally received the accolades from the buying public that had so long eluded it, it was outsold by its upstart cousin, the Challenger. Chrysler got it right just under the wire, as there were dark days on the horizon for the American performance car.

\* \* \*

*Top and above:* The Plymouth 'Cuda AAR (top) and Dodge's Challenger T/A (AAR 'Cuda photo courtesy Hankster's Hot Rods, Indiana, PA; Challenger T/A photo courtesy Fast Lane Classic Cars, St. Charles, MO).

Chrysler wasn't the only car maker that gave their pony cars a cosmetic overhaul, as GM also apparently decided that after three model years, it was time for a change with its two F-bodies. The reskinning of the Camaro and Firebird lines for 1970 would be the last for quite some time, as the basic form the General gave the cars would remain the same until 1982. That reshaping would also be the earliest

**Strobe striping and bright callouts identified Plymouth's AAR 'Cuda. The "X" shaped pattern is reflected fencing behind the photographer (courtesy Vanguard Motors, Plymouth, MI).**

versions of a shape that would endure to become one of the most recognizable body styles of American automobile history. The longevity and enduring popularity of the 1970 restyle is both a testament to its design, but also an admission that times were changing in the world of car design. In years past, cars, particularly General Motors cars, were restyled every couple of years to keep them fresh. In an era of declining sales and increased foreign competition, the frequent restyles simply weren't cost effective. Thus, the second generation F-body and its twelve year run.

The new-for-1970 108-inch wheelbase Camaro was beset with production issues and was delayed in its release until mid-year, finally showing up on dealers' lots in February of 1970. There was no convertible option, but the standard pony car long hood/short deck proportions were retained, and the car was obviously influenced by the sports cars of Europe. The new semi-fastback Camaro was longer, lower and wider (and heavier) than its first generation, mirroring what was going on with the Mopar pony cars. In fact, the curb weight of the 1970 Camaro was only slightly less than that of the mid-sized 1964 GTO.

The basic pony car formula of offering a wide range of options for personal customization was retained, and the Camaro was available with a wide range of engine choices, from economical six-cylinders to more potent options, and naturally, the performance versions of the Camaro wore the SS badge.

The SS Camaro started with a 350 cubic inch block producing 300 horses. Two 396 options were available as well, producing 350 or, more potently, 375 horses. For 1970, the Z/28 option gave up on the 302 cubic inch engine of the past and snatched the LT-1 engine from the Corvette, a potent 350 cubic inch block producing an impressive 360 horses. Any engine could be backed with the 3-speed Turbo-Hydromatic automatic or 4-speed manual transmission, and power front disc brakes were standard on all SS Camaros.

Pontiac's 1970 Formula Firebird 400 (photo by sicnag, wikimedia Commons).

1970 Chevrolet Camaro Z/28 (courtesy Vanguard Motor Sales, Plymouth, MI).

A Rally Sport appearance package was available as well, as in years past, and it provided a distinctive grille and front end. Round taillights, reminiscent of the Corvette, were used for the first time on the Camaro. The interior was redesigned as well, again inspired by European sports cars, and featured all vinyl seat coverings clothing redesigned seats. Gauges were all moved to the dashboard, as opposed to some having been located on the console in previous years, all within easy view of the driver.

Despite the well-received redesign, sales of the Camaro still fell from 1969 numbers, with just shy of 125,000 sold, of which 12,476 were SS cars and another 8,773 were Z/28s. While the general pressure on the market was part of this fall, Chevy didn't help itself with the late delivery of the new Camaro. The gremlins in the design would, unfortunately, not be the last of the second generation Camaro's problems in the waning years of the muscle car era.

Pontiac followed suit in the F-body redesign and reskinned its Firebird line, and like the Camaro, the new Firebird was delayed in its introduction, having shared the same production difficulties inherent in a radical new design. The Pontiac, on the same 108-inch wheelbase as the Camaro, tracked the lower-longer-wider stance of the Chevy, but there were substantial differences beyond that. The Firebird continued what was by then a Pontiac staple Endura bumper design that had started with the 1968 GTO. The Endura nose gave the Firebird a cleaner, bumper-less appearance. The external antenna was also removed, and all radio-equipped Firebirds had the antenna mounted in the windshield. The single headlamps flanked two yawning grille openings divided in the center in classic Pontiac style.

As in years past, Pontiac differentiated its Firebird levels with individual

**1970 Pontiac Firebird Formula (courtesy the Pontiac-Oakland Museum, Pontiac, IL).**

**1970 Pontiac Trans Am (courtesy Rocky Rotella).**

nameplates. Ignoring the base Firebird with a Chevy-built six-cylinder, the Firebird Esprit offered a two-barrel 350 cubic inch engine that produced 255 horsepower.

The first true performer in the lineup was the Firebird Formula, which replaced the Firebird 400 of 1969. The Formula came standard with a 400 cubic inch four-barrel producing 330 horses, and a unique hood featuring non-functional twin scoops placed far forward, which created a truly menacing appearance. The Ram Air III with 335 horses was optional on the Formula and made the scoops functional. A stiffer suspension was optional as well. A Hurst shifted, 3-speed manual transmission was standard, with a 4-speed manual and Turbo-Hydromatic 3-speed automatic offered as transmission options on the Formula. Like the Camaros, power front discs were standard, and positive traction rear ends were optional as well. Bucket seating was standard, with a console and gauge package as options. Air conditioning and power steering were optional, as was a whole smorgasbord of Pontiac creature comforts.

The top performer in the Firebird line was the Trans Am. The Trans Am featured one of two Ram Air engines breathing through a shaker hood that would become ubiquitous among 1970s era Pontiacs. The base Trans Am engine was the 335 horse Ram Air III and the 345 horse Ram Air IV was optional. The Trans Am also featured fender vents and body colored mirrors, as well as a heavy-duty suspension featuring front and rear stabilizer bars. The Trans Am featured full vinyl interior with engine turned dash inserts surrounding a new rally gauge cluster. A Hurst shifter worked the 4-speed manual, or the car could be optioned with a 3-speed automatic transmission. Power brakes and power steering were standard.

Like the Camaro, the newly designed Firebird was well received, but it didn't sell well, in part due to its late introduction. The popularity of the Mustang was still strong, and the new Mopars sucked a lot of the oxygen out the pony car market before the Firebirds and Camaros were even available. Consequently, fewer than 30,000 Firebirds were sold, including 7,708 Formulas and 3,196 Trans Ams.

\* \* \*

For the 1970 model year, American Motors was riding high with the recent successes it had enjoyed in the performance car arenas. The SC/Rambler was a moderate success, bringing exposure to the company if not sales numbers, and The Machine was holding its own in the intermediate performance car class. The real success story of AMC however, continued to be its pony car, the Javelin.

For 1970, AMC decided it was time to freshen up the Javelin ahead of a total restyle on tap for 1971. AMC refreshed the already successful look of the 1968–69 models with a longer hood atop a redesigned grille and a return to traditional chrome bumpers. The tail end was redesigned as well, featuring full width tail lamps and a center mounted reverse light. The road-hugging suspension common to pony cars was upgraded as well. The three Big Bad colors were available again for 1970. The SST package upgraded the interior to full vinyl seating, as well as other high end accouterments.

Thanks to redesigned cylinder heads, the 390 cubic inch engine jumped to a respectable 325 horses, which represented the top of the Javelin engine options. Behind that was a 245 horse, new-for-1970 360, a two-barrel 304 and a couple of insignificant six-cylinders. The Go Package was again available and netted the buyer front disc brakes, dual exhaust, heavy-duty suspension with sway bars, 3:54 limited slip rear and a power blister, cold air induction hood. Transmission choices included three or 4-speed manuals or a 3-speed automatic.

For 1970, AMC used its Javelin as the basis for a pair of special edition cars. The first was a special Javelin SST called the "Mark Donohue," in celebration of AMC stealing the famed Trans Am driver of the same name, as well as Roger Penske, from behind the wheel of Chevy's Z/28s to pilot 304-powered Javelins on the Trans Am racing circuit. In the world of motorsports, this coup by tiny AMC was even more earth-shattering than Richard Petty leaving Plymouth for Ford on the NASCAR circuit. The Donohue package featured a spoiler emblazoned with Mark Donohue's signature, chin spoiler, special side striping, Go Pack and either the 360 or 390 engine.

The second special edition Javelin was a homologation edition to satisfy SCCA's production number requirements to allow Mark Donohue and Roger Penske to pilot Javelins on the Trans Am circuit. As appropriate as it was unimaginative, these were called Trans Am Javelins. In keeping with the over-the-top patriotic theme of the SC/Rambler and The Machine, the Trans Am Javs were draped in red, white and blue colors. The 325 horse 390 was the only engine available, and a heavy-duty cooling package was standard. Strangely, the Go Package was optional. The only transmission available was a Borg-Warner 4-speed rowed by a Hurst shifter. A 3:90 positive traction rear end was standard as well.

AMC's final performance offering for 1970 was again the unusual little AMX. AMC's two seat sport coupe's engine choices were overhauled for 1970. The 290 horse, four-barrel 360 was the base engine in the AMX, with the 325 horse 390 as the

**1970 AMC Javelin (courtesy Streetside Classics, Charlotte, NC).**

top engine offering. The base transmission was the same Borg-Warner 4-speed available in the Javelin, stirred with a Hurst shifter. Because the AMX was essentially a chopped off Javelin, the suspension received the same rework the Javelin did because it was easy and, more importantly, cheap for cash strapped AMC. The AMX had 10 inch drum brakes standard, though 11 inch discs were available with the Go Package, as was a limited slip rear end available in several different gear ratios.

On the outside, the AMX got a slight restyle that mimicked the Javelin with new tail lamps and a restyled front end. A power bulge hood with non-functional scoops, which became functional with the Go Package, was a prominent feature. Big Bad colors were available, but were surprisingly unpopular, with just a total of 310 AMXs cloaked in one of the three paint schemes. A new paint option called the "shadow mask" incorporated a satin black hood and window surrounds along with silver striping. The shadow mask scheme was available with any regular color. The interior was similar in all respects, save the back seating area, of which there was none, to the Javelin, including bucket only seating.

An interesting bit of legend about the 1970 AMX was that AMC reserved the first fifty serial numbers for special dignitaries, movie and sport stars, politicians and the like, to give them their opportunity to have their own unique car with a serial number as unique as the celebrity him or herself. Sadly and somewhat embarrassingly, no one took them up on the offer. Sad as in sending birthday party invitations and no one showing up.

**1970 AMC AMX (courtesy Vanguard Motor Sales, Plymouth, MI).**

The AMC cars of 1970, like all AMC cars of the era, are overlooked in a world dominated by Mustangs and Camaros, Chargers and Chevelles and the like. Thankfully, they are getting their due today. American Motors performance cars have always enjoyed a loyal, if small, following. Today, there is an emerging fan base that has discovered AMC products. With the price of performance models of the muscle car era from the Big Three spiraling out of control, folks have discovered that American Motors products can be obtained for significantly less and carry the added advantage of being somewhat rare and unusual. One can attend any car show and see literally scores of Camaros, Mustangs and Chevelles, but literally go to hundreds of shows without seeing a Javelin or an AMX, much less a Machine or SC/Rambler.

Unfortunately, that is now, and 1970 was 1970, and buyers then were significantly less enthusiastic. The market was slipping from American Motors as it was for everyone else, and with AMC's smaller production capacity and lower profit margin per vehicle, the diminishing market impacted it more. Compounding the problem, American Motors was hit with labor issues in the fall of 1969 that delayed the release of the 1970 cars. Like the Camaro and Firebird, the late arrival on the scene had a profound impact on sales. People in those days anxiously awaited the arrival of the new models, and many made their buying decisions early in the model year. For AMC, there were no 1970 Javelins on the lots until much later in the model year. The perfect storm of labor union difficulties, the on-time release of the Chrysler E-bodies, the roughly simultaneous release of the GM F-bodies and the ubiquitous popularity of the Mustang simply swamped the Javelin and AMX sales. Consequently, AMC placed only 28,210 Javelins in new homes, including 19,714 SSTs, 2,501 Donohue cars and 100 Trans Am versions. It sold 4,116 AMXs.

* * *

As pressures mounted on the performance car market and sales waned for performance mid-sized cars, the car makers struggled for a response. One of the adaptations was the emergence of the "junior" muscle cars offered by GM. These cars were built on the same A-body platforms as the premier performance models but were cheaper to buy. Being simply option packages on more timid models like the Cutlass and Tempest, they were cheaper to insure. As it turned out, however, the "junior" muscle car concept wasn't terribly popular.

Another source of relief from the skyrocketing insurance premiums was the performance compact—small, lightweight cars powered by performance small blocks that flew, more or less, under the radar of the insurance agent. The performance compact was similar in size to the pony car, but without the range of options—engine, interior, transmission, comfort, etc.—or the inherent sex appeal; no one but the most ardent disciple of the Pentastar would have ever put a Dodge Dart on par with a Mustang in terms of motorized sexiness.

From the early 1960s there had always been a performance compact market. Chevrolet was hanging SS badging on its otherwise harmless little Chevy II Nova, complete with a six-cylinder, since 1963. By 1964, the diminutive SS received Chevy's surprisingly potent 283 producing up to 220 horsepower. Then 1965 saw a 300 horse 327. By 1966, along with a significant restyle, the Nova received the 350 horse 327 and became a little sleeper of wolverine-like ferocity that caught many an unsuspecting lumbering GTO or 4-4-2 by surprise. The SS Nova would continue into the next decade as perhaps the premier compact performance car and would be available with most Chevrolet performance engines along the way—predominantly the 396 and even the 427 (but not the 454).

Ford had its 289 powered Falcons and Mercury its Comet, though Dearborn was more interested in its pony cars than, seemingly, anything else. There was some market overlap between pony cars and performance compacts, and Ford wasn't going to compete against the wild popularity of its own Mustang.

Dodge, while not a player in the pony car field until 1970, had the Dart, which was Chrysler's answer to the performance Nova. The fearsome Darts of the early 1960s, powered by 413s and early Hemis, were large cars. By 1963, the Dart was downsized to 111 inches and entered the compact arena. In 1964, the Dart was available in a GT configuration, with a 180 horse 273 as the top engine option. Like the Nova, the little A-body Dodge became available with bigger and more powerful engines as the 1960s went on. For the 1968 model year, the GTS was introduced, with a standard 275 horse 340 cubic inch power plant. Performance 383s and even 375 horse 440s and the fearsome 426 Hemi were available in the GTS Dart on a limited basis.

As the '60s went on and engines of bigger and bigger displacements were stuffed into compacts, the insurance companies caught on, and the large cube compacts didn't escape the notice of the ever vigilant insurance companies. By 1970, the top performing Dodge compact was the very-1970s named Dart Swinger, with the 340 as the top performance option.

With Dodge receiving its E-body Challenger to fight alongside Plymouth's 'Cuda, Plymouth was given a performance A-body of its own. The Duster, the performance variant of the Valiant line, was adorned with decals that looked suspiciously like Warner Brothers' Tasmanian Devil when he was in a rage (perhaps Plymouth wanted to go the cartoon character route again, but without the royalties). The Duster was originally to be called the Beaver, until Plymouth wisely thought to research the various alternate meanings of that particular name, and it was essentially an updated version of the old A-body Barracuda, which is to say a sporty Valiant. The Duster was available in a variety of engines and cleverly named trim levels such as Gold Duster. The performance model was the Duster 340, with, surprisingly enough, the 275 horse 340 as its prime mover.

The 327 powered Novas and 340 equipped Mopars best represented the compact performance market, but there were other noteworthy cars like the 302 powered Ford Maverick and even the new-for-1970 AMC Hornet SST with a 304. These cars represented a shelter of sorts for a market unable or unwilling to shoulder the increasing operating costs of the dying muscle cars, yet still wanted to drive something fun. As the 1970s wore on and the muscle car and the muscle ponies marched toward their doom, the sporty compacts survived. The performance compacts certainly didn't possess the thunder of large cube intermediates or pony cars, but by the early 1970s, the muscle cars and muscular ponies didn't either.

* * *

Graphics identifying yet another of Ford's legendary cars in America's most legendary car line, the Boss 302 Mustang (courtesy Gateway Classic Cars, St. Louis, MO).

By just about any measure, 1970 was the high water mark for the class of cars now known as "muscle cars." In fact, the American automobile industry had never witnessed a year like 1970. The ever increasing engine displacements, horsepower ratings, wild colors and designs, and the sheer number of performance models all reached a simultaneous crescendo that will never be seen again.

After 1970, the American muscle car began its rapid decline in terms of performance as the forces that would eventually kill them began to consolidate and gather strength. As 1970 drew to a close, the last of the performance titans began to filter off of dealers' lots and out of the showrooms to make room for the incoming 1971 models. While 1971 certainly had its capable performers, a survey of the landscape of the American performance car left one with a palpable sense that the end was rapidly nearing. As it played out, the extinction of the American muscle car was far closer than anyone realized. Thankfully, the end was still in the future as the calendar flipped to 1971, and the car makers and the performance cars that defined a generation had one last curtain call to make, for 1971 would be the last stand of the American muscle car.

\* \* \*

# 10

# Swan Song

## *The Last Stand of the American Muscle Car*

Though the calendar showed that a new decade had begun once it flipped to 1971, there were still echoes of the previous unhappy decade that resonated with the American public. There was still unfinished business to be taken care of, challenges yet to be met.

The most obvious of that unfinished business was the continuing national canker sore of the Vietnam War. In 1968, President Nixon had promised to bring it to an honorable end by handing the heavy lifting over to the South Vietnamese, on the theory that if they truly wanted to be protected from Communism, they'd get their act together and protect themselves. Following up on that promise, Nixon did just that. Troop levels had fallen to 196,700 in 1971, the lowest number since the great Johnsonian escalation in 1966. More and more of the war effort was turned over to the South Vietnamese, though they spent as much time fighting among themselves as they did stemming the spread of Communism. South Vietnam did, however, manage to invade Laos, with considerable American aerial and artillery firepower in support.

The domestic terrorist organization the Weather Underground was not impressed with the expansion of the war and in what was to every good leftist terrorist group an appropriate form of protest, they bombed the men's crapper in the U.S. Capitol. The *New York Times*' untimely release of the Pentagon Papers definitively establishing that the Johnson Administration knew the U.S. was losing the war all along, yet still sent thousands and thousands of American boys to their deaths, didn't help the war effort. In fact, a 1971 Harris poll found that more than 60 percent of American had soured considerably on the war effort. Yet, despite all of this, the beast fought blindly on. At least, the nation finally had the sense to realize that if eighteen year olds could be sent off to fight an unpopular war, they ought to be able to express their preference as to who would send them off. Consequently, the 26th Amendment was passed, lowering the voting age from twenty-one to eighteen.

William Calley, the officer on whom 1969's My Lai massacre was pinned, was convicted by a military tribunal and sentenced to life imprisonment. Charlie Manson was convicted as well, but that is where their stories diverge. Calley was eventually pardoned, and Manson was sentenced to death, courtesy of the state of California. When the U.S. Supreme Court temporarily decided the death penalty constituted cruel and unusual punishment, Manson's capital sentence was commuted to life in prison. Despite the Court later changing its mind, California is California and rather than letting Manson ride the lightning or get the needle, old Charlie was spared and periodically trotted out to have his parole repeatedly denied until his death in 2017.

On television, cigarette advertisements were out, and America's favorite racist Archie Bunker was in. *All in the Family*, the masterpiece of social-commentary-via-situation-comedy, made its debut; Archie's iconic easy chair throne now resides in the Smithsonian. The Montreux Casino in Switzerland gave Deep Purple the inspiration for their best known song by burning down, and the great poet-musician Jim Morrison of the Doors joined Jimi Hendrix and Janis Joplin in the Great Gig in the Sky, as he was found dead of a drug overdose in Paris. Coincidentally, Led Zeppelin gave us their fourth studio album and bequeathed us *Stairway to Heaven*, a song that would achieve nails-on-chalkboard ubiquity, imperfectly echoed in music stores by aspirational beginning guitarists the world over.

Disney World opened in the relatively unknown central Florida town of Orlando, and the *Mariner 9* Mars orbiter disabused us of the notion that little green men abounded on the red planet, simultaneously destroying the basis of countless episodes of *The Twilight Zone*. Intel created its first processor, and the first email was sent between two computers. We are still flocking to Orlando. We are still using Intel inside our computers, and we are thrown back to the Stone Age when our email goes down. Clearly, 1971 was a big year.

\* \* \*

For the crippled muscle car market, it was a big year as well, if for no better reason than it was the last real year of the American muscle car and its big cube, big horsepower pony car cousin. The 1970 model year had seen sales fall precipitously due to the rising rates of the vampiric insurance companies and with the prices of the cars themselves steadily rising as the car makers passed on the costs of meeting the ever increasing government safety mandates. The federal government's new Environmental Protection Agency was as eager to protect the environment as it was to enforce automobile safety, and there was the specter of unleaded fuel mandates on the horizon. The high compression engines powering the performance cars of the era wouldn't run well on polluting, unleaded fuel. In preparation for the coming fuel mandates, many of the once-great engines were fitted with lower compression pistons, and the result was lower horsepower. For performance car buyers of the muscle car era who understood such things as compression ratios, this was, to put it lightly, a turnoff, and damaged the enthusiasm to buy performance models. Some car makers didn't help themselves, and some damage to sales was self-inflicted as some popular car models still enjoying relatively strong sales were given restyles that were less popular with the buying public.

In military strategy, armies conducting a strategic defense try their best to shorten their lines to eliminate bulges and salients by increasing the concentration of what forces are available along a shorter, straighter line of defense. In 1971, some of the car makers executed the automotive equivalent. In an effort to maximize concentration of effort and reduce fraternal competition, such as that between the GTX and the Charger R/T, the car makers began to restructure their performance car lines in an effort to increase sales. Some of the great performance name plates were merged into another performance model. Some, having been made their own models earlier in the '60s, reverted to being simple options on more mundane models. Others morphed into a different car entirely and moved out of their performance intermediate or pony car niche and into an entirely new class in a desperate effort to find a niche in the market. Sadly, some of the great muscle cars did not come back for 1971 and simply disappeared.

Despite the outlandishness of high water mark of 1970, with the giant engine displacements and commensurate horsepower ratings, the wild colors and the whimsicality of the graphics, the American muscle car was dying. The 1971 model year was the Charge of the Light Brigade for the American muscle car. It was the automotive equivalent of Tolkien's Last March of the Ents, or perhaps Pickett's charge at Gettysburg, for 1971 was truly the last stand of the American muscle car.

* * *

General Motors was first off the sinking ship, caving on compression ratios in the face of increased government emissions regulation. GM lowered the compression in all of its performance large displacement engines across the board, with a resulting loss in horsepower, trying to get ahead of the coming catalytic converters and unleaded gasoline that loomed on the horizon. Compounding the actual loss in horsepower from lower compression, General Motors changed the way it rated horsepower production of its engines. GM began using net horsepower, which meant that horsepower production was measured with the air cleaner, alternator, exhaust and other engine accessories installed, all of which sapped horsepower in one way or another. The result of the *actual* decrease in horsepower from the lower compression and the *perceived* lower horsepower ratings from the switch to net horsepower did nothing to boost the public's perception of the cars. However, despite all of this, the General wasn't dead yet, and, while somewhat neutered, still offered a range of large cube power in its flagship muscle cars.

The reliable SS Chevelle was again the standard bearer for Chevrolet. The Chevelle was slightly restyled from the 1970 version, featuring round taillights, single headlamps and standard hood pins. Hood stripes and cowl induction were still available, while the standard interior and options on the inside were essentially identical to the previous year.

The SS Chevelle could be had with a dizzying number of engine options, some of which were less than intimidating. Perhaps in an effort to cover this up, on most SS cars, the legendary Super Sport badges with engine callouts beneath were dropped in favor of just a simple "SS," leaving potential competitors to wonder what exactly was under the hood. However, Chevrolet was proud enough of the 454 equipped cars to include the engine callout beneath the badge.

Aside from the engine displacement, that 454 for 1971 was not the same as it had been in 1970. In 1970, there had been two different 454 options—the LS5 and the much more lethal 450 horse LS6, one of the greatest engines of all time. If there were ever a reminder of the sword of Damocles hanging above the heads of the high-performance engines in the early '70s, it was the fate of the LS6—it couldn't pass

**1971 SS 454 Chevelle (courtesy Fast Lane Classic Cars, St. Charles, MO).**

emissions requirements and thus was discontinued. With the demise of the LS6, the last 454 standing was the LS5 producing 365 gross horsepower. Despite the decrease in compression from 10.25:1 to 8.5:1, the LS5 actually was rated at 5 more gross horsepower than it was in 1970, but the net ratings used by Chevrolet advertised an uninspiring 285 horses. Despite the increase in horsepower, torque output was far less, and the overall result was a much tamer engine.

Continuing down the SS engine option sheet, the SS 396—one of Chevrolet's most storied engines—was put to pasture after a career of terrorizing the streets since 1965. The engine that replaced it was something called the Turbo Jet 400. For some reason, Chevy couldn't quite get their advertised displacements straight: the 396 in 1970 actually displaced 402 cubic inches, and Chevy still didn't get it right with the Turbo Jet 400 because it still displaced 402. Most likely, Chevy was tapping into goodwill built up by 400 cubic inch performance engines from Pontiac, Olds and Buick that had powered their muscle cars since 1967. Regardless, it suffered from reduced compression as well, producing a mere 300 horsepower. In a sign of where things were for performance intermediates in 1971, Chevy offered two small block SS options for the first time since 1965. Both were 350 cubic inch engines, the best of which produced only 270 horses, with single exhaust. The other 350 would have been considered sacrilege in an earlier time—a two-barrel, single exhaust embarrassment. The standard transmission for the 454s was a heavy-duty 4-speed manual unit, with a 3-speedspeed Turbo-Hydromatic automatic optional. Beneath the 454, transmission choices varied depending on the engine, but included a 3-speed manual, one of two Turbo-Hydromatic 3-speed automatics or the 4-speed manual. Rear end gearing

1971 Heavy Chevy Chevelle (courtesy Ron Brundies, Keosauqua, IA).

options were plentiful, and limited slip was available. Standard braking was still manual drums all the way around with power and/or front discs as options.

By 1971 the reality was that the SS package had morphed into what was essentially an appearance package, sort of what the Rally Sport package had been on the Camaros and not necessarily indicative at all of performance. Indeed, only the LS5 454 mandated the SS package, and all other engines were available on cars without the SS option. Basically, by 1971, the intimidating SS badges of the past were nothing to be afraid of.

Figuring that late was better than never, Chevrolet finally got into the budget muscle car game in 1971. Judging by the declining sales of the Road Runner and the anemic sales of the budget and junior muscle cars of her sister divisions, the market for youth friendly, loudly colored and striped budget muscle cars had run its course, but Chevy paid no heed. Chevy's entry level muscle car was an option on the Chevelle which bore the unfortunate name "Heavy Chevy," a peculiar choice for a performance car operating in a world where heavy was bad. Chevrolet explained this away, telling potential buyers that the Heavy Chevy was "heavy on looks and long on price." In defense of Chevrolet, historical context helps; "heavy" in the late '60s and early '70s meant "cool" or "hip."

Avoiding the high insurance premiums of the SS badge, and replete with bright colors, stripes and graphics, the Heavy Chevy was essentially a base Chevelle outfitted with a domed, pinned hood and blacked-out grille. The Heavy Chevy option could be had on any V-8 powered Chevelle except the 454, which was reserved for the SS package. Therefore, engine choices were the two-barrel Turbo-Fire 307—obviously more sizzle than steak—or either the two or four-barrel 350s available on the SS. The top engine offering for the Heavy Chevy was the Turbo Jet 400. The more serious Heavy Chevys—meaning the 350s and the 400—came standard with a 3-speed manual transmission, but this could be swapped out for either a 4-speed manual or a Turbo-Hydromatic 3-speed automatic. Cars equipped with the 307 had the old two-speed Powerglide as the base automatic, though the Turbo-Hydromatic was an option. In keeping with its budget-friendly concept, the Heavy Chevy came standard with manual drum brakes and manual steering. Bucket seating and a console were unavailable. Carpet was replaced by a rubber floor mat.

Chevrolet sold 80,000 or so SS Chevelles in 1971, but this number is illusory. Because the SS package essentially became an appearance option available on any optional Chevelle engine, production numbers for SS Chevelles are notoriously hard to trace. It is safe to assume that not all SS cars were "muscular," and SS versions of the Chevelle based El Camino light pickup are included. Chevrolet managed to sell 6,727 Heavy Chevys, which is actually a respectable number given the way GM's junior muscle cars sold the year before. "Respectable," however, is not synonymous with "good," and taken as a whole, the SS Chevelle as a popular, top performing muscle car was a thing of the past.

Pontiac's GTO may have been eclipsed as the gold standard for intermediate performance, but Pontiac dutifully put it in its place alongside the SS Chevelle in its slow march into oblivion. Like the Chevy, the GTO also received a facelift for the new model year, and the result was arguably the most aggressively styled GTO Pontiac had yet built. The Endura bumper, a staple since 1968, was redesigned to exclude the quad headlights housed in nacelles above the body color bumper. The grille housing itself bulged out from the front of the car and sat under the most prominent change to the GTO, which was the hood. The result of the new front end treatment was as sinister an appearance as had ever been seen on a GTO.

For 1971, the storied Ram Air engines were gone. In their place were three engine offerings, all of them of the lowered compression variety. The base engine was a four-barrel 400 cubic inch, producing 255 net horsepower, or 300 gross. There were two different 455 cubic inch engine offerings as well. The first was rated at 260 net horses, and the second, the HO 455, was rated at 310 net horses. The 400 equipped GTOs came standard with a 3-speed manual transmission, with a choice of close or wide ratio 4-speed manual or 3-speed Turbo-Hydromatic automatic as options. The non-high output 455 had only the automatic transmission available, while HO 455 cars received the 3-speed standard and only the close ratio 4-speed or automatic available as options. The GTO was equipped with an upgraded heavy-duty suspension, including front and rear sway bars. Manual drum brakes were standard, but discs were optional, as was power assist.

Inside, woodgrain surrounded the gauges and the area beneath the gauges was accented with engine turned trim, harking back to the original GTO of 1964. A rally gauge option was available, as was the usual list of interior and power options. Bucket seating was standard.

For buyers who were still attracted to the bright-colors-and-graphics thing, Pontiac brought back The Judge for another season. For $395, the Judge package netted the standard Judge "eyebrow" recycled from 1970, bright color options, and a rear deck spoiler. All Judges were of the 455 variety, either HO or non–HO, with the same transmission choices. The Judge, like the GTO, was offered in both hardtop and convertible.

To appeal to the other end of the price point spectrum, Pontiac again brought out its GT-37 budget beater, again based on the LeMans coupe. Not much changed from the 1970 model. The GT-37 came standard with a bench seat and 3-speed manual transmission, manual steering and drum brakes, and a wide "saber stripe" along its flanks. The GT-37 had a flat, unadorned hood, but it was held down with sporty, chrome hood pins. Engine options for the 1971 GT-37 were expanded. As in 1970, the base engine was still a two-barrel 350 cubic inch engine, but with the horsepower dialed back to 250. Up from that were a two-barrel 400 producing 265 horses, and a four-barrel 400 produced 300. The two 455s offered on the GTO were available as well, and transmission choices mirrored that of the GTO.

Neither the restyle nor Pontiac's willingness to go out on a very thin limb and claim the 1971 H.O. 455 GTO was the fastest GTO ever did much to rescue the Goat from the sales miasma suffered by the performance intermediate cars of the early 1970s. Sales dropped cataclysmically for 1971, from over 40,149 in 1970 to 10,532 in 1971. In what would ultimately prove to be its swan song, the 1971 Judge didn't fare any better, with only 374 cars made. The cheap GT-37 added another 6,589 units, the vast majority of those being the two-barrel 350, most assuredly to escape the insurance premiums; only 69 were equipped with 455s. To put all this in perspective, just five model years previously, in 1966, the GTO sold nearly 97,000 units. By 1971, the noble GTO, the legend that started it all, was suffering a slow and agonizing death.

Over at Oldsmobile, things were not much better, but Doctor Olds did what he could. The "junior" muscle car offerings were dropped for 1971, leaving only the august old 4-4-2 as Olds' performance intermediate. Though there wasn't much to differentiate the '71 4-4-2 from a '70, it did gain new mirrors and some minor revisions to the front end. The major cosmetic changes included a blacked-out grille, silver headlight bezels, and round parking lights. The Sport Coupe body style was deleted, and the car was only available in convertible and hardtop form. Cold air induction got the buyer a fiberglass hood with yawning twin scoops set forward on the hood, similar to the 1970 hood, and it could be adorned with wide striping.

As with Oldsmobile's sister divisions, the biggest difference between the 1970 and 1971 models lay under the hood, as decompression was eroding the performance of the 455 offerings available in the venerable 4-4-2. The standard engine on the 4-4-2 was once again a 455 cubic inch unit, but compression was dropped from 10.25:1 to 8.5:1 to prepare for the coming of unleaded fuel. The result was that horsepower ratings were reduced from 365 to 340 in gross terms, or even uglier, 270 net horsepower. The "Force-Air" W-30 option was still available. The dragon's breath W-30 of 1970 was gone, and in its stead was an emasculated shadow, detuned and producing only 350 gross horsepower, or 300 net. The standard 4-4-2 transmission was a 3-speed manual, which was not available on the W-30, or two optional 4-speeds. Also available was the GM standard 3-speed Turbo Hydromatic automatic transmission. W-30 models got a heavy-duty 4-speed manual standard, and the Turbo-Hydromatic was optional. All floor shifters were built by Hurst, unsurprising given the long history of collaboration between Olds and George Hurst. With Oldsmobile being Oldsmobile, front disc brakes were standard, with power assist available unless a manual transmission was chosen.

**1971 Oldsmobile 4-4-2 W-30 (courtesy Vanguard Motor Sales, Plymouth, MI).**

Standard seating was a bench covered in full vinyl, but this could be ordered with power and bucket seating, with or without power, was optional as well. Oldsmobile offered a full list of luxury options: power windows, air conditioning, extra seat padding, and deluxe arm rests. Oldsmobile even offered an option on seatbelts, which traded out standard black for belts matched to the interior.

Oldsmobile's 4-4-2 had always lived in the shadow of the GTO and SS Chevelle, and if the dying muscle car market hit those two models hard, it would be worse for the Oldsmobile. Indeed, it was for the fading 4-4-2. Doctor Olds sold only 7,589 4-4-2s in 1971. A pitiful 920 of those were W-30 models, a clear indication of how far and fast things had fallen for Oldsmobile's performance intermediate.

At Buick, the Tri-shield guys stuck with their elegant street brawler, the GS. Like her sister divisions, Buick didn't do a lot to alter the appearance of the exterior of the GS, with a redesigned grille featuring horizontal bars being the most predominant change. As with the rest of the A-body line, the Buick's major changes were in the castration of its engines.

Buick was long the champion of the "junior" muscle car, and, as it was a relatively strong seller in 1970, the GS 350 was brought back for 1971. In fact, the GS 350 proved to be the enduring Buick performance intermediate, as it was the starting point for all GS cars for 1971; the GS 455 was relegated back to an option. The 350 cubic inch, four-barrel block produced a respectable 260 horsepower, all the more respectable when one considers that the other two GS engine options, both 455 cubic inch offerings, were much closer in output to the GS 350's 260 horsepower than they had been previously.

The first of these 455s was the base GS 455 engine, a four-barrel unit detuned to 8.5:1 compression and producing 315 rated horsepower. The top dog in the Buick yard was again the Stage 1, but where it had been a pit bull in 1970, it was closer to an angry boxer in 1971—still to be given a wide berth, but nowhere near as dangerous. Where the 1970 455 Stage 1 produced an unbelievable—literally not to be believed—360 horsepower and 510 foot-pounds of torque, for 1971, with compression lowered to 8.5:1, horsepower dipped to 345, and torque reduced to 450 foot-pounds.

The GS 350 came with a standard 3-speed manual transmission but could be upgraded to a 4-speed manual or the 3-speed Turbo-Hydromatic automatic. The 455 equipped cars, including the Stage One, passed on the 3-speed manual and had as standard equipment the heavy-duty 4-speed manual standard with the Turbo Hydromatic as a popular-with-genteel-Buick-buyers option. The rollback of high-performance standard options included a return to drum brakes all around, though front disks were optional, as was power assist.

The base GS interior was scaled back to that of the Skylark Custom for 1971, so gone were the standard black vinyl covered bucket seats, replaced by a basic bench seat. Standard Skylark instrumentation allowed the driver to monitor things, though a tach or clock could be chosen. But the GS was still a Buick, so the familiar bucket seating, air conditioning, power windows, steering and door locks, and a choice of a full length or truncated console were optional.

The GSX, the crown jewel for Buick for the muscle car era, was available again for 1971, though it was considerably watered down. The color palette was expanded from the iconic two choices to nine, and in reality, the GSX package was more of an appearance package than a performance one. The hood tach and meaty 15 inch wheels, standard in 1970, were optional, though the striping and the rear deck spoiler remained. Painted headlamp bezels, rear deck spoiler and special rocker trim were also part of the package. Additionally, the GSX package could be ordered on any GS car, even the little GS 350. In truth, like the SS package offered by Chevrolet, for 1971 the GSX was more of an appearance package than a performance one, emphasizing form over substance.

The market evaporation affecting mid-sized performance sales all across the GM spectrum didn't forget Buick. Buick sold only 9,170 GS cars of all engine varieties, including only 124 GSXs and 882 Stage 1 equipped 455s. Clearly, the end was near for the Buick's elder statesman of the muscle car world. While this was likely not too bitter a pill for Buick to swallow—performance cars didn't pay the bills at Buick, after all—it was shaping up to be a sad ending for one of the most underrated nameplates of the muscle car era.

* * *

For 1971, the GM A-body performance intermediates were but shadows of what they had been just a year previous. Things weren't as bad as they were going to get, as there were days ahead for the GTO, 4-4-2, SS Chevelle and GS cars that would make 1971 seem positively wonderful.

Regardless, it was bad, and with the close of the 1971 model year, it was clear to GM brass that the performance intermediate was the sick man of the lineup, and

The warning decal of Chevy's budget bruiser (courtesy Ron Brundies, Keosauqua, IA).

while they would linger on for a bit longer, plans were being made to revamp the intermediate line, and performance cars were not a part of that plan.

The giant car builder General Motors could better afford the losses it was incurring as a result of the dying muscle car market. GM's rivals, with less profit margin, were not as lucky.

* * *

If General Motors was willing to wave the white flag in the face of the coming reality of unleaded fuel and tightening of emissions restrictions, her arch-nemesis at Dearborn was not. Ford—who reluctantly entered the performance intermediate arena back in 1966—would enthusiastically advance to occupy the ground given up by GM, led by its 429 Cobra Jet and Super Cobra Jet power plants as barbaric in 1971 as they ever had been.

The Torino line would again provide a vehicle upon which Ford mid-sized performance was based. As in years past, the Torino line did a lot of heavy lifting for Ford and represented Ford's multipurpose line, much like Chevrolet's Malibu line. In total, there were fourteen different flavors of Torino for 1971. The Torino badge was hung on everything from six-cylinder sedans to station wagons, and, like Chevrolet's El Camino, included a car/truck hybrid, the Ranchero, first introduced in 1957. The Falcon and Fairlane nameplates were dropped from the Torino line in 1971, bringing to an inglorious end to two of the more storied badges of the 1960s. The Torino was left practically unchanged from the 1970 model year; perhaps all the design guys at Ford were locked in a room to hammer out what the next generation Mustang would look like. Regardless, only minor changes were made to trim and the grille, which was now divided by a vertical bar. On the Cobra models, even this was absent in favor of the recycled 1970 grille. Hideaway headlamps were an option on some models, and the GT models sported a longer laser stripe.

The performance versions of the Torino family began with the Torino GT, which could be had in either hardtop "Sportsroof" or convertible. The GT sported a non-functional hood scoop, and a rear deck spoiler was optional. The GT also came with heavy-duty suspension, extra capacity radiator, and dual exhaust. While manual front disc/rear drum brakes were standard, power discs up front were mandatory on convertibles and available on any GT.

Though advertised performance ratings on Ford's most lethal engines were down slightly from 1970, the top of the Torino line still had plenty to offer; those horsepower ratings from previous years were widely believed to be lies anyway. The base engine for the Torino GT was the 302 two-barrel small block producing 210 horsepower, which isn't much to talk about. Up from this was a two-barrel, 351 cubic inch Windsor rated at 240 horses. A four-barrel version of the 351 Cleveland could be opted for to produce 285 horses. The standard tranny for 302 equipped cars was a 3-speed manual, with the C4 3-speed automatic optional. In a reversal of the norm, 351 cars came standard with the FMX 3-speed automatic. Two different 4-speeds were optional on all GTs, regardless of engine.

The top GT offerings were still the 429s, either in Cobra or Super Cobra Jet form, defiantly sporting 10.5:1 compression ratios in the face of the coming government mandates. The Cobra Jet produced 370 horses, while the Super Cobra Jet, with different internals and a Holley carb, produced 375. Either engine could be had with cold air induction, which Ford insisted resulted in no horsepower difference. Transmission choices for the 429s were the heavy-duty C6 or "Toploader" 4-speed manual. "Traction-Lok" limited slip differentials were available on all Torino GTs, as was rear end gearing in a wide variety of ratios. Front disc brakes were standard, with drums in the rear, and power assist was optional.

**1971 Ford 429 Super Cobra Jet Torino GT (courtesy Gateway Classic Cars, St. Louis, MO).**

**1971 Ford Torino Cobra, owned by Todd Hollar of Thackerville, OK (photo by owner).**

The Torino Cobra was brought back as the top intermediate performance offering for Ford's 1971 model year. The engine offerings for the Cobra were revised for 1971, as the 429 Thunder Jet was deleted from the option list. In an effort to take care of the buyer that wanted a Cobra but didn't want the insurance rate of a Cobra Jet engine, Ford downgraded the standard Cobra engine. For 1971, in Ford's continued inability to line up the names of its Cobra cars with those of its Cobra Jet engines, the four-barrel 351 Cleveland was the base engine. Things got clearer with the top engine options, and Ford thankfully made either its 429 Cobra Jet or Super Cobra Jet available. The Cobra shared the same transmission choices and suspension and brake setups as the Torino GT.

Inside, the interiors of the Torino GT and Cobra models were a blend of comfort and sportiness. A full vinyl bench seat was standard, with buckets optional. Matching door panels, bright armrest bases, and a standard sport steering wheel rounded out the interior package, as did brightwork on the pedals. Air conditioning and power steering were popular options as well. The full range of Ford's color palette was available, including the Grabber colors.

The 429 powered Torino GT and Cobra cars of 1971 were what Ford should have built in 1969 but didn't. While Ford could boast that it had finally emerged from the shadow of the GM cars and offered arguably the best performers for the 1971 model year, hardly anyone cared, as Torino GT and Cobra production numbers tumbled with everyone else's. Only 33,254 Torino GTs of all engine displacements were sold for 1971, and a paltry 3,054 Cobras rolled off the line, down by more than half from 1970.

By 1971, Ford's junior division Mercury was under new divisional leadership. As a consequence, with the performance car market dying, Mercury was put on a different path. The new trajectory at the "sign of the cat" took it away from performance cars, an area in which Mercury was decidedly a fringe player, and solidly into the realm of family luxury cars, to compete with the upscale Buicks, Oldsmobiles and Chryslers. In 1971, performance Mercurys were quietly fading into oblivion.

However, while most of the sand was in the bottom of the hourglass for an intermediate performance Mercury, one still existed for 1971. For one last sortie, Mercury brought out its Montego-based Cyclone, available in three forms: the Cyclone GT, which according to Mercury logic somehow fit below the "base" Cyclone, and top-of-the-line Cyclone Spoiler.

The 1971 Cyclone variants received few cosmetic changes from the 1970 model, with the only one of significance being an even larger gunsight in the grill and a performance hood with an integrated scoop. Cyclones and Cyclone Spoilers received new body striping as well.

The performance versions of the Cyclone were the GT and the Spoiler. The GT came standard with the two-barrel 302, identical to the Ford's base Torino GT offering. The standard engine for the Cyclone GT was the same two-barrel 351 Windsor that powered base Torino Cobras, with the four-barrel 351 Cleveland optional. The four-barrel 351 Cleveland was the base engine for the confusingly named "base" Cyclone, as well as for the Cyclone Spoiler. In a departure from Ford, Mercury offered not two but only one optional 429 in any of the three Cyclones—the non-cold air breathing 429 Cobra Jet; the Super Cobra Jet was not available. Transmission options were identical to those available on the Ford. Indicating Mercury's new direction, a softer "Cross Country" ride package was standard for Cyclones and Cyclone Spoilers, and was optional on the Cyclone GT. Spoiler cars featured spoilers on the chin and rear deck, and side stripes with "Cyclone Spoiler" identification forward on the fender.

Inside, it was all Mercury, with standard bucket seats, full instrumentation, including the addition of race inspired toggle switches, and a sport steering wheel. A full line of creature comforts was available as well.

When everything was tallied up, it was clear that the performance mid-sized Mercury was dead, as 1971 sales were especially bleak. In fact, when compared to Cyclone production, Ford's weak sales numbers for its Torino GT and Cobra seem downright bountiful. For 1971, Mercury sold only 444 base Cyclones, 2,287 Cyclone GTs, and a minuscule 353 Spoilers.

The Blue Oval folks could read the handwriting on the wall as easily as everyone else. Sales of smaller, more economical cars were brisk, indicating the drift of the market. While sales of the midsized Ford powered cars were declining, the Maverick and even the Pinto, with its danger of bursting into flames at any moment, were powering Ford's bottom line.

\* \* \*

For 1971, Chrysler had big changes in store for its B-body line of mid-sized cars, including its performance models. The entire line was treated to its first wholesale restyle since 1968, and the convertible was now a thing of the past. The new "fuselage"

1971 Cyclone GT (photo by dave_7, Wikimedia Commons).

By 1971 Ford's Cobra may have lost its wheels, but the model is widely considered to be the best looking of Ford's muscle car efforts (courtesy Vanguard Motor Sales, Plymouth, MI).

body style, coming only pillarless hardtop, featured voluptuous curves replacing the harder lines of the previous generation, new flowing lines, long hood and short deck and thick C pillars that resembled the fighter aircraft of the day. The fuselage cars featured flush door handles and windshield wipers. Going against the grain of the trend of performance cars getting ever bigger, the fuselage cars were actually an inch shorter in wheelbase than the previous generation of B-bodies, though the new stance appeared beefier than the previous B-bodies. While not as popular—back then or today—as the 1968–1970 B-body design, the "fuselage" cars sold well as a whole, particularly the standard, non-performance versions sold for everyday duties.

Like Ford, Chrysler refused to go quietly into the performance wilderness of the 1970s. Chrysler too refused to lower compression in its top of the line performance cars, and Chrysler stoically faced the gathering storm that doomed the American muscle car.

For 1971, Plymouth killed off the less-than-inspiring Belvedere name for its B-body line, sticking the whole line with the Satellite name. All told, there were thirteen different variants of the Satellite; with the exception of the light car/truck hybrid, the Satellite family spanned the entire spectrum of applications, just as Chevrolet's Chevelle and Ford's Torino did. Of the Satellite line, there were two purposely designed performance variants, just as there had been since 1968—the Road Runner and the GTX. In a move common by 1971, however, Plymouth made most of its performance engines available in lesser siblings of the Satellite family, like the Satellite Sebring, thereby allowing buyers who could live without both performance badging and performance insurance rates an alternative.

As it always had been, the Road Runner was the entry level mid-sized performance offering from Plymouth. "Entry-level" meant something different in 1971 than it did in 1968. When the Road Runner was introduced, it was designed to be a bare bones, lightweight street brawler with few options available and an even shorter list of standard features. By 1971, the Road Runner had drifted from that original concept. While a stripped Road Runner could still be had, it would take some effort in the deletion of standard equipment. The curb weight of a standard 1971 Road Runner was an outlandish (for a Road Runner) 3,640 pounds, nearly 250 pounds heavier than the original 1968 version. There were over fifty options available on the Road Runner's option sheet, allowing the purchaser to be just about as comfortable as an Oldsmobile driver while piloting the '71 bird.

The 1971 restyle gave the Road Runner an aggressive, more purposeful look than it had in its boxier years of 1968–70. The thick C-pillar could be spruced up with a strobe stripe that wrapped from quarter panel to quarter panel over the roof; otherwise, it was a simple Road Runner decal and badge on the car's quarter panel. The Road Runner featured a bulged hood, and the blacked-out "Air Grabber" hood was still an option. The iconic "beep-beep" horn was still standard, as was the looped chrome bumper resembling that of the 1970 Charger. Optionally that bumper could be ordered in a coating to match the body color, giving it an appearance similar to that of the Endura nosed GTOs.

The Road Runner still came with a standard 383 cubic inch, four-barrel engine, as it always had, but it was hardly the same engine as in years past. Compression was lowered to 8.5:1, and the result was a loss of 35 rated horses, down to 300. In a sign of the times, the first small block was offered in a Road Runner, with the still reasonably insurance friendly 275 horse, four-barrel 340 a no-cost option. The 440 Six Barrel survived into 1971, and while compression was lowered, it wasn't by much and at 285 horses, power was down just five from previous years. The top of the line engine option was still the revered 426 Hemi, still as ill-tempered and barbarous as it ever had been, producing 425 horsepower. Heavy-duty suspension was standard, as was a 3-speed manual tranny, with the heavy-duty A-833 4-speed or TorqueFlite 3-speed automatic optional. Manual drum brakes were standard, though front discs and power assist were optional. Limited slip 'Sure-Grip" rear ends in a variety of gear ratios were also available, as was the heavy-duty "Dana" rear end.

Despite the range of options available on the '71 Road Runner, the basic package was still more or less true to its roots; at least a bench seat was standard. Rally gauges were standard as well. Bucket seating, air conditioning, power steering, and a choice of radios and steering wheels were among the extensive list of interior choices.

If buyers didn't notice the revamped styling—and judging by the sales numbers they didn't—they likewise failed to notice that the 1971 Road Runner was only about 100 bucks more expensive than the base '68 version, which is remarkable in and of itself. Sales of the 1971 Road Runner were sluggish, plummeting to just 13,644 units, down from over 41,484 in 1970, including 1,681 340 cars equipped with the 340, 246 with the Six Barrel 440 and only 55 Hemi cars. The attractive fuselage-sided second generation Road Runners suffered the misfortune of ill-timing, coming as they did when the muscle car market was dying. The second-generation Road Runners have only recently been gaining in popularity relative to the 1968–70 models. This may be in response to the premiums commanded by the first generation Road Runners, or perhaps they're simply being seen as the attractive, aggressively styled cars they have always been.

Plymouth's luxury-muscle car, the GTX, made its final appearance as a stand-alone model in 1971. Based as it was on the Satellite line, it shared the lines of its Road Runner cousin, replacing the Road Runner's decals with the GTX emblems unchanged from its inception in 1967. It shared the same chrome bumper as the Road Runner, with the body color option available as well. The GTX shared the hood, including the "Air-Grabber," and it shared the long list of options. The GTX did, however, come with standard bucket seats. In truth, the gap between the bare-bones Road Runner and the upscale GTX was closing quickly, and this did not bode well for the GTX.

The 1971 GTX did not compromise when it came to engine choices, even in an age when big cube, big horsepower engines were becoming passé. The base engine for the GTX was still the 440 four barrel, slightly detuned and now producing 370 horses, down from 375 in previous years. The 385 horse Six Barrel was optional, as was the Hemi. There was no small block available on the GTX. The standard transmission was the TorqueFlite automatic, with the heavy-duty 4-speed as an option. Also standard was the heavy-duty, sway bar equipped suspension and heavy-duty drum brakes, with power or power front discs optional.

Inside, the GTX was still as plush as anything Plymouth made in a mid-sized

**1971 Plymouth GTX (courtesy Steven Anastos, Red Hills Rods and Classics, St. George, UT).**

car. The standard bucket seats were covered in full vinyl; leather was optional. Wood graining adorned the dash and door panels, and a console was a popular option. Air conditioning, power steering and even a sunroof were among the list of features that could be had on a '71 GTX.

The GTX always tried to cater to a muscle car buyer with a more refined taste. Throughout the history of the GTX, Plymouth found few of those buyers, who were more likely to be interested in an Oldsmobile, Buick or Mercury than a Plymouth. Luxury is just not what Plymouth did, and the GTX is a car that never really caught fire. This unfortunate reality carried into 1971 but was compounded by the general downturn for performance intermediates. Plymouth sold only 2,703 GTXs, including 135 440 Six Barrel cars and 30 with the 426 Hemi. For 1972, Plymouth decided to kill off the lavish GTX as its own line, and for 1972, it became a mere option package on, of all things, the Road Runner.

Dodge, Chrysler's volume division, with more performance models offered, suffered correspondingly more with the dwindling of the performance intermediate market than did Plymouth. Last year, sales of some of Dodge's performance car lines were alarmingly sluggish, and for 1971, Dodge took measures to protect what was left by consolidating or outright eliminating some of its lines.

The first casualty of Dodge's effort to protect its market share was the entire Coronet family as a true midsized line. For 1971, the Coronet line was exclusively 118-inch wheelbase four door or station wagon vehicles. Throwing the baby out with the bathwater, this meant that the esteemed old Coronet R/T was killed off for the model year.

In truth, the Coronet R/T had its death warrant signed back in 1968 when Dodge re-introduced the world to its Charger, reskinned for 1968. The Coronet R/T and the performance Chargers were squabbling over the same market territory, though the misfires of the 1966–67 fastback Chargers didn't impact the Coronet R/T too profoundly. The enormous popularity of the second generation Charger, which endured through 1970, however, effectively vanquished the Coronet R/T, though it took Dodge until 1970 to fully realize it. By 1971, however, Dodge was fully aware that the 1970 Coronet R/T was a corpse, and it was buried for 1971. Thus, the Coronet R/T was one of the earliest of the great name plates to fade into automotive history. Unlike some muscle car nameplates that were subsequently resurrected, the Coronet R/T was never heard from again.

The end of the sluggish-selling Coronet R/T was one thing, but cancellation of the performance versions of the Coronet line had another, far more popular casualty—the Super Bee.

Dodge's budget super car never quite got the traction of its corporate cousin the Road Runner. By the time Dodge was given the green light to let the Super Bee loose in 1968, a good chunk of the model year was gone and the Road Runner's head start allowed it to cement its place at the entry level point of the muscle car market. The Super Bee wasn't the marketing home-run the Road Runner was and didn't have the advantage of an instantly recognizable Saturday morning friend gracing its sides or a gimmicky horn. Additionally, while Dodge was certainly not Buick, the idea of a budget muscle car felt more natural coming from Plymouth than it did from Dodge. So, with the end of the Coronet as a mid-sized line, the Super Bee went with it, and the scowling, angry looking 1970 Super Bee was the last of its kind.

Unlike the Coronet R/T, however, Dodge considered the Super Bee to be redeemable and was not willing to let it go completely away. The Super Bee survived Dodge's 1971 purge by merging the helmeted insect with the Charger. That the Charger, as high end a muscle car as Chrysler built, would absorb the bare-bones Super Bee is a bit counterintuitive, but the Super Bee survived.

Like the rest of Chrysler's B-body family, the Charger got the fuselage restyle for 1971. It shared the same basic shape as Plymouth's Satellite family, with its long hood, short deck and thick C-pillars. The Charger, however, took the long front end look to extremes; while it rode a shorter wheelbase than it had in previous years, the car simply *looked* bigger. Huge, in fact. The 1971 Charger line carried a lot of water for Dodge; it had to in order take up the slack left to it by the Coronet's departure. The Charger line included several different trim or performance models, from the Spartan Charger Custom, the Charger 500 (not to be confused with the NASCAR specific Charger 500 of 1969), the opulent Special Edition and the performance variants, the R/T and the Super Bee.

True to its budget roots, the re-imagined Super Bee was the entry-level, performance option package on the Charger line. In a mild case of changing things remaining the same, the Charger Super Bee soldiered on as Dodge's analog to Plymouth's Road Runner, right down to the engine options. The base engine was the 300 horsepower 383 Magnum; the 275 horse 340 was a no-cost option. For those wishing to pay for optional engines, there were three, which included one unavailable on the Road Runner. These were the 385 horse 440 Six Pack, the 425 horse 426 Hemi. The

**1971 Dodge Charger R/T (courtesy Fast Lane Classic Cars, St. Charles, MO).**

availability of the four barrel, 370 horse 440 was the deviation from the Road Runner, and it was available by virtue of it being available on the Charger R/T. The 383 cars came standard with a 3-speed manual transmission, but all other engines had the heavy-duty A-833 4-speed standard. All Super Bees, regardless of engine application, could be had with the 727 TorqueFlite 3-speed automatic or the 4-speed manual. The Charger Super Bee came standard with a heavy-duty suspension, including sway bars, and manual drum brakes, though power and front discs were available.

On the outside, the Super Bee got a blacked-out power bulge hood with side facing engine callouts or with the optional "Air Grabber" vacuum operated scoop. The Air Grabber was standard on cars with the 426 Hemi. Hideaway headlamps and front and rear spoilers were optional. The Super Bee sported side stripes, and while the familiar bumble-bee-in-high-gear emblem was gone from its familiar place on the car's quarter panels, the emblem was moved to the center of the hood, just ahead of the bulge. As an entry level performance option, the interior was shared with the decidedly low buck Charger 500, which meant bench seats, though buckets were optional and rally gauges were standard.

The Charger R/T continued to be the flagship of the line and continued to represent Dodge's best—in 1971, Dodge's only—luxury muscle car effort, particularly paired with the Special Edition (SE) package.

The R/T, which started at about $1,000 north of the Charger Super Bee, shared the same body as the Super Bee. The R/T hood was the same power bulge hood as the Super Bee, but a series of louvers set it apart from that of the budget option. An Air Grabber hood was also available and was standard on Hemi cars. The doors featured a set of molded louvers accented by stripe tape, and hideaway head lamps and chin and deck spoilers were optional.

The base engine for the R/T was the 370 horse, four-barrel 440 Magnum engine, with the Six Pack 440 and the Hemi optional. There was no 383 or 340 available in the R/T Charger. The car's standard transmission was the 3-speed TorqueFlite automatic, but the A-833 4-speed manual was optional. The R/T included the same suspension as the Super Bee, but heavy-duty power front disc brakes were standard. Rear ends on both the Super Bee and R/T were available with "Sure-Grip" in a variety of gear ratios, and the indestructible Dana rear end was available as well.

Inside, the Charger was as opulent as Dodge got: simulated wood on the door panels and dash, standard bucket seats, rallye dash and optional lighting packages. A console was standard, and light packages and a choice of radio and steering wheel were available.

Charger sales were robust for 1971, though most of those sold—by far—were of the lower performance variety. Performance models did not fare well, even with the reduction of internal competition from the elimination of the Coronet based performance intermediates. Of the Chargers that count, Dodge built 4,325 Super Bee Chargers, including 22 with the 426 Hemi and 99 with Six Pack 440s, and 2,745 Charger R/Ts, 178 of which were Six Pack 440s and 63 Hemis.

Chrysler continued to offer compact sales performance with its small A-body platform based Plymouth Duster, a member of the Valiant line, the most potent of which were equipped again with the small block, 275 horse 340. In 1968 Dodge learned that pitching a fit was a perfectly effective method of getting its way when it

**1971 Dodge Charger Super Bee (courtesy Vanguard Motor Sales, Plymouth, MI).**

wanted its own low buck B-body super car, and in 1971 Dodge went back to that well again to get its own version of the Duster. As with its 1968 tantrum that resulted in the Super Bee, it got what it wanted in the form of the Demon.

The 1971 Dodge Demon, with a grinning, pitchfork wielding little devil adorning its lower fenders, also netted a hell of a lot of heat from the Religious Right, offended at the blasphemy of the moniker. Dodge took its chances that not a lot of devout Christians were buying performance compacts so they soldiered on with their little imp. The Demon was available with a weak slant six but could be had with the same high winding, 275 horse 340 powering the Duster. The Demon certainly wasn't a muscle car in the traditional sense, but with the fading of the performance intermediate, it stood as an example of the direction that buyers would have to look if they wanted to purchase a performance car in the coming years.

Despite Chrysler's defiance in stubbornly offering barely detuned—or, in the case of the Hemi, not detuned at all—versions of its performance engines in its intermediates, the muscle car offerings from the Pentastar fared no better than those from GM or Ford. Chrysler didn't help itself any with the redesign of the B-body line, as there are two kinds of fans of Mopar B-body muscle cars—those who like the fuselage design and those that don't—with very little crossover between the two camps. For one reason or another—either the unpopularity of the 1971 restyle, the withering of the market, or both—there weren't many people buying fuselage Mopar mid-sizes in 1971.

This year would see the last of some of the good things from Chrysler, and 1972 would see the extinction of some of the icons of Chrysler's muscle car years. The retirement of the High Impact colors would prove to be the least of them.

\* \* \*

(Photo courtesy Steven Anastos, Red Hills Rods and Classics, St. George, UT).

Beginning in 1967, the car makers tied their pony cars to the large cube, high horsepower performance wagon alongside the performance intermediates. The short term results were resoundingly successful; while they continued to offer pony cars in six-cylinder or small-block form, it was the 396 powered Camaros, 390 and 428/249 Mustangs, and Chrysler E-bodies with 383s, 440s and Hemis that got the most attention then and certainly still do now.

In the long term, however, the big-block pony cars suffered right along with their mid-sized cousins. The emissions and safety regulations affected them just the same, and the insurance rates were no lower for performance pony cars. Fortunately, the very nature of the pony car—a personally customizable, smaller car with a wide range of engines and comfort options—somewhat blunted the impact of the catastrophe being suffered by the performance intermediates. Pony cars were better situated to survive the steadily decreasing horsepower of the big-block intermediates because of simple physics. Being smaller and lighter—though by 1971 they weren't *that* much smaller or lighter—they did not suffer as noticeably from the loss of horsepower as did the heavier, and getting heavier all the time, midsized models. Regardless, the pony car concept, as originally conceived back in 1964, was getting stale by 1971, and sales across the pony car spectrum suffered; the performance variants of the pony cars suffered the most.

Coming into 1971, Ford finally decided the Mustang in its current form had run its course. Though its dimensions had grown over the years, one could glance at a 1970 Mustang and recognize it as a Mustang. The 1970 Mustang and the 1964 Mustang were clearly not the same car, but there was a definite family resemblance. GM may have had problems launching the newly restyled Camaro and Firebird, but they were new and exciting. Chrysler's Challenger and Barracuda were enjoying a level of success that a Mopar pony car had never experienced, largely at the expense of the Mustang. The Mustang was still the king of the hill to be sure, but in a world used to major restyles every two to three years, Ford felt it was a time for a change.

Ford's planners could read their crystal balls as well as anyone else, and they understood that the federal emissions and safety mandates scheduled for implementation over the coming years of the early 1970s would not be good for performance cars. Ford determined that the substitute for brute force, high horsepower performance would naturally be in road-hugging handling. Building cars that corner and stop well, never much of a priority in previous years, didn't require high horsepower and they were unlikely to receive some knee-jerk regulation edict from the government. In fact, better handling and braking would make both the safety advocates and the Environmental Protection Agency happier. The Mustang, with its storied road racing past, would be particularly suited for the switch in performance emphasis from straight line acceleration to better road handling characteristics. Covering all of its bases, Ford believed that if power was out, more luxury was the way of the future—if people had to go slower, they'd rather do so in more comfort. With these things in mind, Ford's engineers went to work reinventing the Mustang.

The result was a car that radically veered from the cute little pony car of 1964 and was, by Mustang standards, a behemoth. Ford's engineers, perhaps remembering the pain of restructuring the suspension of previous Mustangs to accommodate the largest Ford engines, designed the '71 with that in mind. The car's wheelbase was lengthened by an inch, its width was increased by three inches, and its overall length by more than two. Weight increased by over 100 pounds. That wider stance, however, lowered the center of gravity of the car and allowed it to improve on its road huggability. The dimensional expansions of the Mustang don't seem like much, but the 1971 Mustang seemed to dwarf anything that came before it.

True to its pony car roots, the 1971 Mustang could be had in one of three body styles: coupe, fastback, and convertible, in various trim levels. The new-for-'71 fastback has proven to be one of the most recognizable profiles of any car of the era. There had been a lot of fastback or semi-fastback designs in the muscle car era, but none like what Ford designed in 1971. The 1971–'73 Mustangs are known today, perhaps derisively, as "flat tops" because the nearly horizontal roofline of these fastback Mustangs combined with the Mustang's larger size make it sort of resemble an aircraft carrier. People either loved or despised the 1971 Mustang.

Like any good pony car builder, Ford offered a cornucopia of options for the Mustang, allowing the buyer to customize the car as desired. The base engine was a "Thriftpower" six-cylinder, but Ford's entire engine lineup was available in any Mustang. V-8 engine choices included a 302, a variety of 351s and the same two 429s that were available on Ford's Torino Cobras.

For 1971 Ford reduced the number of performance Mustangs, with the fabulous, limited production Boss 302 and 429 put to pasture. For buyers looking for a performance Mustang, that left only two options. The first of these was the Mach 1.

Like previous Mach 1's, the 1971 model was available only in fastback form. The Mach 1 received bumpers that matched the exterior color of the car, racing mirrors that matched the body color as well, a special honeycomb pattern grille with integrated driving lights, fender and deck lid decals and lower body and valence paint treatment in either black or argent, depending on body color. The standard hood featured what Ford called "NACA-type," low profile hood scoops. NACA was the predecessor of NASA and had developed the distinctive duct shape for air inlets on aircraft to produce minimal aerodynamic drag.

The standard engine for the 1971 was downgraded to a feeble two-barrel 302, producing 210 horsepower. That wasn't much power to haul around the chunky fastback, so many Mach 1 buyers wisely paid the 45 bucks to upgrade to a two-barrel 351 Cleveland with 9.0:1 compression producing 240 horses. Serious 1971 Mach 1 buyers, however, opted for the four-barrel, 10.7:1 compression version of the 351 Cleveland that produced 285 horses. For those buyers still hanging on and demanding performance on par with previous years, the Mach 1 dropped the 428 for 1971 and offered instead either of two 429s. The first was the 429 Cobra Jet, identical to that offered in the Torino line. The second, as part of Ford's "Drag Pak 3.91" or "Drag Pak 4.11" packages, got the buyer the 375 horse 429 Super Cobra Jet, along with Traction-Lok limited slip differential and rear end gearing corresponding to the Drag Pak package chosen. Cold air induction was standard on 429 equipped cars and was optional on Mach 1's equipped with the 351.

The standard transmission for the Mach 1 was a 3-speed manual for cars equipped with the 302 or two-barrel 351, with a 4-speed as an option. The 3-speed manual wasn't available on more powerful Mach 1's, however, and the base tranny for four-barrel 351s and 429 powered cars was Ford's un-destroyable "Toploader" 4-speed manual. Cruise-O-Matic 3-speed transmissions were available as options, with the heavier duty C6 being applied to the more powerful cars. All 4-speeds were equipped with Hurst t-handle shifters. Standard braking was manual drums at all four corners, though after an early run, 429 powered cars got power front discs standard. Power assisted drums and the power front disc setup were optional on all Mach 1's.

Ford's performance alternative to the Mach 1, for those who wanted to pony up for the additional cost, was what would be the last of the great Boss line, called the Boss 351. Like the Mach 1, the Boss 351 was available only in fastback form. The Boss 351 shared its hood with the Mach 1, with functional hood scoops. In the place of the Mach 1's fender callouts, the Boss 351 got its own decals to identify it. A rear deck and chin spoiler were mandatory.

Naturally, the Boss 351 was powered by a modified 351 Cleveland that featured four-barrel carburation, mandatory Ram Air and, incredibly in an era of lowering compressions, an 11.7:1 compression ratio. The Boss 351 produced 330 horsepower, which, by the standards of any year, was impressive; Ford's earlier 428s carried a horsepower rating only a bit higher. The standard transmission was Ford's "Toploader" 4-speed manual, with a Hurst shifter. Options for rear ends were similarly limited, with only Ford's 3.91 with Traction-Lok available. Braking was handled by power front discs and rear drums.

The last of Ford's Boss line, the 1971 Mustang Boss 351 (courtesy Vanguard Motor Sales, Plymouth, MI).

Reflecting Ford's gravitation toward more plush performance cars, all Mustangs received high-back, full vinyl bucket seating, deluxe door panels, full carpeting and a standard mini-console. Hidden wipers and racing mirrors were standard. Optional, and standard on high-performance Mustangs, was a full length console incorporating oil, temperature and alternator gauges. Standard instrumentation could be upgraded to replace the standard clock with a tachometer. Ford offered different steering wheels and a choice of radios, in addition to the standard fare of options commonly available. Rear window louvers and a rear deck spoiler were also optional on Mach 1's.

If Mustang fans could put aside their bias and refrain from holding the 1971 restyle against the car, they'd have to admit that the flat-top Mustang with NACA hood and optional striping was an impressively pugnacious looking car, especially when dressed in Ford's Grabber colors. Be that as it may, buyers were decidedly unimpressed with the 1971 revision to their beloved pony car. Mustang sales, which once upon a time had exceeded 600,000, continued to plummet. Ford sold 149,678 Mustangs in 1971, which was a very strong number. Digging deeper, however, will reveal that the high-performance Mustang was dying, just like all other high-performance vehicles in 1971. Ford sold only 36,499 Mach 1's of all engines varieties and 1806 Boss 351 cars. Ford president Lee Iacocca claimed that the market hadn't moved away from the Mustang, but that the Mustang had moved away from the market. Either way, the Mustang was fading.

Sadly, the new Mustang would be Dearborn's only representative in the pony car market. Mercury's Cougar, the Mustang's upscale pony car companion since 1967, outgrew the class. The early Cougars were magnificent vehicles, and the motor press agreed to the point that it was bestowed with the honor of being named *Motor Trend's* Car of the Year, something no other pony car of the muscle era accomplished. Despite this, the Cougar never really caught fire, standing as it always had in the long shadow of the Mustang, and being introduced simultaneously with the Camaro and Firebird. The Cougar had its moments on the track as well, nearly topping the Mustang in the 1967 Trans Am racing series. That Ford pulled the plug on Mercury's Trans Am racing efforts after so close a call was a backhanded compliment, but it served to cripple the Cougar by taking from it public visibility and self-promoting advertising material.

Like the Mustang, the Cougar was redesigned for 1971, and in accordance with the new style-before-performance direction Mercury was taking, the result was a Cougar even porkier than the Mustang. The Cougar's wheelbase was stretched out two inches to 113 inches, which was four inches longer than that of the Mustang. Actual length was nearly 200 inches. A fully equipped Cougar, as most Mercurys tended to be, had a curb weight pushing 4,000 pounds. The new Cougar was aiming squarely at the market segment that bought Oldsmobiles and Buicks, and so came with a long list of standard equipment, which got even longer when the popular XR7 package was chosen. In truth, the Cougar for 1971 was a junior Ford Thunderbird—too big and heavy to be a pony car any longer, yet too small to be considered a mid-sized muscle car.

None of this meant that the buyer absolutely insistent on purchasing a

**The last of Ford's legendary Boss line, the Boss 351 (courtesy Vanguard Motor Sales, Plymouth, MI).**

performance Cougar was without options. That option—the only option—came in the form of the Cougar GT, as the Eliminator was eliminated for 1971. The Cougar's form resembled that of the Mustang coupe, unless, of course, the convertible was chosen. Its iconic hidden headlamps were gone, and the front end of the car featured a huge center grille flanked by quad headlamps. The unique sequential taillights remained, and the GT scored a scooped hood, dual racing mirrors, stiffer suspension and sport instrumentation.

The Cougar GT had for its base engine either the 351 Windsor or Cleveland, each with two-barrel carburation and producing 240 horses. The only option above that was the 429 Cobra Jet with cold air induction, producing 370 horsepower. The standard transmission was a 3-speed manual for 351 equipped cars, with a 3-speed automatic or "Toploader" 4-speed manual as options. The 429 powered cars got the Toploader standard and a heavy-duty C6 3-speed automatic as an option. Braking options mirrored the Mach 1: standard manual drums with power or power front discs as options.

Declining sales and Mercury's drift in another direction meant that the 1971 Cougar GT would be the final version of the car that could reasonably be considered a performance car. The 429 was off the option list for 1972, and though it was replaced by a new, high output 351, it just wasn't enough engine to motivate the fat cat. As the '70s droned on, the Cougar would diverge even further from its performance roots, and veer more and more into the luxury car arena. By 1974 the Cougar had grown to a 114 inch wheelbase and by 1977, it was 118 inches—nearly as long as the biggest full-sized Mercurys when the pony car market was born in 1964. By then

**1971 428 Cobra Jet powered Mercury Cougar (courtesy Steven Anastos, Red Hills Rods and Classics, St. George, UT).**

it had become a full-fledged land liner, a true Mercury badged Thunderbird. For 1971, Cougar sales continued to recede. Only 787 GT models were sold, which includes 401 powered by the Cobra Jet 429.

Throughout the muscle car era, Mercury suffered from somewhat of an identity crisis, wedged as it was between the lower priced offerings from Ford and the high end, luxury offerings from Lincoln. Mercury seemed never to be able to decide if it built performance or luxury cars and always attempted to strike a balance and appeal to a more "sophisticated" market that still wanted the thrill of Ford performance but also to be comfortable while being thrilled. With the Cougar as the only real example, Mercury performance cars had little to differentiate themselves from their Ford counterparts. While the Cougar wasn't exactly a Mustang clone, throughout the era the mid-sized Mercury offerings were little different than those of Ford, save for price. Sales figures throughout the era seem to indicate that many people saw little sense in paying more when essentially the same car was offered by Ford. This unhappy circumstance would plague Mercury through the ensuing decades and would finally result in the lights being turned off at Mercury in 2011.

* * *

As it struggled with production obstacles leading into the 1970 model year, General Motors must have believed the automotive gods, like much of the public, disapproved of the reskinning it gave its F-body pony cars. Then when the restyled Camaros and Firebirds finally started showing up in dealers' showrooms months overdue, GM must have believed everything was going to be all right for its pony

The Boss 351 Mustang emblem (courtesy Vanguard Motor Sales, Plymouth, MI).

cars heading into 1971. Alas, just like clockwork, the gods smote GM's F-bodies again, in the form of a late 1970 labor dispute that delayed the delivery of the new model year cars for the second straight season. Incidentally, this was no coincidence—labor unions understand that a strike timed to the release of a new model year will get the attention of management.

When the 1971 Camaro finally did show up on dealers' lots, not much had changed. The car was only in its second year of its restyle and because it got such a late start in the 1970 model year, there really wasn't any point in changing much.

The biggest change to the 1971 Camaro line was the switch to high back seating with integrated headrests on the standard buckets. Other than that, the deck lid emblem went from "Camaro by Chevrolet" to simply "Camaro," Chevy having decided that in its fifth model year, most people knew who built the Camaro. Even the sales brochures were nearly identical to 1970. Mechanically, however, the Camaro—built, in case it has been forgotten, by Chevrolet—was a different car.

The base Camaro engine continued to be a 145 horse Turbo-Thrift six-cylinder, and the first V-8 in the lineup was a 200 horse two-barrel 307. There was also a two-barrel 350 putting out 245 horses. Performance engines started with an 8.5:1 compression four-barrel 350 at 270 horsepower. Also optional was the detuned 396 generating 300 horsepower, the same engine powering Chevelles but called a 400. Six-cylinder and 307 cars could be had with either a 3-speed manual or optional two-speed Powerglide automatic. A 4-speed manual transmission was standard on all 350 and 396 cars, and the 3-speed Hydromatic was optional with the 307, 350 and 396.

The Super Sport and Rally Sport packages were carried over to 1971. The SS package, as with the Chevelle, was becoming more of an appearance package than a true performance group. It did, however, net the 270 horse 350 or the optional 396, SS trim and a blacked-out grille. The SS package also got the buyer dual exhaust and a heavy-duty suspension and mandated the 4-speed manual over the base 3-speed or the 3-speed Turbo-Hydromatic automatic transmission. SS braking was in the form of power front discs and rear drums.

The RS package, which had always been an appearance group, included a distinctive front end treatment that included a blacked-out grille with body color wrap-around and a front bumper split around the beak of the grille instead of a full width bumper. RS buyers also got a distinctive headlight setup that included a parking light in the grille and bright molding on the cowl edge of the hood. An RS specific steering wheel was also included in the package.

As in years past, the ultimate '71 Camaro was the Z/28. The Z/28 car came standard with a 330 horse, four-barrel 350-cubic inch power plant and Hurst shifted 4-speed manual transmission, with the Turbo-Hydromatic optional. The package came with heavy-duty suspension and quick ratio steering, befitting a car born for the Trans Am racing series. It came as well with a standard rear deck spoiler, limited slip rear end and special wheels and striping. Power assisted front discs with rear drums were standard.

The Camaro wasn't any more popular in 1971 than it was in 1970, which should have been expected given the lack of changes that might draw the interest of the market. Sales of the Camaro were down across the line with just over 103,000 V-8 units of all types sold. Most of these were sold to people more interested in looking fast and paying lower insurance premiums while doing so. Of 8,377 SS Camaros sold, only 1,533 had the 396. Chevy managed to convince a mere 4,862 to buy a Z/28.

At Pontiac, planners likewise saw no need to change much on the late-to-the-party 1970 Firebird. The Camaro's high back bucket seating was installed in the Firebird, but aside from that, not much was different for 1971. New soon-to-be-legendary honeycomb wheels were added to the Firebird option list. Pontiac didn't even have the need to clarify who built it by redoing any external badging, as Chevrolet did with the Camaro.

The Firebird was available in four different varieties—the base Firebird, Firebird Esprit, Formula, and Trans Am—and engine choices differed based on these. All engines available in the Firebird had their compression lowered in preparation for the coming age of low octane, unleaded fuel, and for 1971, Firebirds with Ram Air engines were extinct.

The base Firebird came standard with a 250 cubic inch six-cylinder producing 155 horses. Optional was a two-barrel 350 that upped the horsepower production to 255. The standard transmission for the base Firebird was a 3-speed manual. Optional transmissions were a heavy-duty 3-speed manual, 4-speed manual or Turbo-Hydromatic 3-speed automatic. The Esprit was built to be a more sumptuous version of the Firebird, concentrating on interior appointments that included special seat covers and wood grained dash instrument panel inserts. Engine availability was a standard two-barrel 350 cube block producing 250 horses or a two-barrel 400 for

**1971 Formula Firebird (courtesy Streetside Classics, Charlotte, NC).**

265 horses. Transmission choices were identical to the base Firebird. Base and Esprit cars exhaled through single exhaust.

Performance began with the Formula Firebird. The Formula series came in three varieties—the Formula 350, Formula 400 and Formula 455—and these designations naturally correspond to engine displacements. The Formula 350 was powered by the same two-barrel 350 available in the Esprit. The Formula 400 engine was Pontiac's four-barrel 400 that was rated at 300 horsepower.

The 455 cubic inch engines Pontiac put in its Firebirds were the biggest engines ever offered in a pony car. The 455 powered Pontiac Firebird, coming as it did in the dying days of the muscle car era, is somewhat poetic and in a sense brings things full circle for Pontiac. Way back in 1964, a lifetime ago in the car business, the underdog car maker fired the first shots of the muscle car wars when it stuffed its big car engine, the 389, into its intermediate Tempest. John DeLorean's act of defiance in the face of GM mandates gave the world the GTO and all the great cars that tried to duplicate it. Likewise, the Formula 455 Firebird was Pontiac's act of defiance in the face of the various forces trying to kill the American muscle car.

The Formula 455 could be had with a choice of two different 455s. The first was a base four-barrel 455 that produced 325 horsepower. The other was the cold air breathing 455 H.O. built by Pontiac's engineers from leftover Ram Air IV pieces that were bolted onto the 455. This added ten more horsepower, which brought it up to a respectable-for-1971 335.

All Formulas shared the same transmission choices as the base or Esprit models. They came standard with heavy-duty suspensions and unique "engine compartment extractors" which was car-speak for fender vents which, in theory, allowed hot air from the engine to escape through the fenders. They looked cool but were more form than function; regardless, they remained a part of the Firebird line on Trans Ams until 1982. All Firebird Formulas were dual exhaust. Formulas came with a unique hood featuring twin scoops mounted far out on the leading edge of the hood, and the Formula 455 with the H.O. engine made these functional, giving the engine a nostalgic Ram Air vibe.

The Trans Am was again the top-of-the-line Firebird and was again only available in blue or white with stripes of the same, contrasting color. The Trans Am standard rear facing shaker hood was also still standard. Engine and transmission choices were simple: 455 H.O. and 4-speed manual or 3-speed Turbo-Hydromatic automatic. That was it. Naturally, heavy-duty suspension and front disc/rear drum brakes were standard. A full range of options was available on all Firebird models, including air conditioning, power steering, and power brakes.

Breaking with the trend of flagging sales, overall Firebird sales actually ticked up slightly in 1971, though they still could not be considered strong. Pontiac sold 23,022 base Firebirds, 20,185 Esprits, and 7,802 Formulas, of which 671 had one or the other 455. Trans Am numbers slipped by nearly 1,100 to 2166.

The H.O. 455 Pontiac produced for 1971 was one of the last true GM muscle car engines, but Pontiac wasn't going to go quietly from the muscle car era. Indeed, in the waning years of the era, Pontiac had one last card to play.

\* \* \*

Chrysler entered the 1971 pony car arena riding on the momentum of its 1970 restyle of Plymouth's Barracuda line and its Dodge analog, the Challenger. These two vehicles represented the pinnacle of Chrysler's pony car effort, and it is unfortunate

**1971 Pontiac Firebird Trans Am (courtesy Gateway Classic Cars, St. Louis, MO).**

that they came along so late in the era, because there wasn't much time left before the end, and for the E-bodies, particularly the Challenger, they had just gotten started. For the Barracuda, it was a redemption story, having suffered at the hands of the Mustang and, well, every other pony car after it, since its inception in 1964. Despite their magnificence, their fortunes would not fare much better than anyone else in 1971.

For 1971, the Barracuda line, including the high-performance 'Cuda models, didn't change much from 1970. The standard hood was a twin scooped unit, and on 'Cudas, the fenders were adorned with four faux openings, appropriately called "gills." The grille was reworked as well, most notably with the addition of twin headlamps, and could be had in body color. The flanks of any 'Cuda could be decorated with a wide flat black or white "billboard" stripe that covered most of the quarter panel and dramatically called out engine displacement, or "HEMI" if so equipped. As in 1970, the 1971 Barracuda line was available in either coupe or convertible forms, including the 'Cudas.

Standard for 1971 'Cudas was again the 383 cubic inch engine, though detuned to 8.5:1 compression, which resulted in a 35 horsepower drop in gross ratings to 300 horses. A no cost option was the 340 small block with 10.5:1 compression, still rated at 275 horses. The 440 four-barrel was not available in 1971, but the Six Barrel 440 was still available, though down five horses from 1970's 390. Finally, the mighty Street Hemi was available once again, producing its unapologetic 425 horsepower. A shaker hood was available with any engine choice; the Hemi mandated the shaker hood, heavy-duty suspension and radiator, and Dana limited slip rear end. All 'Cudas could be had with either the bombproof A-833 manual 4-speed transmission, topped with the iconic Hurst Pistol Grip shifter, or the equally tough TorqueFlite 727 3-speed automatic. All 'Cudas were stopped by heavy-duty drum brakes, with power and/or front discs optional, and were equipped with dual exhaust. "Sure-Grip" limited slip rear differentials were available in a range of gearing, as was the heavy-duty Dana rear end.

On the inside, 'Cudas were equipped with high back bucket seating standard, but could be ordered with a bench seat, though that mandated a column mounted automatic transmission. An upscale "Gran Coupe" option featured leather interior. The standard instrument panel could be upgraded to a rally gauge cluster as well.

After the flurry of 1970 sales driven by the 'Cuda's restyle, sales of the Barracuda plummeted again in 1971, dropping an astonishing 66 percent for 1971. Plymouth sold only 5,675 'Cudas, the vast majority of which were 340 powered cars with only 114 being Hemis. Plymouth has the bittersweet distinction of providing what many consider to be the Holy Grail of muscle era performance cars—the 1971 Hemi 'Cuda convertible, of which only 7 were made.

Dodge's Challenger had barely gotten itself off the ground before facing the same afflictions that were hurrying the American performance car toward its annihilation. The Challenger had a successful debut, by 1970 standards, but for the little Dodge, there was to be no honeymoon.

Like its Barracuda sister, the Challenger saw few changes for 1971; the same held for the performance minded Challenger R/T. Perhaps the biggest change was the deletion of the convertible for the R/T, though it was still available on the base

**1971 Challenger R/T (courtesy Fast Lane Classic Cars, St. Charles, MO).**

Challenger. The cosmetic changes that were made included alterations to the grilles and headlamps and the addition of fake brake cooling vents in the quarter panels. R/Ts came standard with a power bulge hood equipped with twin non-functional scoops, with a shaker scoop available with any engine. Optional striping was a narrow, contour hugging stripe that ended with "R/T" lettering below the back edge of the quarter glass. R/T striping could be had on the standard hood as well, mimicking the optional hood treatment of Charger R/T.

For the Challenger R/T, the available engine and transmission choices were exactly what they were in the 'Cuda: 330 horse, 383 cubic inch engine standard, with the 275 horse 340, 385 horse 440 "Six Pack" or 426 Hemi optional. Transmissions were limited to the A-833 4-speed or TorqueFlite 727 automatic and all R/T Challengers got heavy-duty suspensions and drum brakes, with power and/or discs optional. "Sure-Grip" limited slip rear differentials were available in a range of gearing, as was the heavy-duty Dana rear end. Unlike the Plymouth, Rallye gauges came standard. Unlike the 'Cuda, the Challenger R/T came standard with bucket seating and rally gauges.

Selling the Challenger proved to be less challenging than Plymouth's effort at selling the Barracuda. That said, sales of the Challenger line still plunged by nearly 65 percent from 1970. When it came to performance versions, however, the 'Cuda was more popular, as Dodge sold only 3,903 R/T Challengers, including only 70 Hemi equipped cars.

After the optimism born of the resurgent sales of the 1970 Challenger and Barracuda lines, closing the books on 1971 revealed that the bottom was clearly falling

**One of Chrysler's most memorable features of the muscle car era, the Hurst "Pistol-Grip" shifter (courtesy Steven Anastos, Red Hills Rods and Classics, St. George, UT).**

out all across the pony car market. Chrysler's pony car offerings were hit particularly hard, as the Challenger and Barracuda settled back into their familiar places near the bottom of the stack for sales. Mother Mopar faced some tough decisions regarding the future of the Barracuda and Challenger lines, and those decisions would not be long in coming.

\* \* \*

The rapidly disintegrating market for performance mid-sized and pony cars impacted American Motors more acutely than it did its much larger competitors. AMC's production capacity was much smaller, and the lack of mass production meant that the profit margin per vehicle sold was much thinner. Simply put, American Motors could not absorb the economic losses suffered by GM, Ford, and even Chrysler when the market for performance cars tanked. Added to the economic disadvantages tied to scale or production, American Motors had some reputational barriers to overcome as well. Despite some great performance cars of the previous years, AMC always struggled to overcome its stodgy and unexciting image carried over from its Rambler days. Indeed, by 1971, many people still referred to AMC as Rambler, though that marque was phased out in favor of AMC in 1966. In fact, old timers *still* refer to AMC products as Ramblers. Naming its 1969 performance car SC/Rambler didn't do a lot to exorcise the Rambler image, but, ironically, it was Rambler/AMC's solid reputation for building safe, reliable but utterly unexciting vehicles—a reputation that AMC still took seriously throughout the muscle car era—that provided an almost insurmountable barrier to creating a performance image for AMC; the two competing images for AMC were incompatible. The lack of production capacity and AMC's unexciting image resulted in the great AMC performance cars being rarely seen on the streets, and they suffered from a lack of a widespread image and street credibility. The law of averages mandated that every town or cruise route of consequence would have a performance Ford or Chevy lurking on its dark boulevards. The reverse was also true—AMC performance cars were unlikely to be found on any given car haunt. Even today, most people heavily involved in the muscle car hobby have never laid eyes on an SC/Rambler or Rebel Machine.

With the market dissolving beneath it, AMC made two major efforts to shore up the flagging sales of its performance cars of 1971. The first was to abandon the Rebel-based Machine altogether, as well as the AMX as a stand-alone model, and to focus the resulting savings in resources squarely on the second effort, a complete redesign of the Javelin.

There are two kinds of people with regard to the new-for-1971 Javelin—those that absolutely hate it and those that love it. Either way, there is no mistaking the profile of a 1971 Javelin. Compared to the first generation Javelins, the restyle was quite dramatic as the 1971 model grew in both girth and length. The most conspicuous feature of the new Javelin was the prominent bulges in the fenders and quarter panels, somewhat reminiscent of the contemporaneous "C-3" Corvettes. Despite the radical new look, many body panels were actually shared with the 1970 Javelin, including

**1971 Javelin AMX (courtesy CZmarlin/Christopher Ziemnowicz, Wikimedia Commons).**

doors, windshield, door glass and valence panels. The fastback design was retained as well, and chin and deck lid spoilers were standard.

Though base Javelins came with a choice of two six-cylinder engines, the AMX name lived on as the performance option on the Javelin line. The standard engine in the Javelin AMX was a 210 horse, two-barrel 360, breathing through cowl induction and exhaling through single exhaust. The 360 could be traded up to a four barrel, dual exhaust version that produced 285 horses. The top option in the AMX was the four-barrel, 401 cubic inch unit that produced a very respectable 330 horses. The base tranny was a 3-speed manual, with a Hurst shifted, 4-speed manual optional, as was a Shift Command 3-speed automatic. The cars were stopped by 10 inch drums all around, with power assist and front discs, or both, as options. The optional Go-Package provided either of the two high-performance engines, special instrumentation, heavy-duty suspension, power disc brakes, limited slip "Twin-Grip" rear end, as well as a T shaped hood stripe and blacked-out taillight panel.

The inside of the Javelin and Javelin AMX was as unique as the outside. The most prominent feature was the wrap-around instrument panel, obviously inspired by fighter aircraft. Full vinyl bucket seating was standard on the Javelin, and AMX buyers could opt for a domino pattern cloth/vinyl seat covering.

If one were going to buy a performance car in 1971, it was unlikely to be a Rambler. Little AMC produced roughly 21,000 Javelins powered by V-8s of one type or another. Of those, only 2,054 Javelins were equipped with the AMX package.

\* \* \*

Companies, regardless of the product they produce, exist for one purpose. That purpose is not to provide jobs, or health insurance, or day care for its employees, or retirement plans. Businesses do not exist as a tax revenue stream to fund whatever good idea program which the government has devised. Companies exist to generate a profit, and that is it. Nothing else. As much as performance car enthusiasts would like to believe otherwise, car makers are companies, and they don't exist to build cars. They exist to make a profit, and the production of vehicles is the avenue they have chosen to do that. If they don't sell cars they go bankrupt. That the climax of the muscle car era was 1970 is generally accepted, and in terms of style, power and sheer number of muscle car models, it certainly was. In economic terms—the only terms that mean anything with the car makers—the muscle car and performance pony cars were walking the Green Mile in 1970. In terms of sales, the apogee of the muscle car era was much earlier, in 1967 or 1968.

The reality is that 1971 was the final year for true performance intermediates and pony cars. The market for those cars had grown so feeble that there were no longer sufficient financial incentives to produce them, and the car makers began to look elsewhere for market share. For a variety of reasons, the tastes of the buying public had evolved, and while the car companies would continue to build them in ever decreasing numbers over the few years following 1971, the market was dead. That isn't to say that the car makers gave up and suddenly, in unison, quit building performance intermediates and pony cars—there still might be some gold dust left in the mine after all—but the effort was no longer a priority.

**The shaker hood scoop that would adorn Pontiac's Trans Ams in one form or another through the 1979 model year (courtesy Gateway Classic Cars, St. Louis, MO).**

When the curtain dropped on the 1971 model year, it dropped to a large degree on the muscle car as well. To borrow a term from the Vietnam War, the "body count" for the 1971 model year was extensive. Chrysler's mythical 426 Hemi was gone forever after 1971. Its Chevrolet rival, the LS6, was planned for the model year but fell victim to the increasing stringency of the government's emissions standards. Ford's magnificent Boss 302 and 429 Mustangs were put to pasture, and the 429 engine itself would not come back for 1972. Mercury's Cougar Eliminator was terminated, and the Cougar itself might as well have been. The AAR 'Cuda and T/A Challenger were not brought back for 1971. AMC pulled the plug on its Machine and morphed the AMX with the Javelin. Dodge killed off the Coronet R/T and relegated its legendary Super Bee to a mere option package on the Charger. In the coming year, the list of casualties would only get longer.

The fall of the American muscle car was breathtaking, from its performance and style peak in 1970 to what it had become with the close of the 1971 model year. From that 1970 high, the muscle car roared into 1971. The mythical American muscle car—the greatest performance cars in the history of the American automotive industry—would stagger bravely into 1972 to face the final reckoning.

# 11

# A Stroll Among the Ruins

## *What Goes Up Must Come Down*

Two years removed from the turbulent 1960s, in many ways things felt largely the same in 1972 as ghosts of the '60s remained like unhealthy lesions on the national mood. There was the Vietnam War, ever-present and seemingly not going away, still raging unabated. By year's end however, President Nixon kept his promise to turn the show over to the South Vietnamese and withdrew the last U.S. ground troops. The South Vietnamese immediately began fumbling things, enthusiastically retreating in the face of a North Vietnamese invasion. Late in the year, in an effort to get the North Vietnamese to the negotiating table to end the long national nightmare, Nixon ordered the two Linebacker bombing campaigns against the North, hammering the previously off-limits cities of Haiphong and Hanoi. American anti-war liberals understandably failed to understand how B-52s raining bombs on North Vietnam represented the best path to peace, and the massive war protests continued. Grace Slick managed to get herself maced while protesting, and Jane Fonda cemented herself as "Hanoi Jane" after, among other things, musing about shooting down American aircraft while sitting at a North Vietnamese anti-aircraft gun.

Aside from winding down Vietnam, Nixon had himself a pretty big year. On the upside were his visits to China and the Soviet Union, a brilliant diplomatic coup arranged by Henry Kissinger, which played America's two Communist rivals off against each other while simultaneously causing North Vietnam to question the dedication of its two biggest benefactors. Nixon signed off on the paperwork that set in motion a program to build a reusable space vehicle, known to us today as the space shuttle. The Democratic National Committee pinned the rose on George McGovern to take one for the team in the 1972 presidential election, and that is exactly what happened—Nixon won 49 states, 520 electoral votes, and more than 60 percent of the popular vote.

The bigger result of that 1972 presidential election was the most serious Constitutional crisis since the Johnson Administration—the Andrew Johnson administration in the late 1860s—known to us today simply as "Watergate." After a group of Republican operatives were arrested for breaking into the Democratic National Committee headquarters in the Watergate Hotel complex in Washington, D.C., Nixon huddled with key staff and decided the only prudent course of action was to cover up the whole affair and his knowledge of it. The cover-up and the protracted legal fight over his secret Oval Office tape recordings would certainly have led to his impeachment;

in August of 1974, Nixon decided that discretion was the better part of valor and resigned the Presidency, while still maintaining his innocence. Thus, the nation was bequeathed to Gerald Ford, who almost immediately pardoned Nixon, leaving Americans to wonder what previously undiscovered levels of paranoia Nixon must have suffered to cause him to cheat in an election he in no way could lose.

The year had its share of tragedies, but perhaps none so astounding as what occurred at the Summer Olympic Games in Munich, Germany, when Palestinian radical group Black September kidnapped and murdered 11 Israeli athletes attending the games. The event had a sinister irony, set as it was in the city that gave birth to the Nazi party. Once the games moved ahead in the aftermath of the tragedy, American Mark Spitz—of Jewish origin—became the first Olympian ever to win seven gold medals, surpassed only by Michael Phelps' eight in the 2008 Beijing games.

The sports landscape of 1972, however, was more than the Olympics. The Miami Dolphins completed the first undefeated NFL season, many of those games witnessed from on high by the Goodyear blimp, which made its maiden flight that year.

The Supreme Court of California abolished the death penalty as contrary to its state constitution, assuring such luminaries as Charles Manson and Sirhan Sirhan a taxpayer funded minimum standard of living until they died naturally, as Manson did in 2017. The U.S. Supreme Court followed suit, holding in *Furman v. Georgia* that the death penalty amounted to cruel and unusual punishment. The Supreme Court also held in *Eisenstadte v. Baird* that single people had the same right to contraception as married couples; the need of a Supreme Court ruling to determine that is astounding enough and the fact that the *Eisenstadte* decision struck down a state law from liberal Massachusetts is even more so. The Equal Rights Amendment was approved by both houses of Congress, but we are all still waiting for it to be ratified by the requisite number of states to bring it out of the legal limbo in which it has remained since.

Explosions-as-statements seemed to be popular again in 1972. The northern Irish regularly blew up Englishmen, in addition to some of themselves due to wayward detonations. The Soviet Union and the United States traded nuclear weapons tests, which made sense after signing a treaty that limited their ability to defend themselves against nuclear ballistic missiles.

It was a year ripe with miscellaneous events, the knowledge of which would be useful in any bar trivia game. Senator, pro-segregation crusader, and father of a mixed race child Strom Thurmond of South Carolina wanted to deport John Lennon. The environmental activist group Greenpeace was founded. Anti-war sitcom *M\*A\*S\*H* and *Sanford and Son*, with its near death experiences, debuted on TV. Georgia's monument to the heroes of the Confederacy at Stone Mountain was completed. The United States began selling grain to the Soviet Union, the first evidence of the cracks in the Soviet system that would spell its doom nearly 20 years later.

Finally, contrary to the popular belief that World War II ended on the USS *Missouri* in September of 1945, that great conflict found finality. History's greatest True Believer and model of patriotic dedication, Sergeant Shoichi Yokoi of the Imperial

Japanese Army surrendered to U.S. authorities on the island of Guam, where he had been hiding and carrying on the struggle for 27 years.

* * *

By 1972, all that was left was to survey the devastation and pick through the wreckage of what had once been a vibrant performance car market only two model years previously. The American muscle car had suffered a spectacular fall in just two years, and a survey of the 1972 model year primarily serves to measure how far things had fallen, and what was lost.

Many of the great car models of the earlier era were gone, as were the ferocious, high compression engines that had once powered them. There were cars bearing the once great nameplates, but they were mere ghosts of what they once were, and few were buying them. Performance could still be had in the form of sporty compacts like Dodge's Demon, Plymouth's Duster, Chevy's Nova, the Ford Maverick and even Gremlins and Hornets from AMC, but the great cars of earlier years were rapidly going extinct. For 1972, there was nothing left of the muscle car market but the smoldering ruins of what once was.

* * *

Chrysler, for all its 1971 defiance, folded the tent pretty quickly in 1972. Chrysler switched to net horsepower ratings in 1972, and while the net numbers looked far worse than they were, particularly to a generation accustomed to higher gross horsepower numbers, by 1972 the great Chrysler engines of the muscle care era were a whisper of what they had been, regardless of how horsepower was measured. The legendary 426 Hemi was no more, a welcome occurrence for Chrysler's competitors. The Six Pack 440s were for all practical purposes gone as well; they were offered in sales literature, but ultimately Chrysler couldn't get the blessing of EPA emissions sniffers, and the 440 Six Pack went the way of the LS6 454 the year before. There have been rumors that a few 1972 Six Pack cars snuck out, but none have been accounted for. The venerable old four-barrel 440 survived into 1972, but it was castrated by 8.2:1 compression and rated at 280 net horsepower. The 383, the workhorse, entry level performance engine on muscle Mopars since the dawn of the muscle car era, was gone as well, bored out to 400 cubic inches and rated 205 horses when equipped with four-barrel carb and dual exhaust.

The weakening of engines wasn't the only change to Chrysler's performance lines. All R/T models were gone, and those intimidating two letters that had graced muscle Dodges since 1967 were no more. The Super Bee option, on life support as a Charger option in 1971, was finally done away with in any form in 1972, though it would re-emerge—again as a Charger option—in 2007. Plymouth's GTX was no longer a stand-alone model, but was an option package on the Road Runner. The gulf that existed in 1968 between the cheap Road Runner and the high end GTX had finally closed as the list of standard equipment and available Road Runner options grew longer. The winnowing of Chrysler's muscle era performance models in 1971 and 1972 left standing only Dodge's Charger and Challenger, and Plymouth's Road Runner and 'Cuda.

With the R/T badge gone, Dodge replaced it on both the Charger and Challenger line with something called a "Rallye" package. The Rallye package, in truth, was an appearance package rather than a performance one, as on neither car did the Rallye package mandate a high-performance V-8. The Rallye Dodges could still be had in what were once called High Impact colors; by 1972 only Top Banana yellow and Hemi Orange were left.

The basic form of the fuselage Charger was unchanged from the previous model year; it was still big and getting bigger and moving away from its persona as a luxury-performance model, and instead focusing on the luxury side of things. The Rallye package meant special instrumentation, dark grille paint, domed hood, simulated door louvers, sway bars and a special suspension. The standard power plant for a Rallye package-equipped Charger was the 150 horse 318 cubic inch engine. Options from there were a two-barrel 400 cubic inch engine producing a paltry 190 horses, or a four-barrel version of the 400 at 225 horsepower. The most powerful options were the 340 cubic inch 4 barrel, producing a modestly impressive 240 horses, and the big 440 four barrel. The 440 produced 280 horses and was available only on the Rallye and the luxury-themed SE packaged Chargers. Transmission choices were determined by engine option—a column mounted 3-speed manual was standard on 318 and two-barrel 400 cars, while the A-833 4-speed manual was standard with the four-barrel 400 and 440. The 3-speed TorqueFlite automatic was available as an option with any engine. By 1972 the Charger was well into the plus-sized category, and it is telling of the state of things in 1972 that the Rallye Charger, heir to the distinguished R/T badge, was available with a little 318.

For the Challenger, little was changed in appearance from 1971. There were slight revisions to the taillights and grille treatments, but aside from this, the car looked like a '71. Engine choices across the line were reduced from 10 to 3, as Chrysler eliminated all large cube engines from its Challenger and Barracuda lines. The Rallye package got a scooped hood, strobe striping along the flanks and faux air extractors behind the front wheels. The standard engine for the Rallye was the same 318 available in the Rallye Charger. The only option for the Challenger Rallye was the 240 horse 340 engine. All Challenger Rallyes came standard with a column mounted 3-speed manual transmission, but buyers who sprang for the 340 could opt up for the 4-speed manual, and the 3-speed TorqueFlite automatic was available with either engine.

Dodge managed to sell nearly 8,128 Rallye Challengers and another 3,891 Rallye Chargers, both increases over the R/T variants of 1971. The Rallye package was an appearance package, however, and did not mandate a high-performance engine as the old R/T option once did, and most of these cars were equipped with the lesser, more easily insured engines available to them. The sales numbers reflected more the affordability of small displacement Rallyes than any kind of market rebound.

For 1972, Plymouth also thinned out its performance line, and it only offered two of its traditional stand-alone models—the Road Runner and the 'Cuda. The high end GTX was relegated to an option on the Road Runner, as the latter continued its drift away from its bare-bones roots and solidly into luxury-performance territory.

Aesthetically, the 1972 Road Runner was a copy of the 1971 model. In base form the Road Runner came equipped with the four-barrel 400 cubic inch engine under

1972 Challenger Rallye (courtesy Motor Car Company, San Diego, CA).

1972 Plymouth Road Runner (courtesy Vanguard Motor Sales, Plymouth, MI).

a power bulge hood with two thin, non-functional hood scoops. An "Air Grabber" hood was also an option.

When it came to engine choices, the Road Runner didn't offer as many as did the Charger. The 318 and two-barrel 400 cubic inch offerings were left to the Road Runner's parent Satellite line. The base engine for the Road Runner was the four-barrel 400 that produced 225 horsepower. There were two options for the Road Runner—the same 240 horse 340 found on the Dodge offerings, or, if the GTX option was selected, the 280 horse 440 cubic inch four barrel. If the GTX was gone as a stand-alone model, its spirit survived; the GTX option also netted bucket seating over the Road Runner's standard bench as well as additional luxury accouterments. Road Runners, with or without the GTX option, came equipped with a heavy-duty suspension, sway bars, and a standard 3-speed manual, with 4-speed manual and 3-speed TorqueFlite automatic optional. The 3-speed manual was unavailable on the Road Runner GTX. The iconic "beep-beep" horn was retained and the same two formerly High Impact colors were available on the Plymouths as on the Dodges, though in Plymouth vernacular they were called Tor-Red and Lemon Twist yellow.

Road Runner sales plummeted from 13,644 in 1971 to only 7,628 in '72. Road Runners equipped with the GTX package fell to 672.

Outward appearances didn't show much change to Plymouth's once heralded pony car, the 'Cuda, with only slight revisions. The quad headlamps of 1971 were swapped out for singles, and the tail end received an upgrade of twin round tail lamps on each side. The "gills" adorning the fenders of the 1971 model were gone as well.

The most drastic changes to the 'Cuda were under the hood, as the long list of available engines was reduced. As with the Challengers, there were no more big-block engine options for the 'Cuda. The base engine was the 318, and the only optional engine available was the 225 horse 340. Either engine was backed by the standard 3-speed manual, with optional 4-speed manual or TorqueFlite 3-speed automatic.

Sales for the 1972 'Cuda are an outlier, and, while still weak, actually rebounded somewhat from 1971 numbers. Sales increased to 7,828 including 5,864 powered by the optional 340.

The two bright color options and the Hurst "Pistol Grip" shifter on manual transmission cars were about as flashy as it got for what had been Chrysler's top performance models in previous years. Over the next few model years, as sales continued to diminish, Chrysler's muscle car models would continue to fade away with the performance of their engines.

The Road Runner would continue limping on in various forms for the next eight model years. The Road Runner's GTX option was killed off after 1974, before the Road Runner was moved to a bigger platform and itself made an option on the Fury. The Road Runner would later become an option on the compact Volare before mercifully being put down for good after the 1980 model year.

The Charger would be the only semi-consistent legacy of the glory years of Chrysler performance. After having its name applied to a Dodge version of Chrysler's Cordoba personal luxury car from 1975 to 1978, it would show back up in 1983, as a small 96-inch wheelbase hatchback that would last through the 1987 model year. None other than Carroll Shelby had a hand in the creation of performance versions

1972 Plymouth 'Cuda (courtesy of Vanguard Motor Sales, Plymouth, MI).

of the little Charger. To help bolster the perpetually ailing Chrysler Corporation, the Charger would come back from the dead a second time in 2006, this time with four doors, complete with R/T and Super Bee options. Cleverly designed to hark back to the glory days of the 1960s, the Charger is still with us. Its performance variants, particularly the Hellcat Chargers, put to shame any Charger from the muscle car era, despite having too many doors. In fact, the 2014 Hellcat Charger claimed the distinction of being history's fastest 4 door sedan. Interesting praise indeed.

The Barracuda and Challenger lines disappeared after 1974. The Challenger name was applied to a small Mitsubishi-built coupe marketed by Dodge from 1978 to 1983, then went dormant until being resurrected in 2008 for a car directly modeled on the original 1970 model. Since then the Challenger has been available in several flavors, including in re-animated R/T form, and with the old High Impact colors as options. The ultimate modern Challenger combines the Challenger badge with that of another performance Dodge from the past, the Demon. The Demon Challenger comes equipped with a supercharged 6.2 liter Hemi engine that produces a reported 840 horsepower and 770 ft. pounds of torque, capable of quarter mile times of 9.65 seconds. The Demon is one of the most powerful American production cars ever built, and its performance is something that would have been inconceivable in the muscle car era.

Chrysler would stagger through the 1970s, and suffer a near death experience in the late 1970s until rescued from financial ruin by the genius of none other than Lee Iacocca, the father of the Ford Mustang. Chrysler, seemingly always in need of resuscitation, would again face financial catastrophe in the mid–2000s. The Plymouth brand was shut down in 2001. Regardless of Chrysler's chronic economic trouble and questionable quality of muscle era bodies, its vehicles made an indelible impact on the muscle car era. The legendary name plates of the era—the Road Runner and Super Bee, R/T Challengers, Chargers and Coronets, the GTX, and the long suffering Barracuda—have found a place among the immortals on the Olympus of American performance cars

\* \* \*

Coming into the 1972 model year, Ford faced the same crisis of declining mid-sized car sales that was seen across the entire American automotive landscape. Ford was selling plenty of its Pintos and Mavericks, which were offered to counter the flood of small, economical and cheap Japanese imports. Ford's intermediate line was in trouble, and in order to save its mid-sized line Ford gave its Torino a makeover.

The new Torino was noticeably bigger than it had been in 1971. Though its wheelbase had been trimmed to 114 inches it was beginning to emphasize comfort over performance. It rode on a newly designed frame and softer suspension in the interest of ride. Ford offered nine Torinos in 1972, from station wagons to land barges. A large "fish mouth" grille opening was flanked by quad headlamps, and the quarter panels were flared. All in all, the car looked bigger, more rounded and voluptuous than the previous body style, and people either loved it or hated it. One need look no further than the central object in Clint Eastwood's 2008 movie *Gran Torino* to get a good look at the new Ford intermediate.

The Torino's muscle car incarnation was the Gran Torino Sport, as the old GT and Cobra versions of the Torino were discontinued. The Gran Torino Sport was available in either fastback or formal roofline. The Gran Torino Sport was an upscale version of the basic Torino, and included front disc brakes, full carpeting, a deluxe steering wheel, and other high end trim pieces. The Gran Torino Sport included all of the goodies the of the Gran Torino, plus special door trim, woodgrain steering wheel, grille and hood scoops.

The base engine for the Gran Torino Sport was a 302 two-barrel producing 140 horses. Up next was a pair of 351 Cleveland options. The first was a two-barrel option that produced 161 horsepower. The other was a cold air breathing, four-barrel, 351 "Cobra Jet," an unabashed attempt to reclaim the glory of previous years, which produced 266 horsepower which was respectable for 1972. A 172 horse, two-barrel, 400 cubic inch block was available, as was an engine displacing 429 cubic inches that shared only displacement with the legendary Ford 429s of the past; this 429 produced a paltry 205 horses; in other words, the largest displacement engine on the Gran Torino Sport produced 50 fewer horses than the much smaller four-barrel 351s.

Transmission choices varied by engine. The base 302 came standard with a 3-speed manual shifted on the column, and 4-speed manuals topped with Hurst shifters were available only on all other engines. Three-speed automatics—of either the C4 or FMX variety—were likewise available on all engine options. Suspensions across the entire Torino line were soft, indicating the drift Ford was taking toward luxury, but a stiffer suspension with front and rear sway bars could be had. The Gran Torino Sport featured standard power front disc brakes with drums in the rear.

Ford pushed more than 92,033 Gran Torino Sports of both rooflines out the door in 1972. This is an impressive number in light of the rapidly declining sales for performance intermediates that had taken shape over the previous model years. However, the precise breakdown according to engine choice is unavailable, and most assuredly the majority of them were of the lower performance variety. Interestingly, the Torino line outsold its Chevrolet competitor, the Chevelle, marking the first time a Ford mid-size had topped the Chevy since the latter's introduction in 1964. It took until the end of the muscle car era for Ford to catch Chevy, but in the eternal battle between the Bowtie and the Blue Oval, a win is a win.

Mercury's analog to the Torino was the Montego. In accordance with longstanding Mercury tradition, the Montego was essentially a clone of the Torino. Like the Torino, the Montego was reduced in wheelbase to 114 inches, and it wore a restyled front end devoid of the huge grille and featured scalloped molding just behind the doors. The performance version of the Montego was the Montego GT, with the Cyclone being put to pasture and unceremoniously made an option package on the base two-door Montego, Montego GT and Montego MX hardtops. The Montego GT also got a scooped hood, so it at least looked the part of a performance car.

The base engine for the Montego GT was the two-barrel, 140 horse 302 cubic inch unit. Optional was a two-barrel 351 Cleveland good for 163 horses. Four-barrel 351 Cleveland options included a four-barrel producing 262 horsepower or the cold air breathing 351 Cobra Jet at 266 horsepower. The two-barrel, 172 horse 400 and neutered 205 horse 429 were available as well. If the Cyclone package was opted for, the Montego GT netted either the 351 Cobra Jet or a cold air 429, plus appropriate Cyclone striping and badging. Befitting Mercury, a 4-speed manual transmission was available only on the 351 Cobra Jet; otherwise it was a 3-speed automatic. The Montego GT shared the Gran Torino Sport's front disc/rear drum setup.

Whereas sales for the Gran Torino Sport were relatively strong, the market was not so kind to the Montego GT. Mercury built 5,820 Montego GTs, including only 30 with the Cyclone package.

The Montego would soldier on deep into the 1970s, carrying Mercury's mid-sized banner until 1977, when it was finally replaced by the ever-growing Cougar. The Montego nameplate would re-emerge in the 2005 model year as a Mercury-badged Ford 500, designed as a full-sized model to replace Mercury Sable, but the Cyclone was lost to history after the 1972 model year.

Like the Montero, the Torino would remain as Ford's midsized line through the 1976 model year, when it was killed off. To date, there has been no re-emergence of the storied Torino.

For the Mustang line, little changed for 1972 after the radical restyle of the previous year. The Boss 351 was gone, leaving the Mach 1 as the Mustang's sporting incarnation, again available only in the fastback body style. With ample striping, optional blacked-out hood and prominent rear deck spoiler, the Mach 1 for 1972 looked the part of a premium performer. However, the mechanical motivation of the big pony represented the big changes for the new model year.

Mach 1 engine choices were substantially curtailed for the 1972 model year, as there was no large cube option and the Boss 351 had been retired. The base engine for '72 was the same two-barrel 302 as found in the Gran Torino Sport and Montego GT.

**1972 Ford Mustang Mach 1 R–Code (courtesy Vanguard Motor Sales, Plymouth, MI).**

With the exception of the 400 and 429, engine choices for the Mach 1 were the same as for the intermediate Gran Torino Sport, but there was an additional, limited production version of the 351 Cleveland available in the Mach 1. This was the R–Code, a cold air breathing, four-barrel, 351 H.O. that produced a very respectable 275 horses. Transmission choices included the base console mounted 3-speed manual for 302 and two-barrel 351 powered cars, and with a 4-speed manual on all others, or some variation of Ford's 3-speed automatic. All Mach 1's came with front disc/rear drum brake systems, with power assist optional.

Inside, the Mach 1 was reminiscent of a grand touring car, with full vinyl bucket seating standard, as well as full carpeting on the floor and lower door panels. A short console was standard, but a full length one was optional. Secondary gauges were located on the console. Power steering, power windows, and power locks were optional as well.

Ford built a respectable number of Mach 1's in 1972, though most were of the base 302 variety. In all, the Blue Oval built 27,675 of its flat top Mach 1's for the model year.

The Mustang's historical twin, the Cougar, continued its departure from the realm of the performance car and toward that of luxury tourer and the big cat only continued to grow for 1972. For the new model year the Cougar was available in hardtop or convertible trim, and its performance version was the Cougar GT.

The base engine for the Cougar GT was the two-barrel, 163-horse 351 Cleveland. Engine options included the four-barrel 351 and the most potent engine offering, the 266-horse Cobra Jet 351. As with the Mach 1, there was no 400 or 429 option available.

Transmission choices were the standard 3-speed manual, which was upgradable to a 4-speed manual or a Select-Shift 3-speed automatic. The Cougar shared the Mach 1's power front disc/rear drum brake system.

Illustrative of the direction in which the Cougar was heading, Mercury bragged that what were considered luxury extras on other cars were standard on the Cougar—bucket seats, console, and the like. The XR-7 upgrade netted even more: leather trimmed buckets, locking steering column, bright pedal trim, map and courtesy lights and a lot of other things rarely found on the muscle cars of old.

Mercury sold 53,684 copies of all varieties of Cougar in 1972, which is a respectable number, illustrating that Mercury was wise to move its Cat out of the cratering pony car market. However, it sold only 300 Cougar GTs of one engine or another. The 1972 Cougar truly was an ersatz Thunderbird, and was a far cry from the menacing Eliminators of old.

The flat top Mach 1 would continue into the 1973 model year with few changes, save for a continued slide in performance. In 1974 Ford redesigned the Mustang yet again, this time as an unpopular and thoroughly unmuscular compact called the Mustang II, and the Mach 1 survived the restyle, lasting until the Mustang was redesigned yet again in 1979. The venerable old nameplate would resurface again in 2003, just in time to appeal to the generation that cut their eye teeth on the original Mach 1 in 1969, and perhaps more importantly, in time to intercept some of that graying generation's disposable income.

\* \* \*

For tiny American Motors, the end of the muscle car was tough. For a company unable to compete with the Big Three in terms of production or sales volume, the losses taken by the performance car market in the early '70s were all the more acute. Despite this, AMC continued to compete in the dying market, bringing back its Javelin. For 1972 there was no "base" Javelin—there were only the more upscale SST and the performance Javelin AMX.

On the outside, the Javelin AMX sported flush grilles painted black, and the taillights were covered with chrome molding. A rear deck spoiler was standard, as was a cowl induction type hood. The optional leather interior was dropped, but a quintessential 1970s corduroy seat cover option was available. The unique, curved instrument panel reminiscent of an aircraft cockpit was retained as well. Interestingly, AMC also offered the first of what are today the ubiquitous "bumper to bumper" warranties, offering to fix anything wrong with the car, save tires, for a year or 12,000 miles.

For 1972, the base engine in the Javelin AMX was a two-barrel, single exhaust 304 cubic inch unit that produced a feeble 150 horsepower. Up from that was a pair of 360s: a two-barrel that produced 175 horsepower or a four-barrel at 220. The top engine available in the 1972 Javelin AMX was again the 401, producing 255 horsepower. All Javelin AMXs came standard with a 3-speed manual transmission shifted through a console, and a 4-speed with Hurst shifter was optional. For 1972, AMC farmed out its automatic transmission offerings to Chrysler. The 304 equipped cars used a lighter duty Torque-Command 3-speed, while 360 and 401 equipped units had

1972 Javelin AMX (photo by Greg Gjerdingen, Wikimedia Commons).

the bombproof 727 TorqueFlite. Manual drum brakes were standard all around, but power assist was available as were power front discs. AMC still offered the performance Go-Package option in 1972. This required either the four-barrel 360 or the 401 cubic inch engine, functional cowl induction hood, larger tires and wheels, unique striping and limited slip "Twin-Grip" rear end.

American Motors sold 26,184 Javelins in 1972, and this number includes 3,220 Javelin AMX models. Of the Javelin AMX models, only 825 were equipped with the 401. The Javelin and its AMX sub-species would survive two more model years before AMC pulled the plug on it after the 1974 model year. From there, AMC would concentrate on special, niche-specific cars such as the Gremlin, Hornet and otherworldly Pacer, the latter of which, with a back glass area that would make a first generation Barracuda envious, would become one of the poster boys for the outlandish styling of the 1970s.

* * *

The sister divisions at General Motors, which had recognized early the trends toward unleaded gasoline and stricter emissions and adjusted accordingly, did not see the catastrophic downturn in respectability in their high-end engines in 1972 that were suffered by Ford and Chrysler. That was because General Motors had felt that downturn in respectability a year previous. The performance nameplates of old— GTO, SS, GS, Trans Am and the like—continued into 1972 far more on momentum than on their own performance merit. The performance A-bodies offered by General Motors were essentially copies of the 1971 models, as the entire A-body platform was due for a major overhaul for the 1973 model year; the famous (or infamous) "colonnade" cars would be the hallmark of GM intermediate styling though much of the 1970s. Adding to the woes of 1972, as if things couldn't get any worse for the dying muscle cars, General Motors plants that produced the Firebird and Camaro lines suffered from catastrophic labor issues. The issues with the autoworker's unions were so severe that production was crippled and GM seriously considered killing off the Camaro and Firebird in 1972.

All things considered, 1972 was a craptastic year for what remained of GM's performance cars.

At Chevrolet, the Chevelle line once again carried the banner for mid-sized performance. In the final year of a body style that had remained substantially the same since 1968, Chevrolet didn't spend much time revamping the Chevelle line. The only significant changes were to the grilles and parking lights.

Like the previous year, the SS package was available on all V-8 Chevelles, and engine choices were identical to the previous year as well. True performance in the Chevelle line, such as it was, began with a four-barrel 350 that cranked out 175 horsepower. Next up was the still-misnamed 400 cubic inch block topped with a 4-barrel carb, actually displacing 402 cubes and producing 240 horses. Finally, the LS5 454, only available with SS option, produced 270 horsepower. The SS 454 wasn't available in California, as it wouldn't pass that state's stricter emissions requirements. The SS package for 1972 netted a domed hood, blacked-out grille and locking hood pins; it was again more of a show than a go package, though the SS was the only way to acquire a 454.

The budget friendly version of the Chevelle, the Heavy Chevy, was trotted out for one last foray. Introduced late in the 1971 model year, the '72 Heavy Chevy was virtually identical to the '71. As in '71, the Heavy Chevy could be had with any available V-8, with the exception of course of the SS-only 454.

Across the Chevelle line, with the exception of the LS6 454, the base transmission was a 3-speed manual, Cars powered by the 350s, 400 and 454 could be shifted by a 4-speed manual, or by the Turbo-Jet 400 automatic transmission.

Chevy's Chevelle sold well in 1972, but as the Chevelle was Chevrolet's most versatile line there was a lot of variance. Just over 500,000 Chevelles of all flavors were sent out the door, including 4 doors, station wagons and El Camino trucks. However, given the state of the market for performance mid-sized cars in 1972, sales were relatively strong for performance Chevelles. Just under 25,000 SS equipped Chevelles were sold, though presumably most of those were of the 307 or 350 variety, and that number includes SS equipped El Caminos. Chevrolet sold another 9,508 Heavy Chevys in that model's swan song.

Chevrolet's other performance offering not named Corvette was again the Camaro, the hottest of which were the venerable SS and Z/28 options. The 1972 Camaro seemed to be a cursed vehicle from the start, suffering from labor difficulties that crippled production. Of the few that were built, over 1,000 had to be scrapped or were donated to vocational schools because they did not conform to ever-tightening emissions and bumper mandates meted out by Uncle Sam.

Cosmetic changes for 1972 included a new eggcrate grille, and the RS package

**1972 Chevelle SS 454 (courtesy Vanguard Motor Sales, Plymouth, MI).**

continued to offer the split front bumper, virtually identical to the previous year. Three-point seat belts were used for the first time, and Chevrolet, most likely in a nod to insurance pressure, installed a 130 max speedometer, replacing the 150 MPH gauge of previous years.

Performance-wise, the Camaro continued to wither. This would be a year of finality in many ways. It would be the last year for the SS option on the Camaro until 1997, though Chevrolet somehow saw fit to put the SS badge on a station wagon in later years. It would also be the last year for a big-block Camaro for quite some time, and Chevrolet even thought to delete the Hurst shifter on manual transmission cars. The guys at the Bowtie left no stone unturned in neutering the Camaro.

As with the Chevelle, the SS package was more of an appearance package than a performance group. The SS Camaro netted the buyer a 200 horsepower Turbo-Fire 350 four-barrel engine, with the 240 horse Turbo-Jet 396 cubic incher optional. The Z/28 was powered by the 350 cubic inch Turbo-Fire power plant producing 255 horsepower. Any of these engines could be mated to a 3-speed Turbo Hydramatic automatic transmission or 4-speed manual. The Z/28 offered the same split bumper as the Rally Sport as well as racing stripes, while the SS included SS badging and a deck lid spoiler; a deck lid spoiler was no longer standard for the Z/28.

Chevrolet's labor troubles and a dying market conspired to nearly destroy the 1972 Camaro. Chevrolet produced 58,544 Camaro copies of all models, including the entry level six-cylinder powered Sport Coupes. Chevrolet sold only 2,575 Z/28s, as well as another 6,562 SS models of one engine or another.

The Chevelle SS was trotted out one more time for 1973 and it frankly was an embarrassment to the storied SS badge. In a cheap bid to increase sales, the SS badge was even whored out to Chevelle-based station wagons, an inglorious end to a veritable legend. While there would never be another SS Chevelle, the SS badge has reappeared every now and again on Chevrolet products, including the resurrected Impala of the 1990s and various versions of Chevrolet pickups. That Camaro line would continue on into the early 1990s, before being killed off in 2002, only to be raised from the dead again for the 2010 model year. Even in the dark days of the 1970s and '80s, the Camaro line produced some fine cars, such as the IROC Z/28 of the 1980s or the SS Camaros of the mid–1990s. In a respectful tip of the cap to its predecessor born in 1967, the SS badge today confidently rides on the current generation of Camaro, still tussling with its ancient enemy, the Ford Mustang.

The 1972 model year would be the end of the trail for Buick's unlikely supercar, the GS, as a performance option on its Skylark, and the Stage One would make one more sentimental launch, for posterity's sake if nothing else.

The 1972 Buick GS was essentially a rehash of the previous model year, as GM didn't sink much investment into a dying line and with the imminent release of its entirely restyled A-body line scheduled for 1973. As Buick had always done with its muscle line, it hedged its bets by offering an affordable GS 350 as well as its more Buick-like GS 455, with or without the Stage One option. The GS 350 was powered by a four-barrel 350 producing 195 horsepower, while the 455 option netted a sickly 250 horses. The Stage One package to the 455 upped this to 270. All GS cars received cold air induction, regardless of engine. Turbo-Hydromatic 3-speed automatics were standard on any GS car, with the 4-speed manual as an option.

The GSX returned again for 1972, though no one seemed to notice. The GSX option could be had on any GS, including the GS 350. The GSX option included the standard striping, black bucket seating, floor mounted shifter (with either the

1972 Buick GS 455 (courtesy Gateway Classic Cars, St. Louis, MO).

automatic or manually shifted transmission) and a deck mounted spoiler. Buick continued to offer the full range of Buick luxury accouterments, such as power assisted everything, air conditioning, and the like.

Buick might as well not have even tried in 1972. The performance intermediate market was one to which Buick was particularly ill-suited, even back in the halcyon days of the late 1960s, and Buick suffered the same declining sales as all other car makers, pushing only 8,575 copies out the door. This number includes 6,542 budget-and-fuel friendly GS 350s, 1,225 GS 455s, and 809 copies of the Stage 1 455. Most astoundingly, only 44 GSX models were sold.

The GS badge, including the GSX, would shift to the smaller X-body Apollo for 1973. The GSX badge would disappear entirely after 1974. The GS nameplate would continue on various Buick models into the 1990s, but Buick would quietly retreat to doing what it did best—building expensive luxury cars for high end buyers—in the mid–1970s. However, Buick made sure the performance community remembered it by releasing some out-of-nowhere performance monsters from time to time, just as it did with the 1970 Stage One GSX. Buick was responsible for perhaps the most fearsome car of the performance-lacking 1980s—the completely black, bad-boy Grand National and its terrifying ultimate incarnation, the GNX. Buick would survive the great GM restructuring of the late 2000s and survives today filling the niche between Chevrolet and Cadillac in the GM line. Sadly, there is currently no Buick occupying GM's luxury-performance niche. That honor, as strange as it may seem to anyone remotely familiar with the muscle car era, belongs to Cadillac, a division that didn't even field a vehicle to take part in the muscle car wars.

Like Buick's GS, the legendary Oldsmobile 4-4-2 was reduced to simply an option on the Olds' various A-body models, with the exception of the Cutlass Supreme notchback. Like its GM cousins across the A-body line, the 4-4-2 for 1972 was a whisper of what once was.

Sadly for a car with such a past, the base engine for the 4-4-2 was a 350-cube unit topped by a 2 barrel carb on the Cutlass and Cutlass S models, producing 160 horses. The next engine up was not a whole lot better, being another 350, producing 180 horses with a four-barrel carb. This was the base engine for Cutlass Supreme based 4-4-2s. Luckily, at least in terms of displacement, there was a pair of 455 cube engines available as well—a 270 horse four barrel, and the venerable W-30, which produced a respectable-for-1972 300 horsepower. The 350s were standard with a 3-speed manual shifted on the column, with a console at extra charge. Optional transmissions were a 4-speed manual shifted through a console or Turbo-Hydromatic 350 3-speed automatic. The 455 offerings had only the floor mounted 4-speed or 3-speed automatic available. Continuing the 4-4-2's tradition as one of the best handling of all mid-sized muscle cars, it came standard with heavy-duty suspension and brakes.

Thankfully, the 1972 4-4-2 was still a formidable appearing car. The standard hood was molded with faux louvers, side striping and redesigned taillights, divided into 3 sections. Available on all engines was the locking fiberglass hood with prominent scoops that made its debut in 1970, complete with striping. The interior was all Olds, with wood grained dash, and a lengthy list of creature comforts.

Oldsmobile sent 9,843 4-4-2s of various body styles out its doors in 1972, including 1,171 drop-tops and 770 W-30 cars. Unlike many of its A-body brethren, the 4-4-2 would continue on in various forms throughout most of the life of Oldsmobile, which was put to death in 2004. Olds and its 4-4-2 were the first to react to Pontiac's assault in 1964; it is unjust that the great Olds spent the muscle car years in the shadow of its GTO cousin. Despite this, the 4-4-2 is revered by collectors today, and rightly holds a prominent place in the pantheon of the American muscle car.

Finally, there was Pontiac's GTO, the old man of the genre, and the car that started the spectacular muscle car wars of the 1960s and early 1970s, the greatest of all American automotive eras. Sadly, for 1972 The Great One lost its status as its own model and came full circle, once again being an option on the sedate LeMans. The convertible was put to pasture as was the short-lived but magnificent Judge.

The '72 GTO looked very much like the 1971 model, with only slight revisions to the grilles, which were blacked-out for 1972 similar to those of the 1966 model. The retention of the aggressive hood made the GTO one of the more threatening-looking muscle cars of 1972; the looks of the 1972 GTO were writing checks its driveline could not cash.

What performance it had was provided by essentially the same engine options as in 1971: a standard 400 cubic inch engine producing 250 horses, and a pair of 455 engines. The first of these was a base 455 producing 250 horses and a 300 horse, High Output 455. Any of these engines could be had with optional cold air induction. The 400 had as its standard transmission a 3-speed manual, but optional trannies included a close or wide ratio 4-speed manual or the Turbo-Hydromatic 3-speed automatic. The base 455 could only be had with the automatic, while the H.O. 455 could be tied to the 3-speed manual, a close ratio 4-speed or the automatic. Drum brakes were standard, though power disc brakes were commonly ordered. All GTOs were equipped with upgraded, performance suspensions. The interior option list was a long one, as the GTO followed the general trend of becoming more luxurious as the performance waned. Bucket seating, consoles, 8 track tape players, and power everything were included on the list.

The GTO continued its death spiral in 1972. Sales for the 1972 offering were halved again from the paltry numbers of 1971, with only 5,807 GTOs built. Clearly, the GTO was not what it had once been, and by 1972 it was essentially an afterthought in the Pontiac line. Over the next two years, the GTO would see a sad, agonizing death—one that would see the great acronym pasted on two different platforms over the last two model years before going into hibernation for the next three decades. When the GTO did emerge again in 2004, it was more of an effort to tap into the nostalgia of the first wave of aging Baby Boomers than a genuine effort at building a performance car in the image of its ancestors. The last years of the GTO were truly tragic, a sad, dispiriting coda to one of the greatest nameplates in the history of the American automobile.

Pontiac returned its E-body Firebird line for 1972, and as if things weren't bad enough in the world of performance pony cars, the plants building the Firebird line, as with the Camaro, suffered from an episode of the chronic labor controversies. The difficulties with the unions substantially impacted the effort to produce Firebirds for what market there was left.

**1972 Pontiac GTO (courtesy the Pontiac-Oakland Museum, Pontiac, IL).**

A honeycomb grille was the most noticeable upgrade over the 1971 model and marks the easiest external identifier of the 1972 model. Like the 1971 line, the '72 Firebird line started with the base Firebird, and the next model up was the luxury-oriented Esprit. The base 'Bird could be had with a base 250 cubic inch six-cylinder not worth discussing, or optional 350 cube two-barrel producing 160 horses. The Esprit could be ordered with the same 350 available in the base Firebird, with a 175 horse, two-barrel 400 cubic inch unit as an option.

The Formula model was where true performance started. The base Formula engine was the 350 cubic inch two barrel, but this could be cast aside in favor of a four-barrel 400 with 250 horses or the same 300 horse H.O. 455 available in the GTO. The top of the Firebird line was again the Trans Am, available only in blue on white or white on blue and with H.O. 455 as the only available engine.

Base Firebirds and Esprits were standard with a 3-speed manual, with a 4-speed manual or the 3-speed Turbo-Hydromatic automatic as options. Formula and Trans Am models could be had with the automatic or a heavy-duty 4-speed. Formula models featured the same twin scoop adorned hood as they had in 1971, while the Trans Am featured a shaker hood with 455 H.O. callouts. The Trans Am also came equipped with fender air extractors. Both the Formulas and the Trans Ams came complete with standard bucket seating and heavy-duty suspensions.

The labor bosses helped hobble Firebird production to the tune of a mere 29,951 units, including 5,249 Formulas and a mere 1,286 Trans Ams.

Eclipsing the revered GTO, it would be the Firebird and especially its Trans Am variant replete with giant "screaming chicken" hood decals that would carry the

**The last gasp of the muscle car era—Pontiac's 1974 Super Duty 455 Trans Am (courtesy Vanguard Motor Sales, Plymouth, MI).**

Pontiac banner into the performance wilderness of the 1970s and beyond until the death of the Firebird in 2002. The Firebird even proved more popular in the short and long term than did its corporate rival the Camaro, helped along as it was by its conspicuous placement on both the big and small screens in iconic '70s popular culture fare such as *The Rockford Files* and *Smokey and the Bandit.* The Firebird line would provide some good performance cars where they were least expected, most notably the 1977–1981 Trans Ams and the Trans Am GTA cars of the late 1980s and early 1990s.

It is a fitting footnote to the muscle car era that Pontiac would build the last true muscle car. Based on its Firebird line, the '73–74 Super Duty 455 Formulas and Trans Ams would hold out long after other performance models died away. Poetic and historical justice demanded it would be Pontiac that would build such an insolently defiant car, though perhaps more so had it worn the GTO emblem. Be that as it may, the SD 455 was the last true muscle car, rated for 1973 at 310 horses. This was widely regarded as an out and out lie by Pontiac, as the true measure is believed to be closer to 370. It was detuned to a rated 290 horses for '74, but regardless, the SD 455 served as a last echo of the remarkable history of the American muscle car.

\* \* \*

The year 1972 was the last desperate stand of the American muscle car. While there is rampant debate on the date of the end of the muscle car era, the 1972 model year is the last that could plausibly be argued is a part of the previous years dating back to 1964. Many enthusiasts stop counting after 1971 because the decline in

**Dashboard Hurst emblem of Oldsmobiles so equipped (photo by author).**

performance from 1971 to 1972 was so precipitous, while some date the muscle car era to the lifespan of the car that started it, the GTO, which endured from 1964 to its painful death in 1974. Regardless, the truth is that entering 1973, the muscle car era was unequivocally dead. Many of the great names ceased to exist and many of those that remained were merely appearance packages on baser models. The greatest engines of the era were gone, and a very few of what remained could barely manage 300 horsepower.

The year 1972 represented a sad end of a glorious era and saw the American performance car standing at the edge of a vast performance desert in which it would wander, with few exceptions, for the better part of the next 20 years.

By any measure, 1972 was the end of the American Muscle car.

# 12

# Autopsy of an Era

## *The Death and Rebirth of the American Muscle Car*

By 1973, the United States finally seemed to have put the tempestuous '60s behind them. Despite what proved a relatively calm year, the weary nation was on the precipice of yet another round of public convulsions that would come with the mid–1970s. The United States military, tail tucked neatly between its legs, withdrew from the wreckage of Vietnam, leaving the Vietnamese to take their chances with themselves. The corrupt and virtually defenseless Republic of South Vietnam continued halfheartedly in the struggle against North Vietnamese communism, often fighting with itself as well as its northern enemies. Predictably, that endeavor didn't end well. The South fell in 1975, and, as was predicted in justifying the whole Southeast Asian misadventure in the first place, the surrounding countries of Laos and Cambodia fell to Communism as well. Hundreds of thousands paid for the transition to Communism with their lives, particularly in Cambodia. The psychological impact on the self-esteem of the U.S. military, suffering its first unquestioned defeat, was acute and would not be salved over until the pummeling given to Saddam Hussein in the 1991 Persian Gulf War.

The political front of American society didn't offer much respite. Richard Nixon, who had been elected in 1968 by promising to restore law and order to a beleaguered nation, felt the need to openly convince people that he himself was no crook while under investigation in the Watergate Hearings. His presidency wouldn't even last as long as the South Vietnamese government would. The U.S. Supreme Court, supposedly having taken a look at the Constitution, revealed a heretofore undiscovered constitutional right to abortion, apparently written in invisible ink. Its *Roe v. Wade* decision is arguably the most controversial decision since 1857 and the *Dred Scott v. Sanford* case, the jurisprudential catastrophe that declared that blacks are not human beings.

No year is without highlights, and 1973 was no exception. In a landmark symbolic victory for feminism and women's rights, female tennis star Billie Jean King defeated Bobby Riggs, casting women's athleticism in a new and favorable light. Thoroughbred horse Secretariat accomplished the rare feat of winning horse racing's Triple Crown. Riding the momentum from the successful *Apollo* missions (the tragedy of *Apollo I* notwithstanding), the *Mariner 10* spacecraft explored Mercury en route to orbit the sun, and the little spacecraft is still standing post today. British rockers Pink Floyd released their landmark album *Dark Side of the Moon*, and movie goers terrorized themselves with *The Exorcist*.

Another 1973 film of note is *American Graffiti*, a tribute to American youth and car culture set in the late 1950s. The popularity of *American Graffiti* says quite a bit about the rapidly changing culture. By the film's release, people were already reminiscing about the earlier, simpler times of the '50 and early '60s—a scant ten years previous—when all there was to worry about was impending college attendance and out-of-town hot rodders.

People reminisce about how they wish things still were. They reminisce about what they recall as better times. By the mid-1970s, that the great endeavors of the 1960s were mostly failures became increasingly clear—the war in Vietnam, the Great Society, and in some parts of the country, the Civil Rights Movement. From the vantage point of 1973, with the Baby Boomers being forced into grown-up responsibility and faced with grown-up things, the era of fast cars and carefree nights cruising the streets as depicted in *American Graffiti* certainly seemed better times.

*       *       *

The ten model years from 1964 through 1973 were arguably the high point of the American automotive industry in terms of style, marketing, image and performance. In the years since, there have been cars that have performed better, having the benefit of emerging technology, but they have done so without the style or the flair—and in an atmosphere completely unlike the 1960s. The cultural elements that made up the environment that we remember as "The '60s" produced an alchemy that gave birth to many things that define that incredible time—the Space Race, the Civil Rights Movement, the Great Society, the war in Vietnam, the Counterculture; the list goes on and on. The muscle car was just one of those things, another thread in the tapestry that made up the '60s.

During the muscle car era, virtually every major American car maker entered the fray. The exceptions were Ford's Lincoln division, GM's Cadillac, and Chrysler's eponymous line and Imperial. Because "performance" was not a part of the mission of these car makers, these divisions would not likely have participated had they had an intermediate size platform on hand to build a muscle car around. The mid-sized wheelbase was basically 116 inches, with some exceptions. In 1964, the shortest wheelbase car Cadillac offered was 129.5 inches. Lincoln's Continental was 126 inches. The Chrysler line offered one at a comparatively tiny 122 and let the Imperial line handle the really big cars, with the smallest being 129 inches. Imperial's Crown Imperial stretched it out to an incredible 149.5 inches. Not to be outdone, Cadillac's Series 75 was 149.8 inches.

Clearly, mid-sized performance was not the specialty of these divisions, but neither was it the specialty of Buick. For the most part, Buick didn't build performance cars with heavy-duty components; "heavy-duty" for Buick usually meant that they were capable of hauling an extra green bean casserole to a church social. By 1965, however, even Buick was in the muscle car game, trying to cash in by scratching the Baby Boomer itch for performance mid-sized vehicles. That even Buick would get involved in the muscle car competition illustrates the intense competition between the car makers, even between divisions of the same parent corporation. Ford and Chevy had battled for decades. That was nothing new. In the muscle car era, the

Plymouth GTX tried to encroach on the territory occupied by the Mercury Cyclone. Cheap Plymouth and tasteful Mercury rarely competed for the same market segment, but they did in the '60s. This is but one example. These rivalries between car makers that generally stayed in their own yard were a hallmark of the era, and are overlooked in most muscle car histories.

There is a harsh reality that car enthusiasts are sometimes reluctant to admit, and that is that the goal of the car makers in the 1960s wasn't to build performance cars, *per se*. The goal was to sell cars, and because performance intermediates and pony cars were hot sellers *du jour*, that is what they built. These cars were simply a means to a profitable end. While the engineers and the salespeople may have been excited about building and selling performance cars, at the highest levels of the car business all that really mattered was that cars sold, profits were made, and shareholders were happy. It just so happened that in the era of the mid-'60s and early '70s, muscle cars are what sold, at least for a while. If flatbed pickup trucks had been selling, that's what would have been built.

The 1960s was an era in which performance cars were deeply embedded in popular culture—think Beach Boys car songs and the chase scene in *Bullitt*. The '60s were a time in which the social lives of young people took place on cruise strips and drive-ins. It was an era in which young people were actually *identified* by the cars they drove. In this climate, naturally building muscle cars was an effective avenue to generating profits. When even Buick—the great builder of cars driven by business executives or the moderately prosperous family—realized that there was profit to be made selling mid-sized performance cars and that they had a pre-existing platform on which to build one, the Gran Sport was born.

Coming into the 1964 model year, no car maker specialized in the performance intermediate. No maker mass produced a mid-sized performance car for public consumption before Pontiac did so in 1964. Prior to 1964, the performance cars were all big cars with powerful engines—cars like Ford's 406 powered Galaxies, Chevy's 409 Impalas, Pontiac's Super Duty Catalinas and Max Wedge Mopars.

Taking the longer view of the history of the era, it is easy to see the snowball effect that began when John DeLorean kicked the pebble down the mountainside with his GTO in 1964. Once Pontiac let its GTO loose and Olds quickly responded with its 4-4-2, the muscle car era provided its own momentum. What John DeLorean did was simply take an existing engine that had powered big cars—Pontiac's 389— and put it in a smaller body. That was it: brilliance in simplicity. Since most car makers had mid-sized cars, all they had to do to respond to the GTO was sift through the parts bins and stuff their own big car engine into them. Even Buick—not known for performance cars—could get into this game buy using what was on hand.

Things quickly escalated. By 1965, Pontiac was using foam to channel cold air through the hood scoops to the carb—the first of its famous Ram Air engines—to increase performance. Chevrolet put a few of the new, vicious 396 engine intended for the Corvette in its Malibu, just for funsies. Clearly, Chevy liked what happened, because by 1966, the SS 396 was common and dominating, and the Corvette never saw the 396 engine again.

As the competition intensified, car makers moved from using whatever big car engine happened to be lying around to building engines specifically designed as street racers. Chrysler performance cars could be had with what had previously been a race-only engine, the 426 Hemi. Olds responded with its W-30, Buick its Stage 1, and so on and so on as each car maker ratcheted things up in response to each other. By 1970, things had gone completely haywire with LS6 454s producing 450 horsepower, multiple carb 440s and torque-monster Buicks, all to the benefit of the performance car buying market.

That market—the young, normally male, Baby Boomer—allowed the snowball effect to take place. To stick with the analogy, the market was the slope of the mountain that the snowball rolled down. By the early 1970s, the slope was flattening as the market withered away. By the 1973 model year, the ground had completely flattened out. Without the market, there were no more muscle cars, because there was no more profit to be made in building them. Car makers follow the market, because the business of the car companies is business, so the era of the muscle car faded away, a golden era never to be seen again.

What caused the death of the muscle car market? What was the Sword of Damocles that eventually fell? Just as the birth of the muscle car was the product of its time and context, its death was as well. The American car builders did not wake up in 1973 and decide to stop building them. The market simply eroded out from under them, and faced with the law of diminishing returns, the automakers let the muscle car genre die.

In reality, no single factor was the cause of the mass extinction of those marvelous machines. Instead, a perfect storm of forces that steadily gained strength during the years of the muscle car era forced an armistice on the warring car builders.

Among muscle car historians, three basic causes have been articulated *ad nauseam*, and these can be recited by rote by even the most pedestrian of muscle car fans: insurance rates, government regulation, and fuel prices. However, these factors tell an incomplete story; there are other influencing elements that are rarely, if ever, identified. The tempest of forces arrayed against the street antagonists was both undeniable and inexorable.

\* \* \*

The most easily identifiable and most commonly discussed of factors that conspired to deal the American muscle car its death blow was the meteoric rise in insurance premiums. Premiums on performance cars had been rising since the 1964 GTO was set loose but really gained momentum as the cubic inch and horsepower wars amped up though the mid–1960s. Anyone who has ever owned a car understands how the game is played: rates are set by a myriad of factors, and few outside of the insurance industry can explain or even understand the algorithm used to determine insurance rates. Some factors include the age of the driver, the driving history of the insured, and the area in which the insured lives. In a bit of sanctioned sexism never mentioned by the equal rights crowd, the sex of the driver is also a factor, with higher premiums for male drivers.

Perhaps as important as anything else, the type of car is factored in, and horsepower to weight ratio. In the muscle car era, insurance companies' ears pricked up when cars carried a horsepower-to-weight ratio less than ten pounds of car per horsepower. All of these variables are plugged into what must be a great and powerful calculator that spits out a rate to be paid, based on something cryptically referred to as a "risk factor," which is invariably much higher than expected.

In defense of the insurance industry, it is made up of insurance businesses. Like all companies, they exist to generate profits. Insurance companies cannot keep the lights on for long if they are paying out more in claims than they are bringing in in premiums. In fairness, these companies provide a vital public function in that they assure that the life or property is protected in the event of negligence or buffoonery on the part of the people they insure. Insurance companies protect wealth. Socially speaking, this is a good thing.

Insurance companies, being companies, are always looking for ways to increase profit margins while reducing costs. As the 1960s moved along, and the car makers built more and more powerful cars driven by more people, the insurers ratcheted up the rates on those cars and their drivers, who usually were young men. Young men driving powerful cars in an assumedly unsafe manner were a gold mine for car insurers, and they knew it. It did not help that necessities like brakes were often moved down the priority list by the car makers. By the height of the muscle car wars in 1970, the insurance premiums matched the craziness of the vehicles. On certain cars driven by certain drivers, with whatever other factors went into the Great Risk Factor Calculation, the premiums were more than the monthly car payment. Buyers were literally priced out of the market, and not by the price of the car.

Between the years 1964 and 1972, Americans travelled nearly 83 billion miles. Given that performance car production was but a tiny fraction of the overall U.S. automobile production, relatively few of those miles were driven by muscle or pony cars, particularly when many of them only travelled a quarter of a mile at a time. During those years, the rate of people killed in car accidents generally rose, but it actually fell in 1967, 1970 and 1971. While drag racing is an inherently dangerous way to spend one's time, particularly in the cars of that era, a tiny fraction of the time spent in a performance vehicle is actually spent doing idiotic things. People don't, and didn't, drive their performance cars with reckless abandon from points of departure to destination every single time they drove them. The vast majority of the time, performance cars were not driven in a manner any more unsafe than, say, a pickup truck or a Volkswagen Beetle. The insurance companies, however, began with the assumption that every time a muscle car was in motion, it was driven in some unsafe way, and set rates accordingly. The assumption was that if the car was moving, it was an unsafe metal box hurtling its occupants to an early demise, or at the very least, to the destruction of the insured vehicle that would have to be paid for by the insurance company.

With the advantage of hindsight and comparing those cars to those we have today, this is understandable. The truth is, those cars were borderline unsafe. A high horsepower car rolling on bias ply tires bolted to an antique suspension with manual drum brakes, manual steering and with only lap belts (if any belts at all) can be pants-crappingly scary and makes one wonder how the human race survived at all. In their time, however, all these cars were generally as safe as the next one. They all labored under the same limitations to safety. It is true that a '69 440 powered Coronet R/T is more dangerous than, say, a Rambler of the same vintage. When the R/T is being used for anything other than actual racing, however, such as for getting from point A to point B, the Dodge was only marginally more unsafe than the Rambler. By the standards of today, both were pretty unsafe.

The insurers didn't see it that way. To them, driving a muscle car was only marginally safer than cutting Tony Soprano off in traffic. The customers of those companies that didn't drive muscle cars—say, the guys driving Ramblers—were perfectly happy to stick the performance car buyers with an inflated bill, because it kept their own premiums down. The exorbitant rates charged by the insurance companies on performance vehicles as the muscle car era moved along were essentially price gouging, sanctioned by the various state insurance regulators, heavily influenced by the robust insurance lobby.

All of this was rationalized by the simple notion that no one was forced to drive a high-performance car, and if he or she insisted on buying one, they acquiesced to the higher rates. It was just the way it was (and the way it still is). If one didn't want to pay the high rates, buy a performance car. Or, apparently, a Chevrolet Corvair.

The Corvair remains America's timeless monument to automotive deadliness. Any car whose maker insisted that tire pressures be maintained outside the tire's recommendations for the sake of drivability cannot be classified in any other way. To a modern plaintiff's attorney, putting the Corvair into the stream of commerce is equivalent to selling lead catheters or asbestos underwear—a veritable gold mine of litigation. The high probability of something going horrendously wrong by intentionally putting a Corvair in motion was ably pointed out by consumer advocate and twice failed Presidential candidate Ralph Nader, who wrote a book called *Unsafe at Any Speed*. A large segment of his book spoke to the certainty of death of driving a Corvair, but in one of automotive history's greatest ironies, for the average driver insurance premiums were lower for the 1968 Corvair than for a Chevrolet SS 396 Chevelle.

The performance car market did justify some increase in premiums. The cars, after all, were powerful and were driven in ways that a Rambler wouldn't be. However, the insurers overplayed their hand, and the well was gone to too often and for too long, as premiums on performance cars reached absurd levels and far outpaced the payouts. Unable to afford the insurance rates, people just stopped buying the cars. By the early 1970s, the insurance companies helped kill the geese laying the golden eggs.

\* \* \*

The second of the most commonly cited reasons for the demise of the American muscle car was the always helpful interference of the federal government. For the federal government, the presumption seems to be that the American people are imbeciles incapable of taking care of themselves. Therefore, federal regulators are obligated to ensure that the public does not cause itself to go extinct due to its stupidity. With the very survival of the species at stake, the role of the government is the issuance of a never-ending stream of paternalistic regulations, all designed to protect us from ourselves.

Government helpfulness that affected the American muscle car came in two broad areas. The first of these areas was the increasing safety regulations imposed on American car builders in the wake of the 1966 National Traffic and Motor Vehicle Safety Act. This law established the supremacy of the federal government in setting safety standards for American automobiles and requirements to meet those standards.

Up to that point, the operation of the free market regulated vehicle safety. If safety was important to the market, unsafe cars would be hard sells. The market forced safety on the car builders and over the years the car makers had developed a long list of standard safety features. The car builders knew full well that no one was going to buy a death trap, and the safer the car, the better it would sell.

For the federal government, however, and particularly one headed as it was by the left-leaning Lyndon Johnson administration, the market was never good enough and was not to be trusted. Enter the National Traffic and Motor Vehicle Safety Act and the paternalism of federally mandated safety regulations, because the government just knows safety better than the market. "We're the government, we know best, and we are here to help."

After the passage of the National Traffic and Motor Vehicle Safety Act, the safety mandates issued from on high came fast and furiously. Immediately came the requirement for padded instrument panels, seat belts of the lap variety and reverse lights. Required for 1967 were dual circuit brake master cylinders (in fairness, not such a bad idea; one was forced to rely on the Fred Flintstone method of stopping the car if a single circuit brake system craps out). For 1968 car makers were required to equip cars with collapsible steering columns and side marker lights. In 1969 came mandatory, whiplash preventing headrests. The early 1970s saw the introduction of bumper standards with minimum impact requirements that steadily increased over the years. These are all great strides in safety and undeniably increased the survivability rate of those involved in automobile accidents. With more and more baby boomers coming of age and driving, and millions more total miles being driven each year, these standards were undeniably necessary. Had the market been allowed to work things out for itself, car manufacturers would have been forced to come up with safety features on their own, at possibly a faster rate, and certainly more cost effective manner. Governmental decrees to be met on an arbitrary timeline are rarely cost effective. Car makers may have even developed more safety features; they had created a laundry list of safety features on their own prior to 1966.

Government regulations work as a double-edged sword. They set universal minimum safety standards, to be sure. With government mandated minimums, whatever the government mandated was "good enough," and as long as the minimum safety standards were met, the car makers were relatively free of fear from product liability lawsuits and government scrutiny. The bar had been met. The creative energy at, say, AMC, that would have otherwise been dedicated to making sure AMCs were safer than Fords was redirected elsewhere. Setting universal minimum safety requirements also stifles ingenuity and the potential for features that exceed the minimum.

A secondary effect of government mandates, regardless of the industry upon which those mandates are imposed, is increased cost of production. Mandates act as a de facto, regressive tax, regardless of the product regulated. This is something that seems to be lost on those in the ivory towers arbitrarily creating regulations. The assumption seems to be that the industry will simply eat the increased costs of whatever regulation the government decides is necessary. This is not how things work.

At least, that is not how things work if a company wants to remain a company and not in bankruptcy court. Because of increasing safety regulations, car builders were forced to spend millions in research and development to meet government standards, and exactly zero of that investment would lead to increased profits. Government standards were the same for each manufacturer, so Ford couldn't say to the public, "Hey! We have side marker lights and collapsible steering columns!" as a selling point. Everyone else had side marker lights and collapsible steering wheels, too. Government mandates would only be exceeded when cost-benefit analysis of spending R&D dollars indicated higher sales, and that didn't happen often. As long as the minimums were met, the car makers were protected.

In an outstanding case of government counter productivity, Federal anti-trust laws and the threat of their application kept the car builders from collaborating and sharing the costs of research and development. Absurdly, everyone had to invent the wheel for themselves, at their own cost, to meet the exact same regulation. Allowing the car makers to pool their resources and maximize economy of effort could have resulted in more effective safety measures produced and implemented at a faster rate, if safety were truly a motivation of the federal government.

This inability to pool resources affected the smaller car builders, with less volume sold, disproportionately. American Motors, until its death in the mid–80s, and Chrysler, the smallest of the Big Three, were the most profoundly affected; the R&D costs to meet new regulations were roughly the same for each car maker, but General Motors, with much higher production, could spread that R&D cost over millions more cars than AMC or Chrysler. By 2008, the American auto industry as a whole was on the verge of bankruptcy in no small part due to strangling government regulation. This point was made in the late 1970s by then-Chrysler chief Lee Iacocca when begging Congress for federally guaranteed loans to resuscitate Chrysler in the late 1970s.

Federal mandates, like minimum wage laws or any other increase in the cost of production, are not absorbed by manufacturers as many apparently believe. Manufacturers simply pass the increased cost on to the consumer. This increases the cost of the product and impacts those with less money in the budget to purchase the item than those with more. The poor pay proportionally more than the wealthy for a given product. For example, a headrest the government forced Chrysler to put in its high-end Imperial in 1969 cost about the same as the headrest it was forced to put into its cheapest Plymouth Valiant. Therefore, proportionally, the headrest increased the cost of the Plymouth more. The guy buying the Valiant caught the sharp end of the government's regulatory stick.

Cars of the muscle car era were not immune to this effect, and coupled with the rising insurance rates, the cars became unaffordable to the preferred market. Demand was reduced, and supply soon followed. The original 1964 GTO base coupe cost approximately $2,852. In 1970 dollars, that same '64 GTO coupe would have cost $3,570, a difference of $718—roughly 25% of the car's original price, and a significant sum at the time. Inflation was accelerating in the mid- to late 1960s as the Johnson Administration attempted to simultaneously implement the Great Society and fight the Vietnam War, while paying for neither. Regardless of inflation, collapsible steering columns, side marker lights and whatever other safety mandates the government thought would be a good idea didn't come free, and the net effect of the government's paternalism was to increase the cost of the cars of the era, including the muscle cars.

The regulatory assault of the government on the car industry continues today. Take backup cameras, for one example. During the height of regulatory activity of the Obama Administration, the federal government mandated that, by May 1, 2018, all new vehicles will come with "rear-view visibility systems," which is a fancy term for a backup camera. Whether installed on a high end German import or a basic transportation Ford Focus, backup cameras cost about the same—by government estimates, between $132 and $142 per vehicle, not including the increased cost of labor to actually install the things.

What is the gain of this mandate? The National Highway Travel Safety Administration estimates that 58 to 69 lives will be saved each year once the entire on-road vehicle fleet has rear-view systems, which it believes will come about forty years down the road in 2054.

To be clear, losing but one life to an accident is too many. However, a simple cost-benefit analysis illustrates the absurdity of mandating the expenditure of billions of dollars to equip millions of cars from now until 2054 to save 69 lives per year, if those estimates even turn out to be accurate. Generally speaking, however, the federal government has only a casual relationship with common sense. The truth is that the backup camera mandate was a knee-jerk reaction to an unfortunate rash of people backing over and killing children, and in fact, the child for which the law was named would not have been saved by a backup camera.

Regardless, people, and legislators in particular, feel better about mandating such things because they feel like they are doing something about the problem. Feeling many times trumps the inconvenience of fact. People feel they are making a difference about the perceived scourge of back-over deaths, regardless of the cost. Since the vast majority of people forced to pay for backup cameras in their new cars will never have the devices keep them from backing over anyone, that cost will be for nothing. Further, because the cost to install a backup camera is $140 in either a $70,000 Lincoln or a $20,000 Ford, the cost will fall disproportionally on those buying the cheaper cars—de facto tax on the poorer car buyers. Progressive paternalism, indeed.

\* \* \*

The second area of government interference that severely impacted the performance car market of the early 1970s went straight to the beating heart of what made the muscle cars what they were—their engines.

In addition to a deep public distrust of government and all its institutions, a feeling carefully cultivated by politicians of all stripes to the present day—one of Richard Nixon's most enduring legacies is the Environmental Protection Agency, or EPA, born in 1970. The EPA was the result of a burgeoning support of all things environmental that had its basis in the 1950s and had reached a crescendo by the late 1960s. The purpose of the EPA was, and is, to draft regulations pursuant to federal law and to ensure the enforcement of those regulations. Though initiated by a Republican administration, the EPA didn't take long to infuriate most of the Right, something it continues to do with astounding efficiency today. Through its regulations, the EPA did its part to kill the American performance car.

Performance vehicles have always been anathema to the green Left. In fairness to the environmental movement, the performance cars of the 1960s and early 1970s were an appropriate nemesis. They were environmentally terrible; they were horrendously inefficient, with most models barely capable of more than 15 miles per gallon with a stiff tailwind, going downhill. Their primitive exhaust systems belched filth into the sky, the automotive equivalent of dumping raw sewage into a koi pond. Anyone who has checked an old car for "a miss"—meaning a cylinder that is not properly firing—by the tried and true method of sticking one's face in the exhaust pipe to hear the rhythm of the exhaust—knows how rich with unburnt hydrocarbons old car exhaust can be. There were other things that incensed the green Left, and in general, they are the same things that still piss them off today—coal, oil, drilling, people who like coal, oil or drilling and generally anything that uses anything but sunshine or wind for energy. When the EPA was given the shillelagh of 1970's Clean Air Act, the environmental movement really got excited, and with that the EPA immediately set about screwing with cars. Of particular interest to the EPA, through the Clean Air Act's regulated air quality standards were "criteria pollutants"—carbon monoxide and especially lead.

Lead was added to gasoline as early as the 1920 to boost octane, which, in simplified terms, allowed for higher compression engines. Higher compression engines increased performance. Lead also served to protect valves and acted as an anti-knock agent. The leaded fuel burning performance cars of the '60s and early '70s were apparently causing everything from cancer to solar flares, and the EPA set about to rectify this, requiring car makers to install catalytic converters to the exhaust systems to increase their efficiency. More importantly, the EPA mandated a transition to unleaded fuel.

The high compression engines of the muscle car era did not run well on unleaded fuel. By the early 1970s, to comply with the coming unleaded fuel mandates, car makers began to reduce the compression ratios in performance engines. Compounding that, the addition of catalytic converters reduced the free flow of exhaust from the engine and created was what essentially a low water dam in the exhaust. The reduced flow in the exhaust increased back pressure on the engine, further eroding performance. By 1972, about the best compression ratio available was 8.5:1, and some were worse than that, and, as with the safety regulations being decreed, catalytic converters and other emissions control measures weren't free. The government mandated but didn't offer any suggestions as to how to pay for those mandates, and so the costs were simply passed through to the consumer, raising the price of all cars.

In the face of these crippling federal edicts, the car makers shot themselves in the foot with the shift from using gross horsepower ratings to net ratings. Gross horse-power ratings, used exclusively before 1971, measured the horsepower of any partic-ular engine when it was running on a stand, with no air cleaner, exhaust, driveline or accessories. Basically, gross horsepower was a measurement of power at the engine itself under ideal conditions. Net horsepower, used exclusively beginning in 1972, measured horsepower with air cleaner, exhaust system and accessories (such as the water pump and alternator) attached.

The resulting difference was huge. The addition of accessories, the restrictive factors of air cleaners and exhaust systems, and the use of stock ignition timing com-bined to produce much lower numbers that more accurately reflected an engine's real-world output when installed in a vehicle, as opposed to the unrealistic ideal fig-ure of gross horsepower. (Both systems, incidentally, measured horsepower at the engine, not at the wheels, thus not accounting for driveline losses to friction.) Unfor-tunately for buyers' perceptions, at the very time that car makers were reducing com-pression to reduce emissions and use low octane unleaded fuel, they went out of their way to make their engines seem even weaker by advertising net rather than gross horsepower ratings. Suddenly, the Mopar 440 that produced 375 horses in 1970 was producing an advertised 280 horses in 1972, a combination of reduced compression and the new net horsepower rating. The government was killing the performance engines, and the car builders worked very diligently to make sure people knew it.

* * *

The American muscle car stood under the gallows on a three-legged stool. Insur-ance premiums and government mandates were the first two legs, and the third was the steady rise in the price of fuel, which then shot up to catastrophic levels by late 1973. The rise in fuel prices was in part the product of natural inflation, but events that took place on the world stage also affected the cost to feed the hungry performance V-8s.

Economic warfare had been a frequently employed tactic of the Cold War era since it began in 1945. Things like economic warfare are what made the Cold War cold; the Soviets and Americans were not actively shooting each other—though at various times their proxies did—but resorted instead to non-lethal means to pro-jecting national power. The natural ebbs and flows of the world economy affected the price of everything, but the various thrusts and counterthrusts between the two superpowers did as well. It is hard to imagine events on the world stage affecting the American muscle car, but one in particular did. Way back in 1947, in the aftermath of World War II, the state of Israel was born and has existed in a state of conflict with its neighbors since. This conflict—the "Arab-Israeli conflict"—would eventually pro-duce effects that would help to kill the muscle car by affecting the price of oil and therefore the price of the gasoline that fueled them.

To get from 1948 to the death of the muscle car requires a bit of history. Israel disappeared as a political entity in the year 66 when the Roman Emperor Nero sent a legion to put down a Jewish revolt in the province of Judea. The Jewish population was then dispersed around the Roman Empire, which was most of Europe, where they developed flourishing communities for the next 2,000 years. The establishment of Israel in 1948 was the result of the "Zionist" movement—the emigration of Jews to Palestine, which began in the last half of the 19th century and gained momentum after Palestine was placed under English administration in the wake of World War I. After World War II and the attempted extinction of European Jewry and the much less publicized Soviet anti–Jewish pogroms of the 1930s and 1940s, Jews world-wide flowed into Palestine and began pressuring the English government for independence. A combination of political pressure, Jewish tactics that would accurately be labeled terrorism today, and the economic exhaustion of the British after the war persuaded the English to sign off on the creation of the Jewish state in 1948.

The indigenous Arab population and surrounding Arab nations then being established, already alarmed at the flow of Jews into Palestine, immediately attacked the nascent state. Using Western equipment, including, ironically, German Tiger II and other varieties of *panzers* bought and paid for by the Third Reich and transferred to the Jewish state, Israel fought back and eventually defeated the Arab powers, assuring its existence.

Since that time, and up to today, Israel has relied upon Western and especially U.S. military and economic aid. The Israelis, backed militarily by France and Britain, fought a conflict with Egypt in 1956 over control of the Suez Canal. In 1967 came the Six Day War, the most serious of the Arab-Israeli conflicts, which resulted in a resounding defeat of Egypt, Syria and Jordan at the hands of the Israelis and the occupation of Egypt's Sinai Peninsula as a buffer zone between Egypt and Israel proper. More importantly, Israel occupied the city of Jerusalem for the first time in 1900 years; Jerusalem might as well be the center of the universe to Jews and Christians, and ranks right up there with Muslims as well.

Having failed—spectacularly—to destroy the Jewish state of Israel in the 1967 Six Day War, in October of 1973 the Arab states of Egypt and Syria girded up their loins and took one last shot (so far) at destroying Israel. In what is now known as the Yom Kippur War, Egypt and Syria launched an attack on Israel on the Jewish holy day that gave name to the conflict, and after some initial success, the Yom Kippur War ended much like the Six Day War—quickly and in with a resounding Israeli victory.

The result of all of these events, and specifically of the staunch support of Israel by the U.S. and the West, drove the Arab states into the arms of the Soviet Union and fostered a virulent anti–Western sentiment that has not abated to this day. The Arab states realized that they did not have the military strength to challenge an Israeli state armed by the United States, but they also realized they sat atop perhaps the most valuable commodity on earth—most of the world's then-known oil reserves. After the Six Day War and especially after the Yom Kippur War, the Arab dominated Organization of Petroleum Exporting Countries, or OPEC, lashed out in fury at the world supporting Israel with the only truly effective weapon it had—an oil embargo on any nation that offered material support to the Jewish state.

The result in the U.S. of the Arab Oil Embargo of 1973 was much more acute than the general price rise of gasoline in the wake of the 1967 Six-Day War. Gasoline was rationed in the U.S., and in some instances lines to buy a few gallons of fuel stretched for miles. Prices soared more than 200 percent. The 1960 price of regular leaded gasoline in the United States stood at 31 cents a gallon. In 1966, on the eve of the Six Day War, it was 32 cents a gallon. By 1974, however, after the turmoil in the Middle East and the flexing of OPEC's muscles, gas prices had risen 53 cents, or $2.59 in today's terms.

The Arab Oil Embargo and the catastrophic rise in gas prices put a final bullet in what was left of the mid-sized muscle car and pony car market, which by 1973 admittedly wasn't much. Thirsty performance cars, such as they were in 1973, were passed over in favor of fuel economy. As incredible as it may seem today, if people didn't actually prefer a new Ford Pinto to a new Trans Am, economic realities forced them to opt for the more practical and less ravenous Ford. The Embargo also drove down the popularity of the earlier, better performing models that were still relatively new. The incredible muscle cars and powerful ponies of the '60s and early '70s were suddenly rendered nearly worthless and undesirable—parked behind buildings to rot in the elements, or just crushed outright for scrap—literally only worth their weight in metal. While the embargo would eventually prove a boon to the domestic petroleum production as "grasshopper" oil pumps sprang up all across the swamps of Louisiana and the wastelands of western Oklahoma and Texas, the mid-'70s price rise was the kill shot that extinguished what life was left of the American muscle car.

\* \* \*

In the myriad histories of the muscle car era, much ink has been spilled convicting the federal government for its part in killing the American muscle car. To be sure, this condemnation is deserved. The federal government, under the guise of saving everyone from killing themselves in car crashes while breathing polluted air, enthusiastically did its part to kill performance cars. However, there is one area of federal involvement, universally overlooked by muscle car histories, that actually buoyed the performance car market and perhaps helped the muscle car era become more than it otherwise would have. Alas, it is time to give the federal government some overdue credit for its positive role in the story of the American muscle car.

From the beginning of American involvement in Southeast Asia in the 1950s and hitting its stride in the mid-'60s before winding down in the early '70s, hundreds of thousands of American males were treated to a government funded vacation to Vietnam. Increasingly as the war dragged on, many were sent against their will, having been unfortunate enough to be without any of the various deferments. To a large extent, the Vietnam War was a poor man's war, as the government granted draft deferments for college students, and in those days only those relatively well-off went to college.

Soldiers of the Vietnam War were relatively well paid, but they had very little to spend their money on in-country. As opposed to today's deployed service members, there was no internet access to Amazon, Walmart.com or any other online seller. There were no post exchanges within easy reach of service members in country. Iraq and Afghanistan today are littered with post exchanges, big or small, and mail order goods will eventually make it to even the most remote outpost. While today's deployed service members still suffer many of the hardships their predecessors did, such as a separation from family and proximity to imminent danger, easy access to most of the consumer goods available back home is not generally one of them. Big screen high-definition televisions and internet access are common in the hooches of today's service members.

In Vietnam, access to consumer goods existed only on larger bases and installations or if the service member was in close proximity to Saigon. The mail did run, however, and in the mail came car magazines, and through them, the service members were aware of what was going on in the automotive world back home. Many of these service members, ripped right out of high school, yearned to return home—preferably in one piece—and live the life the government had forced them to put on hold. Not having much opportunity to spend their very hard-earned government paychecks in country, many anxiously anticipated getting home and spending the money they'd squirrelled away on a new performance car. To them, a new performance car was a well-deserved reward for a tour of duty in service to country.

There is no way to quantify the impact on muscle car sales of the Vietnam War and the infusion of cash to young males, and the evidence there is entirely anecdotal. Anecdotal evidence is still evidence, however, and there is a lot of it. One cannot peruse a modern magazine dedicated to '60s era muscle cars and not be struck by the sheer volume of remarkably similar narratives of original muscle car owners—"When I got back from Vietnam, the first thing I did was go out and buy myself a brand new...." Story after story, issue after issue. Neither can it be ignored that the pinnacle of muscle car sales, from 1966 through 1968, roughly tracks with the rapid escalation of the war and the peak of young men receiving a government paycheck. Likewise, the decline in demand for the muscle car models, which began in 1969 and continued precipitously into the early '70s also tracks with the Nixonian withdrawal from Southeast Asia. While the true impact of government pay for service men and women in Vietnam on the muscle car market may never been known, there can be no doubt that the war did indeed have an indirect impact on the vitality of the performance car market of the late '60s and early '70s. Undoubtedly, thousands of performance cars were purchased by returning service members, and without the war, the muscle car market would not have been the same.

* * *

The predatory insurance rates, increased government mandates in safety and emissions and the skyrocketing price of fuel in the wake of the Arab oil embargo have been rightly identified as the triumvirate that dealt simultaneous blows to the American performance car market. The muscle car market simply could not survive the damage. There is yet another factor, one usually overlooked by fans and historians of the American muscle car. The truth is, by the late 1960s and especially into the early 1970s, the underlying culture that had given birth to the muscle car era simply eroded over the years.

Taking the long view of history, ten years is a blink, a mere moment in time. When we analyze, say, the fall of Rome, we examine the degradation of Latin culture in terms of centuries, not decades. We look at how things were different in the year 410, when Rome was sacked by Alaric and his marauding Visigoths, from, say, 306 when Constantine became emperor of the Empire. We don't look at the difference in Roman culture in ten-year spans. Too little changed in a decade to be noticed looking backward through 2,000 years of history. As we move closer to our own era, the historical benchmarks that define eras become shorter periods of time. Differences in those shorter periods become more relevant to our own time, and a lot of important things can happen in ten years. In the ten years between 1964 and 1973, a lot of important things did happen.

Nineteen sixty-four, the year that spawned both the muscle car and pony car revolutions, was far more similar, culturally speaking, to 1954 than it was to 1974. It still carried the momentum of drive-ins, cruising, and the lighthearted and saccharine music of the late 1950s. In 1964, when the war in Vietnam was still popular with the majority of the public—the Haight-Ashbury crowd was never a fan—Staff Sergeant Barry Sadler had a hit song lionizing the martial fierceness of the Green Berets. By 1969, Country Joe McDonald thrilled the Woodstock crowd and reminded the nation that parents could be "the first one on the block to have your boy come home in a box." Television shows were more similar to those of the late 1950s, shows like *The Andy Griffith Show* and *The Twilight Zone*. Even the Kennedy Administration, hailed as it is today by the American Left as some kind of great proto-progressive force, was in fact much more similar to the conservative Eisenhower Administration it replaced than to the truly progressive Johnson years that followed. Kennedy, revered as a great social activist and civil rights champion, wasn't. Little brother Bobby, the Attorney General, was the prime mover in that arena, not the President.

Cars were very much a part of that culture. Guys worked on their cars themselves, and they built their own customized hot rods, assuming they had the mechanical acumen to do so. If they didn't, they bought factory racers, which until 1964 meant full size barges like the Pontiac Catalina or the Ford Galaxie. In 1964, cars and letter jackets were the measure of cool for young males, just as they had been in 1955; America still retained quite a measure of its innocence of the 1950s. The ten years between 1964 and 1973 were ten of the most violently convulsive in the history of the nation, convulsions driven primarily but not exclusively by the Vietnam War. The Vietnam War years happened to coincide precisely the years of the muscle car wars. The events of those ten years were both progressive and scarring, and in many ways, the nation has yet to recover. The impactful events came one after the other, giving the nation little time to recover or to adapt to the new realities in their wake before being struck by the next.

The assassination of Kennedy in late 1963 was preceded by the percolating Civil Rights Movement, with Freedom Riders, forced desegregation of schools and the events on the Edmund Pettus Bridge in Selma, Alabama. Kennedy's burial was immediately followed by Johnson's Great Society, and the Texan's twin wars—those on poverty and on the Vietnamese Communists. Soon after was the Civil Rights Act of 1964, which outlawed discrimination of any kind based on race, color, religion, sex or national origin, followed closely by the Voting Rights Act of 1965. These pieces of legislation were aimed squarely at the states of the Old Confederacy, and while their passage was nearly 100 years past due, they served to sow division along regional and racial lines. The unpopularity of these bills in the South also destroyed the southern Democratic Party as it was then known. They also set the stage for the return of Richard Nixon from the political wilderness and for twenty-four years of Republican presidential administrations, excepting the thoroughly ineffective 1976–1980 hiatus of the administration of Georgia's most famous peanut farmer. There was the burgeoning counterculture, a full-blown liberal revolution against the conservatism of previous years, with its iconic hippies, music festivals, tie dye and acid rock. The oral contraceptive, also known as The Pill, was approved for use in 1960, freeing women from the fear of unplanned and unwanted pregnancies. A sexual revolution soon followed. Indeed, by the mid–1960s, there were more revolutions going on than one could keep track of.

By the late 1960s, people simply had more to do than worry about cars and drive-ins. The rapid rise of television ownership and viewership played a large part of that. In 1960, television had surpassed radio as the dominant mass medium in the United States. In that year, the average household consumed more than five hours of television per day. That number would climb by an average of twenty-three minutes a day in the years between 1960 and 1965. The average weekly attendance at movie theaters plunged from 44 million in 1965 to 17.5 million by 1970. The same demographic that supported the muscle car market—generally males—was instead at home watching baseball, boxing or, especially, the new National Football League. Consequently, attendance at drag strips and road tracks plunged as well. There were simply more things to occupy one's free time.

Of course, there was the ever-present elephant in the decade—the cancerous war in Vietnam, looming like a specter, just out of the main line of sight, but always there. The war, popular in the early 1960s, had become an albatross around the neck of the Johnson Administration by 1968. So burdensome was the war that Johnson, possessed of legendary political instincts, was instinctual enough to know he was headed for a cataclysmic defeat in the election of 1968. Deciding that discretion was the better part of valor, Johnson declined to run for President in 1968. To the extent that the American Left criticizes Johnson at all, it is for handing the 1968 election to Nixon. This is unfair. Given all the damage Johnson had inflicted on the Democratic Party with the Vietnam War and the acrimony his civil rights legislation caused in the South, Nixon likely would have won anyway.

Then there was Tet. In 1968, as the war was devouring mass quantities of American blood and treasure, the Tet Offensive by Vietnamese communist forces showed the nation that the war effort, portrayed as rosy and with victory imminent, was anything but. Tet illustrated that, far from the thorough beating American machines and masculinity were assumed to be inflicting on the red hordes, the U.S. was actually losing the war in Vietnam. More dangerously, Tet exposed the government as fundamentally dishonest and eroded the faith of the population in it. This put the younger generation at odds with the previous one, which had, to a large extent, seen government as a benevolent savior whose New Deal saved the nation from starvation in the '30s and who eradicated Nazism in the '40s.

The Vietnam War gradually tore the nation apart as other specific events ripped it quickly. With the U.S. distracted in Vietnam, an emboldened Soviet Union crushed an uprising in Czechoslovakia, alarmingly close to NATO's Austrian frontier. The assassinations of Robert Kennedy and Martin Luther King, Jr., cast a pall of cynicism over the public, and this was followed quickly by the violence at the 1968 Democratic

National Convention. With 1969 came the antics of the Weather Underground and the Manson murders. People began to overwhelmingly believe the country was headed in the wrong direction. The Nixon Administration was supposed to rectify all of this, only to betray the trust of a distrustful nation once again with the Watergate scandal. In terms of trust in the government, one needs to look no further than the modern American Right and its propensity to believe any government conspiracy to see that the nation has never fully recovered its faith after Tet and Watergate.

By 1973, the national psyche was battered and bruised and left forever altered by the events of the previous decade. Some of those changes were profoundly for the good, and imminently necessary, but others were destructive. The nation of 1973 was not the nation of 1964. In the dark and cynical cultural atmosphere of the early 1970s, which car was more capable of going stop light to stop light fastest no longer seemed important. The American public had been violently jolted out of its innocence.

Finally, there is the simple fact that markets are rarely monolithic, and the tastes gradually change over time. Generally speaking, the typical performance car buyer is male, and young males tend to start noticing cars in their early teen years. The Baby Boomers who came of driving age in the mid- to late '60s, the height of the muscle car era, were by 1972 less concerned with elapsed times and trap speed, and more concerned with safety features and fuel economy as they set out in their life's journey of real jobs and families. The Vietnam veteran returning in 1967, having cleaned himself of the spit of an ungrateful public—the treatment of returning veterans was another disgrace of the 1960s—that bought himself a new GTO was by 1973 shopping for a full-sized Bonneville, or perhaps a station wagon of some sort, something capable of hauling around one or more car seats and a wife. By the early 1970s, the Baby Boomers that fueled the performance car market were growing up.

Tastes in style evolve as well. The 1950s had its styles. The elegant (or outrageous) tail fins, wide white sidewall tires, pastel "ice cream" colors, AM radio (complete with nuclear era CONELRAD (which stood for Control of Electromagnetic Radiation) triangles indicating frequencies to be turned to in order to find out which parts of the country had been vaporized by a Soviet ICBM strike) and fender skirts. These eventually gave way to Coke-bottle flanks, redline tires, hideaway headlamps, emerging FM radio and extreme color schemes of the 1960s. These hallmarks of '60s performance styling would give way to whatever it was that was attractive about cars of the 1970s. Market tastes aren't static and they are ever shifting. Even without the unique external pressures the performance car market faced in the late 1960s and early '70s, the American muscle car would have eventually died. Instead of a respectable, dignified natural death, however, the muscle car was torturously executed.

The forces arrayed against the American muscle car were formidable indeed—the obscene insurance rates, skyrocketing gas prices and government mandates that increased the price of the vehicles themselves to a point out of reach of the youth market that had supported the market in earlier years. However, the profound changes in the national landscape that forced the maturation of the American culture underpinning the muscle car market had an effect. Biology dictates that species adapt in the face of changing circumstances, or they die out. The forces of a free market are remarkably similar in this respect. The very thing that made the American muscle car what it was precluded it from being able to adapt, and, unable to cope with its new environment, it went extinct.

* * *

The great party known as the muscle car era, kicked off so gloriously in 1964 with the Pontiac GTO, had come to an inglorious end by 1973. Its crash left nothing but the automotive equivalent of a smoking hole in the ground. A few of the legendary nameplates remained, but those name badges were like mahogany veneer over particle board. Dodge's Charger soldiered on, but it had grown to obscene proportions—quite an accomplishment for what was one of the heaviest muscle cars ever built back in its heyday. Its Mopar stablemates—Super Bee, Coronet R/T—were gone by 1973, though the Road Runner did survive. Plymouth built it through the 1980 model year, when it was taken out back and shot, presumably after Warner Brothers demanded Plymouth remove its little bird from such a pathetic vehicle. Olds still built its 4-4-2 and would well into the '80s, but it was hardly the thundering Olds of the past. The Mustang was redesigned and re-badged Mustang II in 1974, a tacit admission by Ford that the original pony car had (de)evolved into something other than what it once was. The Mustang's cousin, the Cougar, evolved into a family car; by the late 1970s, Mercury affixed the Cougar nameplate to four doors and station wagons. Chrysler's twin pony cars, the Barracuda and the Challenger, would live through the 1974 model year, but they were mere ghosts of what they once were, and the father of the genre, the legendary GTO, would stagger on, mortally wounded, as well. Sadly, by 1974 DeLorean's machine had come full circle—from a docile little Tempest option in 1964 to a completely neutered little Ventura option in 1974. Mercifully, Pontiac euthanized it after the 1974 model year.

In the mid–1970s, the American performance car industry stood on the edge of a very large wasteland, one in which it would wander for the better part of the next twenty years. The environmental movement, the skyrocketing cost of fuel, and the rising insurance rates caused American car builders to redirect their efforts from raw horsepower and toward safety and fuel economy. During this dark era—what we now call "the Seventies"—the old boulevard brawlers that prowled the streets and strips of the 1960s were merely old, impractical cars, relics of another era, left to atrophy in garages or behind barns or otherwise sold for pennies on the dollar. They were scavenged for parts, or in many cases, they just deteriorated into rusting hulks and left for dead, never to be resurrected. As hard as it would have been a few short years earlier, or certainly today, the muscle cars of the 1960s and early '70s were unwanted and scorned.

This sorry state of affairs lingered into the mid–1980s, when the cars that had survived the times of troubles of the 1970s enjoyed a revival of sorts. The United States, in the aftermath of the Arab Oil Embargo and the economic paralyzation of the Carter Administration, had rediscovered its domestic petroleum production and a general economic revival under Ronald Reagan. Suddenly, fuel was more affordable, and, as if intentionally timed, the young men who originally bought the cars in the 1960s were entering their late 30s and early 40s; the revival of the muscle cars occurred just in time for the beginning of the Boomers' midlife crisis years. As the

**The sad end of the original "Great One": the 1974 Pontiac GTO (courtesy Streetside Classics, Charlotte, NC).**

original fans of the muscle car era began to reanimate the corpses of the warriors of the muscle car era in an enthusiastic effort to recreate their youth, an entire restoration industry to support the resurgent muscle car market developed. Restoration parts suppliers and services abounded, serving those bringing dilapidated old muscle cars, previously left for dead, back to their original glory.

The American performance car market continued to gain momentum through the late 1980s and into the 1990s. By 1998, it was Pontiac—appropriately—that was confident enough to declare in its Trans Am advertising campaign that "the muscle car is back." Nearly simultaneous with this grand proclamation, the American car builders dusted off many of the legendary nameplates of the muscle car past, a not-so-veiled attempt to attract the attention, yet again, of the empty nester Boomers with their increased amount of disposable income. Mercury brought back the Cougar after a brief hiatus in 1999, and Ford built a retro-looking Thunderbird from 2002 through 2005, a fitting if not particularly popular tribute to the original 1955–57 Thunderbird designs. In 2010, Chevrolet resurrected the Camaro after putting it down after the 2002 model year, a car obviously inspired by its 1969 model ancestor. There were helmeted, gear-grinding bumble bees seen on the flanks of new Dodges. In perhaps the most anticipated return of a legendary nameplate, Pontiac announced the return of the original legend, the GTO, in 2004, and Ford introduced a retro-styled Mustang in 2005.

But did the late 1990s and early to mid–2000s truly represent the return of the muscle car? Was the muscle car, as Pontiac claimed, "back"? The answer is unequivocally no. In terms of performance, there is no doubt that the modern incarnation of American performance cars would easily turn the muscle cars of the past into bits of scrap metal. The steady march of technology assured that. In the muscle car era, the power necessary to hurl heavy cars with all the aerodynamic qualities of an anvil at great rates of speed was produced by simply dumping more fuel into bigger engines. Over the past thirty years, advances in metal alloys, turbochargers, fuel injection, engine aspiration, intercoolers and a whole host of other whiz bang technologies allow the same horsepower to be created by engines of half the displacement in substantially lighter vehicles. Today's vehicles, even those not considered performance vehicles, can literally outrun stock muscle cars of the '60s and '70s without a lot of effort. In this sense—pure performance—the muscle car was back.

But the muscle car era was more than simply the performance of the cars. To view muscle cars simply in terms of performance cheapens them. That time had an aura that went beyond mere horsepower ratings and time slips and was an atmosphere in and of itself. It was an epoch. Despite Pontiac's confident declaration, the disparate elements that made up the '60s cannot be recreated. Jan and Dean and the Beach Boys and their songs about cars are gone. The audacious advertising is absent. The punch and counterpunch of the car builders, each one trying to outdo the other, has not been recreated. Even the tragedy of Vietnam played an indispensable role in creating that aura; thankfully that could not be re-created either, though the second Bush administration did its dead level best. The inextricable weaving of the American performance car into the fabric of American popular culture cannot be recreated any more than the Fabulous '50s or the Renaissance or the glory of Augustus' Rome can be. All we are left with are the stories and the mental recreations of those times, aided by what artifacts of the time that can still be seen and touched, like the surviving drive-in theater, full service "filling station," or the occasional muscle car sitting at an opposite stoplight.

With the benefit of hindsight, the rebirths of some of the glorious nameplates of the past are revealed as desperate efforts to boost sales in the face of declining revenue in the weak car market of the early 2000s. Some car makers failed to save themselves, and some of the most legendary car brands of the past would not survive the economic catastrophe that opened the second decade of the new millennium.

There had been changes to the American car builder landscape well before the 2000s. Tiny American Motors finally lost the David-versus-Goliath battle it had waged with the Big Three. AMC, builder of the defiant AMX and Javelin, was purchased and absorbed by Chrysler in 1987. The entire AMC line was eventually killed off, except Jeep, which survives as a division of Chrysler's parent Stellantis.

Even before the calamity of the late 2000s, some car builders were in trouble. Plymouth, builder of the legendary Road Runner, GTX and Barracuda, was extinguished by Chrysler in 2001. General Motors pulled the plug on Oldsmobile, progenitor of the 4-4-2, in 2004. Mercury, maker of the Cyclone and Cougar, Spoiler and Eliminator, ceased to exist after 2011.

By 2008, the American car industry was literally on death's door. Ford wisely had seen the storm coming and had husbanded resources to weather it. The Chrysler

Corporation, chronically on the brink of oblivion and left for dead several times in its history, was threatened with joining Plymouth in the boneyard in 2010. To try to save itself, Dodge revived its legendary Charger and Challenger nameplates, including the R/T badge. The cars sold, and sold well, but Chrysler still needed substantial federal loans—again—and a major sell-off to Italy's Fiat to keep the Reaper at bay, but, as it did in the early 1980s, Chrysler came back. In fact, Chrysler's resurgence was celebrated in a 2015 commercial featuring the Dodge Brothers racing each other in various Dodges of the past, including an angry 1969 Super Bee. General Motors, whose huge size and sales volume usually provided better economic insulation against market volatility than Chrysler or even Ford, was forced by the federal government to restructure in order to stave off destruction. Pontiac, the father of the original muscle car, was killed in the government mandated bankruptcy reorganization of 2010.

Today, the American car industry is back on its feet, and many of the old name plates of the past are thriving. Dodge's Hellcat Chargers and Challengers offer literally twice the performance—at double the fuel economy—as their ancestors; the Demon is on another planet in terms of performance. Chevrolet's Camaro continues its historic role as the performance Chevy of the masses, slotted right behind the venerable Corvette in the performance lineup. And, of course, the Mustang—the most famous of American automobiles—continues to be Ford's performance flagship, a banner it has carried since the middle of the 1964 model year.

* * *

The old muscle cars are relics of an earlier era, conspicuously out of place on the roads today. Technology allows car builders today to engineer amazing vehicles, with science that was literally unimaginable in the 1960s. What can be done today is as removed from that era as *Star Trek* was in its time. Back then, horsepower was produced in essentially one way—pour more fuel into ever more cavernous cylinders—but today's cars, with computer controlled fuel injection and engine control systems, are more complex than the most advanced fighter aircraft in combat over Vietnam. Today, six and even four-cylinder engines, through technology, are producing more horsepower than the greatest engines of the muscle car era. While the old muscle car survivors of the '60s and early '70s could still hold their own through the 1980s, they are completely outclassed—even laughably so—by today's cars. There are—literally—minivans today that can turn quarter mile times faster than some muscle cars of old. What they are missing, though, is the mystique, the spirit that those old cars had and still retain today. A Pontiac was a Pontiac then. An Oldsmobile was an Oldsmobile. Each make and model had characteristics that made them different from one another and made them unique. There was a muscle car for everyone. A person with discriminating tastes could drive a formidable, well-built Buick in plush comfort. At the other end of the spectrum, there was a Plymouth, devoid of sound deadener and screwed together by someone for whom craftsmanship seemed to be no priority, subjecting anyone trapped inside to an experience similar to that of the agitator ball in a can of spray paint. Each car had its own mystique, its own individualism that bordered on a personality. Today, one is hard pressed to tell one from the other, regardless of make.

They all look substantially the same from model year to model year and from make to make. Today's new car landscape is, in large part, a sea of mediocrity and sameness, with very few islands of uniqueness.

Today, the old street warriors enjoy a well-earned retirement, having survived the beatings they took in the muscle car era and the apathy they suffered in the '70s. The former terrors of the boulevards are now more often found in museums or serving weekend duty at car shows or cruises. They may occasionally be spotted on a long deserted small town cruise route, a specter of an earlier age haunting the street in search of a stoplight race that will never come. Their drivers rarely rev them to anything even remotely approaching the tachometer's redline, being terrified of throwing a rod or some other catastrophic failure to the priceless engines, all the more so if the car is still equipped with its original driveline. The muscle car hobby, if an endeavor that underpins hundreds of millions in revenue each year can be called a simple "hobby," is healthy and vibrant, fueled mainly by quickly graying Baby Boomers with plenty of disposable income who can now afford the cars they couldn't in their youth.

Biology mandates that that particular demographic and its enthusiasm for the hobby, as dedicated as it is, is fading. Once that generation is gone, so goes the original generation of muscle car enthusiasts—the people who were there, that worked on the cars, that saw them new on the streets and serve as the war correspondents to the street battles of the car builders. People who saw, in their time, the wild Grabber and Big Bad colors draping Fords and AMCs, the subtle threat of the crossed flag engine callout on the fender of a SS Chevelle, or the smiling cartoon countenance of a bird of the American southwest happily churning up dust on the side of a Plymouth. These living primary sources won't be with us forever to tell the tales of these cars safely stored away in the depths of memory.

The survival of the hobby depends on that enthusiasm being passed on to the younger generation, the so-called Millennials, to carry it forward. This is much more easily said than done. While muscle cars generally draw large crowds at car shows and cruises, these events are disproportionately attended by first or second-generation enthusiasts, meaning Boomers and their children, rapidly aging themselves. For most Millennials, fifty-year-old cars just aren't that special. They are just old cars.

Millennials must be inspired. With every generation wedged between the muscle car era and the current day, the enthusiasm for those cars fades, and when the Boomers are gone, they're gone. The generation after the Boomers, those brought up on the myths of the muscle car era, are aging themselves. The passing of time is a threat to the hobby, and the need to pass the torch to the next generation is imperative to the survival, not only of the old car hobby but of the cars themselves.

A further danger to the future of the American muscle car comes from its ancient nemesis, the federal government, which has been actively trying to kill muscle cars since they were young. In 2009, the federal government began a program called the "Car Allowance Rebate System," cutely shortened to C.A.R.S., which was known colloquially as "cash for clunkers," with the term "clunkers" likely chosen intentionally for its negative connotations to negatively influence and condition the public *zeitgeist*.

Cash for Clunkers provided three billion dollars in taxpayer money for car owners to trade in older, less fuel-efficient vehicles for rebates on newer, more environmentally friendly vehicles. In reality, it was an environmental program designed to reduce emissions and combat climate change, sold to the public under the guise of then-trendy "economic stimulus." Cynics decry it as a further, indirect bailout of the auto industry, specifically the reliably Democratic voting auto workers unions. Either way, there was no direct danger to the muscle cars from the Cash to Clunker program, as no one not outside of an insane asylum would ever consider trading a classic muscle car for a rebate to purchase a Hyundai. The Cash for Clunkers program, and ideas like it, do represent a potential danger to the muscle car hobby, and an insidious one at that. Cash for Clunkers, passed by a Democratic Congress allied with the environmental movement and signed into law by a likeminded president, represented unprecedented government action against vehicles it found to be unacceptable in terms of emissions and fuel consumption.

To be clear, Cash for Clunkers was not government confiscation. The government is limited by the Constitution in its ability to confiscate private property. It was, however, the direct use of public funds—taxpayer funds—to incentivize the destruction of vehicles arbitrarily found to be a threat to the environment. Time will tell if it was the first step down a very slippery slope, but it does not take a lot of mental gymnastics to imagine the government moving from mere incentivizing to outright confiscation.

If there were any doubt that classic cars are on the targeting radars of environmental activists, one need only look to Paris, France. Citing growing pollution and environmental concerns in the City of Lights, Parisian officials enacted a citywide ban on "old cars," which was defined as any car built before 1997(!). Such offending vehicles could not enter the city during the weekdays, and further restrictions would be enacted in the future. French classic car enthusiasts negotiated an exemption for registered historic vehicles, but the direction of the winds is clear.

France, to be sure, does not have the enthusiastic classic car base that is present in the United States, but it doesn't take a lot of imagination to see places like Los Angeles, San Francisco or Seattle wishing they'd thought of that first. The Parisian measure represents an attack on the enjoyment of historic vehicles, and an intermediate step between an incentive program like Cash for Clunkers and outright confiscation. While the government is limited in its ability to confiscate private property, such as cars it does not like, the government is not precluded from doing so. Confiscation can be accomplished, relatively easily, through the use of a Constitutional provision called "eminent domain."

Eminent domain is the jurisprudential method of taking property, with "just compensation," if that taking is to the benefit of the public. It is usually used to confiscate private land for public works, such as highways or airports or the like. Eminent domain has also been used more questionably, such as taking of private land, only to hand it over to private real estate developers or Indian tribes on which they build shopping malls or casinos, with the justification that the economic windfalls constitute a public benefit. It is not hard to imagine a green-friendly federal or state government determining that the taking of vehicles below a certain fuel economy level or producing an unacceptable level of emissions would be to the benefit of the public. That would satisfy the requirements of eminent domain. The owner of the vehicle thus confiscated would of course be magnanimously "justly compensated" for a price set by the government, an amount surely nowhere near the actual value of the vehicle, particularly when sentimentality is not factored in.

Eminent domain is a potential danger to any automotive hobby, not only muscle car restoration, but also off-roading, racing, etc., in the future, and it may get here faster than one would think. In 2016, the EPA, under—surprise, surprise—the Clean Air Act, proposed a set of regulations to prevent the modification of factory vehicles for racing purposes. The measure was eventually withdrawn, but only the most obtuse car enthusiast would fail to recognize that warning.

The threat of "national emergency" is another threat to the continuation of the classic car hobby. Some argue that when Republican President Donald Trump declared illegal immigration a national emergency in 2019, over vociferous opposition by Democrats, it set a precedent for using the tool of "national emergency" as a means of circumventing an uncooperative Congress to achieve policy goals. Some have warned that under a future, Democratic presidential administration, "climate change" could likewise be declared a national emergency, with possible repercussions for the decidedly non-green classic car hobby. This remains to be seen, but it makes sense.

*  *  *

Looking back through the lens of history, and with the resurgent popularity of the American muscle car, there is an impression that every other car on the street in the 1960s and early '70s was a Six Pack powered Super Bee or a 396 Chevrolet or some other of the legendary cars of the era. However wonderful that is to imagine, the truth is that there were literally millions of cars built and sold in the United States in the years 1964–1972, and only a very, very small fraction of them would have been considered muscle cars. The incredible variety of cars with a diversity of engines, styles, colors and options within the performance car world of the '60s and '70s has led to a perception out of sync with reality. For a thinning number, that misperception is the product of memory peering through the haze of fifty years. For a growing number, it is purely the product of imaginations of those too young to have seen them firsthand, relying on stories and secondhand accounts of the time. Yet, perception is what it is, and we can have much more fun remembering the muscle car era as we wish to, reality be damned. There is nothing wrong with that. The reality of the muscle car era was indeed fantastic, unlike any time before or since.

Like all things, the muscle car era had to come to an end.

# Epilogue

Unfortunately, I missed the muscle car era, and I am reduced to imagining the way things were. I have to cobble together a mental narrative based on stories from my parents and my uncle and from what I can glean from other car people. Ironically, I may have it better than those who actually were there, as I can imagine it the way I want. In my mind's eye, the streets and cruise routes were teeming with the performance vehicles I have discussed in the previous pages.

I was brought up listening to car stories told by my mom and dad and my uncle. I can practically recite who drove what cars at El Reno High School in the mid-'60s, people whom I don't know from Adam but whose cars I do know. Hearing these stories and the adventures of my uncle's apparently awesome 1966 327 Nova SS, I imagine another time, one in which the streets simply teemed with big-block performance models and muscular ponies. As that generation fades, unfortunately so will the enthusiasm, with the exception of people like me who grew up with the cars and with car people.

I worry about the muscle car hobby fading with the passing of the rapidly graying generation that lived the muscle car era. As an amateur historian, I understand that as generations pass, enthusiasm for the things of the past does as well. That original generation is fueling today's surge in the popularity of muscle cars of from the '60s and early '70s. Thirty years ago, there was a flurry of enthusiasm for cars of the 1950s too. That enthusiasm of twenty years ago has diminished and is a shadow of what it was when I was growing up in the 1980s. I worry that as that generation fades, so too will the interest in the American muscle car. This book has been an effort to prevent that.

* * *

I own two of these fantastic cars—a 1966 GTO and a 1969 Road Runner. For me, an old history teacher, these cars are archaeological relics, no different than an Egyptian funeral mask or a Roman coin. They are pieces of history, and pieces of art.

As I removed the standard single speaker from the dash of my 1969 Road Runner, I wondered what news had passed through that speaker. News of deaths in Vietnam, of the moon landing, of Nixon's resignation, the Manson atrocities and fifty years of the evolution of music. The earliest muscle cars had radios that transmitted the death of a president. The news of the deaths that president's brother and of Martin Luther King, Jr., may have come through one of my car's radios.

My GTO would have seen even sadder things. Its only previous owner worked on Fort Sill in southwest Oklahoma, home of the Army's field artillery and a major induction station. He drove that GTO back and forth to Fort Sill every day. When I bought it, it still carried the Department of Defense sticker on the front bumper. I wonder how many kids got off the buses at Sill for basic training, headed to Vietnam. I wonder for how many of those boys, eaten up with muscle car fever as so many were in those days, my GTO might have been the last muscle car they ever saw. I wonder how many of them vowed to buy one like it when they got back to the States, and I wonder how many of those never made it back. That is how I think of my cars. I think of the things they have seen.

I am blessed to have a family that is into cars and that encouraged my passion for these amazing machines. The first old car brought into the family wasn't even that old when it was adopted. That's my dad's 1957 Thunderbird, which he bought in 1965 while still in high school. Since then, my family has brought together a modest collection that still includes the old workhorse T-bird, veteran of two generations of proms, plus a 1966 427 Corvette, a 1967 H.O. GTO, and a 1978 Trans Am, in addition to my two cars. Most of these are owned by my dad, one of those graying Boomers with disposable income. In fact, Dad provides the storage for most of them and the base of operations for our car adventures. My mom even owns an example of modern Mopar muscle, a 2018 Hellcat Charger. She's afraid of it, but she owns it.

For many families, by the time the kids reach adulthood, there is little common ground left with their parents. For us, the cars are the generational bridge. I spend countless hours with my dad working on this or that old car, usually screwing up whatever it is we are trying to do, or detailing cars to go to some local car show. My family, including my mom who is underrated in her knowledge of old cars, spend too much time watching car shows on TV, or televised auto auctions, or just simply talking about cars. I was even pleased—very pleased—when my niece and nephew asked me to help them build scale models of a 1959 Cadillac and a 1966 Charger (building models is another of my vast array of nerdy talents). I am truly hoping to turn their interest in cars of a miniature scale to an interest in those of actual size. I have good reason for this hope as this past summer my youngest nephew enthusiastically helped me wax Dad's '66 Corvette. If a six-year-old will enthusiastically help wax a car—one of the most boring and tedious of car husbandry exercises—there is hope indeed.

Dad and I attend a lot of car shows. These are always a good time, and I could go to one every weekend if my schedule allowed. Generally speaking, car shows are made up of vintage cars brought there by vintage people. I am somewhat of an exception, though I am getting more and more vintage myself. Car shows are a great place for car people to talk to each other, and to other car fans, which can be interesting in and of itself. Without fail, I will talk to at least one guy per show who "had one just like it" back in whatever year or when he got back from Vietnam. I am convinced if you counted all the 1966 GTOs that people claim to have bought new that that the number would wildly exceed the number Pontiac actually built, but that's part of the fun.

Car shows do have their rare annoyances, but even these are entertaining. A particular aggravation are the people who seem to believe that whatever car they own is somehow better than all the others, and, look down on whatever I happen to have brought. I don't understand an old car owner who looks down on other old cars. I may not *like* a particular old car model, but I *love* all of them. For example, I am personally not a fan—at all—of pre–1966 Chrysler cars. I do not find them the least bit attractive, and I personally would not spend the thousands and thousands in monetary and sweat equity to restore one. After all, whether one is restoring a '60 Fury or a '70 455-powered Buick GS, generally the same amount of work has to be done. If you are restoring the former, when you are done you still have a '60 Plymouth Fury, so personally, I'd much rather work on the Buick. The Buick is a legendary car worth far more than a '60 Fury, a car that has generally been lost to history. But that's me, and I am awfully glad someone else loves the '60 Furys or the '63 Ramblers or any other car I don't have a passion for, because those cars—all classic cars—deserve to be preserved.

Another source of car show annoyance is the guy is the one who is more of an expert on your car than you are, and all of us who take a car to a car show know the type. For example, Dad and I had the pleasure of meeting a guy that insisted my dad's 1967 GTO wasn't correct because … it had a Pontiac engine. According to him, it should properly be equipped with an Oldsmobile engine of some type or another. While they did indeed put Olds engines in Pontiacs in the late 1970s, they did not do so in 1967.

Dad's '67 GTO always causes confusion, because that car is an odd duck. There may not be another one like it in fact. It is a post car, with a bench seat and the high output 360 horse engine. Based simply on that, one might reasonably assume that someone back in 1967 ordered a stripped-down GTO especially for the track, but that car's peculiarity doesn't stop there. It also has air conditioning, power steering, power brakes and an automatic transmission, shifted on the column no less. It is as odd a GTO as you will see. So odd, in fact, that it attracted the attention of the most obnoxious car show "expert" we have yet run into, a guy who spent the better part of one afternoon trying to convince my dad that it was really a 1964 Chevy Impala with GTO badging. Dad patiently continued the discussion until he finally just settled it with an agreement to disagree, and The Authority went on to tell someone else what was wrong with their car. Such is the car show experience. Even the annoyances are fun.

Surprisingly, so is working on old cars. "Surprisingly" because I possess a breathtaking level of mechanical ineptitude. Any project I start on my cars begins with a two part analysis: whether I can successfully complete the project and what it will cost to complete it when I inevitably fail.

I enjoy failing at my projects, however, and as I am failing, I am always surprised by the mechanical simplicity of the cars of that era. Today's cars, even the lower priced ones, put an amazing amount of technology at the fingertips of the driver: On board Wi-Fi, television, game systems, touch screens, and navigation systems that have made maps obsolete. There is—literally—more computing power and technology in a basic Ford Focus than there was in the first space shuttle, the *Columbia*. Today, technologically speaking, we are closer to George Jetson than we are to the muscle car

**Lynn Fees (right) with his black GTO and Clay Fees (left) with his '66 GTO at an Indian Nations Pontiac Oakland Club Chapter event in Tulsa in July 2011. July in Oklahoma explains the sweat-drenched clothing (photo by author).**

era. As I write this, plans are being made for remains of John Glenn, World War II fighter pilot, astronaut and former U.S. senator from Ohio, to return to space. I am in awe at the astonishing bravery of men like him hurling themselves out into space, relying on the primitive technology found in, say, a rheostat or a dimmer switch.

My first car, that 1968 Road Runner that was the mechanical equivalent of Frankenstein's Monster, still holds a special place to me. It was my high school car, and it was a large part of my emerging identity as a teenager. I loved that car, though it is the biggest piece of crap I have ever owned; when I think of it, I am always reminded of the nemesis in Stephen King's *Christine* being referred to as a "mechanical asshole." In fairness, it had had a hard life, owing to an early career as a drag racer. That Road Runner was without most of its original equipment and with a lot of extra good ideas like a heavy I-beam welded above the differential for added weight over the rear tires. Every time I hit a bump, the differential slamming into that I-beam would break your teeth. Though it was truly a mechanical turd, it was my car and it is to this day my favorite car that I have ever owned. My dad and I worked on it together. My Chrysler hating uncle painted it for me—*gratis*—bitching about Mopars the entire time (the man may despise Chrysler products more than even Fords, or his hatred of the Pentastar may just be something to give me crap about). It was the vehicle that took me through my youth.

I sold that car in the fall of 1991 to one of my dad's high school friends, who bought it for a reason common to people of that era—his dad had owned a Plymouth Fury, and the

The author's youngest brother Cody, owner of a 1977 Pontiac Trans Am, tearing down the Chrysler 383 from the author's '69 Road Runner in the fall of 2011. Due to mechanical ineptitude, the author was not allowed near the project (photo by author).

Road Runner reminded him of that car. A bit drama that is hard to imagine is that as I drove the Road Runner out of my grandmother's driveway in El Reno to deliver it to its new home across town, I saw a road runner—the avian kind—standing in her yard.

I had no idea how much I would miss that car. Over the next twenty-five years, I would occasionally drive by the house where I dropped it off, hoping to catch a glimpse of it. I was thrilled in 1994 when it appeared in a Route 66 themed calendar in front of the now-gone Big 8 Motel in El Reno. Aside from that calendar though, I never saw that car again.

That is, until the spring of 2015 when, again stalking the house where I'd left my car back in '91, I saw the garage door opened a couple of feet, and in that space I glimpsed a Magnum 500 road wheel. I stopped and knocked on the door.

That day, I saw my car again. I slid onto the bench seat, and I gripped the incorrect pistol grip shifter taken from an E-body, a Christmas gift in 1988 that went nicely with my Mopar Repair Kit. I unlatched the J.C. Whitney hood pins I bought for myself as a birthday present that same year. I lifted the hood adorned with 1969 style stripes, and gazed upon the incorrect 440 engine. The car was a mess, covered with twenty-five years of accumulated garage junk, but it was my car.

Seeing my Road Runner again was truly was a surreal experience. I am not sure the owner has ever driven it since I left it with him on that cold November day back in 1991. The wing window was still adorned with the maroon vinyl sticker of the number one, my high school baseball number. The old Alpine radio was still there, the one I bought hot from Tommy Turner and wisely installed under the dash so as not to alter the original instrument panel. The homemade floor mats that Dad and I had made were still in it, complete with the rubber letters spelling "Road Runner" peeling off. I think the one on the driver's side said "O AD UN ER." Dad and I never did figure out how to get those letters to properly stick.

The owner, my dad's friend, asked about my parents and other members of my family, and through the course of conversation, I found out that it might be possible for me to re-acquire my old car.

To my surprise, I was uninterested. I discovered in that moment, after a quarter century of periodic reminiscence about that car, that I didn't want it back. My taste in old cars had grown and evolved, as had my hair line and my belt size. My GTO was purchased from the original owner's widow, and I restored it to factory condition. The 1969 Road Runner is being restored to precise factory condition as well. That is my taste now. My cars are archaeological relics from 1966 and 1969. My old car was not that and never would be. It was about as far from factory original as it could be.

I ran my hand along the flared hips of its quarter panels and the door mounted black and white road runner decals my car crazy grandmother got for me for Christmas in 1988. I got a lot of car gifts in 1988. I touched the steering wheel, still wrapped in the cheap faux leather cover I installed in 1989. I gazed at the black grille and thought of the time Dad and I painted it that way in the garage in the winter of 1988. I remember Tulsa's K-107 radio was playing George Michael's "Father Figure" on the radio while we painted that grille. Hearing that song always reminds me of that particular project. I thought of all the street races I was lucky to have survived, driving on used bias ply tires, and of the hours wasting time cruising the circuit in Sapulpa. I thought of how mad I'd get at it when it quit me—I was often mad at it.

Some might say, "It's just a car, for God's sake," but it's not just a car. Not to me, and I believe to car people, their beloved cars, particularly their first one, are never "just cars." To me, that red Plymouth was an old friend, one I had not seen for far too long. But like all friends reunited after so long a time, after the reminiscences, there was nothing but awkward, empty space.

I appreciate that car for being such a large part of my youth. Because of that car, people called me "Road Runner." I smiled at that old car as I rifled through the memories of the youth this old Plymouth represented, barely visible under a mountain of junk. I still love that car, just as I did in 1987 when I was allowed to drive it no further than a few feet in and out of the garage for its weekly bath.

As I looked at my old companion, I thought of a book I read when I was a kid—A.A. Milne's *House at Pooh Corner*. That book that made me very sad when I was

**Lynn Fees dragging the author's 1969 Plymouth Road Runner out of its 5 year hibernation in 2011 to begin its restoration. As of January 2020, the restoration is ongoing (photo by the author).**

little. In it, Christopher Robin told Pooh that he was growing up and wouldn't come back to the Hundred Acre Wood to see him. He promised Pooh that though he was grown up, he would never forget him. Their time together had come to an end. I thought of that book as I looked at my old car, draped in the paint my uncle put on it, because he wanted to do that for me. I realized that old Road Runner was my Winnie the Pooh. I had to tell that old Road Runner goodbye once more, just as I did in 1991. I knew that it was unlikely I'd ever see my old Plymouth again. Like Christopher Robin, I had outgrown that old car. I thanked its owner for allowing me the time with my old Road Runner, gave my friend a long last look, and then I got in my car and drove away.

Indeed, they are not just old cars to us.

\* \* \*

# Bibliography

Adolphus, David T. "Hemmings Feature: Assault with a Deadly Weapon—1969 Torino Talladega." *Hemmings Muscle Machines*, Dec. 2008, www.hemmings.com/stories/article/assault-with-a-deadly-weapon-1969-torino-talladega.

_____. "Hemmings Feature: 1970 Ford Mustang Boss." *Hemmings Muscle Machines*, Feb. 2009, www.hemmings.com/stories/article/american-legend-1970-ford-mustang-boss.

_____. "Hemmings Feature: 1971 Dodge Charger R/T." *Hemmings Muscle Machines*, May 2011, www.hemmings.com/stories/article/1971-dodge-charger-r-t.

Bonsall, Thomas E. *Firebird: A Source Book*. Baltimore, MD, Bookman Publishing, 1981.

Bumbeck, Mike. "Buyer's Guide: 1973 Pontiac GTO." *Hemmings Muscle Machines*, Feb. 2011, www.hemmings.com/stories/article/1973-pontiac-gto-2.

_____. "Hemmings Feature: Double X Hemi Four-Speed Fast Top—1969 Dodge Charger 500." *Hemmings Muscle Machines*, Jan. 2012, www.hemmings.com/stories/article/double-x-hemi-four-speed-fast-top-1969-dodge-charger-500.

_____. "Hemmings Feature: Restored, Original—1972 AMC Javelin AMX." *Hemmings Muscle Machines*, Feb. 2016, www.hemmings.com/stories/article/restored-original-1972-amc-javelin-amx.

Consumer Guide, Auto Editors. *American Cars of the 1960s*. Morton Grove, IL: Publications International, 2010.

_____. *Encyclopedia of American Cars*. Morton Grove, IL: Publications International, 2006.

Contributor, Hemmings. "Hemmings Feature: Back in the Day—1970 Dodge Coronet R/T." *Hemmings Muscle Machines*, Jan. 2018, www.hemmings.com/stories/article/back-in-the-day-1970-dodge-coronet-r-t-convertible.

_____. "Hemmings Feature: High-Stakes Successor—1967 Ford Mustang GT." *Hemmings Muscle Machines*, Feb. 2017.

_____. "Hemmings Feature: Sophomore Surprise—1971 AMC Javelin AMX." *Hemmings Muscle Machines*, Feb. 2016, www.hemmings.com/stories/article/sophomore-surprise-1971-amc-javelin-amx.

_____. "Hemmings Feature: Superstitious Super Sport—1969 Chevelle Sport Coupe." *Hemmings Muscle Machines*, July 2008, www.hemmings.com/stories/article/superstitious-super-sport-1969-chevelle-sport-coupe.

_____. "Hemmings Feature: A V-code 440 Six-Barrel Makes This 1970 GTX Interesting, but the Father-Son Connection Makes It Special." *Hemmings Muscle Machines*, May 2020, www.hemmings.com/stories/article/many-thanks-dad.

_____. "Tech: Standing the Test of Time—1969 Plymouth GTX." *Hemmings Muscle Machines*, Dec. 2016, www.hemmings.com/stories/article/standing-the-test-of-time-1969-plymouth-gtx.

Conwill, David. "Buyer's Guide: 1966–'67 Fairlane GTA." *Hemmings Muscle Machines*, May 2019, www.hemmings.com/stories/article/1966–67-fairlane-gta.

_____. "Buyer's Guide: 1967 Plymouth GTX." *Hemmings Muscle Machines*, Feb. 2019, www.hemmings.com/stories/article/1967-plymouth-gtx-4.

_____. "Buyer's Guide: 1968 Plymouth Road Runner." *Hemmings Muscle Machines*, Jan. 2021, www.hemmings.com/stories/article/1968-plymouth-road-runner.

_____. "Buyer's Guide: 1969 Chevrolet Camaro SS 396." *Hemmings Muscle Machines*, Oct. 2018, www.hemmings.com/stories/article/1969-chevrolet-camaro-ss-396.

_____. "Buyer's Guide: 1969 Hurst/Olds Buyer's Guide." *Hemmings Muscle Machines*, Mar. 2019, www.hemmings.com/stories/article/1969-hurst-olds-4.

_____. "Buyer's Guide—1969 SC/Rambler." *Hemmings Muscle Machines*, June 2019, www.hemmings.com/stories/article/1969-amc-sc-rambler-3.

_____. "Drivable Dreams: Affordable Exclusivity—1965 Rambler Marlin." *Hemmings Classic Car*, Jan. 2020, www.hemmings.com/stories/2014/11/21/amc-designer-vince-geraci-on-the-marlin-theres-a-very-fine-line-between-unique-and-strange.

_____. "Hemmings Feature: A Merc for All Seasons—1969 Mercury Cyclone GT." *Hemmings Muscle Machines*, Oct. 2017, www.hemmings.com/stories/article/a-merc-for-all-seasons-1969-mercury-cyclone-gt.

DeLorean, John Z., and Ted Schwarz. *Delorean*. Zondervan Publishing House, 1985.

DeMauro, Thomas A. "Buyer's Guide: 1963 Pontiac Catalina." *Hemmings Muscle Machines*, June 2014, www.hemmings.com/stories/article/1963-pontiac-catalina.

_____. "Buyer's Guide: 1964 Pontiac GTO." *Hemmings Muscle Machines*, Oct. 2016, www.hemmings.com/stories/article/1964-pontiac-gto-2.

_____. "Buyer's Guide: 1965 Plymouth Barracuda V-8 Buyer's Guide." *Hemmings Muscle Machines*, Apr. 2020, www.hemmings.com/stories/article/1965-plymouth-barracuda-v-8-buyers-guide.

_____. "Buyer's Guide: 1965 Pontiac GTO." *Hemmings Muscle Machines*, Dec. 2017, www.hemmings.com/stories/article/1965-pontiac-gto-4.

_____. "Buyer's Guide: 1966 Pontiac GTO." *Hemmings Muscle Machines*, Aug. 2016, www.hemmings.com/stories/article/1966-pontiac-gto-2.

_____. "Buyer's Guide: 1968 Plymouth Barracuda Formula S 340 and 383." *Hemmings Muscle Machines*, July 2014, www.hemmings.com/stories/article/1968-plymouth-barracuda-formula-s-340-and-383.

_____. "Buyer's Guide: 1969 Pontiac GTO." *Hemmings Muscle Machines*, Aug. 2015, www.hemmings.com/stories/article/1969-pontiac-gto.

_____. "Buyer's Guide: 1970 Dodge Challenger R/T." *Hemmings Muscle Machines*, Sept. 2018, www.hemmings.com/stories/article/1970-dodge-challenger-r-t.

_____. "Buyer's Guide: 1970 Mercury Cougar Eliminator." *Hemmings Muscle Machines*, Apr. 2018, www.hemmings.com/stories/article/1970-mercury-cougar-eliminator-3.

_____. "Buyer's Guide: 1970 Plymouth Road Runner." *Hemmings Muscle Machines*, July 2017, www.hemmings.com/stories/article/1970-plymouth-road-runner-2.

_____. "Buyer's Guide: 1970 Pontiac GTO Judge." *Hemmings Muscle Machines*, Aug. 2018, www.hemmings.com/stories/article/1970-pontiac-gto-judge-2.

_____. "Buyer's Guide: 1971 Ford Mustang Mach 1." *Hemmings Muscle Machines*, Mar. 2017, www.hemmings.com/stories/article/1971-ford-mustang-mach-1-2.

_____. "Buyer's Guide: 1971-'72 Pontiac Trans-Am." *Hemmings Muscle Machines*, Nov. 2020, www.hemmings.com/stories/article/1971-72-pontiac-trans-am.

_____. "Buyer's Guide: 1972 Plymouth Road Runner and Road Runner GTX Buyer's Guide." *Hemmings Muscle Machines*, Jan. 2018, www.hemmings.com/stories/article/1972-plymouth-road-runner-and-road-runner-gtx.

_____. "Hemmings Feature: Affordable Moderate Muscle: The 1971 Buick GS 350 Hardtop." *Hemmings Muscle Machines*, Jan. 2020, www.hemmings.com/stories/article/1971-buick-gs-hardtop.

_____. "Hemmings Feature: GSX2—1971 Buick GSX." *Hemmings Muscle Machines*, Feb. 2016, www.hemmings.com/stories/article/gsx2-1971-buick-gsx.

_____. "Hemmings Feature: Long-Term Commitment 1971 Dodge Charger R/T." *Hemmings Muscle Machines*, Feb. 2018, www.hemmings.com/stories/article/long-term-commitment-1971-dodge-charger-r-t.

_____. "Hemmings Feature: 1964 GTO and 1964 4-4-2." *Hemmings Muscle Machines*, Aug. 2014, www.hemmings.com/stories/article/1964-gto-and-1964-4-4-2.

_____. "Hemmings Feature: 1967 Buick GS 400." *Hemmings Muscle Machines*, Sept. 2013, www.hemmings.com/stories/article/1967-buick-gs-400.

_____. "Hemmings Feature: The 1968 Dodge Hemi Super Bee Was Budget Muscle Made Legendary with Optional 426 Hemi Power." *Hemmings Muscle Machines*, Aug. 2020.

_____. "How Ford's Budget Supercar—the 1969 Cobra—Compared to the Competition." *Hemmings Muscle Machines*, Feb. 2018, www.hemmings.com/stories/2018/02/01/how-fords-budget-supercar-the-1969-cobra-compared-to-the-competition.

Ernst, Kurt. "The 1972 Dodge Charger: Muscle Car or Family Car?" *Hemmings Blog*, Hemmings.com, 26 Feb. 2015, www.hemmings.com/stories/2015/02/26/the-1972-dodge-charger-muscle-car-or-family-car.

Fitzgerald, Craig. "Hemmings Feature: The Lonely Bull—1967 Buick GS-400." *Hemmings Muscle Machines*, May 2004, www.hemmings.com/stories/article/the-lonely-bull-1967-buick-gs-400.

Glastonbury, Jim. *The Ultimate Guide to Muscle Cars*. Edison, NJ: Chartwell Books, 2004.

Gunnell, John. *Muscle Cars Field Guide*. Iola, WI: Krause Publications, 2004.

Herd, Paul. *Charger, Road Runner and Super Bee Restoration Guide*. St. Paul, MN: MBI Publishing, 1994.

Holder, Bill, and Phil Kunz. *GTO*. Osceola, WI, USA, Motorbooks International, 1997.

Holder, Bill, et al. *Muscle Car Legends*. Ann Arbor, MI: Lowe and B. Hould, 2002.

Hunting, Benjamin. "Your Definitive 1968–70 Dodge Charger Buyer's Guide." *Hagerty Media*, 13 June 2018, www.hagerty.com/media/car-profiles/definitive-1968–70-dodge-charger-buyers-guide/.

Iacocca, Lee, and William Novak. *Iacocca: An Autobiography*. New York: Bantam, 1984.

Kinnan, Rob, and Diego Rosenberg. *Cobra Jet: The History of Ford's Greatest High-Performance Muscle Cars*. Forest Lake, MN: Cartech, Inc., 2020.

Koch, Jeff. "Buyer's Guide: 1967 Dodge Coronet R/T." *Hemmings Muscle Machines*, Sept. 2011, www.hemmings.com/stories/article/1967-dodge-coronet-r-t-2.

_____. "Buyer's Guide: 1969 Mustang Mach 1." *Hemmings Muscle Machines*, Sept. 2014, www.hemmings.com/stories/article/1969-ford-mustang-mach-1-4.

_____. "Buyer's Guide: 1970-'71 Dodge Challenger R/T." *Hemmings Muscle Machines*, Oct. 2009, www.hemmings.com/stories/article/1970–71-dodge-challenger-r-t.

_____. "Buyer's Guide: 1971 Dodge Super Bee." *Hemmings Muscle Machines*, May 2007, www.hemmings.com/stories/article/1971-dodge-super-bee-2.

_____. "Hemmings Feature: All Hail the Kings(s)—1970 Chevrolet Chevelle SS, 1970 Plymouth Hemi 'Cuda." *Hemmings Muscle Machines*, Apr. 2011, www.hemmings.com/stories/article/all-hail-the-kings-1970-chevrolet-chevelle-ss-1970-plymouth-hemi-cuda.

_____. "Hemmings Feature: Class Transit—1970 Olds 4-4-2 vs. 1970 Buick GS 455." *Hemmings Muscle Machines*, July 2019, www.hemmings.com/stories/article/class-transit-1970-olds-4-4-2-vs-1970-buick-gs-455.

_____. "Hemmings Feature: Go Mod Big Bad—1969 AMC Javelin." *Hemmings Muscle Machines*, Oct. 2019, www.hemmings.com/stories/article/go-mod-big-bad-1969-amc-javelin-st.

_____. "Hemmings Feature: Gunsight Grandiosity." *Hemmings Muscle Machines*, Nov. 2007, www.hemmings.com/stories/article/gunsight-grandiosity.

_____. "Hemmings Feature: It's a Bird! It's a Plane! It's ... 1970 Dodge Super Bee." *Hemmings Muscle Machines*, Sept. 2017, www.hemmings.com/stories/article/its-a-bird-its-a-plane-its-1970-dodge-super-bee.

_____. "Hemmings Feature: Just a Second—1968 Chevrolet Camaro Z/28." *Hemmings Muscle Machines*, Aug. 2008, www.hemmings.com/stories/article/just-a-second-1968-chevrolet-camaro-z-28.

_____. "Hemmings Feature: Leather and Torque—1969 Mercury Cougar XR7." *Hemmings Muscle Machines*, Aug. 2013, www.hemmings.com/stories/article/leather-and-torque-1969-mercury-cougar-xr-7.

_____. "Hemmings Feature: Mr. Stealth Vs. the Showoff—1969 Hemi Road Runner, 1969 Mustang 428CJ." *Hemmings Muscle Machines*, May 2007, www.hemmings.com/stories/article/mr-stealth-vs-the-showoff-1969-hemi-road-runner-1969-mustang-428cj.

_____. "Hemmings Feature: More Than Merely Muscle—1963 Dodge 330 Max Wedge." *Hemmings Muscle Machines*, Nov. 2017, www.hemmings.com/stories/article/more-than-merely-muscle-1963-dodge-330-max-wedge.

_____. "Hemmings Feature: 1965–'66 Pontiac Catalina 2+2." *Hemmings Muscle Machines*, Dec. 2008.

_____. "Hemmings Feature: 1966 Rambler Marlin." *Hemmings Classic Car*, Mar. 2010, www.hemmings.com/stories/article/1966-rambler-marlin.

_____. "Hemmings Feature: 1966–'67 Ford Fairlane GT/GTA." *Hemmings Muscle Machines*, Sept. 2008, www.hemmings.com/stories/article/1966–67-ford-fairlane-gt-gta.

_____. "Hemmings Feature: 1970 Chevrolet Chevelle SS, 1970 Plymouth Hemi 'Cuda." *Hemmings Muscle Machines*, Apr. 2011, www.hemmings.com/stories/article/all-hail-the-kings-1970-chevrolet-chevelle-ss-1970-plymouth-hemi-cuda.

_____. "Hemmings Feature: 1970 Chevrolet Chevelle SS396 (L34), 1970 Pontiac GTO Judge Ram Air III." *Hemmings Muscle Machines*, Oct. 2011, www.hemmings.com/stories/article/dna-bodies-1970-chevrolet-chevelle-ss396-l34–1970-pontiac-gto-judge-ram-air-iii.

_____. "Hemmings Feature: 1970 Dodge Challenger T/A and Plymouth 'Cuda AAR." *Hemmings Muscle Machines*, Feb. 2012, www.hemmings.com/stories/article/t-aar-1970-dodge-challenger-t-a-and-plymouth-cuda-aar.

_____. "Hemmings Feature—1970 Rebel Machine." *Hemmings Muscle Machines*, Mar. 2015, www.hemmings.com/stories/article/1970-amc-rebel-machine.

_____. "Hemmings Feature: Production-Proboscis Plymouth with Provenance—1970 Plymouth Superbird." *Hemmings Muscle Machines*, Jan. 2011, www.hemmings.com/stories/article/production-proboscis-plymouth-with-provenance-1970-plymouth-superbird.

_____. "Hemmings Feature: Scoop vs. Ornament—1965 Pontiac GTO, 1965 Plymouth Satellite." *Hemmings Muscle Machines*, June 2012, www.hemmings.com/stories/article/scoop-vs-ornament-1965-pontiac-gto-1965-plymouth-satellite.

_____. "Hemmings Feature: Trans-Am Toughs—1970 Plymouth AAR Cuda, 1969 Chevrolet Camaro Z/28." *Hemmings Muscle Machines*, Aug. 2007, www.hemmings.com/stories/article/trans-am-toughs-1970-plymouth-aar-cuda-1969-chevrolet-camaro-z-28.

_____. "Hemmings Feature: Un-SS 1970 Chevrolet Chevelle Malibu 400." *Hemmings Muscle Machines*, Dec. 2010, www.hemmings.com/stories/article/un-ss-1970-chevrolet-chevelle-malibu-400.

_____. "Special Section: Chrysler E-Body." *Hemmings Muscle Machines*, June 2018, www.hemmings.com/stories/article/chrysler-e-body.

_____. "Year, Make and Model—1967 Dodge Coronet R/T." *Hemmings Motor News*, Nov. 2013, www.hemmings.com/stories/2016/09/19/year-make-and-model-1967-dodge-coronet-rt.

LaChance, Dave. "Buyer's Guide: 1971 Ford Mustang Boss 351." *Hemmings Muscle Machines*, Aug. 2006, www.hemmings.com/stories/article/1971-ford-mustang-boss-351–2.

_____. "Hemmings Feature: Flying Fish—1967 Plymouth Barracuda." *Hemmings Muscle Machines*, Oct. 2008, www.hemmings.com/stories/article/flying-fish-1967-plymouth-barracuda.

_____. "Hemmings Feature: 1967 Dodge Charger." *Hemmings Muscle Machines*, Dec. 2008, www.hemmings.com/stories/article/1967-dodge-charger.

_____. "Hemmings Feature: 1972–'73 Ford Gran Torino Sport." *Hemmings Muscle Machines*, Mar. 2006, www.hemmings.com/stories/article/1972-73-ford-gran-torino-sport.

_____. "Hemmings Feature: Rhymes with Orange—1971 Dodge Challenger." *Hemmings Muscle Machines*, Aug. 2008, www.hemmings.com/stories/

article/rhymes-with-orange-1971-dodge-challenger.

Litwin, Matt. "Buyer's Guide: 1964½–'67 Ford Mustang K-Code 289." *Hemmings Muscle Machines*, Dec. 2013, www.hemmings.com/stories/article/1964-1-2-67-ford-mustang-k-code-289.

——. "Buyer's Guide: 1965 Chevelle Malibu SS." *Hemmings Muscle Machines*, June 2017, www.hemmings.com/stories/article/1965-chevrolet-chevelle-malibu-ss-3.

——. "Buyer's Guide: 1965 Oldsmobile 4-4-2." *Hemmings Muscle Machines*, Feb. 2015, www.hemmings.com/stories/article/1965-oldsmobile-4-4-2-2.

——. "Buyer's Guide: 1966 Buick Skylark Gran Sport." *Hemmings Muscle Machines*, Sept. 2006, www.hemmings.com/stories/article/1966-buick-skylark-gran-sport.

——. "Buyer's Guide: 1966–'67 Dodge Charger." *Hemmings Muscle Machines*, Apr. 2016, www.hemmings.com/stories/article/1966-67-dodge-charger-2.

——. "Buyer's Guide: 1966–'67 Oldsmobile 4-4-2 Buyer's Guide." *Hemmings Muscle Machines*, Jan. 2021.

——. "Buyer's Guide: 1967 Plymouth GTX." *Hemmings Muscle Machines*, Sept. 2010, www.hemmings.com/stories/article/1967-plymouth-gtx-2.

——. "Buyer's Guide: 1968 Hurst/Olds." *Hemmings Muscle Machines*, Mar. 2013, www.hemmings.com/stories/article/1968-hurst-olds-2.

——. "Buyer's Guide: 1968 Mercury Cougar XR7-G." *Hemmings Muscle Machines*, July 2011, www.hemmings.com/stories/article/1968-mercury-cougar-xr7-g.

——. "Buyer's Guide: 1968 Pontiac GTO." *Hemmings Muscle Machines*, Aug. 2013, www.hemmings.com/stories/article/1968-pontiac-gto-3.

——. "Buyer's Guide: 1968–'69 Buick GS 400." *Hemmings Muscle Machines*, Nov. 2002, www.hemmings.com/stories/article/1968-69-buick-gs-400.

——. "Buyer's Guide: 1968–'69 Dodge Coronet R/T." *Hemmings Muscle Machines*, Dec. 2010, www.hemmings.com/stories/article/1968-69-dodge-coronet-r-t.

——. "Buyer's Guide: 1968–'69 Dodge Coronet Super Bee." *Hemmings Muscle Machines*, Dec. 2014, www.hemmings.com/stories/article/1968-69-dodge-coronet-super-bee.

——. "Buyer's Guide: 1968–'69 Ford Torino GT." *Hemmings Muscle Machines*, Dec. 2018, www.hemmings.com/stories/article/1968-69-ford-torino-gt-2.

——. "Buyer's Guide: 1968–'69 Plymouth Road Runner." *Hemmings Muscle Machines*, Nov. 2011, www.hemmings.com/stories/article/1968-69-plymouth-road-runner.

——. "Buyer's Guide: 1969 Chevrolet Camaro Z/28." *Hemmings Muscle Machines*, July 2015, www.hemmings.com/stories/article/1969-chevrolet-camaro-z-28-4.

——. "Buyer's Guide: 1969 Ford Cobra." *Hemmings Muscle Machines*, Jan. 2012, www.hemmings.com/stories/article/1969-ford-cobra-2.

——. "Buyer's Guide: 1969 Ford Mustang Boss 302." *Hemmings Muscle Machines*, Oct. 2012, www.hemmings.com/stories/article/1969-ford-mustang-boss-302.

——. "Buyer's Guide: 1969 Hurst/Olds." *Hemmings Muscle Machines*, Mar. 2019, www.hemmings.com/stories/article/1969-hurst-olds-2.

——. "Buyer's Guide: 1969 Mercury Cougar Eliminator." *Hemmings Muscle Machines*, Jan. 2010, www.hemmings.com/stories/article/1969-mercury-cougar-eliminator.

——. "Buyer's Guide: 1969 Oldsmobile 4-4-2." *Hemmings Muscle Machines*, May 2016, www.hemmings.com/stories/article/1969-oldsmobile-4-4-2-2.

——. "Buyer's Guide: 1969 Pontiac Firebird H.O." *Hemmings Muscle Machines*, June 2016, www.hemmings.com/stories/article/1969-pontiac-firebird-h-o.

——. "Buyer's Guide: 1969 Pontiac Firebird Trans Am." *Hemmings Muscle Machines*, May 2015, www.hemmings.com/stories/article/1969-pontiac-firebird-trans-am.

——. "Buyer's Guide: 1969½ Dodge A12 Super Bee." *Hemmings Muscle Machines*, Mar. 2009, www.hemmings.com/stories/article/1969-1-2-dodge-a12-super-bee.

——. "Buyer's Guide: 1970 AMC Javelin SST Mark Donohue." *Hemmings Muscle Machines*, Oct. 2015, www.hemmings.com/stories/article/1970-amc-javelin-sst-mark-donohue.

——. "Buyer's Guide: 1970 AMC Trans-Am Javelin." *Hemmings Muscle Machines*, Jan. 2014, www.hemmings.com/stories/article/1970-amc-trans-am-javelin.

——. "Buyer's Guide: 1970 Buick GS 455 and GS 455 Stage 1." *Hemmings Muscle Machines*, Dec. 2014, www.hemmings.com/stories/article/1970-buick-gs-455-gs-455-stage-1.

——. "Buyer's Guide: 1970 Buick GSX." *Hemmings Muscle Machines*, Feb. 2018, www.hemmings.com/stories/article/1970-buick-gsx-2.

——. "Buyer's Guide: 1970 Ford Torino Cobra." *Hemmings Muscle Machines*, Aug. 2016, www.hemmings.com/stories/article/1970-ford-torino-cobra.

——. "Buyer's Guide: 1970 Ford Torino GT." *Hemmings Muscle Machines*, Aug. 2017, www.hemmings.com/stories/article/1970-ford-torino-gt.

——. "Buyer's Guide: 1970 4-4-2/4-4-2 W-30." *Hemmings Muscle Machines*, Oct. 2017, www.hemmings.com/stories/article/1970-oldsmobile-4-4-2-4-4-2-w-30.

——. "Buyer's Guide: 1970 Mercury Cougar and Cougar XR7." *Hemmings Muscle Machines*, Mar. 2015, www.hemmings.com/stories/article/1970-mercury-cougar-cougar-xr-7.

——. "Buyer's Guide: 1970 Mustang Boss 429." *Hemmings Muscle Machines*, Apr. 2014, www.hemmings.com/stories/article/1970-ford-mustang-boss-429.

——. "Buyer's Guide: 1970 Oldsmobile F-85/Cutlass W-31." *Hemmings Muscle Machines*, Jan. 2011, www.hemmings.com/stories/article/1970-oldsmobile-f-85-cutlass-w-31.

———. "Buyer's Guide: 1970.5–'71 Pontiac GT-37." *Hemmings Muscle Machines*, Apr. 2009, www.hemmings.com/stories/article/1970-5-71-pontiac-gt-37.

———. "Buyer's Guide: 1970–'71 Plymouth 'Cuda." *Hemmings Muscle Machines*, Apr. 2013, www.hemmings.com/stories/article/1970-71-plymouth-cuda-2.

———. "Buyer's Guide: 1971–'72 Buick GS 455." *Hemmings Muscle Machines*, Apr. 2011, www.hemmings.com/stories/article/1971-72-buick-gs-455.

———. "Buyer's Guide: 1971–'72 Buick GSX." *Hemmings Muscle Machines*, Jan. 2013, www.hemmings.com/stories/article/1971-72-buick-gsx.

———. "Buyer's Guide: 1971–'72 Javelin AMX." *Hemmings Muscle Machines*, Apr. 2017, www.hemmings.com/stories/article/1971-72-amc-javelin-amx.

———. "Buyer's Guide: 1972 Charger Rallye." *Hemmings Muscle Machines*, Jan. 2015, www.hemmings.com/stories/article/1972-dodge-charger-rallye-2.

———. "Buyer's Guide: 1972 Ford Gran Torino Sport." *Hemmings Muscle Machines*, Feb. 2016, www.hemmings.com/stories/article/1972-ford-gran-torino-sport-2.

———. "Buyer's Guide: 1972–'73 Mercury Montego GT." *Hemmings Muscle Machines*, Feb. 2013, www.hemmings.com/stories/article/1972-73-mercury-montego-gt.

———. "Buyer's Guide: 1973–'74 Challenger Rallye." *Hemmings Muscle Machines*, July 2016, www.hemmings.com/stories/article/1973-74-dodge-challenger-rallye.

———. "Buyer's Guide: 1974 Pontiac GTO." *Hemmings Muscle Machines*, Dec. 2012, www.hemmings.com/stories/article/1974-pontiac-gto-2.

———. "Happy 50th birthday, Plymouth Barracuda." *Hemmings.com*, 14 Mar. 2014, www.hemmings.com/stories/2014/03/14/happy-50th-birthday-plymouth-barracuda.

———. "Hemmings Feature: 1965 Buick Skylark Gran Sport." *Hemmings Muscle Machines*, Aug. 2008, www.hemmings.com/stories/article/1965-buick-skylark-gran-sport-2.

———. "Hemmings Feature: 1965 Chevelle Malibu SS." *Hemmings Muscle Machines*, Sept. 2008, www.hemmings.com/stories/article/1965-chevrolet-chevelle-malibu-ss-2.

———. "Hemmings Feature: 1965 Plymouth Barracuda." *Hemmings Motor News*, Sept. 2010, www.hemmings.com/stories/article/1965-plymouth-barracuda.

———. "Hemmings Feature: 1969 Dodge Charger R/T." *Hemmings Muscle Machines*, May 2017, www.hemmings.com/stories/article/1969-dodge-charger-r-t.

———. "Hemmings Feature: 1969 Ford Cobra." *Hemmings Muscle Machines*, June 2012, www.hemmings.com/stories/article/1969-ford-cobra.

———. "Hemmings Feature: 1969 Plymouth 383 'Cuda." *Hemmings Muscle Machines*, Sept. 2007, www.hemmings.com/stories/article/1969-plymouth-383-cuda-2.

———. "Hemmings Feature: 1970 Ford Mustang Boss 302." *Hemmings Muscle Machines*, Apr. 2008, www.hemmings.com/stories/article/1970-ford-mustang-boss-302-2.

———. "Hemmings Feature: 1970 Plymouth Road Runner Superbird." *Hemmings Muscle Machines*, Mar. 2007, www.hemmings.com/stories/article/1970-plymouth-road-runner-superbird.

———. "Hemmings Feature: 1970–'71 Ford Torino GT Sportsroof." *Hemmings Muscle Machines*, Feb. 2007, www.hemmings.com/stories/article/1970-71-ford-torino-gt-sportsroof.

———. "Hemmings Feature: Buick's California GS: West Coast Style and Performance, on a Budget." *Hemmings Muscle Machines*, June 2020, www.hemmings.com/stories/article/1967-buick-california-gs-340.

———. "Hemmings Feature: Common Bond—1972 Chevrolet Chevelle." *Hemmings Muscle Machines*, July 2009, www.hemmings.com/stories/article/common-bond-1972-chevrolet-chevelle.

———. "Hemmings Feature: Gran Sport Rising—1967 Buick GS 400." *Hemmings Muscle Machines*, July 2008, www.hemmings.com/stories/article/gran-sport-rising-1967-buick-gs-400.

———. "Hemmings Feature: Small Block Muscle—1969 Buick GS 350." *Hemmings Muscle Machines*, May 2011, www.hemmings.com/stories/article/small-block-muscle-1969-buick-gs-350.

———. "Hemmings Feature: Underrated!—1969 Buick GS 400 Stage 1." *Hemmings Muscle Machines*, May 2014, www.hemmings.com/stories/article/underrated-1969-buick-gs-400-stage-1.

———. "Tech: 1967 Buick GS 340." *Hemmings Muscle Machines*, Feb. 2009, www.hemmings.com/stories/article/1967-buick-gs-340-2.

———. "This or That: 1966 Mercury Comet Cyclone GT versus 1967 Mercury Comet 202." *Hemmings.com*, 1 Dec. 2016, www.hemmings.com/stories/article/1969-mercury-cyclone-cj.

Mattar, George. "Buyer's Guide: 1970 Oldsmobile Rallye 350." *Hemmings Muscle Machines*, Oct. 2007, www.hemmings.com/stories/article/1970-oldsmobile-rallye-350-3.

———. "Hemmings Feature: The Boss of Bosses—The 1969 Mustang Boss 429." *Hemmings Muscle Machines*, July 2007, www.hemmings.com/stories/article/the-boss-of-bosses-1969-mustang-boss-429.

———. "Hemmings Feature: GeeTeeX—1968 Plymouth GTX." *Hemmings Muscle Machines*, June 2007, www.hemmings.com/stories/article/geeteex-1968-plymouth-gtx.

———. "Hemmings Feature: GM's Other Pony Car—1969 Pontiac Firebird." *Hemmings Muscle Machines*, May 2007, www.hemmings.com/stories/article/gms-other-pony-car-1969-pontiac-firebird.

———. "Hemmings Feature: Mercury Cougar." *Hemmings Muscle Machines*, Sept. 2007, www.hemmings.com/stories/article/mercury-cougar.

_____. "Hemmings Feature: 1963 Plymouth Max Wedge 426." *Hemmings Muscle Machines*, Oct. 2006, www.hemmings.com/stories/article/1963-plymouth-max-wedge-426.

_____. "Hemmings Feature: 1965 Mercury Comet Cyclone." *Hemmings Muscle Machines*, July 2005, www.hemmings.com/stories/article/1965-mercury-comet-cyclone-2.

_____. "Hemmings Feature: 1966 Mercury Comet Cyclone GT." *Hemmings Muscle Machines*, Feb. 2008, www.hemmings.com/stories/article/1966-mercury-comet-cyclone-gt.

_____. "Hemmings Feature: 1969 Dodge Super Bee." *Hemmings Muscle Machines*, Dec. 2006, www.hemmings.com/stories/article/1969-dodge-super-bee-3.

_____. "Hemmings Feature: 1969 Mercury Cyclone." *Hemmings Muscle Machines*, Sept. 2005, www.hemmings.com/stories/article/1969-mercury-cyclone.

_____. "Hemmings Feature: 1970 AMC AMX." *Hemmings Muscle Machines*, Aug. 2007, www.hemmings.com/stories/article/1970-amc-amx-3.

_____. "Hemmings Feature: 1970 Buick GSX." *Hemmings Muscle Machines*, Nov. 2005, www.hemmings.com/stories/article/1970-buick-gsx.

_____. "Hemmings Feature: 1970 Oldsmobile 4-4-2." *Hemmings Muscle Machines*, Mar. 2007, www.hemmings.com/stories/article/1970-oldsmobile-4-4-2.

_____. "Hemmings Feature: 1970–72 Olds Cutlass 4-4-2 W-30." *Hemmings Muscle Machines*, Aug. 2005, www.hemmings.com/stories/article/1970-72-olds-cutlass-4-4-2-w-30.

_____. "Hemmings Feature: 1971 Dodge Super Bee." *Hemmings Muscle Machines*, Oct. 2007, www.hemmings.com/stories/article/1971-dodge-super-bee.

_____. "Hemmings Feature: Personal Luxury Muscle—1970 Oldsmobile Cutlass SX." *Hemmings Muscle Machines*, Dec. 2005, www.hemmings.com/stories/article/personal-luxury-muscle-1970-oldsmobile-cutlass-sx.

_____. "Hemmings Feature: Six Barrels, One Family—1969 Plymouth Road Runner." *Hemmings Muscle Machines*, May 2008, www.hemmings.com/stories/article/six-barrels-one-family-1969-plymouth-road-runner.

_____. "Hemmings Feature: Six Pack Highjack—1971 Dodge Super Bee." *Hemmings Muscle Machines*, July 2005, www.hemmings.com/stories/article/six-pack-highjack-1971-dodge-super-bee.

_____. "Hemmings Feature: Sizzling Satellite—1966 Plymouth Sport Satellite." *Hemmings Muscle Machines*, Feb. 2007, www.hemmings.com/stories/article/sizzling-satellite-1966-plymouth-sport-satellite.

_____. "Hemmings Feature: Z Best Original? 1970½ Camaro Z/28 RS." *Hemmings Muscle Machines*, Sept. 2006, www.hemmings.com/stories/article/z-best-original-1970-1-2-camaro-z28-rs.

McCourt, Mark J. "Buyer's Guide: 1971-'74 Plymouth Satellite Road Runner and GTX." *Hemmings*

*Muscle Machines*, Feb. 2011, www.hemmings.com/stories/article/1971–74-plymouth-satellite-road-runner-and-gtx.

_____. "Hemmings Feature: Fish Under Glass." *Hemmings Motor News*, Dec. 2006, www.hemmings.com/stories/article/fish-under-glass.

_____. "Hemmings Feature: Matchless Mercury—1967 Cyclone." *Hemmings Muscle Machines*, Apr. 2011, www.hemmings.com/stories/article/matchless-mercury-1967-cyclone.

_____. "Hemmings Feature: 1966–67 Pontiac GTO." *Hemmings Muscle Machines*, Nov. 2004, www.hemmings.com/stories/article/1966–67-pontiac-gto.

_____. "Hemmings Feature: 1967 AMC Marlin." *Hemmings Motor News*, July 2014, www.hemmings.com/stories/article/1967-amc-marlin-2.

_____. "Hemmings Feature: 1967 Pontiac GTO." *Hemmings Motor News*, June 2007, www.hemmings.com/stories/article/1967-pontiac-gto-2.

_____. "Hemmings Feature: 1967–'68 Mercury Cougar." *Hemmings Muscle Machines*, Jan. 2004, www.hemmings.com/stories/article/1967–68-mercury-cougar.

_____. "Hemmings Feature: 1968–1970 Dodge Charger." *Hemmings Muscle Machines*, May 2004, www.hemmings.com/stories/article/1968-1970-dodge-charger.

_____. "Hemmings Feature: 1969 Chevrolet Camaro." *Hemmings Muscle Machines*, Oct. 2004, www.hemmings.com/stories/article/1969-chevrolet-camaro-2.

_____. "Hemmings Feature: 1970 Pontiac GTO." *Hemmings Muscle Machines*, Oct. 2004, www.hemmings.com/stories/article/1970-pontiac-gto.

_____. "Hemmings Feature: 1970–'71 Plymouth Cuda." *Hemmings Muscle Machines*, June 2006, www.hemmings.com/stories/article/1970–71-plymouth-cuda.

_____. "Hemmings Feature: 1970–1972 Chevelle SS 454." *Hemmings Muscle Machines*, July 2004, www.hemmings.com/stories/article/1970–1972-chevelle-ss-454.

_____. "Hemmings Feature: 1971–1973 Ford Mustang." *Hemmings Muscle Machines*, Sept. 2004, www.hemmings.com/stories/article/1971–1973-ford-mustang.

_____. "Hemmings Feature: 1971–'74 AMC Javelin/AMX." *Hemmings Muscle Machines*, Mar. 2004, www.hemmings.com/stories/article/1971–74-amc-javelin-amx.

McGean, Terry. "Hemmings Feature: 1967 Buick GS 340." *Hemmings Muscle Machines*, May 2009, www.hemmings.com/stories/article/1967-buick-gs-340.

_____. "Hemmings Feature: 1968 Dodge Charger R/T." *Hemmings Muscle Machines*, Jan. 2019, www.hemmings.com/stories/article/1968-dodge-charger-r-t-2.

_____. "Hemmings Feature: 1969 Plymouth Barracuda 383." *Hemmings Muscle Machines*, Mar. 2014, www.hemmings.com/stories/article/1969-plymouth-barracuda-383.

_____. "Hemmings Feature: Oldsmobile's W-31 350."

*Hemmings Muscle Machines*, Oct. 2010, www.hemmings.com/stories/article/oldsmobiles-w-31-350.

_____. "Hemmings Feature: Stealth (Cobra) Jet—1968 Ford Torino GT." *Hemmings Muscle Machines*, May 2014, www.hemmings.com/stories/article/stealth-cobra-jet-1968-ford-torino-gt.

McNessor, Mike. "Buyer's Guide: 1965–'66 Ford Mustang." *Hemmings Motor News*, Feb. 2020, www.hemmings.com/stories/article/1965–66-ford-mustang.

_____. "Buyer's Guide: 1966–'67 Chevrolet Chevelle SS 396." *Hemmings Muscle Machines*, Mar. 2012, www.hemmings.com/stories/article/1966–67-chevrolet-chevelle-ss-396.

_____. "Buyer's Guide: 1967–'69 Chevrolet Camaro SS." *Hemmings Muscle Machines*, Dec. 2011, www.hemmings.com/stories/article/1967–69-chevrolet-camaro-ss.

_____. "Buyer's Guide: 1968–'69 Chevrolet Chevelle." *Hemmings Muscle Machines*, Mar. 2012, www.hemmings.com/stories/article/1968–69-chevrolet-chevelle.

_____. "Buyer's Guide: 1970 Pontiac GTO Judge." *Hemmings Muscle Machines*, Feb. 2012, www.hemmings.com/stories/article/1970-pontiac-gto-judge-3.

_____. "Buyer's Guide: 1971–'72 Chevrolet Chevelle." *Hemmings Muscle Machines*, Sept. 2012, www.hemmings.com/stories/article/1971–72-chevrolet-chevelle.

_____. "Buyer's Guide: 1971 Dodge Challenger R/T." *Hemmings Muscle Machines*, Apr. 2018, www.hemmings.com/stories/article/1971-dodge-challenger-r-t.

_____. "Buyer's Guide: 1971 Plymouth Road Runner." *Hemmings Muscle Machines*, Oct. 2019, www.hemmings.com/stories/article/1971-plymouth-road-runner.

_____. "Hemmings Feature: Bronze Bomber—1972 Oldsmobile 4-4-2." *Hemmings Muscle Machines*, Sept. 2008, www.hemmings.com/stories/article/bronze-bomber-1972-oldsmobile-442.

_____. "Hemmings Feature: 1968–'72 Oldsmobile 4-4-2." *Hemmings Muscle Machines*, Dec. 2013, www.hemmings.com/stories/article/1968–72-oldsmobile-4-4-2.

_____. "Hemmings Feature: 1970 Dodge Challenger T/A." *Hemmings Muscle Machines*, Dec. 2015, www.hemmings.com/stories/article/1970-dodge-challenger-t-a-2.

_____. "Hemmings Feature: 1970 Dodge Coronet." *Hemmings Muscle Machines*, July 2013, www.hemmings.com/stories/article/1970-dodge-coronet.

_____. "Hemmings Feature: 1970 Dodge Super Bee." *Hemmings Muscle Machines*, Oct. 2016, www.hemmings.com/stories/article/1970-dodge-super-bee.

_____. "Hemmings Feature: 1970 Mercury Cyclone Spoiler." *Hemmings Muscle Machines*, May 2014, www.hemmings.com/stories/article/1970-mercury-cyclone-spoiler.

_____. "Hemmings Feature: 1971 Buick GS." *Hemmings Muscle Machines*, Dec. 2018, www.hemmings.com/stories/article/1971-buick-gs.

Mehta, Sajeev. "Your Handy 1965–73 Ford Mustang Buyer's Guide." *Hagerty Media*, Hagerty.com, Apr. 2020.

Mueller, Mike. *Muscle Car Source Book*. Minneapolis: Quarto, 2015.

Newhardt, David. *Mopar Muscle*. Ann Arbor, MI, Lowe & B. Hould Publishers, 2005.

Oldham, Scott. "Your definitive 1964–67 Pontiac GTO buyer's guide." *Hagerty Media*, 2 Oct. 2018, www.hagerty.com/media/buying-and-selling/your-definitive-pontiac-gto-buyers-guide/.

Rosenberg, Diego. *Selling the American Muscle Car*. Forest Lake, MN: Cartech, 2016.

Sessler, Peter C. *Dodge and Plymouth Muscle Car Red Book*, 2d ed. Osceola, WI: MBI Publishing, 2001.

_____. *GTO Red Book 1964–1974*. Osceola, WI, USA, Motorbooks International, 1992.

Shea, Terry. "Buyer's Guide: 1968 Ford Mustang GT/CS California Special." *Hemmings Muscle Machines*, July 2018, www.hemmings.com/stories/article/1968-ford-mustang-gt-cs-california-special.

_____. "Buyer's Guide: 1968–'69 AMC AMX." *Hemmings Muscle Machines*, June 2018, www.hemmings.com/stories/article/1968–69-amc-amx.

_____. "Buyer's Guide: 1969 Mercury Cyclone CJ." *Hemmings Muscle Machines*, Aug. 2012, www.hemmings.com/stories/article/1969-mercury-cyclone-cj.

_____. "Buyer's Guide: 1971–'72 Pontiac GTO." *Hemmings Muscle Machines*, Feb. 2012, www.hemmings.com/stories/article/1971–72-pontiac-gto.

_____. "Buyer's Guide: 1973–'74 Pontiac Firebird Formula and Trans Am SD-455." *Hemmings Muscle Machines*, June 2020, www.hemmings.com/stories/article/1971–72-pontiac-trans-am.

_____. "Hemmings Feature: Killer Bee—1968 Dodge Super Bee." *Hemmings Muscle Machines*, May 2013, www.hemmings.com/stories/article/killer-bee-1968-dodge-super-bee.

_____. "Hemmings Feature: Redemption X2—1966 Ford Mustang GT Fastback." *Hemmings Muscle Machines*, Feb. 2013, www.hemmings.com/stories/article/redemption-x2–1966-mustang-gt-fastback.

_____. "Hemmings Feature: A Tale of Two Hemis—1966 Dodge Coronet 500, 1966 Plymouth Belvedere II." *Hemmings Muscle Machines*, Dec. 2012, www.hemmings.com/stories/article/a-tale-of-two-hemis-1966-dodge-coronet-500–1966-plymouth-belvedere-ii.

Strohl, Daniel. "AMC Designer Vince Geraci on the Marlin: 'There's a very fine line between unique and strange.'" *Hemmings.com*, Hemmings.com, 21 Nov. 2014, www.hemmings.com/stories/2014/11/21/amc-designer-vince-geraci-on-the-marlin-theres-a-very-fine-line-between-unique-and-strange.

_____. "Buyer's Guide: 1967–'68 Pontiac Firebird." *Hemmings Muscle Machines*, Dec. 2009, www.hem

mings.com/stories/article/1967–68-pontiac-fire bird-400.

_____. "Buyer's Guide: 1968–'69 Ford Torino GT." *Hemmings Muscle Machines*, Oct. 2006, www.hemmings.com/stories/article/1968–69-ford-torino-gt.

_____. "Buyer's Guide: 1968–'70 AMC AMX." *Hemmings Muscle Machines*, Jan. 2007, www.hemmings.com/stories/article/1968–70-amc-amx.

_____. "Buyer's Guide: 1969 AMC SC/Rambler." *Hemmings Muscle Machines*, June 2008, www.hemmings.com/stories/article/1969-amc-sc-rambler.

_____. "Buyer's Guide: 1969 Dodge Charger Daytona." *Hemmings Muscle Machines*, June 2006, www.hemmings.com/stories/article/1969-dodge-charger-daytona.

_____. "Buyer's Guide: 1971–1974 Javelin and AMX." *Hemmings Muscle Machines*, Mar. 2015, www.hemmings.com/stories/article/1971–1974-amc-javelin-and-amx-2.

_____. "Hemmings Feature: Balancing Act—1971 Mercury Cougar." *Hemmings Muscle Machines*, Apr. 2018, www.hemmings.com/stories/article/balancing-act-1971-mercury-cougar.

_____. "Hemmings Feature: Big Bad Brothers—1969 AMC Javelin SST, 1969 AMC AMX." *Hemmings Muscle Machines*, Jan. 2011, www.hemmings.com/stories/article/big-bad-brothers-1969-amc-javelin-sst-1969-amc-amx.

_____. "Hemmings Feature: The Cat That Swallowed a Cobra—1968 Mercury Cougar GT-E." *Hemmings Muscle Machines*, Nov. 2006, www.hemmings.com/stories/article/the-cat-that-swallowed-a-cobra-1968-mercury-cougar-gt-e.

_____. "Hemmings Feature: Fast but Forgotten—1970 Dodge Super Bee." *Hemmings Muscle Machines*, Nov. 2006, www.hemmings.com/stories/article/fast-but-forgotten-1970-dodge-super-bee.

_____. "Hemmings Feature: Mel's AMX—1969 AMC AMX." *Hemmings Muscle Machines*, May 2006, www.hemmings.com/stories/article/mels-amx-1969-amc-amx.

_____. "Hemmings Feature: Muscle for the Jet Set—1968 AMC AMX." *Hemmings Muscle Machines*, Aug. 2011, www.hemmings.com/stories/article/muscle-for-the-jet-set-1968-amc-amx.

_____. "Hemmings Feature: Now Take a Deep Breath—1969 Buick GS400." *Hemmings Muscle Machines*, Apr. 2007, www.hemmings.com/stories/article/now-take-a-deep-breath-1969-buick-gs400.

_____. "Hemmings Feature: Objectified Oldsmobile—1964 Oldsmobile F-85 4-4-2 Convertible." *Hemmings Muscle Machines*, Nov. 2005, www.hemmings.com/stories/article/objectified-oldsmobile-1964-oldsmobile-f85–4-4-2-convertible.

_____. "Hemmings Feature: The Ol' Razzle Dazzle—1965 Pontiac GTO." *Hemmings Muscle Machines*, Jan. 2009.

_____. "Hemmings Feature: Small Wonder—1972 Plymouth Road Runner." *Hemmings Muscle Machines*, Jan. 2009, www.hemmings.com/stories/article/small-wonder-1972-plymouth-road-runner.

_____. "Hemmings Feature: Trawling for Success—1967 AMC Marlin." *Hemmings Motor News*, Aug. 2007, www.hemmings.com/stories/article/trawling-for-success-1967-amc-marlin.

_____. "Hemmings Feature: An Uncommon Path—1968 AMC Javelin." *Hemmings Muscle Machines*, Apr. 2008, www.hemmings.com/stories/article/an-uncommon-path-1968-amc-javelin.

_____. "Hemmings Feature: Up with the Rebellion—1970 Rebel Machine." *Hemmings Muscle Machines*, Oct. 2007, www.hemmings.com/stories/article/up-with-the-rebellion-1970-rebel-machine.

_____. "Periodic Reminder: 4-4-2 Stood for Many Things Over the Years." *Hemmings Motor News*, 30 Sept. 2019, www.hemmings.com/stories/2019/09/30/periodic-reminder-4-4-2-stood-for-many-things-over-the-years.

Wangers, Jim. *Glory Days: When Horsepower and Passion Ruled Detroit*. Cambridge, MA: Bentley Publishing, 1998.

Zazarine, Paul. *Illustrated GTO Buyer's Guide*. Osceola, WI: Motorbooks International, 1994.

_____, and Chuck Roberts. *Pontiac GTO Restoration Guide, 1964–1972*, 2d ed. Osceola, WI: Motorbooks International, 1995.

# Index